ISBN 978-0-266-04859-6
PIBN 10954828

English
Français
Deutsche
Italiano
Español
Português

www.forgottenbooks.com

Mythology Photography **Fiction**
Fishing Christianity **Art** Cooking
Essays Buddhism Freemasonry
Medicine **Biology** Music **Ancient
Egypt** Evolution Carpentry Physics
Dance Geology **Mathematics** Fitness
Shakespeare **Folklore** Yoga Marketing
Confidence Immortality Biographies
Poetry **Psychology** Witchcraft
Electronics Chemistry History **Law**
Accounting **Philosophy** Anthropology
Alchemy Drama Quantum Mechanics
Atheism Sexual Health **Ancient History**
Entrepreneurship Languages Sport
Paleontology Needlework Islam
Metaphysics Investment Archaeology
Parenting Statistics Criminology
Motivational

REPORTS OF CASES

DETERMINED BY

THE SUPREME COURT

OF THE

STATE OF NEVADA

DURING JULY AND OCTOBER TERMS, 1919,
AND JANUARY TERM, 1920

REPORTED BY

WM. KENNETT
CLERK OF SUPREME COURT

AND

JOHN E. RICHARDS, Esq.
ATTORNEY AT LAW AND OFFICIAL REPORTER

VOLUME XLIII

CARSON CITY, NEVADA
STATE PRINTING OFFICE—JOE FARNSWORTH, SUPERINTENDENT
1920

1919-1920

Justices of the Supreme Court

HON. B. W. COLEMAN..............................CHIEF JUSTICE

HON. J. A. SANDERS }
HON. E. A. DUCKER } ....ASSOCIATE JUSTICES

Officers of the Court

HON. LEONARD B. FOWLER.........ATTORNEY-GENERAL

HON. ROBT. RICHARDS....DEPUTY ATTORNEY-GENERAL

HON. WM. KENNETT ....CLERK

JOHN E. RICHARDS, ESQ.................OFFICIAL REPORTER

MR. JOSEPH STERN ....BAILIFF

DISTRICT JUDGES, 1919-1920

HON. FRANK P. LANGAN......................FIRST DISTRICT

HON. THOMAS F. MORAN...............SECOND DISTRICT

HON. E. F. LUNSFORD.........................SECOND DISTRICT

HON. PETER BREEN.............................THIRD DISTRICT

HON. E. J. L. TABER...........................FOURTH DISTRICT

HON. MARK R. AVERILL.......................FIFTH DISTRICT

HON. J. A. CALLAHAN...,......................SIXTH DISTRICT

HON. J. EMMETT WALSH................SEVENTH DISTRICT

HON. T. C. HART....................................EIGHTH DISTRICT

HON. C. J. McFADDEN...........................NINTH DISTRICT

HON. WM. E. ORR.................................TENTH DISTRICT

TABLE OF CASES REPORTED

TABLE OF CASES CITED
In the Opinions Reported in This Volume

FROM NEVADA REPORTS
(ALPHABETICAL ORDER)

FROM NEVADA·REPORTS
(NUMERICAL ORDER)

FROM OTHER REPORTS

CONSTITUTION AND STATUTES CITED

NEVADA

REVISED LAWS OF NEVADA (1912)

UNITED STATES

REPORTS OF CASES

DETERMINED BY

THE SUPREME COURT

OF THE

STATE OF NEVADA

JULY TERM, 1919

[No. 2326]

GEORGE W. GILL, APPELLANT, v. THE GOLDFIELD CONSOLIDATED MINES COMPANY (A CORPORATION), RESPONDENT.

[176 Pac. 784; 184 Pac. 309]

1. STATUTES—CONSTRUCTION—LEGISLATIVE KNOWLEDGE — PRESUMPTION.
 It may be presumed that the legislature adopted Civ. Prac. Act, sec. 386 (Rev. Laws, 5328), requiring that a motion for new trial must be made and determined before an appeal based on insufficiency of evidence can be taken, with full knowledge that the existing practice was otherwise.

2. CONSTITUTIONAL LAW—JUDICIAL AUTHORITY—CONSTRUCTION OF STATUTES.
 Whether a statute was repealed by a later one is a judicial, and not a legislative, question.

3. STATUTES—REPEAL—LEGISLATIVE INTENTION.
 Whether one statute was repealed by another is a question of legislative intention, which is to be determined by acknowledged rules.

4. STATUTES—REPEAL BY IMPLICATION.
 Stats. 1915, c. 142, revises the subject-matter of Rev. Laws, 5343 (Civ. Prac. Act. sec. 401), respecting statements on appeal, and substitutes therefor in toto a system of bills of exception, and hence repeals by implication the earlier statute.

5. STATUTES—REPEAL BY CODIFICATION—REVISION—OMITTED PARTS.
 Where a statute is revised or one act framed from another, some parts being omitted, the omitted parts are considered annulled.

6. STATUTES—REPEAL—REPUGNANT ACT.

One statute is not repugnant to another unless they relate to the same subject and are enacted for the same purpose.

7. STATUTES—IMPLIED REPEAL.—CONFLICT IN OBJECTS.

Although Civ. Prac. Act, sec. 386 (Rev. Laws, 5328), and Stats. 1915, c. 142. relate to the same subject, both being designed to correct errors on appeal, the purpose of the former was to require a motion for new trial before taking appeal, while the object of the latter was to provide the method of appeal by bills of exception, so that the latter does not repeal the former by conflict in objects.

8. APPEAL AND ERROR—METHOD OF APPEAL—STATUTES.

Where the method of appeal is prescribed by statute, it must be followed, and the assumption that a ceremony is useless will not justify a departure therefrom.

9. APPEAL AND ERROR — REVIEW — ASSIGNMENTS — NECESSITY OF MOTION FOR NEW TRIAL.

Where an appeal is based upon alleged errors relating to evidence as pointed out under Rev. Laws. 5323 (Civ. Prac. Act. sec. 381), a motion for a new trial must be made and determined before the appeal is taken, as required by section 5328 (section 386).

ON REHEARING

1. APPEAL AND ERROR—JURISDICTION ACQUIRED BY APPEAL ON JUDGMENT ROLL.

Though an appeal was taken on the judgment roll alone, and the appellate court did not acquire jurisdiction to review errors other than those appearing on the face of the judgment roll, the appellate court acquired jurisdiction of the appeal.

APPEAL from Seventh Judicial District Court, Esmeralda County; *J. Emmett Walsh,* Judge.

Action by George W. Gill against the Goldfield Consolidated Mines Company, a corporation. Judgment for defendant, and plaintiff appeals. **Motion to dismiss appeal sustained.**

On rehearing, **former judgment affirmed.**

John F. Kunz, for Appellant:

Not only has the respondent failed to interpose his attack against the appeal in the manner provided by law, but the appeal itself has been taken in strict accordance with the recent legislative enactment.

There has never been before the court a motion to dismiss, only a notice of intention to move to dismiss the appeal having been filed.

An appeal may be taken from the judgment alone, under the practice which prevailed prior to the enactment of the statute of 1915. Also, there are certain assignments of error set forth by respondent, which under the old practice could be reviewed without first making a motion for a new trial as formerly required under section 5328, Revised Laws. Therefore, if the respondent desired to assail the method of appeal, it could not be reached by a motion to dismiss. Written objections and exceptions, as set forth in rule 8 of the supreme court rules, should have been filed at least one day prior to the argument. In the absence of a statute, the rules of the supreme court have the same force and effect as statutory enactments.

Hoyt, Gibbons, French & Springmeyer and *Benj. J. Henley,* for Respondent:

Motion for a new trial not having been made, this court has no jurisdiction to entertain or consider the appeal. Rule 8 of the supreme court has no application. Said rule requires that only those exceptions or objections which might be "cured on suggestion of diminution of the record" must be noted in the written or printed points of respondent and filed at least one day before the argument, or they will not be regarded, and the error here referred to cannot be cured by this court. Skaggs v. Bridgman, 39 Nev. 310.

The statutes are express and specific in their terms, providing that, where an appeal is based upon the ground of error assigned, a motion for a new trial must be made and determined before an appeal is taken, and that no errors other than those specified in the memorandum of errors, required by section 5322, Revised Laws, shall be considered, either upon the motion for a new trial or upon the appeal.

By the Court, SANDERS, J.:

The plaintiff brought this action to recover from the defendant corporation the sum of $10,000 as damages for the wrongful death by drowning of his child, 9 years of age, in a reservoir erected and maintained by the defendant upon its premises for the purposes of fire protection to the defendant's milling plant or reduction works situated near by. The plaintiff sought to recover the sum stated, upon the theory that the reservoir was in law and in fact an "attractive nuisance," and that at the time of the drowning of the child the reservoir was not safeguarded as required by the statute entitled "An act to secure persons and animals from danger arising from mining and other excavations." Rev. Laws, 3233. At the trial the jury returned a verdict in favor of the defendant, and judgment was entered accordingly. This appeal is taken from the judgment alone.

Upon calling the case for argument in this court, the respondent, upon notice previously given, moved the court to dismiss the appeal, upon the ground that no motion for a new trial was ever made in the lower court before the appeal was taken, and that no memorandum of errors was filed and served as contemplated by section 5322, Revised Laws.

1-5. Section 386 of our civil practice act (Rev. Laws, 5328) upon which the motion is based, provides:

"Where the appeal is based upon the ground that the evidence is insufficient to justify the verdict or decision of the court, or to support the findings, or upon alleged errors in ruling upon the evidence, or upon instructions claimed to be erroneous, a motion for a new trial must be made and determined before the appeal is taken. In all other cases the party aggrieved may appeal with or without first moving for a new trial; but by appealing without first moving for a new trial, the right to move for a new trial is waived."

It is admitted that no motion for a new trial was made in the court as contemplated by this section, and it is conceded that the appeal in this case is based upon alleged errors in ruling upon the evidence, the giving of instructions claimed to be erroneous, and the refusal to give instructions claimed to be correct. The question raised by the motion to dismiss, therefore, is: Is it essential to the jurisdiction of this court on an appeal from a judgment that it should affirmatively appear from the record that a motion for a new trial was made and determined before the appeal was taken? Manifestly the legislature by the adoption of section 386 clearly evinced an intention that an appeal which is based upon certain errors raising questions dependent upon the evidence for determination should not be considered in the appellate court unless the court below had been afforded an opportunity to correct such errors by motion for a new trial. The section as adopted had no place in the old procedure. What is made by it a statutory rule was once characterized by this court as being entirely unnecessary. Cooper v. Pac. Mutual Life Ins. Co., 7 Nev. 116, 8 Am. Rep. 705. In that case the court said:

"It is the everyday practice under the new system, as well as the old, to take cases to the appellate courts upon bill of exceptions, upon which all rulings raising legal questions may be reviewed. Will it be argued, for example, that a question growing out of the instructions or charge to the jury cannot be reviewed, except when a motion for a new trial is made? Certainly not. * * *"

It may be presumed that the legislature adopted section 386 with full knowledge of the state of the practice then existing. By a subsequent contemporaneous section of the practice act (section 401; Rev. Laws, 5343) it is provided, inter alia, that at the time a decision, order, or ruling is made, and during the progress of the cause, before or after judgment, a party may take his bill of exceptions to the decision, order, admission, or exclusion of testimony or evidence, or other ruling of the court or judge on points of law, and any party aggrieved may appeal from the judgment without further statement or motion. By section 386, where the appeal is based upon the same errors as those embraced in section 401, the party aggrieved must first move for a new trial before taking his appeal. By section 401 the same errors may be reviewed on appeal from the judgment without such motion. We are not here called upon to reconcile the obvious inconsistency of these provisions, except as incident to the solution of the main question presented in opposition to the motion to dismiss the appeal, namely, that section 386, upon which the motion to dismiss is based, was repealed by the approval of a subsequent act entitled:

"An act supplemental to and to amend an act entitled 'An act to regulate proceedings in civil cases in this state and to repeal all acts in relation thereto,' approved March 17, 1911." Stats. 1915, p. 164.

Section 2 of the act provides:

"Any party to an action or special proceeding from the time said action or proceeding is called for trial, and until including final judgment has been entered therein, may object and except to any ruling, decision, or order of the court or judge made therein, and, within twenty (20) days after such objection and exception, serve and file a bill of exceptions to such ruling, decision, or action of the court, which bill of exceptions shall be settled and allowed by the judge or court, or by stipulation of the parties, as in the preceding section provided, and when so settled and allowed shall be and become a part of the record of said action or proceeding."

Section 7 of the act provides:

"Bills of exception provided for by section 2 of this act may be prepared, served, and filed within twenty (20) days after a motion for a new trial has been determined by the court, and all errors relied upon which may have occurred at the trial, or which may be alleged against the findings, or exceptions to the findings as made, and all errors based upon any ground for a new trial, may be included therein, and all such errors may be reviewed by the supreme court on appeal from the judgment or order denying the motion for a new trial."

Section 15 of the act provides:

"Sections 389, 390, 391, 392, 393, 394, 395, 396, and 397 of the above-entitled act, and all provisions of law in conflict herewith, are hereby repealed; but nothing contained herein shall affect or invalidate any proceedings already had in any action or special proceeding now pending, but said action or proceeding may be finally heard and determined upon the record made under the existing law."

It will be observed that neither section 386 nor section 401 of the practice act are expressly repealed by the act of 1915. Whether a statute was repealed by a later one is a judicial, not a legislative, question. It is therefore a question of judicial construction whether section 386 is in conflict with the statute of 1915, and whether section 401 was repealed by said act. Repeal or no repeal is a question of legislative intention; and there are acknowledged rules for ascertaining that intention. From the framework of the statute of 1915 it is apparent that the legislature designed it to be and to operate as a complete revision of the practice then in vogue respecting statements on appeal, and to substitute therefor, in toto, a system of bills of exception. The act specifies with much particularity how and when exceptions may be taken, how they may become a part of the record, how to be prepared and served, and what may be included therein to be reviewable on appeal from the judgment or order denying the motion for a new trial. The act is a complete revision of section 401, and operates to enlarge the common acceptation of bills of exception so as to make it perform the function of a statement on appeal. Section 5 of the act provides, inter alia, that the shorthand report of the proceedings in any action, when certified to, may, at the option of any party, be submitted to the court for allowance and settlement, as the bill of exceptions required under the provisions of the act, and become a part of the record. The option is usually exercised. Prior to the act of 1915 section 401 was declared by this court to be a separate and distinct method of appeal. Ward v. Silver Peak, 39 Nev. 80, 148 Pac. 345, 153 Pac. 434, 154 Pac. 74. It will be observed that the provision contained in section 401 that makes it a separate and distinct method of appeal was not carried into the act of 1915. The latter act provides in detail how the record may be placed in condition to be reviewed on appeal from the judgment or order denying a motion for a new trial, but, unlike section 401, it is silent as to the method of appeal. In this state of the law the question whether it is necessary to first move for a new trial before taking an appeal from the judgment is vexatiously doubtful. The two provisions relate to the same subject-matter, and it cannot be said that they are different in purview; neither are they repugnant or inconsistent, but the latter statute is clearly intended to prescribe the only rule which should govern the cases provided for in the former, and omits the provision of the section: "The party aggrieved may appeal from the judgment without further statement or motion." What, then, is the effect of the statute of 1915 upon section 401? The rule is that, if the new statute revises the subject-matter of the old, and is plainly intended as a substitute, it will operate as a repeal of the old statute. Thorpe v. Schooling, 7 Nev. 15; State v. Rogers, 10 Nev. 322; Swensen v. So. Pac. Co. (Or.) 174 Pac. 158; Strickland v. Geide, 31 Or. 373, 49 Pac. 982; Road Co. v. Allen, 16 Barb. (N.Y.) 15; Roche v. Mayor, etc., 40 N. J. Law, 257; Swann v. Buck, 40 Miss. 268; Daviess v. Fairbairn, 3 How. 636, 11 L. Ed. 760; Murdoch v. City of Memphis, 20 Wall. 592, 22 L. Ed. 429.

In the case of Roche v. Mayor, etc., supra, the court said:

"The rule does not rest strictly upon the ground of repeal by implication, but upon the principle that, when the legislature makes a revision of a particular statute, and frames a new statute upon the subject-matter, and from the framework of the act it is apparent that the legislature designed a complete scheme for this matter, it is a legislative declaration that whatever is embraced in the new law shall prevail, and whatever is excluded is discarded. It is decisive evidence of an intention to prescribe the provisions contained in the later act as the only ones on that subject which shall be obligatory. Sacramento v. Bird, 15 Cal. 294; State v. Conkling, 19 Cal. 501."

Manifestly it was the intention of the legislature by the act of 1915 to prescribe the only regulations to be observed in the preparation of a record for review in the appellate court. When a statute is revised, or one act framed from another, some part being omitted, the parts omitted are not revived by construction, but are to be considered as annulled. Eureka Bank Cases, 35 Nev. 85, 126 Pac. 655, 129 Pac. 308; State v. Wilson, 43 N. H. 419, 82 Am. Dec. 163; Farr v. Brackett, 30 Vt. 344; Pingree v. Snell, 42 Me. 53.

Tested by the above standards of construction, section 401 is repealed by the statute of 1915.

6. What, then, is the effect of the statute of 1915 upon section 386? It is a general and well-established rule of construction that one statute is not repugnant to another unless they relate to the same subject and are enacted for the same purpose. If the objects of both statutes are not the same, the two statutes will be permitted to stand, although they may refer to the same subject. United States v. Claflin, 97 U. S. 546, 24 L. Ed. 1082; McMillan v. Payne Co., 14 Okl. 659, 79 Pac. 898; Swensen v. So. Pac. Co., supra. Undoubtedly section 386 and the statute of 1915 relate to the same subject, in so far as both are designed to correct errors on appeal, but it is clear that the object of section 386 was to provide when a motion for a new trial must be made before appeal is taken, and when not necessary. The statute of 1915 relates to bills of exception. Since the object of section 386 relates solely to new trials, and the statute of 1915

to bills of exception, we conclude that they may stand together without either conflicting with the other. When exceptions are taken as required by the act, and they fall within the cases pointed out by section 386, it becomes a simple matter to move for a new trial before taking an appeal from the judgment. This interpretation is the only one consistent with the context and spirit of both enactments, and the only one that harmonizes and makes consistent the several provisions of the practice act.

7. It is insisted by counsel for appellant that the decisions of the Supreme Court of California construing the California act of 1915 (page 209) may well be followed in the construction of our statute of 1915 with reference to the discontinuance of the practice of first moving for a new trial on an appeal from a judgment. We learn from the decisions cited that in California there is no longer an appeal from an order denying a motion for a new trial. Allen Co. v. Wood, 32 Cal. App. 76, 162 Pac. 121; Nathan v. Porter (Cal. App.) 172 Pac. 170. Unlike our statute, a motion for a new trial and an appeal therefrom is clearly recognized.

8. This court has repeatedly held that, where the method of appeal is prescribed by the statute, it must be followed. Coffin v. Coffin, 40 Nev. 347, 163 Pac. 731; Gardner v. Pac. Power Co., 40 Nev. 344, 163 Pac. 731; Ward v. Silver Peak, 39 Nev. 89, 148 Pac. 345, 153 Pac. 434, 154 Pac. 74. Exceptional cases may, and doubtless often do, arise wherein it would be an idle and useless ceremony, so far as the trial court is concerned, to move for a new trial; but this assumption does not justify a departure from the statutory method of taking appeals. Burbank v. Rivers, 20 Nev. 87, 16 Pac. 430.

9. It is useless to repeat what has so often been said by this court, that it is as unsatisfactory to the court as it is to counsel (and litigants) to have cases disposed of upon mere questions of practice, but, as the point involved arises upon the construction of a recent statute

designed for the working over of earlier acts, and is one of such general importance, we are impelled to lay down a rule for guidance in future cases.

Entertaining the views as herein expressed, we are of the opinion that, where an appeal is based upon alleged errors, as pointed out in section 5323, Revised Laws, a motion for a new trial must be made and determined before the appeal is taken. As this was not done in this case, nothing remains for us to do but to sustain the motion to dismiss the appeal.

The motion is sustained.

ON REHEARING

By the Court, SANDERS, J.:

We granted a rehearing in this cause for the purpose of giving further consideration to the point raised in opposition to the conclusion reached.

Appellant insists that as the appeal was taken upon the judgment roll alone, and the errors sought to be reviewed being made a part of the record on appeal from the judgment, as required by section 11 of Statutes of 1915, p. 164, it became and was the duty of the court to review all errors that appear on the face of the judgment roll. Upon further consideration, we are entirely satisfied that the opinion furnishes a full and complete answer to this proposition. By adhering to the express mandate of the statute (Rev. Laws, 5328), we complied with the law. Certainly no more substantial reason could be given for our action. Williams v. Rice, 13 Nev. 235. The appeal was taken upon the judgment roll alone. The court, therefore, certainly acquired jurisdiction of the appeal. It probably would have been more regular to have affirmed the judgment than to have dismissed the appeal; but, in the view we take of the judgment roll, the order of dismissal amounts to an affirmance of the judgment.

The only errors appearing on the face of the judgment roll, other than those enumerated in section 5328,

Revised Laws, are directed to the court's sustaining the challenge of the defendant to certain prospective jurors, Hotchkiss and Perow, upon the ground of implied bias. After reading the exhaustive voir dire examination of these gentlemen, we are in no position to say that the court erred in permitting them to remain in the jury box.

The judgment must be affirmed.

It is so ordered.

[No. 2309]

NELLIE MILLER NICKEL AND J. LEROY NICKEL, AS TRUSTEES UNDER THAT CERTAIN DEED OF TRUST DATED APRIL 17, 1913, MADE, EXECUTED AND DELIVERED BY HENRY MILLER TO NELLIE MILLER NICKEL AND J. LEROY NICKEL, AS TRUSTEES, AND RECORDED IN BOOK 972 OF DEEDS (N.S.), PAGE 170, IN THE COUNTY RECORDER'S OFFICE OF THE CITY AND COUNTY OF SAN FRANCISCO, STATE OF CALIFORNIA, APPELLANTS, v. THE STATE OF NEVADA, RESPONDENT.

[No. 2310]

GEORGE A. COLE, AS STATE CONTROLLER OF THE STATE OF NEVADA, RESPONDENT, v. J. LEROY NICKEL AND NELLIE MILLER NICKEL, AS TRUSTEES, ETC., ET AL., APPELLANTS.

[177 Pac. 409; 185 Pac. 565]

1. TAXATION—TRANSFER TAX—CONSTRUCTION OF DEED OF TRUST.
    In determining whether a deed of trust immediately vested legal title so as to exempt transfer from a transfer tax under inheritance-tax law, the deed will be construed, together with a will executed simultaneously therewith as a single instrument.

2. TAXATION—TRANSFER TAX—DEED OF TRUST—CONSTRUCTION.
    Deed of trust by 86-year-old invalid after enactment of inheritance-tax law, but shortly before law took effect, transferring stock to trustees with directions to pay income to grantor during his life, with directions as to disposition of property after his death, corresponding to provisions of will executed simultaneously with deed, was intended as disposition of property to take effect at or after grantor's death, within inheritance-tax law.

3. TAXATION—TRANSFER TAX—DEED OF TRUST—WEIGHT OF EVIDENCE.

Where, immediately after execution of the will, testator executed deed of trust directing trustees to pay testator income during his natural life and directed disposal of property following his death by provisions corresponding to those in will, evidence that execution of deed was an afterthought to avoid, if possible. an expected increase in the tax rate in California and a probable inheritance tax of federal government. is entitled to weight in action to impose a transfer tax under inheritance-tax law.

4. TRUSTS—REVOCABILITY.

It is only in cases where other parties besides the person creating the trust have an interest therein that the trust becomes irrevocable.

5. TRUSTS—REVOCABILITY—DEED OF TRUST.

Deed of trust transferring stock to trustees, with direction to pay income to grantor during his life and directing disposition after death in manner corresponding to will executed simultaneously, beneficiaries receiving no present interest, grantor could revoke deed of trust.

6. DEEDS—VALIDITY—EFFECT UPON EXECUTION.

A deed to be valid should take effect in interest upon its execution, though the right of possession or enjoyment may not take place until the happening of a certain event.

7. WILLS—DEED OR WILL—FUTURE INTERESTS.

Where interests created do not arise until death of donor or some other future time. the instrument cannot be a deed, although so denominated and accompanied by words of immediate grant, a sufficient consideration, and formal delivery.

8. DEEDS—ESTATES WHICH MAY BE CREATED.

There is no natural right to create artificial and technical estates with limitations over, nor has the remainderman any more right to succeed to the possession of property under such deeds than legatees or devisees under a will.

9. DEEDS—CONSTRUCTION—FEE.

It is the policy of the law to encourage making conveyances in fee.

10. DEEDS—LEGALITY.

It is as lawful to create an estate for life with remainder after death of the grantor as it is to convey in fee.

11. TAXATION—"TRANSFER TAX"—NATURE.

The "transfer tax," imposed by inheritance-tax law. is in the nature of an excise tax, to wit. on the transfer of property.

12. TAXATION—TRANSFER TAX—RIGHTS AND OBLIGATIONS.

The rights and obligations of all parties in regard to payment of inheritance tax under inheritance-tax law are determinable as of the time of the death of the decedent.

13. Taxation—Inheritance Tax—Statute—Operation.

Transfer of stock by deed of trust intended to take effect in possession or enjoyment at or after grantor's death was taxable under the inheritance-tax law, although such law had not taken effect at time of execution of deed; the property having vested at time of death and not at the date of the execution of the deed.

ON REHEARING

1. Taxation—Transfer Tax Not Interference with Comity between States.

Where the devolution of title to property involves a succession or inheritance tax, it is governed and controlled by the laws of the forum imposing the tax, if the transfer sought to be taxed is within the jurisdiction of the tax authorities, and imposition of such tax cannot be denied, on the ground that it would interfere with comity between states, for it is a well-settled rule that no foreign law will be enforced in a sovereign state, if to enforce it will contravene the express statute law or expressed public policy of the forum or is injurious to its interests.

2. Taxation—Tax on Transfer in Contemplation of Death.

Whether a transfer by way of trust is one intended to take effect at or after the grantor's death does not depend on whether the trust is revocable, but the test is whether the property passes with all attributes of ownership, independently of the death of the transferor.

APPEAL from Second Judicial District Court, Washoe County; *R. C. Stoddard*, Judge.

Proceeding by George A. Cole, as Controller of the State of Nevada, against J. Leroy Nickel and another, trustees, and others. From an order and judgment assessing a transfer tax against property involved and from an order denying and overruling motion for new trial, defendants appeal. Affirmed, COLEMAN, J., dissenting.

On rehearing, affirmed, COLEMAN, J., dissenting.

On writ of error to United States Supreme Court.

Cheney, Downer, Price & Hawkins and *Edward F. Treadwell*, for Appellants:

The estates created by the deed and transfer vested before the act in question became effective. The transfer made by the deed of trust dated April 17, 1913, created vested estates in the beneficiaries and in the remaindermen; no power of revocation being reserved, such estates were not subject to be defeated by any act of the grantor, and they vested at the date of the transfer, and not at the date of the death of the grantor. Nichols v. Emery, 109 Cal. 323; Tennant v. Tennant Memorial Home, 167 Cal. 570. No power of revocation was reserved in the deed of trust. Gray v. Union Trust Co., 171 Cal. 637. Future estates, conditional estates, and contingent estates are as much vested property rights as are present, absolute, unconditional estates, and are as much entitled to protection under the constitution. "An estate is vested when there is an immediate right of present enjoyment or a fixed right of future enjoyment." Estate of Stanford, 126 Cal. 122.

The inheritance-tax act by its terms does not apply to any transfer made before it became effective. It is presumed to be prospective, and to apply only to future transactions; not retroactive or applicable to past transactions, in the absence of an express provision to the contrary. 36 Cyc. L. & P., pp. 1205–1208; Milliken v. Sloat, 1 Nev. 573; Hunter v. Savage Mining Co., 4 Nev. 153; State v. Manhattan-Verde, 32 Nev. 474; State v. Eggers, 33 Nev. 535; United States v. Heth, 7 U. S. 399; Chew Heong v. United States, 112 U. S. 536. "It is hardly necessary to say that such statutes are exceptions to the almost universal rule that all statutes are addressed to the future and not to the past. They usually constitute a new factor in the affairs and relations of men, and should not be held to affect what has happened unless, indeed, explicit words be used, or by clear implication that construction be required." Winfree v. Northern P. R. Co., 227 U. S. 296, 57 L. Ed. 518; Ogden v. Blackledge, 2 Cranch, 272; Surgett v. Lapice, 8 How. 48; Murray v. Gibson, 56 U. S. 421; White v. United States, 191 U. S. 545; United States v. American Sugar Refining Co., 202 U. S. 563; United States Fidelity Co. v. Struthers

Wells Co., 209 U. S. 306; United States v. Schofield Co., 182 Fed. 240. "Laws which create new obligations, or impose new duties, or exact new penalties because of past transactions, have been universally reprobated by civil- and common-law writers, and it is to be presumed that no statute is intended to have such effect unless the contrary clearly appears. This is especially so where to give the statute retrospective effect would work manifest injustice." Pignaz v. Burnett, 119 Cal. 157. "Retroaction is never allowed to a statute unless required by express legislative mandate or unavoidable implication." Vanderbilt v. All Persons, 163 Cal. 507; Gates v. Salmon, 28 Cal. 320; Estate of Richmond, 9 Cal. App. 402; People v. Nash, 15 Cal. App. 320; Craycroft v. Superior Court, 18 Cal. App. 781; State Commission v. Welch, 20 Cal. App. 624; Ferlage v. Supreme Tribe, 153 Ky. 645; Heiskell v. Lowe, 153 S. W. 284; Walton v. Woodward, 73. Kan. 238; Denny v. Bean, 51 Or. 180; Casey v. Bingham, 37 Okl. 484; In Re Lamprecht, 137 Mich. 450; Brown v. Hughes, 89 Minn. 150; Harrelson v. W. U. T. Co., 90 S. C. 132; Thomas v. Higgs, 68 W. Va. 152.

The act could not constitutionally be made applicable to the transfer in question. Laws imposing inheritance taxes are to be strictly construed against the state. "In accordance with the well-settled rules of construction, statutes of this character cannot be so construed as to extend their meaning beyond the clear import of the words used." United States v. Watts, 1 Bond, 580, Fed. Cas. 16,653; Fox's Administrators v. Commonwealth, 16 Gratt. 1. "But a law imposing taxes will be construed in favor of the subject and against the sovereign." In Re Cullen's Estate, 21 Atl. 781; In Re Feyerweather, 143 N. Y. 119; In Re Vassar's Estate, 127 N. Y. 12; In Re Enston's Estate, 113 N. Y. 178. "It is an old and familiar rule of the English courts, applicable to all forms of taxation, and particularly special taxes, that the sovereign is bound to express its intention to tax in clear and unambiguous language, and that a liberal construction be given to words of exception confining the operation of duty." Eidman v. Martinez, 46 L. Ed. 697; Disston v. McClain, 147 Fed. 114; Lynch v. Union Trust Co., 164 Fed. 161; People v. Koenig, 37 Colo. 283; Re Harbeck's Will, 161 N. Y. 211; Bailey v. Henry, 143 S. W. 1124; In Re Durfee's Estate, 140 N. Y. Supp. 594; In Re Terry's Estate, 112 N. E. 931.

Laws imposing inheritance taxes are universally held not to be deemed retroactive or to impose a tax on rights which have accrued prior to the passage of such laws. Howe v. Howe, 179 Mass. 546; Carter v. Whitcomb, 74 N. H. 482; Eury's Exrs. v. State, 74 N. E. 650; In Re Forsythe's Estate, 32 N. Y. Supp. 175; Gilbertson v. Ballard, 125 Iowa, 420; Re Hendrick's Estate, 3 N. Y. Supp. 281; Morrow v. Depper, 133 N. W. 729; Lacey v. State Treasurer, 132 N. W. 843; Warrimer v. People, 6 Dem. Sur. 211; In Re Miller, 18 N. E. 139; In Re Appeal of Lambard, 34 Atl. 530; Commonwealth v. Wellford, 76 S. E. 917. "Ordinarily statutes will not be given a retrospective effect unless there is no other reasonable interpretation to be placed upon their language." People v. Carpenter, 106 N. E. 302; Commonwealth v. McCauley's Exr., 179 S. W. 41; In Re Haight's Estate, 136 N. Y. Supp. 557; McLain v. Penn Co., 108 Fed. 618; Keeney v. New York, 222 U. S. 525.

Taxes on transfers made in contemplation of death, or intended to take effect in possession or enjoyment after death, have always been held to be governed by the law in force at the time of the transfer, and not by the law in force at the time of death, and not to be subject to inheritance-tax laws passed after such transfers. Gilbertson v. Ballard, 125 Iowa, 420; Re Hendrick's Estate, 3 N. Y. Supp. 281; Morrow v. Depper, 133 N. W. 729; Lacey v. State Treasurer, 132 N. W. 843; Commonwealth v. McCauley's Exr., 179 S. W. 41; In Re Haight's Estate, 136 N. Y. Supp. 557; In Re Webber, 136 N. Y. Supp. 83; Polhemus's Estate, 145

N. Y. Supp. 1107; Haley's Estate, 152 N. Y. Supp. 732; In Re Keeney, 194 N. Y. 281; Matter of Thompson, 87 Misc. Rep. 539; Matter of Valentine, 91 Misc. Rep. 203. "But the statute does not impose a tax on the property, but on the transfer. The validity of that burden must be determined by the situation as it existed when the deed was made." Keeney v. Comptroller, 56 L. Ed. 299; In Re Hodge's Estate, 215 N. Y. 447; People v. Carpenter, 106 N. E. 302; People v. Griffith, 245 Ill. 532; People v. Union Trust Co., 255 Ill. 168; Ormsby County v. Kearney, 37 Nev. 314; Cowlick v. Shingle, 5 Wyo. 87; Laporte v. Gamewell Tel. Co., 146 Ind. 466.

If the inheritance-tax act be construed to impose a tax on the interests, estates, and property rights which passed by the deed and vested before its passage, it is unconstitutional, being in violation of the Fourteenth Amendment to the Constitution of the United States, section 10 of article 1 of said constitution, section 8 of article 1, section 15 of article 5, and section 1 of article 10 of the Constitution of the State of Nevada. "Legislation which impairs the value of a vested estate is unconstitutional." Re Pell, 171 N. Y. 48; Matter of Lansing, 182 N. Y. 238; Matter of Vanderbilt, 172 N. Y. 69. "That law [inheritance-tax law] is prospective in its operation, and it is beyond the power of the state, even if it so desired, to subject to its operation property which the owner in good faith disposed of before his death." State v. Probate Court, 104 Minn. 268, 113 N. W. 888; Lacey v. State Treasurer, 132 N. W. 843; Pullen v. Wake Co., 66 N. C. 361; In Re Meyer, 83 N. Y. App. Div. 381; In Re Smith, 135 N. Y. Supp. 240; Matter of Craig, 89 N. Y. Supp. 972; Matter of Chapman, 117 N. Y. Supp. 679; Commonwealth v. Wellford, 76 S. E. 917; In Re Haggerty, 112 N. Y. Supp. 1017. "It is immaterial, so far as the question we discussed is concerned, that it is alleged that the transfer was made 'in contemplation of his death and without valuable consideration.' The estate conveyed fully vested at the time of the delivery of the deed in escrow, entirely regardless of the motives of the grantor for the conveyance, and without regard to whether the transfer was without valuable consideration, and there was then no law imposing a tax on any such transfer." Hunt v. Wicht, 162 Pac. 639.

The mere fact that a deed executed before the date upon which the inheritance-tax law became effective is made in contemplation of death, or intended to take effect in possession and enjoyment after death, does not make it taxable. Re Hendrick's Estate, 3 N. Y. Supp. 281; Morrow v. Depper, 133 N. W. 729; Lacey v. State Treasurer, 132 N. W. 843; Commonwealth v. McCauley's Executors, 179 S. W. 41; In Re Haight's Estate, 136 N. Y. Supp. 557; Gilbertson v. Ballard, 125 Iowa, 420; In Re Webber, 136 N. Y. Supp. 83; Polhemus's Estate, 145 N. Y. Supp. 1107; Haley's Estate, 152 N. Y. Supp. 732; State v. Probate Court, 102 Minn. 268; In Re Slosson's Estate, 216 N. Y. 79. The mere fact that a deed was made before the date upon which an inheritance-tax law goes into effect was made with the intention of avoiding the tax, does not make it taxable. State v. Probate Court, 102 Minn. 268. The fact that a deed executed before the date upon which an inheritance-tax law goes into effect created estates which are technically contingent, and do not become vested until after the death of the grantor and after the act became effective, does not make them taxable. Matter of Lansing, 182 N. Y. 238; Matter of Vanderbilt, 172 N. Y. 69; Lacey v. State Treasurer, 132 N. W. 843; In Re Smith, 135 N. Y. Supp. 24; Matter of Craig, 89 N. Y. Supp. 972. The mere fact that the beneficiaries do not come into the actual possession of the property until after the inheritance tax goes into effect, does not make it taxable. Matter of Valentine, 91 Misc. Rep. 203; Commonwealth v. Wellford, 76 S. E. 911.

Geo. B. Thatcher, Attorney-General, and *William McKnight*, Deputy Attorney-General, for Respondent:

It is not necessary that the inheritance-tax statute operate retrospectively in order to tax the transfers herein involved. The tax became due on the date of death, and on that day the right of the state to receive the tax became fixed and vested. Appeal of Lambard, 88 Me. 587. "But the occasion for the tax being the devolution of the property, it ought to attach to such interests only as arise by reason of a death subsequent to the act." Eury's Exrs. v. State, 74 N. Y. 650.

The transfers were intended to and did take effect in possession only upon the death of the testator. The property did not vest in possession or enjoyment until after such death. In Re Masury's Estate, 51 N. Y. Supp. 331; In Re Ogsbury's Estate, 39 N. Y. Supp. 978; Barbey's Estate, 114 N. Y. Supp. 725; Patterson's Estate, 127 N. Y. Supp. 284; Seaman's Estate, 147 N. Y. 69; Green's Estate, 153 N. Y. 223; Bostwick's Estate, 160 N. Y. 489; In Re Douglas County, 84 Neb. 506; Appeal of Bibert, 110 Pa. 329; Crocker v. Shaw, 174 Mass. 266; New England Trust Co. v. Abbott, 91 N. E. 379; State v. Bullen, 143 Wis. 512. "We are equally clear in the conclusion that the trust deed * * * did not vest the beneficiary with any rights of property until the death of the grantor, and that it comes within the provisions of the statute, and is subject to the tax ordered to be collected by the order of the surrogate." In Re Masbury's Estate, supra.

When the possession and enjoyment are postponed during the life of the grantor, that fact subjects the property to payment of the inheritance tax. In Re Moir's Estate, 69 N. E. 905; Reisch v. Commonwealth, 106 Pa. St. 521. The beneficiaries under the deed of trust must trace their succession through the will, and the rights of the parties are determined by the law as it stood at the date of death. In Re Douglas County, supra; In Re Ogsbury's Estate, supra; In Re Brandreth, 169 N. Y. 437; In Re Hart's Estate, 169 N. Y. 716. Whether a deed is made in contemplation of death, is a question of fact on which the finding of the trial court is final. Blackmore & Bancroft, Inheritance

Taxes, sec. 114. The trial court found that the trust deed was made in contemplation of death, and appellants concede that, "if this act had been in force at the time of the transfer, the same might be held to be in contemplation of death." This, in itself, is sufficient to authorize the tax in question. People v. Carpenter, 264 Ill. 400.

The fact that the trust deed and the will were executed on the same day, makes them a single transaction, entered into for the purpose of evading the inheritance tax, and brings the transfer squarely within the law as taking effect after the death of the grantor. In Re Dobson, 132 N. Y. 472; People v. Moir, 207 Ill. 180; Reisch v. Commonwealth, 106 Pa. 521; Conwell's Estate, 5 Pa. Co. Ct. 368. The deed was not recorded until after the death of the grantor. This fact makes the statute applicable. In Re Shearer, 73 N. Y. Supp. 1057.

The test by which the exemption is to be ascertained is not whether a power to revoke was or was not inserted in the trust deed, but upon the passing of the property, with all the attributes of ownership, independently of the death of the grantor. State Street Trust Co. v. Stevens, 95 N. E. 851. A tax on a passing by will is imposed at the date of death, and there is certainly no difference in principle between property passing by deed intended to take effect in possession and enjoyment on the death of the grantor and property passing by will. Crocker v. Shaw, 174 Mass. 245; N. E. Trust Co. v. Abbott, 205 Mass. 279; In Re Line's Estate, 155 Pa. St. 378.

If the inheritance-tax act be construed as imposing a tax on the transfers involved, the same is not unconstitutional nor in violation of any constitutional provision. State ex rel. Gelsthrope v. Turnell, 20 Mont. 219; Stevens v. Brodford, 185 Mass. 439; Attorney-General v. Stone, 209 Mass. 186; Carpenter v. State, 17 How. 456; Attorney-General v. Middleton, 3 Hurl. & N. 125;

In Re Short's Estate, 16 Pa. St. 66; Commonwealth v. Smith, 5 Pa. St. 143; State v. Mollier, 96 Ky. 514.

Since the tax is imposed upon the privilege of receiving or taking property, and not upon the property itself (33 L. R. A. 606), and since the privilege is itself not a natural right, but a creature of law, it follows as a corollary that, except in so far as it is clearly restricted by the constitution, the legislature may impose such burdens upon it as it may see fit. In Re Tuohy's Estate, 90 Pac. 170.

The naked legal title, which is all that passed by the trust deed, is not a vested interest in the sense of a property right which the courts will protect from retroactive legislation. Diamond State I. Co. v. Husbands, 8 Del. Ch. 205. So long as anything remains to be done to complete the transfer, the tax may be imposed, for until then the transfer is not complete. Estates do not vest in the sense of being exempt from an inheritance tax until the time for the vesting occurs. The tax, being based upon the right to receive, may be imposed, and by the Nevada statute is imposed, on all transfers which were not fully completed in possession and enjoyment at the time the act went into effect. Chandler v. Kelsey, 205 U. S. 466; Magoun v. Bank, 170 U. S. 283; Plumber v. Coler, 178 U. S. 115; Runnemarcher v. State, 129 Wis. 190; Westhus v. Union I. Co., 164 Fed. 795; Mertz v. Woodman, 218 U. S. 205; New England Trust Co. v. Abbott, 91 N. E. 379; Minot v. Stevens, 93 N. E. 973.

By the Court, SANDERS, J.:

This was a statutory proceeding brought by Cole as Controller of the State of Nevada, against the appellants under our so-called inheritance-tax law (Stats. 1913, p. 411). The appeal is prosecuted to review an order and judgment assessing and adjudging a transfer tax against the property involved for the sum of $48,149.78, and from an order denying and overruling the appellants' motion for a new trial.

The facts of the case are as follows: On March 26, 1913, the inheritance-tax law was approved, but by the terms of section 31 of the act it did not take effect until thirty days thereafter, or April 25, 1913 (Stats. 1913, pp. 411–422). Prior to April 17, 1913, Henry Miller, deceased, a resident of San Francisco, Cal., was the owner of 119,875.75 shares of stock in Miller & Lux, Incorporated, a Nevada corporation. This corporation owned all of the capital stock of the Pacific Live Stock Company, a California corporation. The latter corporation owned a large amount of real estate and personal property in Nevada, appraised at $1,431,326.86. To the extent that this stock represented the property situated in Nevada, it is taxable under section 1 of the act, which provides:

"For the purposes of this act, the ownership of shares of stock in a corporation owning property in this state shall be considered as the ownership of such interest in the property so owned by such corporation, as the number of shares so owned shall bear to the entire issued and outstanding capital stock of such corporation."

This proposition is not disputed by appellants if the property is otherwise subject to the act.

On April 17, 1913, after the enactment and adoption of the act in question, and eight days before it became effective, Henry Miller, having prior thereto made other wills, published and declared his last will and testament, nominating therein Nellie Miller Nickel, J. Leroy Nickel, and F. B. Anderson as executors thereof without bonds. Immediately after the publication and declaration of his will, Henry Miller executed and delivered to Nellie Miller Nickel and J. Leroy Nickel a deed of trust, by which all of the said stock was transferred to said trustees upon certain trusts. On the same date the trustees accepted the trust in writing. On the same date the stock was transferred on the books of the corporation to the trustees. The deed of trust and stock were thereafter kept in the exclusive custody of the trustees.

At the time of the execution of the will and deed, Henry Miller was 86 years of age, was an invalid under medical care and treatment, and afflicted with physical ailments from which he never recovered, and on October 14, 1916, he died. On June 4, 1913, Henry Miller published and declared a codicil to his last will and testament, whereby the said Anderson was relieved of his trust as executor; he having theretofore expressed his desire to decline the trust. The deed contains substantially the same trusts as the will, and directs the trustees to pay the beneficiaries the amounts therein specified, which are the same as named in the will, and on the same conditions and limitations. The stock was, by the deed of trust, transferred to the trustees:

"To have and to hold the same as such trustees upon the following uses and trusts and for the following uses and purposes, that is to say:

"I. During the lifetime of the said party of the first part the said trustees shall receive the rents, issues and profits of said property and pay the same to the party of the first part, during the term of his natural life.

"II. (1) Upon and after the death of the said party of the first part the said trustees shall take and hold all of said property, and shall convert sufficient thereof into cash to pay the several amounts hereby directed to be paid, and shall collect the rents, issues and profits thereof, and therefrom shall be by them applied in the manner hereinafter set forth:

"(2) From the proceeds of the sale of said property said trustees shall pay the following sums: [Then follows list of persons and amounts to be paid to them. Some of these payments are to be made monthly and shall not extend beyond the lives of designated parties and 'their children living at the time of the death of the party of the first part.' It also provides that upon the death of certain of said parties before receiving said sums, the share of such deceased person shall go to others.]

"(o) They shall pay to the following-named employees of said party of the first part and Miller & Lux, Incorporated, the following sums as soon after the death of said party of the first part as possible: [Then follows list of such employees with the amounts to be paid to each.]

"If any of the above-named persons be not employed by said party of the first part or Miller & Lux, Incorporated, at the time of the death of said party of the first part, the provisions by this subdivision made for him shall lapse. [Then follows list of other beneficiaries, with the amounts to be paid to each, followed by the provisions that all of the income from the said property, except the income from certain specified bequests, 'from the time of the death of said party of the first part shall be paid to the daughter of said party of the first part, etc.']

"III. Nothing herein shall be construed to restrain the free alienation of any of said property and said trustees may sell any of said property at public or private sale, with or without notice, and on such terms as they may see fit. Whenever said trustees are authorized to invest any of said property, they shall invest the same only in real estate, mortgages on real estate, bonds of the United States, or of some county or municipal corporation within the United States, or stock or bonds of the corporations Miller & Lux, Incorporated, Pacific Live Stock Company, or the San Joaquin & Kings River Canal & Irrigation Company, Incorporated. All of the sums directed to be paid by the second (II) paragraph of this deed shall be paid as soon as sufficient money may be realized from the sale of the said property without injury thereto, and the same shall be paid as soon as in the judgment of said trustees it can be done without loss, but not later than ten (10) years after the death of said party of the first part and during the lives of the descendants of said party of the first part living at the time of his death, and said trustees may pay the same in such amounts and at such times as may be most beneficial, and none of said amounts shall bear interest; provided, that at least one hundred and fifty ($150) dollars a month shall be paid on account of the provision for the daughter-in-law of said party of the first part, Sarah E. Miller, from the time of the death of said party of the first part. Nothing herein shall be construed to required or permit the accumulation of the income of said property, but the entire income of said property shall at all times be applied to the purposes herein set forth. If any person to whom any sum of money is directed to be paid dies before the death of said party of the first part, such provision shall lapse except as otherwise provided herein. If any of the sums directed by this deed to be paid to or set aside for the benefit of the persons named herein shall be paid or set aside in whole or in part by any trustees named in the last will and testament of said party of the first part from any estate coming into their possession under said will, such payment shall be deemed to be in satisfaction of the provision herein made for such party, and also in satisfaction of the provision in such will made for such party, in whole or in part, as the case may be, and the parties of the second part shall hold and dispose of the property conveyed hereby upon the remaining trusts designated herein."

It appears that Henry Miller once expressed a desire to change one of the legacies specified in the trust deed, but he was advised by his counsel that it was not possible for him to do so "as no power of revocation had been reserved in the deed."

It is the contention of the State of Nevada that the deed of trust was either made in contemplation of death, or was intended to take effect in possession or enjoyment at or after death within the meaning of the term "contemplation of death" as used in the act, which is defined by the act as follows:

"The words 'contemplation of death' as used in this act shall be taken to include that expectancy of death which actuates the mind of a person on the execution of his will, and in no wise shall said words be limited and restricted to that expectancy of death which actuates the mind of a person in making a gift causa mortis. * * *" Section 30.

Counsel for appellants in reply to this position state in their brief:

"It is not necessary for us to discuss these questions, because for the purpose of this appeal only we are willing to concede that, if this act had been in force at the time of this transfer, the same might be held to be made in contemplation of death, or not intended to take effect in possession or enjoyment at or after death within the meaning of the statute. Section 1. We do this because we have entire confidence in the position which we take in the case, viz, that whether in fact made in contemplation of death, or in law or in fact intended to take effect in possession or enjoyment after death so far as the beneficiaries other than Henry Miller are concerned, the transfer at its date created vested interests to which the act was not intended to apply, and to which it could not constitutionally apply."

If we clearly interpret counsel's admission, the questions to be determined are narrowed down to three propositions: Did the deed of trust create a vested estate? Does the act apply to transfers made before it became effective? Can the act constitutionally be made to apply to such a transfer? Reading the opinion of the trial court in connection with its findings and conclusions, we take it that the last question is eliminated from the case. The district court in its opinion states:

"It will be noted that the statute went into effect April 25, 1913, and is not by its express terms made retroactive. Hence it must be construed as having only a prospective operation, as no intent to make the same operate retrospectively may be inferred from the words therein employed; therefore, if the interests in the property mentioned in the deed passed to and vested absolutely in the beneficiaries therein named upon the date of the execution and delivery of the deed and independently of the death of Henry Miller, no tax may lawfully be imposed thereon."

1-7. In this situation the vital point raised is: Did the deed of trust as of its date create a vested estate so as to exempt the transfer from the operation of the statute? The execution of the will, the deed, and the transfer of the stock was one transaction. To determine whether the indenture mediately vested the legal title to the stock so as to exempt the transfer from a transfer tax under the statute, the instruments must be construed together as a single instrument. In Re Brandreth, 58 App. Div. 575, 69 N. Y. Supp. 142; State v. Pabst, 139 Wis. 561, 121 N. W. 360. While it is true that the nominal sum of $10 is named as the consideration of the deed, we do not apprehend that it would be contended that the deed was intended to be anything more than a voluntary deed of gift to those whom the deceased regarded as the natural and worthy objects of his bounty. Considering the deed and will simultaneously executed, the physical condition of the deceased at the time, and the facts and circumstances attending and leading up to the execution of the indenture and transfer of the stock, as well as the language employed in the deed, construed in connection with that employed in the will, indicates that deceased disposed of his property to take effect in possession or enjoyment at or after his death. From the evidence, the impression is irresistible that the deed of trust was an afterthought to avoid, if possible, an expected increase in the inheritance-tax rate in California, and a probable inheritance tax of the federal government. Clearly the deceased was advised of these possibilities prior to the execution of the deed. This materially affects the weight of the deed as evidence in a case seeking to impose upon the transfer a transfer tax in this or any other court. The deceased, after the execution of the instruments and delivery of the deed, was advised that however much he desired to change any legacy provided for therein he could not do so, because no power of revocation had been reserved in the deed. This tends to indicate that the deceased in the first instance did not regard the indenture as irrevocable. We do not doubt the sincerity of the advice, but we are unable to perceive why the principle of law involved should be arbitrarily applied to the facts of this case, particularly in view of the expressed limitation in the deed that, upon and after the death of the grantor, the trustees shall take and hold all of said property. The paper clearly contemplates posthumous operation. It is only in cases where other parties besides the person creating the trust have an interest therein that the trust becomes irrevocable.

We see nothing in the deed that could have prevented the deceased from revoking the trust had he desired so to do. No beneficiaries or third party, as far as the record shows, had any present interest in the property to prevent the deceased, if necessary to do so, from invoking a court of equity to revoke the trust. The appellants and other appointees under the will had no such interest, because the deceased could have revoked his will and made another in favor of other parties. His beneficiaries in the indenture had no such interest, because the deceased had power by will to secure the property to others, and entirely exclude them from all interest therein. In Re Ogsbury's Estate, 7 App. Div. 71, 39 N. Y. Supp. 981. It is clear from both instruments that the trustees were not empowered to transfer any interest or pay any legacy created by either instrument until the death of the grantor. The property was to all intents and purposes that of Henry Miller, subject to the disposition made of it by his will published and declared simultaneously with the deed. No reason is suggested why Miller should conclude himself from the right of disposing of his property by will, or that the deed should be construed as nullifying his will. We do not say that it is necessary to the validity of a deed that it should convey an estate in immediate possession, but it is necessary that it should take effect in interest upon

its execution, though the right of possession or enjoy-
mènt may not take place until the happening of a certain event. Wall v. Wall, 30 Miss. 91, 64 Am. Dec. 152.
If, however, the interests created do not arise until the
death of the donor, or some other future time, the
instrument cannot be a deed, although it may be so
denominated by the maker, may have express words of
immediate grant, may have sufficient consideration to
support a grant, and may be formally delivered. Babb
v. Harrison, 9 Rich. Eq. (S. C.) 111, 70 Am. Dec. 204.
We do not deny that the donor may convey an interest,
reserving a lifetime estate to himself; but a deed, if
made with a view of the disposition of a man's estate
after his death, inures in law as a devise or will.
Wellborn v. Weaver, 17 Ga. 267, 63 Am. Dec. 242.

We are clearly of the opinion, construing the instruments together and in connection with other evidence,
that the district court correctly found that Henry Miller
did not divest himself of, or relinquish control over, the
interests of the beneficiaries named in the instruments,
and it was not until the death of Miller that the transfer
in any respect became absolute and that the beneficiaries
became irrevocably entitled to the various sums mentioned in the deed after the death of Miller.

8. There is no natural right to create artificial and
technical estates with limitations over, nor has the
remainderman any more right to succeed to the possession of property under such deeds than legatees or devisees under a will. The privilege of acquiring property
by such an instrument is as much dependent upon the law
as that of acquiring property by inheritance. Keeney
v. N. Y., 221 U. S. 534, 32 Sup. Ct. 105, 56 L. Ed. 304,
38 L. R. A. (N.S.) 1139.

9-11. The statute in question taxes the passing of
property, or any interest therein, in the possession,
enjoyment, present or future, by inheritance, descent,
devise, succession, bequest, grant, deed, bargain, sale,
gift, or appointment. Stats. 1913, sec. 31, p. 422. This
statute, taken as a whole, goes further than that of New

York, and the fine distinctions made in the briefs of cases in that and other jurisdictions tend rather to confuse than aid the court in construing a local statute. The statute in terms taxes gratuitous acquisitions of property under trust conveyances intended to take effect in possession or enjoyment at or after death. But however broad and comprehensive its terms, the statute was not intended to restrain persons in their right to transfer property in all legitimate ways. It is the policy of the law to encourage making conveyances in fee, and it is as lawful to create an estate for life with remainder after death of the grantor as it is to convey in fee; but there is a marked difference in "taxing a right and taxing a privilege." By the statute the favorite transfer in fee is not taxed with the privilege. The tax is not a property tax, but is in the nature of an excise tax, to wit, cn the transfer of property. In Re Williams, 40 Nev. 241, 161 Pac. 741, L. R. A. 1917c, 602. The language of the statute manifests its purpose to tax all transfers which are accomplished by will, the intestate laws, and those made prior to death which can be classed as similar in nature and effect, because they accomplish a transfer of property under circumstances which impress on it the characteristics of a devolution made at the time of the donor's death. State v. Pabst, supra.

But it is earnestly insisted that, as the transfer of the property was made before the act became effective, no tax accrued. This leads to the discussion of the question: When does a transfer tax as imposed by the statute accrue? To this there can be but one answer— at the death.

Says Chief Justice White, in Knowlton v. Moore, 178 U. S. 56, 20 Sup. Ct. 753, 44 L. Ed. 976:

"* * * Tax laws of this nature in all countries rest in their essence upon the principle that death is the generating source from which the particular taxing power takes its being, and that it is the power to transmit, or the transmission from the dead to the living, on which such taxes are more immediately rested."

12, 13. From this we conclude that the statute taxes, not the interest to which some person succeeds on a death, but the interest which ceased by reason of the death. Knowlton v. Moore, supra; Hansen's Death Duties, p. 63. Had Henry Miller died testate or intestate between the enactment and taking effect of the act, no tax would accrue; but the weakness of the appellants' position in this connection is that the property did not vest until after the statute became effective. The actual possession or enjoyment by those entitled to Miller's bounty under the will and deed was postponed to take effect at or after his death. Conceding that the law did not become effective until thirty days after its enactment, we are of the opinion that in this, as in other cases, the legislature deemed it best to give notice to the public of its provisions for this period of time before it became effective, and the interval of time was not intended to afford ingenious minds an opportunity to devise schemes to defeat the purpose of the act. The rights and obligations of all parties in regard to the payment of an inheritance tax are determinable as of the time of the death of the decedent (English v. Crenshaw, 120 Tenn. 531, 110 S. W. 210, 17 L. R. A (N.S.) 753, 127 Am. St. Rep. 1053) ; and, as we conclude that the property in question did not vest at the date of the transfer, it follows that the transfer is subject to the tax under the statute in question.

The judgment is affirmed.

COLEMAN, C. J., dissenting:

I dissent from the opinion filed in this case by my learned associates. That opinion is made to turn upon the conclusion that the title to the property in question did not vest in the trustees at the time of the execution and delivery of the trust agreement, but that it vested upon the death of the settlor. That was the very theory upon which the trial court rendered its judgment. If that conclusion is sound, it must necessarily follow that the tax is due and collectible.

Whatever might be my view as to a transaction, such as appears from the record in this case, had it taken place in this state, I think that, in view of the fact that it took place in California, where all of the parties reside, where the property was situated, and where the declaration of trust was executed and delivered, the question as to whether or not the title to the property vested at the time of the execution and delivery of the trust agreement is controlled by the law of California. The supreme court of that state, in Nichols v. Emery et al., 109 Cal. 323, 41 Pac. 1089, 50 Am. St. Rep. 43, laid down the rule which I think is binding upon the court in the case at bar upon the point in question. In that case the settlor reserved the right to revoke the trust, but died without exercising the right. The court said:

"It is undoubtedly the general rule enunciated by the leading case of Habergham v. Vincent, 2 Ves. Jr. 231, and oft repeated, that the true test of the character of an instrument is, not the testator's realization that it is a will, but his intention to create a revocable disposition of his property to accrue and take effect only upon his death and passing no present interest. The essential characteristic of an instrument testamentary in its nature is that it operates only upon, and by reason of, the death of the maker. Up to that time it is ambulatory. By its execution the maker has parted with no rights and divested himself of no modicum of his estate, and per contra no rights have accrued to and no estate has vested in any other person. The death of the maker establishes for the first time the character of the instrument. It at once ceases to be ambulatory. It acquires a fixed status and operates as a conveyance of title. Its admission to probate is merely a judicial declaration of that status. Upon the other hand, to the creation of a valid express trust it is essential that some estate or interest should be conveyed to the trustee; and, when the instrument creating the trust is other than a will, that estate or interest must pass immediately. Perry, Trusts, sec. 92. By such a trust, therefore, something of the settlor's estate has passed from him and into the trustee for the benefit of the cestui, and this transfer of interest is a present one, and in no wise dependent upon the settlor's death. But it is important to note the distinction between the interest transferred and the enjoyment of that interest. The enjoyment of the cestui may be made to commence in the future and to depend for its commencement upon the termination of an existing life or lives or an intermediate estate. Civ. Code, sec. 707. Did the grantor in the present case divest himself, by the instrument, of any part of the estate in the land which he had formerly owned and enjoyed? By the terms of the instrument, an estate was assuredly conveyed to the trustee. The language is appropriate to a conveyance, and the grantor's execution and delivery of the deed (both found), he being under no difficulty, and impelled by no fraud, operated to vest so much of his estate in the trustee as was necessary to carry out the purpose of the trust. The especial purpose was to sell and distribute the proceeds upon his death—a legal purpose, authorized by section 857 of the civil code. The term of the duration of the trust—the life of the settlor—did not violate the provisions of section 715 of the same code.

"We have, therefore, an estate conveyed to a named trustee, for named beneficiaries, for a legal purpose and a legal term—such a trust as conforms, in all its essentials, to the statutory requirements. That no disposition is made by the trust of the interest and estate intervening in time and enjoyment between the dates of the deed and the death of the settlor cannot affect the trust. The trustee takes the whole estate necessary for the purposes of the trust. All else remains in the grantor. Civ. Code, sec. 866. In this case there remained in the grantor the equivalent of a life estate during his own life, and he was thus entitled to remain in possession of the land, or lease it and retain the profits. Nor did the fact that the settlor reserved the power to revoke the trust operate to destroy it or change its character. He had the right to make the reservation. Civ. Code, sec. 2280. But the trust remained operative and absolute until the right was exercised in proper mode. Stone v. Hackett, 12 Gray (Mass.) 232; Van Cott v. Prentice, 104 N. Y. 45, 10 N. E. 257. Indeed, this power of revocation was strongly favored in the case of voluntary settlements at common law, and such a trust, without such a reservation, was 'open to suspicion of undue advantage taken of the settlor. Lewin on Trusts, 75, 76; Perry on Trusts, sec: 104. We think, however, that the circumstances of the reservation of power to revoke, and the limitation of the trust upon the life of the settlor, have operated to mislead the learned judge of the trial court. If the life selected had been that of a third person, and if no revocatory power had been reserved, no one would question but that a valid express trust had been created. But the fact that the designated life in being was the settlor's could not operate to destroy its validity, for he had the right to select the life of any person as the measure of duration. And the fact that he reserved the right to revoke did not impair the ·trust, nor affect its character, since title and interest vested subject to divestiture only by revocation, and, if no revocation was made, they became absolute. A man may desire to make disposition of his property in his lifetime to avoid administration of his estate after death. Indeed, in view of the fact, both patent and painful, that the fiercest and most expensive litigation, engendering the bitterest feelings, springs up over wills, such a desire is not unnatural. And when it is given legal expression, as by gifts absolute during life, * * * or voluntary settlements, there is manifest, not only an absence of testamentary intent, but an absolute hostility to such intent."

Other California cases sustaining the decision quoted are: Tennaht v. Tennant Memorial Home, 167 Cal. 570, 140 Pac. 242, and Gray v. Union Trust Co., 171 Cal. 637, 154 Pac. 306.

Do the circumstances of the case, particularly the

making of the will by Miller, show that it was not the
intention that the trust agreement should operate to
vest title to the stock except upon the death of Miller?
In considering this question, it becomes necessary to
call attention to Matter of the Estate of Stanford,
126 Cal. 122, 58 Pac. 465, 45 L. R. A. 788, another California case, in which it is said:

"An estate is vested when there is an immediate right
of present enjoyment or a * * * fixed right of
future enjoyment."

With the rule laid down in the language just quoted,
and that declared in Nichols v. Emery, supra, in mind,
it is necessary to inquire if, at the time of the execution
and delivery of the declaration of trust and the transfer
of the stock certificates, an estate so vested that the
beneficiaries acquired a "fixed right of future enjoyment." If they did acquire such a fixed right of future
enjoyment, then the contention of the state cannot be
sustained. If the theory of the state is sound, Miller
could, by a will executed subsequent to the trust agreement, have revoked the declaration of trust. Suppose
he had tried to do that very thing, and pursuant to such ·
will the trustees had repudiated the trust agreement, in
what court would the beneficiaries have brought suit to
compel the performance of the trust? Certainly no
other courts would have had jurisdiction than the courts
of California, and they would be bound by the decisions
from that state, to which I have alluded. Would the
court of that state say that under the circumstances
leading up to the execution of the trust, and contemporaneous with it, no estate was so vested under the trust
as to establish a fixed right of future enjoyment in the
beneficiaries named? The only circumstances connected
with the entire transaction which throw any light upon
it are the physical condition of Miller at and shortly
prior to the time of executing the trust and the execution of the will simultaneously with the execution of the
trust. Just how the fact that Miller was in poor health
can aid the court, in determining whether or not he

intended that a fixed right of future enjoyment should vest under the trust, is more than I am able to see; but, if it can, there is nothing in it which justifies the conclusion that he did not so intend. If a fixed right of future enjoyment vested under the terms of the declaration of trust, such right was not, and could not have been, divested by the will.

It seems to me that the strongest circumstance surrounding the entire transaction, throwing light upon the character of the declaration of trust, is the indorsing and delivering of the stock certificates by Miller at the time of executing and delivering the declaration of trust. By that act he completely surrendered control, for all time, of the property in question; for, not having reserved the right to revoke the trust, such revocation was impossible, as shown in the case of Nichols v. Emery, supra, which rule is sustained by the overwhelming weight of authority. See 1 Perry on Trusts (6th ed.) sec. 104; 39 Cyc. 92. But the majority opinion states that the deceased (Miller) "disposed of his property to take effect in possession or enjoyment at or after his death." From this statement it seems that the court concluded that Miller did that which was held in Re Stanford's Estate, supra, to be sufficient to create a fixed right of future enjoyment.

If Miller "disposed" of the property, the title must have vested, in which case there was a fixed right of future enjoyment at the time of the execution of the trust agreement, which was prior to the time the inheritance-tax law of Nevada went into effect, and hence no inheritance tax is collectible, unless the act operates retrospectively. The learned trial judge held that the act does not operate retrospectively, in which, I think, he was clearly right; for it would seem absurd to say that such could have been the intention, when in express terms the act was made to go into effect thirty days after approval; besides, there is absolutely nothing to indicate that it was the intention that the act should so operate, and it is a well-known rule of law that—

"All statutes are to be construed as having only a prospective operation, unless the purpose and intention of the legislature to give them a retrospective effect is expressly declared, or is necessarily implied from the language used. In every case of doubt, the doubt must be solved against the retrospective effect." 36 Cyc. pp. 1205–1208.

See, also, Milliken v. Sloat, 1 Nev. 577; Hunter v. Savage, etc., 4 Nev. 154; State v. Manhattan S. M. Co., 4 Nev. 333; State v. Manhattan V. Co., 32 Nev. 474, 109 Pac. 442; State v. Eggers, 33 Nev. 535, 112 Pac. 699; Chew Heong v. U. S., 112 U. S. 536, 5 Sup. Ct. 255, 25 L. Ed. 770; Winfree v. N. P. R. Co., 227 U. S. 301, 33 Sup. Ct. 273, 57 L. Ed. 518.

However, I do not understand that the learned attorney-general questions the correctness of the rule invoked, but he insists that the provision in the inheritance-tax law which provides that when property shall pass without valuable consideration, and "in contemplation of the death of the grantor * * * or intended to take effect in possession or enjoyment at or after such death," it shall be liable to the tax, subjects the property rights in question to the terms of the inheritance-tax law. To sustain this view, reliance is had upon the following authorities: In Re Masury's Estate, 28 App. Div. 580, 51 N. Y. Supp. 331; In Re Ogsbury's Estate, 7 App. Div. 71, 39 N. Y. Supp. 978; In Re Barbey's Estate, 114 N. Y. Supp. 725; In Re Patterson's Estate, 127 N. Y. Supp. 284; In Re Seaman's Estate, 147 N. Y. 69, 41 N. E. 401; In Re Green's Estate, 153 N. Y. 223, 47 N. E. 292; In Re Bostwick's Estate, 160 N. Y. 489, 55 N. E. 208; In Re Brandreth's Estate, 169 N. Y. 437, 62 N. E. 563, 58 L. R. A. 148; In Re Douglas Co., 84 Neb. 506, 121 N. W. 593; Appeal of Seibert, 110 Pa. 329, 1 Atl. 346; In Re Maris's Estate, 14 Pac. Co. Ct. R. 171, 3 Pa. Dist. R. 38; Crocker v. Shaw, 174 Mass. 266, 54 N. E. 549; New England Trust Co. v. Abbott, 205 Mass. 279, 91 N. E. 379, 137 Am. St. Rep. 437; State v. Bullen, 143 Wis. 512, 128 N. W. 109.

In the first case mentioned (In Re Masury's Estate, 28 App. Div. 580, 51 N. Y. Supp. 331), the deed was executed in 1890, but the inheritance-tax law had been in effect since 1885. The question involved in this case was not presented to the court in that case.

In the Matter of Ogsbury's Estate, 7 App. Div. 71, 39 N. Y. Supp. 978, it appears that the transfer was made to the trustees upon the condition that they should, upon the death of the grantor, transfer and convey the property to such person or persons as the grantor should direct in his will. There is no similarity between that case and the one at bar.

The Matter of Barbey's Estate, 114 N. Y. Supp. 725, was decided in 1908, twenty-three years after an inheritance-tax law had been enacted, and it does not appear that the transfer was made before the act became operative, but it does appear that the sole ground upon which the opinion was based was the fact that the grantor reserved to himself the right of ownership in the trust property until his death. The case is not in point.

In Re Patterson's Estate, 127 N. Y. Supp. 284, is one in which the trust law was enacted after the inheritance act had gone into effect. It is not an authority on the point in question.

In the Matter of Douglas County, 84 Neb. 506, 121 N. W. 593, the inheritance law took effect July 1, 1901, and the trust was created in 1904. Hence the question here involved was not presented.

It appears in Re Maris's Estate, 14 Pa. Co. Ct. 171, 3 Pa. Dist. R. 38, that the inheritance law was passed in 1887, and that the deed was made in 1891. The question here presented was not involved.

In the· Matter of Green's Estate, 153 N. Y. 223, 47 N. E. 292, the trust was created in 1889, four years after the inheritance-tax law had taken effect. It is no authority upon the point involved.

In the Matter of Bostwick's Estate, 160 N. Y. 489, 55 N. E. 208, in the Matter of Brandreth, in the Matter of the Appeal of Seibert, and in Crocker v. Shaw, the trusts were created after the inheritance-tax act had taken effect.

In the case of State v. Bullen, 143 Wis. 512, 128 N. W. 109, the point insisted on in this case was not considered. Furthermore, the court says in its opinion:

"As we have seen, Mr. Bullen reserved the right to direct and control the distribution of the trust property and to revoke the trust at any time during his life."

The opinion in that case is not authority upon the point in question.

The case of New England Trust Co. v. Abbott is not in point. The court says:

"The only part of the property which was finally disposed of in a known and definitely stated way was the income for the period of five years. The disposition of the principal was left subject to contingencies, any one of three of which might terminate the trust and give direction to the payment of the principal."

Nothing became vested until the death of the creator of the trust, which was after the inheritance-tax law had gone into effect. I am unable to see in what way this case sustains the contention of counsel.

As to the case of In Re Seaman's Estate, which it is contended sustains the contention of the state, it may be said that, while it is possible that different deductions may be drawn as to what was really decided, nevertheless the opinion in that case has been interpreted by the New York courts, where a different view from that contended for by the attorney-general is maintained.

In the Matter of Craig's Estate, 97 App. Div. 289, 89 N. Y. Supp. 971, it was held that an act imposing an inheritance tax would not affect an estate which had vested before the act went into effect. In that case the Seaman case was interpreted, and the court said:

"It is true that something is said (in the Seaman case) which may seem to be in conflict with the view I am taking, but I am sure there is nothing in the actual decision to that effect."

This opinion was affirmed by the Court of Appeals of New York in 181 N. Y. 551, 74 N. E. 1116, without comment, thereby approving all that had been said by the lower court. But whatever may be said of the Seaman case, or of the Craig case, the Court of Appeals in Re Pell, 171 N. Y. 48, 63 N. E. 789, 57 L. R. A. 540, 89 Am. St. Rep. 791, held that when an estate accrued before the passage of an amendment providing for a tax, but coming into actual possession after the amendment, the amendment was void. So far as I have been able to learn, there has been no decision holding squarely to the contrary, unless it be the case of People v. Carpenter, 264 Ill. 400, 106 N. E. 302. But the force of the Carpenter case is entirely lost, in view of the fact that the conclusion therein reached is based upon the court's interpretation of In Re Seaman, supra, since the New York court from which the Seaman case emanated has put the interpretation upon the case which I contend for.

But counsel for respondent seek to distinguish the Craig case, supra, from the case at bar. They say the deed in that case was made in contemplation of marriage and not of death, and was designed to make an effective provision in præsenti for the prospective wife and the possible offspring. It is true, as claimed by counsel, that the trust in that case was created in contemplation of marriage, but that was not made the turning-point in the decision. The court in that case says:

"The point presented by the appeal is that the right as a property right to take the gifts when the time for possession and beneficial enjoyment should ultimately arrive had fully accrued at the date of the marriage and the birth of the children free from any existing tax upon the transfer either made or contemplated, and that subsequent legislation imposing such a tax must be deemed unconstitutional, as, in effect, the taking of private property for public use without compensation, or as impairing the obligation of a contract. In other words, the appellants contend that at least as early as May 9,

1885, they had acquired their rights by irrevocable deed; that such rights, whether vested or contingent, then constituted present property interests in future estates, which were vested in the sense that they were secured to them by deed, subject only to contingencies as to time and survivorship; that incident to the ownership of such property was the absolute right to its acquisition in possession and enjoyment at the stipulated time; and that such ultimate right of possession and enjoyment, being absolute, and not merely privileged, could not afterwards be taxed by the state, because of well-settled principles of constitutional law."

The point involved in that case is the identical point point in question here, namely, whether the accrual of the "right as a property right to take the gifts when the time for the possession and beneficial enjoyment should ultimately arrive had fully accrued at the date" of the creation of the trust, or whether it accrued upon the death of the donor. The court held that the right fully accrued under the trust at the time of the consummation of the marriage. In the case at bar the rights of the beneficiaries under the trust, as prospective rights to take the gifts when the time for the possession and beneficial enjoyment should ultimately arrive, accrued at the date of the creation of the trust. They were rights which the settlor could not revoke or defeat, and hence the law which thereafter went into effect providing for an inheritance tax did not apply.

In the case of Hunt v. Wicht, 174 Cal. 205, 162 Pac. 639 L. R. A. 1917c, 961, wherein it appears that William Garms executed a deed of conveyonce to Ulrice Garms, conveying certain property, and deposited it in escrow, to be delivered upon his death, the deed was placed in escrow before his death and before the inheritance-tax act was passed. But William Garms died after the act had become a law, whereupon the deed was delivered to the grantee. It was sought to recover an inheritance tax, upon the theory that the conveyance was a transfer by deed "made without valuable and adequate considera-

tion, in contemplation of the death * * * or intended
to take effect in possession or enjoyment at or after
such death"; it being contended that the grantee in the
deed took pursuant to the terms of the inheritance-tax
law, which provided for the levying of a tax where the
party taking "becomes beneficially entitled in possession
or expectancy to any property or the income therefrom,
by any such transfer, whether made before or after the
passage of this act."

The court held that the tax could not be collected, and
said:

"We have then the case of a grant of land so executed
and delivered on April 12, 1905, as to be fully operative
and effective on that date to vest a present title in the
grantee, subject only to a life interest in the grantor;
'an executed conveyance' (Estate of Cornelius, supra)
of this property in fee simple absolute, subject only to
this life interest. Could the legislature subsequently
lawfully impose a succession tax upon this fully executed transfer of title, such tax accruing at the termination of the grantor's reserved life estate, simply because
in the meantime the grantee was debarred by the intervening life estate from actual possession of the property
conveyed and the other incidents of a life estate? It
appears to us that to state the question is to answer it.
The succession to the property by the grantee which is
the thing attempted to be taxed was complete upon the
delivery of the deed in escrow, notwithstanding the reservation of the life estate. The whole estate conveyed
vested irrevocably in interest at once, notwithstanding
that actual possession of the property itself and enjoyment of the profits thereof were deferred until the death
of the life tenant. His death added nothing to the title
theretofore acquired by the grantee, and there was no
transfer of any property in any legal sense at the time
of such death, or at any time subsequent to the delivery
in escrow. The right of the grantee to have actual
physical possession of the property itself, and enjoyment
of the other incidents of an estate for life upon the death

of the life tenant was absolutely vested by the delivery of the deed in escrow, and nondefeasible, and the legislature could not thereafter lawfully destroy, impair, or burden this property right under the guise of a succession tax on account of the transfer. As said in Matter of Craig, 97 App. Div. 289, 89 N. Y. Supp. 971, affirmed 181 N. Y. 551, 74 N. E. 1116:

" 'The underlying principle which supports the tax is that such right (the right of succession) is not a natural one, but is in fact a privilege only, and that the authority conferring the privilege may impose conditions upon its exercise. But when the privilege has ripened into a right it is too late to impose conditions of the character in question, and when the right is conferred by a lawfully executed grant or contract it is property and not a privilege; and as such is protected from legislative encroachment by constitutional guarantees.'

"It is the vesting in interest that constitutes the succession, and the question of liability to such a tax must be determined by the law in force at that time. This view is not opposed to Estate of Woodard, 153 Cal. 39, 94 Pac. 242, cited by appellant, where the statute in force at the time of death of a testator was held applicable, rather than a later act, simply because it was at the time of such death that the estate vested in the devisee and legatee. What we have said appears perfectly clear on principle, and is sustained by practically all of the authorities in other states where the question has arisen. In New York the matter is thoroughly settled by several decisions. In the Matter of Pell, 171 N. Y. 48, 55, 63 N. E. 789, 791 (57 L. R. A. 540, 89 Am. St. Rep. 791), it is said that such a transfer tax being one not imposed on property, but upon the right to succession, it 'follows that, where there was a complete vesting of a residuary estate before the enactment of the transfer-tax statute, it cannot be reached by that form of taxation,' and also, 'if these estates in remainder were vested prior to the enactment of the transfer-tax act, there could be in no legal sense a transfer of the property at the time of possession and enjoyment. This being so, to impose a tax based on the succession would be to diminish the value of these vested estates, to impair the obligation of a contract, and take private property for public use without compensation.' "

It is my opinion that it was not the intention of the legislature that the inheritance-tax act should apply to such a case as the one at bar; and, furthermore, that if such was the intention, so much of the act as so provides is unconstitutional, null, and void.

ON REHEARING

By the Court, SANDERS, J.:

The above-entitled causes were briefed, argued, submitted, and considered as one case. Because of a change in the personnel of the court it became necessary to resubmit the causes, in order to dispose of the petition for rehearing, and to finally determine the case of Nickel et al. v. State of Nevada; it appearing that the latter case remains undetermined.

No better way is suggested for assisting the court in searching for error, where a rehearing is granted, than to carefully consider a well-directed criticism of the opinion upon which its conclusion is based. In this instance counsel for the losing parties in polite terms insist that the opinion of the majority is in conflict with the well-established principles of comity of decisions between states, and that the opinion is contrary to private international law. The argument, coming as it does from such an eminent source, is worthy of some further consideration.

1. Every owner of property has the inherent right to dispose of his property in such form, such manner, and for such purposes as he may see fit; but where the devolution of title involves a succession or an inheritance tax, it is governed and controlled by the law of the forum, imposing the tax if the transfer sought to be taxed is within the jurisdiction of its tax authorities. The difficulty with the application of counsel's rule of

comity is that there is no foreign element in this litigation, other than it happens that the transfer in question
was made, and the parties thereto and the property
affected thereby were located, in our sister state of California.   The property affected by the alleged transfer
consists of 119,871.75 shares of the capital stock of a
Nevada corporation.   These shares of stock are primarily under the protection of the laws of Nevada, and
the complete devolution of the title thereto ordinarily
takes place according to the laws of Nevada.   In Re
Douglas County, 84 Neb. 506, 121 N. W. 596.   But, aside
from this, it must be conceded that, by the express
terms of the Nevada inheritance-tax law, to the extent
that the said shares of stock represented the property
owned by Henry Miller, deceased, situated in Nevada, it
is taxable.   Section 1, Statutes of Nevada, 1913, p. 141.
What, then, becomes of the rule of comity?   Can it be
employed to pervert the statute law of a sovereign
state?   We do not think so.   "Few general principles of
private international law," says Mr. Minor in his valuable work on Conflict of Laws, sec. 6, "are so well settled
as the rule that no foreign law (even though, under
ordinary circumstances, it be the 'proper law') will be
enforced in a sovereign state, if to enforce it will contravene the express statute law or an established policy of
the forum, or is injurious to its interests."   "If the
policy of the forum," says the author, "has been
expressed in a statute which in terms covers even transactions having a foreign element, no difficulty will be
apt to arise."
    The legislature of this state has spoken.   There can be
no question as to its pronounced policy to cover by its
inheritance-tax law such foreign transactions as are disclosed by this record, and we decline to look to a foreign
jurisdiction for an authority either to uphold the law or
to evade its provisions.   We are not concerned in the lex
loci contractus, if the transfer or devolution of title to
the property in question is taxable under our laws.
    We do not concede that the opinion of the majority

does violence to the rule of comity of decisions between states, in that it conflicts with the opinion of the Supreme Court of California in the case of Nickel et al. v. State of California, 175 Pac. 641. It is true the court held the complaint in that case was good as against the demurrer, but it is inferable from the order and what is said by the court in its opinion that it would be entirely proper and permissible for the State of California, upon issue joined, to show as a matter of fact that the instrument (being the same as that involved in both of these cases) was made "in contemplation of death" and was not made for a "valuable and adequate consideration," and liable to a tax under the statute of California. Stats. 1911, p. 713, sec. 1, subd. 3. In view of the findings of the lower court in the case at bar, and the present status of the case of Nickel et al. v. State of California, it is strange that counsel for appellants should cite this as an authority for the proposition that the conveyance in question is not taxable.

Our attention has not been directed to any decision of our sister state, or that of any other jurisdiction, that goes to the extent of holding that it is not permissible, for the purpose of claiming an inheritance tax, to attack a transfer and show by extrinsic proof that an instrument of conveyance is subject to the lien of such a tax. If such be the law, estates in many cases would pass free from tax. The method usually adopted for the avoidance of such a tax is that pursued in this case. In Re Keeney's Estate, 194 N. Y. 281, 87 N. E. 428.

2. But it is insisted that the trustees accepted the trust; that their active duties began immediately upon the delivery of the deed; that it contained no power of revocation, and under the statute of California it was irrevocable. Section 2280, C. C. Cal. Conceding this to be true as between the parties to the transaction, the weakness of the position is that the test in determining whether, under a deed, grant, or gift, the property was intended not to vest in possession or enjoyment until after the death of the grantor, does not depend upon

whether a power to revoke has or has not been inserted, but upon whether or not the property passes with all the attributes of ownership, independently of the death of the transferor. State St. Trust Co. v. Treasurer and Receiver-General, 209 Mass. 373, 95 N. E. 851.

The learned trial judge in these cases, and the inheritance-tax appraiser of California in the case of Nickel et al. v. State of California, supra, found upon identically the same state of facts that the transfer was made by the decedent, Miller, in contemplation of death, without adequate and valuable consideration, and the same was intended to take effect in possession and enjoyment as to the grantees and beneficiaries therein named, other than the deceased, at or after the death of said decedent. This being true, it is immaterial, in this case, that the deed was dated and executed before the inheritance-tax law of Nevada became effective. It is the vesting of the property in possession and the enjoyment of the same upon the death of the grantor, and after the statute took effect, that renders it liable to the tax; and both those things happened in this case. Crocker v. Shaw, 174 Mass. 266, 54 N. E. 549; In Re Green's Estate, 153 N. Y. 223, 47 N. E. 292; In Re Seaman's Estate, 147 N. Y. 69, 41 N. E. 401; Inheritance Tax (Gleason & Otis) 90, 91. It is this well-recognized principle that distinguishes the case at bar from that of Hunt v. Wicht, 174 Cal. 205, 162 Pac. 639, L. R. A. 1917c, 961.

In view of the above findings, it may have been unnecessary for the trial court to find, expressly, that the deed of trust "was made, executed, and delivered with the express intent on the part of Henry Miller, deceased, to evade the inheritance-tax law of this state," and to find "that said deed of trust is testamentary in character." We concede that if, upon any reasonable hypothesis, we could bring ourselves to the conclusion that as a matter of law the title to the specific shares of stock vested absolutely in the trustees before the act became effective, the motive of the grantor for making the deed would be immaterial; but where it is a question of fact, to be determined by the trial court from the nature and character of the conveyance, and from all the circumstances surrounding its execution, whether the property passed, the motive and the intent of the grantor and the bona fides of the transaction are material elements to be considered in determining whether the transfer is taxable.

We have carefully reviewed the evidence and given the exhaustive briefs our earnest consideration. Our conclusion is that the judgment in the above-entitled causes must be affirmed.

COLEMAN, C. J., dissenting:

I dissent, for the reasons given in my opinion filed when the case was originally before us.

[NOTE—On writ of error to United States Supreme Court.]

[No. 2335]

ARNA FECHT ROBERTSON, APPELLANT, *v.* JAMES CUTHBERT ROBERTSON, RESPONDENT.

[180 Pac. 122]

1. HUSBAND AND WIFE—AGREEMENT SETTLING RIGHTS IN COMMUN-
ITY—BREACH.

Plaintiff wife, defendant in divorce suit, by filing motion
in divorce proceeding to set aside divorce decree in favor of
her husband, together with answer to the merits specifically
asking for attorney's fees and other money, violated contract
whereby she agreed not to demand a division of community
property, or ask for suit money in consideration of husband's
promise to pay her a specified sum in settlement of community
property rights.

2. ELECTION OF REMEDIES—ACTS CONSTITUTING AN ELECTION.

Where plaintiff wife, defendant in divorce suit, instead of
bringing action for husband's breach of contract whereby he
agreed to pay her a specified sum in consideration of her
agreement not to demand a division of community property, or
ask for suit money, instituted proceedings to set aside divorce
decree in his favor, *held*, she cannot maintain suit on the contract; the remedies being inconsistent, and she having made
an election.

APPEAL from Fifth Judicial District Court, Nye
County; *Mark R. Averill*, Judge.

Action by Arna Fecht Robertson against James Cuth-
bert Robertson. Judgment for defendant, and plaintiff
appeals. **Affirmed. Rehearing denied.**

H. R. Cooke, for Appellant:

Defendant's affirmative plea of an agreement changing
contract respecting time and manner of payments is
fatally defective in not alleging facts showing a valid
binding agreement. The statute requires that a complaint shall contain "a statement of the facts constituting the cause of action in ordinary and concise language."
Rev. Laws, 5038. The plea says in effect that there is
a writing which accomplished a certain purpose—effect;
or produced a certain condition or result — that is,
deferred the time of payments. This is fatally defective.
being a mere conclusion. Nester v. Diamond M. Co., 143
Fed. 72; Cal. State Tel. Co. v. Patterson, 1 Nev. 150;
Victor M. & M. Co. v. Justice's Court, 18 Nev. 28. "An

allegation that plaintiffs waived and surrendered their alleged claim of mortgage lien * * * is a conclusion of law." Zorn v. Levesley, 75 Pac. 1056; Cambers v. Bank, 144 Fed. 717; Cassimus v. Scottish Co., 33 South. 163. "Where a pleading is intended to show a waiver of a breach of contract, the facts to sustain the conclusion of waiver must be alleged." Pope Mfg. Co. v. Rubber Goods Co., 97 N. Y. Supp. 73; Crafton v. Carmichael, 64 N. E. 627; Stannard v. Aurora Ry. Co., 77 N. E. 254; People v. Brown, 48 Pac. 661; Bennett v. Lewis, 66 N. W. 523.

Plea of alleged agreement modifying and changing contract is defective in not alleging same was upon valuable consideration. The rule is well settled that where a creditor, who has a complete agreement for the payment of money, agrees to defer or extend the time of payment from time to time as fixed in the contract, such agreement must have a new consideration to support it. 9 Cyc. 593; 13 C. J. 592, 722, 753, 759. Any agreement purporting to discharge the original agreement in whole or in part must have a new consideration. 9 Cyc. 67; 13 C. J. 602; Collier Co. v. Moulton, 98 Am. Dec. 370; Pratt v. Morrow, 45 Mo. 404; McIntyre v. Ajax Mining Co., 60 Pac. 552; Shriner v. Craft, 28 L. R. A. 450; Bartlett v. Smith, 117 Am. St. Rep. 625; Empire State Co. v. Hanson, 184 Fed. 58.

Plea of deferred payments arrangement fatally defective, because of its absolute indefiniteness. Uncertainty made same unenforceable. "If an agreement is so uncertain and ambiguous that the court is unable to collect from it what the parties intended, it cannot be enforced." 9 Cyc. 248, 249; Gaines v. Vandicar, 115 Pac. 721. "A promise to forbear for such time as plaintiff shall elect is not good, for it imposes no obligation to forbear for any length of time." 13 C. J. 349; Sticker v. Evans, 21 Am. Dec. 387; Gates v. Hackerthal, 11 Am. Rep. 45.

Defense of waiver as to time of payments must be specially pleaded and the facts constituting the alleged waiver set forth. "Party relying upon a waiver has the

burden of proving it." 40 Cyc. 269; 13 C. J. 738; Kansas
City v. Walsh, 88 Mo. App. 271; Brock v. Des Moines
Co., 64 N. W. 685; Crandall v. Moston, 50 N. Y. Supp.
145.

"The courts are disinclined to construe stipulations in
a contract as conditions precedent when to do so would
result in injustice." 13 C. J. 569; Front St. Co. v. Butler, 50 Cal. 574. "Forfeitures are looked upon by the
courts with ill favor, and will be enforced only when the
strict letter of the contract requires it." Finley v.
School District, 153 Pac. 1010; 13 C. J. 541. Any condition involving a forfeiture must be strictly interpreted
against the party asserting it and liberally construed in
favor of the party against whom it is to be enforced.
Cleary v. Folger, 24 Pac. 280; Randall v. Scott, 42 Pac.
976; People v. Perry, 21 Pac. 423; Quatman v. McCray,
60 Pac. 855. A condition subsequent, to work a forfeiture, must be created by express terms or clear implication, and is to be strictly construed. 13 C. J. 566;
Davidson v. Ellis, 98 Pac. 254; Behlow v. S. P. Co., 62
Pac. 295. The law abhors forfeitures; courts will never
allow them unless absolutely compelled to do so. 24
Cyc. 1347; Richardson v. Jones & Denton, 1 Nev. 405;
Golden v. McKim, 141 Pac. 676.

A mere tender of money does not operate as a satisfaction of a debt. It merely protects against further interest, costs, or damages. 38 Cyc. 162; Colton v. Oakland
Bank, 70 Pac. 225; Ruppell v. Missouri Co., 59 S. W.
1000.

By filing motion for leave to defend, plaintiff did not
make election precluding recourse on contract. There
must be two or more coexistent and inconsistent remedies. Mark v. Schuman Co.,70 N.E.226. Where only one
remedy actually exists, but through mistake an inappro-
priate one is invoked, the proper remedy is not thereby
waived. Bunch v. Grove, 12 N. E. 514; Agar v. Wins-
low, 69 Am. St. Rep. 84; Chaddock v. Tabor, 72 N. W.
1093; Rowell v. Smith, 102 N. W. 1; Fuller Co. v. Har-
ter, 84 Am. St. Rep. 867. "There is no inconsistency

between different legal remedial rights, all of which are based upon claim of title to property in plaintiff." 15 Cyc. 258; Wood v. Claiborne, 11 L. R. A. 915.

Milton M. Detch and *Frank K. Pittman,* for Respondent:

If the contract was an existing valid contract at the time plaintiff filed her motion to set aside the decree of divorce, did the filing of the motion constitute such a breach of the contract that plaintiff could not recover on it? "Waiver may be accomplished by either agreement or contract. Waiver may be made by an express agreement or promise declaring an intention not to claim the supposed benefit or advantage. * * * The more usual manner of waiving a right is by conduct or acts which indicate an intention to relinquish the right or by such failure to' insist upon it that the party is estopped to afterwards set it up against his adversary." 40 Cyc. 265, 266; Rice v. Maryland Fidelity Co., 103 Fed. 427; Knarston v. Manhattan L. Ins. Co., 56 Pac. 773. Defendant by her actions waived the time of payment of the several monthly payments. Consideration for waiver unnecessary where element of estoppel is present. 40 Cyc. 264; Schwartz v. Wilmer, 90 Md. 136; Pabst Brewing Co. v. Milwaukee, 126 Wis. 110. In the original contract, the mutual promises of the parties constituted the entire consideration for the contract. "When mutual covenants go to the entire consideration on both sides, they are mutual conditions and dependent." 13 C. J. 571; Long v. Addix, 184 Ala. 236; Manuel v. Campbell, 3 Ark. 324; Houston v. Spruance, 4 Del. 117; Dakin v. Williams, 11 Wend. 67.

By the filing of her motion to set aside the decree of divorce, appellant precluded recovery under the contract. "Any decisive act of a party with knowledge of his rights and of the facts, determines his election in case of conflicting and inconsistent remedies. * * * The mere commencement of any proceeding to enforce one remedial right * * * is such a decisive act as constitutes a conclusive election, barring the subsequent prosecution of inconsistent remedial rights." 15 Cyc. 259, 260. "Bringing suit is a decisive act; dismissal does not obviate." Robb v. Voss, 155 U. S. 13; Farwell v. Garrett, 73 N. W. 217; Cunnihan v. Thompson, 111 Mass. 270; Martin v. Boyce, 13 N. W. 386. "Where in one suit plaintiff has asserted that a contract was rescinded, he cannot in a subsequent suit take the ground that it is still operative." Martin v. Boyce, 13 N. W. 386; Turner v. Grimes, 106 N. W. 465. "Intent to elect presumed; no reservation will avail." Clausen v. Head, 85 N. W. 1028; Johnson v. R. R. Co., 50 Mo. App. 407; Daily v. Bernstein, 28 Pac. 764; Know v. Gow, 17 S. E. 654.

By the Court, DUCKER, J.:

This is an action for the breach of a contract. The respondent and appellant were husband and wife, and during the pendency of an action for divorce instituted by the husband entered into a written contract whereby the appellant agreed that in the event a divorce was granted to plaintiff she would not pray, ask, or request in said action for divorce the court to award or allow her any alimony, maintenance, or support of any kind, character, or description, temporary, permanent, or otherwise, from or against said plaintiff, nor any award or allowance for costs in said action nor any allowance or award for attorney's fees therein. It was further mutually agreed between them for the purpose of for all time settling and disposing of their property rights that the respondent should pay the appellant the sum of $3,000 in the following manner: The sum of $50 on the 6th day of July, 1915; the sum of $50 on the 6th day of August, 1915; and the sum of $50 on the 6th day of every month commencing on the 6th day of September, 1915, until the whole of said $3,000 is paid. It is also agreed that, if respondent make default in any of the monthly payments as the same become due and continue in default for the period of thirty days, then in that event the whole of said sum of $3,000 or so much thereof as remains unpaid shall immediately become due and payable and subject to an action by the appellant for the collection thereof; the respondent waiving all defenses to such action other than the defense of full payment. In consideration of the said promises on the part of respondent and the faithful performance thereof, appellant agrees to make no demand for any property of the parties. There is also an agreement in the contract that payments shall cease upon the event of the remarriage of wife.

The contract was executed by the parties on the 30th day of August, 1915, and payment of the sum of $100 for the months of July and August, 1915, is acknowledged in the contract by the wife. In the complaint it is alleged that—

"No portion of the $3,000 specified in said written agreement to be paid by the defendant herein to the plaintiff, in the manner and at the times as in said agreement provided, has been paid by, for, or on behalf of said defendant, save and except the sum of $100, receipt of which is acknowledged in and by said agreement, and an additional $75 subsequently paid in full of the $50 payment by the terms of said agreement due and payable on September 6, 1915, and $25 on account of the $50 payment due and payable by the terms of said agreement on October 6, 1915, leaving a balance due, wholly unpaid, and owing from said defendant to plaintiff in the sum of $2,825, with interest on said sum from November 6, 1915, until paid, at the legal rate of 7 per cent per annum."

The defense is based on the grounds that the payments alleged to be due and unpaid were in writing waived and deferred until such time as the plaintiff should make a demand upon the defendant for payment of the same or until the defendant should voluntarily resume the making of such payments, and that, before such demand or resumption of payments was made, the plaintiff breached her contract. As to the

breach of her contract claimed by defendant, it is
alleged in his amended answer that on the 28th day of
February, 1916, she caused to be filed in the district
court in the divorce proceeding her motion to set aside
the decree of divorce granted to her husband, together
with an affidavit and verified answer wherein she seeks
to set up a defense in the divorce proceeding, and
whereby she asks for an order of the court directing
the plaintiff therein to pay attorney fees, traveling
expenses, maintenance during the pendency of the action
and alimony pendente lite, wherein she seeks a division
of certain community property; that said proceedings
are still pending and undetermined in the court; that
in the preparation of the defense in the hearing of said
motion the plaintiff therein was compelled to and did
employ counsel and expend certain sums of money, and
has been ready at all times to be present to have said
motion heard and determined.

The case was tried in the district court without a jury,
and judgment rendered for the respondent.

Appellant appeals from the judgment and the order
of the district court overruling her motion for a new
trial.

A number of errors are assigned, but, as the judgment
of the district court must be affirmed, we deem it
unnecessary to consider many of the errors claimed by
appellant.

The evidence discloses a state of facts which precludes
appellant from maintaining this action.

It appears that the subject-matter of the said contract
is the community property rights of the parties, and
the contract was entered into for the purpose of settling
and disposing of such rights. This is declared in the
contract in the following language:

"And the said parties above named, for and in consideration of the mutual promises, agreements, and
stipulations herein contained, hereby expressly and
respectively contract, agree, and stipulate as follows
for the purpose of for all time settling and disposing of

the property rights of the said parties above named.
* * * * ".

Then follows respondent's promise to pay in monthly installments the sum of $3,000 and appellant's promise in consideration thereof to make no demand of any kind or character for any community or other property of the said parties.

Clearly it was the intention of the parties that appellant was to receive under the terms of the contract the sum of $3,000 in lieu of her interest in the community property. The judgment roll in the action for divorce which was admitted in evidence on the trial of the case at bar shows that after the execution of the contract a divorce was granted respondent on the default of appellant. It further shows that on the 28th day of February, 1916, and prior to the commencement of this action, appellant caused to be filed in the district court, in the divorce proceeding, a motion to set aside the decree of divorce granted her husband, together with an affidavit and verified answer wherein she seeks to set up a defense in the divorce proceeding. In the prayer of the verified answer she asks for an order of the court requiring the respondent to pay a sufficient sum of money for traveling expenses and for her maintenance during the pendency of the action. She also asks for such other and further relief as the court may deem equitable and just.

It is alleged in the answer filed with the motion that the community property of the parties in possession of respondent is valued at many thousands of dollars.

It appears from the record that this motion to set aside the judgment entered against appellant in the divorce proceeding is still pending and undetermined.

1. From this state of facts we conclude that the district court did not err in holding that the appellant breached her contract as alleged in the affirmative defense set forth in the respondent's amended answer. There is no specific demand in the answer accompanying the motion for a division of the community property. but there is an allegation as to such property and its

value, and a prayer for equitable relief. If the judgment were set aside and a divorce granted either party, the court could, and doubtless would, under a pleading and in an action of this kind, make such division of the community property as appeared to be just and equitable. Her intention to obtain such relief in the event of a decree of divorce is evident from the answer and the nature of the proceedings. She specifically asks for attorney fees and other money to enable her to make her defense. In her contract with respondent she agrees, in consideration of his promise to pay, not to demand a division of the community property, or ask for suit money for any purpose. Her attempt to set aside the decree of divorce and answer to the merits of the action constitute a demand for both, in violation of her contract.

True, it would still require an order of the court to open the case, but, so far as appellant is concerned, she has initiated all the demand that she can make. If it requires an order of the court to ripen it into a real demand, it is certain that appellant intended her motion and answer to have that effect.

2. Appellant insists that, prior to the time she sought to be permitted to answer in the divorce action, the respondent had breached the contract by failing to make certain of the monthly payments as agreed. The trial court held that she had extended the time of payments, and that therefore respondent was not in default in his payments. We need not determine the question, for, as we view the case, if the contract was actually breached by the respondent, then by its terms appellant could have brought an action on the contract for all of the $3,000 remaining unpaid. Instead of choosing this remedy, she elected to institute proceedings to set aside the decree of divorce and defend in that action. If her motion is granted, her interest in the community property may properly be determined. Clearly these remedies are inconsistent, and the appellant by electing to

pursue the latter cannot now maintain an action on the contract. In the one she seeks a division of the community property, and in the other to recover the unpaid portion of the $3,000 which she agreed to receive for her interest in the community property. She is not entitled to both.

"It is certainly the established law, in every state that has spoken on the subject, that the definite adoption of one of two or more inconsistent remedies, by a party cognizant of the material facts, is a conclusive and irrevocable bar to his resort to the alternative remedy." 7 Ency. Pl. & Prac. 364, and cases cited.

"An election once made, with knowledge of the facts, between coexisting remedial rights which are inconsistent, is irrevocable and conclusive, irrespective of intent, and constitutes an absolute bar to any action, suit, or proceeding based upon a remedial right inconsistent with that asserted by the election, or to the maintenance of a defense founded on such inconsistent right." 15 Cyc. 262.

Counsel for appellant urges that her remedy in the divorce proceeding is not available unless the court gives her leave to answer, and that therefore there are not two coexisting alternative remedies. The conclusiveness of her election does not depend upon the chances of success that may attend her suit, but upon the fact that she has resorted to a remedy which is inconsistent with the one she now seeks to maintain, and has made such election with full knowledge of the facts in each case.

Under a statute empowering courts to give relief in appropriate cases, and in an action in which she is a party, she has applied to a court having jurisdiction to determine her property rights for an order to set aside a judgment entered against her, so that she may defend and obtain a determination of such property rights. The motion has been duly made and is still pending. Appellant has made no attempt to dismiss it. It may be pressed at any time regardless of the outcome of the

present action. Appellant considered it an available
remedy. We cannot say that it is not. The remedy
sought may be to some extent hazardous, it is true, by
reason of the judgment entered, but it is an appropriate
remedy, and one which, through no mistake of facts or
misconception of her rights, she breached her contract
to invoke.

It is contended that respondent by his contract bound
himself to the single defense of full payment. The
answer is that appellant, by renouncing her claims under
the contract in electing to pursue her remedy in the
divorce proceeding, released respondent from all of his
covenants.

Judgment affirmed.

SANDERS, J., did not participate.

ON PETITION FOR REHEARING

Per Curiam:

Rehearing denied.

Points decided

[No. 2313]

FRANK LOVE AND MARTIN EVENSEN, RESPONDENTS, *v.* MT. ODDIE UNITED MINES COMPANY (A CORPORATION), APPELLANT.

[181 Pac. 133; 184 Pac. 921]

1. APPEAL AND ERROR—EXCEPTIONS—CERTIFICATE.

A trial court's certificate that statement and bill of exceptions contains all material evidence, except documentary evidence, is insufficient to authorize review of evidence, which will be presumed to support findings and judgment.

ON REHEARING

1. MINES AND MINERALS—QUESTION OF FACT WHETHER WORK DONE IMPROVED CLAIMS.

It is purely a question of fact whether or not development work done in a particular shaft by the locator of claims so tended to improve the entire group of claims as to prevent forfeiture thereof.

2. APPEAL AND ERROR — REVERSAL IN EQUITY FOR ERRONEOUS INSTRUCTION.

In equity cases. a judgment will not be reversed because of an erroneous instruction.

3. MINES AND MINERALS—IMPROVEMENT WORK ON SINGLE LOCATION DEVELOPING ENTIRE GROUP.

Improvement work within the meaning of the federal statute as to the location of mining claims, is deemed to have been performed, whether the claim consists of one location or several, when in fact the labor is performed or the improvements are made for the development of the whole claim, that is, to facilitate the extraction of metals, though the labor and improvements may be on ground originally part of only one of the locations, and it is not necessary that the work "manifestly" tend to the development of all the claims in the group; "manifest" meaning evident or obvious to the mind.

4. MINES AND MINERALS—DEVELOPMENT WORK ON GROUP OF CLAIMS.

In the exercise of judgment as to where development work should be done on a group of mining claims and locations, a wide latitude should be allowed the owners of the property.

5. MINES AND MINERALS—EVIDENCE NOT SHOWING DEVELOPMENT WORK INSUFFICIENT.

In an action to quiet title to a group of eight mining claims, wherein verdict was rendered in favor of plaintiff relocators for four of the claims. evidence that the development work done in one place by defendant company on such claims was insufficient to prevent forfeiture *held* not such as to sustain the judgment.

G. TRIAL—VIEW OF PREMISES BY COURT.

     A view of the premises involved in mining litigation cannot be considered as evidence, but only to enable the court better to understand and comprehend the evidence introduced and intelligently to apply it.

APPEAL from Fifth Judicial District Court, Nye County; *Mark R. Averill*, Judge.

Action to quiet title to mining claims. Judgment for plaintiffs, and defendant appeals. **Affirmed.**

On rehearing, **judgment reversed.**

H. R. Cooke, for Appellant:

The record affirmatively shows, as the trial judge, whose duty it was to settle and allow the bill, certifies, that it contains "all of the evidence admitted at said trial (with the exception of documentary evidence, which was separately certified) material and pertinent to the issue." "But, to enable this court to intelligently pass upon the question whether the findings or verdict are sustained by the evidence, it is necessary that it have all of the material evidence before it." Howard v. Winter, 3 Nev. 549; Eaton v. Oregon Ry. Co., 30 Pac. 311. "If it were stated that it contained all the material evidence offered upon the particular facts claimed to be unsupported, the certificate of the judge to the correctness of the statement would of course be sufficient to establish that fact." Sherwood v. Sissa, 5 Nev. 349; Bailey v. Papina, 20 Nev. 177. "A party cannot complain of omission in a bill of exceptions of evidence not material to questions considered on appeal." Denver & R. G. Co. v. Andrews, 53 Pac. 518. The terms "settling," "allowing," etc., presuppose a discretion in the trial court as to what and how much of the evidence is material and should be contained in the bill. 2 C. J. 1156.

Norcross, Thatcher & Woodburn, for Respondent:

The court should not inquire at all into the evidence in this proceeding, for the reason that no valid motion for a new trial was ever made, and because the bill of exceptions shows affirmatively that it does not contain all the evidence. The functions of the jury were advisory, and did not constitute a verdict or decision. State ex rel. Equitable G. M. Co. v. Murphy, 29 Nev. 247. The notice of intention to move for a new trial should have been directed against the decision of the court. Idem. No valid motion for a new trial having been made, this court may not consider the insufficiency of the evidence to justify the decision of the court. Rev. Laws, 5328; Street v. Lemmon M. Co., 9 Nev. 251.

The bill of exceptions does not show affirmatively that it contains all the evidence. The certificate of the official reporter shows that the testimony transcribed is "a full, true and correct transcription of certain designated testimony." This is not cured by the purported certificate of the district judge. To entitle one to review the sufficiency of the evidence to justify the verdict or decision, the statement or record or bill of exceptions must contain all of the evidence. Howard v. Winters, 3 Nev. 541; Sherwood v. Sissa, 5 Nev. 353; Bowker v. Goodwin, 7 Nev. 137; Libby v. Dalton, 9 Nev. 23. The appellate court will presume that every fact essential to sustain the judgment, order or decision was fully proven. "Such rulings are based upon the presumption that all intendments being in favor of the verdict, the omitted evidence would sustain it." Libby v. Dalton, supra.

•

By the Court, COLEMAN, C. J.:

This is an action to quiet title to certain mining claims. Judgment was rendered in favor of the plaintiffs, from which, and from an order denying motion.for a new trial, an appeal has been taken.

Counsel for respondent object to our considering the merits of the case, for the reason that the bill of exceptions does not contain all of the evidence material and essential to a correct determination thereof.

Before proceeding further, it may not be out of place to say that at different stages of the proceedings in the lower court, including the preparation of the record upon this appeal, three attorneys who are not now connected with the case participated at different times in its management.

We think the objection urged to a consideration of the case upon its merits is well taken. The bill of exceptions contains only about 1½ typewritten pages of the direct testimony of the witness Love, who testified on behalf of plaintiffs, and is confined solely to that portion of his testimony showing his experience as a prospector and miner. It does not contain one word of testimony given by the witness mentioned on direct examination concerning the material and vital issue in the case, but it does contain about 25 pages of his cross-examination upon the vital issue. The bill of exceptions is in substantially the same condition as to the testimony of the witness Evensen.

Following the first 36 pages of the testimony contained in the so-called "statement on appeal and bill of exceptions" is found a statement by the court reporter as follows:

"I hereby certify that I am the duly appointed, qualified, and acting official reporter of the district court of the Fifth judicial district of the State of Nevada, in and for the county of Nye; that I acted as official reporter upon the trial of the above-named cause, and that at such trial I took verbatim shorthand notes of all testimony and proceedings given and had; that the foregoing 36 pages constitute a partial transcription of said shorthand notes, and, so far as this particular portion of the testimony goes, is a correct statement thereof."

On page 205 of the statement is found another certificate of the court reporter, which we quote:

"I hereby certify that I am the duly appointed, qualified and acting official reporter of the district court of the Fifth judicial district of the State of Nevada, in and for the county of Nye; and that I acted as such official reporter upon the trial of the above-named cause, and that at such trial I took verbatim shorthand notes of all testimony and proceedings given and had; that the foregoing is a full, true, and correct transcription of certain designated testimony, and is in all respects a full, true, and correct statement of said designated testimony and proceedings given and had at such trial."

The certificate of the trial judge is as follows:

"I, the undersigned, the judge who tried said action, do hereby certify that the foregoing statement on appeal and bill of exceptions has on due notice been settled and allowed by me, and the same is correct, and that it contains a full, true and correct transcription of all of the proceedings upon the trial of said cause and of all the evidence admitted at said trial (with the exception of documentary evidence) material and pertinent to the issue of whether the work on the Verner and on the New York claim was of such a character that the same tended to develop the adjoining claims and which were in controversy between plaintiffs and defendants in this case."

It will be seen from the two certificates of the official reporter that the purported transcript is but a partial transcript of the evidence, while the certificate of the trial judge shows that the statement and bill of exceptions is a correct transcript of all of the evidence admitted at the trial and pertinent to the issues, with the exception of documentary evidence. We do not feel that it is necessary that we determine whether or not the bill of exceptions shows upon its face that all of the material evidence given on direct examination of the witnesses Love and Evensen is not embodied therein. We are clearly of the opinion, however, that the certificate of the trial judge does not show that all of the evidence material to the issue presented upon this appeal is contained in the bill of exceptions, as contended by counsel for appellant, who relies upon the rule laid down in the case of Bailey v. Papina, 20 Nev. 177, 19 Pac. 33. Eliminating from consideration the certificates of the court reporter, which are not necessary at all, it appears from the certificate of the trial judge that documentary evidence material to the issues is not embodied in the statement and bill of exceptions. This being true, we cannot consider the evidence at all, and it must be presumed that the findings and judgment are supported by the evidence. Gammans v. Roussell, 14 Nev. 171; County of White Pine v. Herrick, 19 Nev. 311, 10 Pac. 215; Bailey v. Papina, 20 Nev. 177, 19 Pac. 33.

It may be asked: What documentary evidence could possibly exist which could have aided the trial court in arriving at a conclusion as to the real question of fact involved in the case? Of course, we need not determine that question, though we think it possible that there might have been reports of mining engineers, or signed statements impeaching the testimony of some, or all, of the witnesses who testified in behalf of appellant. Suffice is to say that, since it appears that there was documentary evidence material to the issue, which is not embodied in the bill of exceptions, we could only speculate as to its character and weight, which we are not called upon to do.

Since it is not contended that any error appears from the judgment roll, it follows that the judgment appealed from must be affirmed; and it is so ordered.

ON REHEARING

By the Court, COLEMAN, C. J.:

This is an action to quiet title to a group of eight mining claims. The complaint is in the usual form. The case was tried before a jury. Verdict was rendered in favor of the plaintiffs for four of the claims. From an order denying a motion for a new trial and from the judgment, an appeal has been taken.

Prior to January, 1911, defendant was the undisputed owner of the ground in question consisting of a group of eight claims, under and by virtue of its location as mining claims and a compliance with the laws, rules, and regulations pertaining thereto. On July 25, 1913, plaintiffs, asserting that the labor for the year 1912 had not been done upon the claims by the defendant company, entered upon and located them. It is admitted by plaintiffs that the defendant company did enough work on one of the claims (the Verner) to constitute the labor upon said group, if such work can be considered, but contend that the work done at that point did not tend to develop the group.

1. It is agreed between counsel that it is purely a question of fact as to whether or not the work done in the Verner shaft in 1912 so tended to improve the entire group of claims as to prevent a forfeiture thereof; and such is the law. Big Three M. & M. Co. v. Hamilton, 157 Cal. 130, 107 Pac. 304, 137 Am. St. Rep. 118.

2, 3. Before proceeding to consider the main question of the case, we will dispose of the error assigned to the giving of that portion of plaintiffs' instruction No. 4, wherein the court told the jury that where work is done upon one claim for the benefit of an entire group, it "must manifestly tend" to the development of all the claims in the group. It is a general rule that in equity cases a judgment will not be reversed because of an erroneous instruction. We might dispose of this phase of the question without saying more; but, in view of the fact that the learned trial judge in his written opinion holds that such is the law, and was evidently controlled by that view of the law in reaching his conclusion, we deem it proper to express our interpretation of the law for the guidance of the courts in the future.

The trial judge, in his written decision, cited section 630 of Lindley on Mines in support of his views. He no doubt accepted the statement of Mr. Lindley without having examined the authorities cited by that eminent author in support of the text, as was most natural, in view of the arduous labors incident to his position; and, while we entertain great deference for the views of Mr. Lindley, we cannot accept his statement of the law. We have examined the decisions of the various courts cited, and do not find that they support the author; nor do we see how such a view can be sustained. The word "manifest" means "evident to the senses; evident to the mind; obvious to the mind." Webster's Int. Dict. The courts uniformly hold that annual labor may be done outside of a claim, or group of claims, upon a patented mining claim, or upon the public domain. Certainly work done outside of a claim, upon a patented mining claim, or upon the public domain, cannot be said to "manifestly" tend to develop such claims; but it is the universal rule that proof may be offered to show that such work was done for the purpose of developing such other claims, and that in fact it tends to develop them, and when so shown it complies with all requirements. If it were the rule that the work "must manifestly" tend to develop a group of claims, work done on the public domain could not count, as by no possible stretch of the imagination could it be said that such work would "manifestly" tend to develop such group, nor could proof cause it to "manifestly" so appear. The correct rule to apply to the situation here presented is declared by the Supreme Court of the United States in Smelting Co. v. Kemp, 104 U. S. 636, 26 L. Ed. 875, as follows:

"Labor and improvements, within the meaning of the statute, are deemed to have been had on a mining claim, whether it consists of one location or several, when the labor is performed or the improvements are made for its development, that is, to facilitate the extraction of the metals it may contain, though in fact such labor and improvements may be on ground which originally constituted only one of the locations, as in sinking a shaft, or be at a distance from the claim itself, as where the labor is performed for the turning of a stream, or the introduction of water, or where the improvement consists in the construction of a flume to carry off the debris or waste material."

Whatever other courts may think or say, the law as laid down by the court mentioned upon this question is final, though, so far as we know, all of the courts of the land are in accord with the view thus expressed, and some of the authorities so holding are Copper Mt. M. & M. Co. v. Butte, etc., 39 Mont. 487, 104 Pac. 540, 133 Am. St. Rep. 595; Chambers v. Harrington, 111 U. S. 350, 4 Sup. Ct. 428, 28 L. Ed. 452; Fredricks v. Klauser, 52 Or. 110, 96 Pac. 679; Big Three M. & M. Co. v. Hamilton, 157 Cal. 130, 107 Pac. 304, 137 Am. St. Rep. 118; Nevada Ex. & M. Co. v. Spriggs, 41 Utah, 171, 124 Pac. 773; Lindley on Mines (3d ed.) sec. 629; Snyder on Mines, sec. 480; Costigan on Mines, p. 278.

4. It may be said that it is the policy of the law to encourage the doing of annual labor on mining claims in a manner which will best develop the property and lead to the discovery of mineral, and for that reason annual labor upon a group of mining claims may be done all in one place, the object of the government being to encourage such development as is most likely to result in the production of the precious minerals; and since depth is usually necessary in the making of a mine, it is much better, as a general rule, to spend $800 in one place than to distribute $800 in eight or more places, provided it is done in an honest effort to make a mine, and in a manner tending to develop all of the claims. And in the exercise of judgment as to where work should be done, we think a wide latitude should be allowed the owners of property, consisting of several claims, as to where the work shall be done to develop a group of claims. And in this view we are sustained by ample authority. In Big Three M. & M. Co. v. Hamilton, supra, it was said:

"Work done on one of a group of mining claims which has a tendency to develop or benefit all of the claims in said group inures to the benefit of each and all of said claims, even though the system adopted may not be the best that could have been devised under the circumstances."

Judge Farrington, in Wailes v. Davies (C. C.) 158 Fed. 667, in determining a case in which the question before us was involved, said:

"The statute does not require * * * that the work shall be wisely and judiciously done."

See, also, Mann v. Badlong, 129 Cal. 577, 62 Pac. 120.

With these observations in mind, we will consider the evidence in the case, as shown by the bill of exceptions. Only three witnesses were called in behalf of the plaintiffs, viz, the plaintiffs themselves and one McCarthy, and the latter testified in rebuttal only. We reiterate here what we said in our previous opinion:

"The bill of exceptions contains only about 1½ typewritten pages of the direct testimony of the witness Love, who testified in behalf of plaintiffs, and is confined solely to that portion of his testimony showing his experience as a prospector and miner. It does not contain one word of testimony given by the witness mentioned on direct examination concerning the material and vital issue in the case, but it does contain about 25 pages of his cross-examination upon the vital issue. The bill of exceptions is in substantially the same condition as to the testimony of the witness Evensen."

But, notwithstanding this fact, the trial judge denied a motion for nonsuit at the conclusion of plaintiffs' testimony in chief.

There being no evidence in the record on direct examination for us to consider, tending to sustain the judgment, we are confined to the cross-examination, replete with asterisks, as it is. From the cross-examination of plaintiffs Love we quote the following extracts:

"Mr. Cooke: Q. * * * All right. Then, if you were not concerned in that land, not interested in it, made no examination of the shaft or the character of the work that was done there, why do you say, as you did say a while ago, that that shaft did not benefit the Daisy and the Jackie ground so as to prevent Evensen from relocating it? * * * A. I didn't think it was; where it is situated in the northwest corner there, I can't see how it can benefit them..

"Q. Is that the best answer you have to that question? A. Well, it is the best I know.

"Q. Well, of course that is all you can say, is what you know. That is the best answer you can make, is it? A. (Witness hesitates.)

"Q. You have no further answer to make to that? A. No full answer?

"Q. No further, I say. A. I don't understand you.

"Q. I want to give you an opportunity to answer that if you want to now, if you have any further answer to make; if not, we will proceed with something else.

"Mr. Sanders: I think that is enough.

"Mr. Cooke: Well, if you are satisfied, I am.

"Mr. Sanders: Well, let us go on with something else. * * *

"Mr. Cooke: Q. * * * That shaft, so far as you know, was within the lines of the Verner claim, wasn't it? A. It was, but pretty near the Halifax.

"Q. Well, what has that got to do with it? A. Well, it shows that it wasn't in a place to develop that group of ground.

"Q. What is the reason you jumped the Verner claim when there was $300 worth of work at least done there during that year? A. Because I couldn't see what there was hardly benefiting any claim; I can't see where it benefited more than one-half of the Verner.

"Q. Not even the claim on which the shaft was sunk? A. Well, it didn't look to me that way; that was my purpose of taking it up; I didn't think the work was in the right place; it was a straight shaft, and right near the corner of the Halifax, and I didn't see where it was even benefiting one claim.

"Q. It didn't even develop the Verner? A. Well, that is my idea.

"Mr. Cooke: Q. Do you undertake to say, Mr. Love, that sinking that shaft fifty feet deep on the Verner claim didn't tend to develop that claim? A. The way it is I can't see where it did; I never could get it into my head where it did.

"Q. Do you say as a miner that the sinking of a fifty-foot shaft on that claim didn't tend to develop it? A. I say it didn't tend to develop the whole claim; it wasn't put there for that purpose; that is my idea of it.

"Q. Did it tend to develop that part of the claim on which it was sunk? A. It would do that if they had anything to show; I don't think they have got anything there to show for it.

"Q. Have they got to find mineral in a shaft before it tends to develop the claim? A. No.

"Q. What do you mean then to show in it? A. Want them to put the work in the proper place for to develop the group, if they are trying to hold it for the group.

"Q. Well, but couldn't they hold the Verner claim, which you jumped, couldn't they hold that whether they could hold the others or not, with that fifty-foot shaft? A. My idea is that they could not.

"Q. Then, Mr. Love, with your experience as a miner, the sinking of a fifty-foot shaft upon a claim, in the rock, and timbering it up, doesn't tend to develop the claim? A. Just as I told you, I can't see where it can— the whole of the claim.

"Q. Well, put it that way, because they made a show, and still spent at least $300 in sinking a shaft on the Verner claim, that you admit was within the lines of the Verner claim, that they ought to suffer the loss of that claim, and you ought to take it—is that your position? A. Yes.

"Q. Now, Mr. Love, coming back to this Verner: There was a shaft put in there, and there were timbers put in there. Now, you say the shaft didn't count for anything because in your judgment it wasn't located in the right place and it didn't tend to develop the ground. Now, then, building a building upon a mining claim tends to develop the ground, doesn't it, isn't that good as annual labor? A. It does as far as it goes.

"Q. How far does this blacksmith shop go? A. Oh, I couldn't tell you. It don't go very far.

"Q. If you couldn't tell, what business had you to jump the ground? A. It couldn't amount to a great deal to hold that whole group, that I know.

"Q. Well, if it held one claim, what right did you have to locate that claim on which the blacksmith shop was located? A. I located it because I did not think the work was done in good faith.

"Q. You then assume to be the judge of the good faith of the work done, and if you conclude that it isn't done in good faith you would go and jump any property, no matter if there was $10,000 worth of work done on it? Is that your style of doing business. A. No, it ain't.

"Q. Well, it was your style in this case, wasn't it, Mr. Love? A. It wasn't for that purpose.

"Q. Well, did you assume to judge about the good faith because this wasn't located in the place where you thought it ought to be, notwithstanding that it was a number of times in excess of the required amount of expenditure for one claim on which these improvements were placed, didn't you? A. I located it because it wasn't done in the right place for good faith; it wasn't located for development; that is why I took it.

"Q. Now, if the work actually does tend to show the presence or the likelihood of the presence of ore in the ground, isn't it annual work, even though it is done with the idea of making a showing? A. It shows the way— that is, to me—and I can't get it any other way; it is not showing good faith, putting it in that corner.

"Q. Then why, when you now admit that the work did benefit the Verner, you now admit it was worth $300, why did you relocate the Verner? A. Because, just where the shaft was I didn't think that it was right to develop it.

"Q. It wasn't the right place to put it? * * *

"Q. Well, if you have two claims adjoining each other, and I wanted to do the work on the two of them—on one of them for the benefit of both, and I sink a shaft in the corner of one of them at a cost of $175, is it your understanding that you could jump both of these claims because $175 wasn't sufficient to include both, and because I had put my shaft in a corner instead of the middle? A. No, if one benefits the other.

"Q. Well, how about the claim on which the shaft is sunk, can I hold that whether I can hold the other one or not? A. Well, yes, you can hold that one.

"Q. Yes. Then why could not the Mount Oddie United Mines Company in this case hold the Verner? A. Because it wasn't done from a good intention.

"Q. Was the Little Billie developed to any extent, or benefited to any extent by the sinking of that shaft in the northwest corner of the Verner? A. I can't see that it was.

"Q. You can't see it. That is all the reason you know of, Mr. Love, that you just can't see it? A. I can't see it that way.

"Q. You know of no other reasons? A. That is all the reasons I have. It don't look possible to me.

"Q. It don't look possible to you that a shaft sunk in the rock 50 feet deep could develop more than 700 feet away? A. No, it don't."

The following extracts we take from the testimony of plaintiff Evensen:

"Mr. Cooke: Q. * * * Well, if the Verner shaft, sunk in 1912, which was worth approximately $300 to sink, and a blacksmith shop was put up there at the valuation you have given us, and the concrete work was done there, and the shaft was timbered, on what grounds do you claim in this case that the Verner was open for relocation in July, 1913? A. It don't develop any group —that shaft.

"Q. Don't develop any group? A. No.

"Q. Because it didn't develop the group that left the Verner open to relocation, is that the proposition? A. Yes; don't see to develop even the Verner.

"Q. Now, right there: Do you say, as a mining man of such experience as you have had, that the sinking of that shaft in the Verner claim did not tend to develop the Verner claim? Just cut out these other claims for the time being. A. No. * * * Well, I don't know. I ain't much of a mining man myself, so far as mining expert or anything. * * *

"Q. Well, if you don't know anything about it, why do you say that this work didn't tend to develop the Verner claim? A. Well, that is what I say, I don't know.

"Q. Well, if you don't know, why do you say that a shaft fifty feet wouldn't develop it? A. Well, I suppose a lawyer ought to know it.

"Q. Just answer the question. A. Well, I got the information from a lawyer, that that shaft didn't develop that group. I went to him and asked him first.

"Q. Asked him if it developed it? A. Yes.

"Q. And you relied upon that rather than your own judgment, in making the relocation. A. Why, sure I did.

"Q. Did Love do the same thing? A. I think he did.

* * *

"Mr. Cooke: Q. Then you didn't know anything about what the effect of sinking a shaft on one claim is, with reference to its developing adjoining claims? * * * A. I don't know."

5. Such is the testimony on cross-examination, as it appears from the bill of exceptions, upon which we must sustain the judgment, if it is to be sustained at all. Notwithstanding the rule that an appellate court is reluctant to reverse a judgment of a trial court purely upon the ground that the evidence does not sustain the judgment, we do not find that this is such a case. The evidence in favor of respondents, as presented to us, consists of nothing but conclusions. There is not a statement of a fact contained in the bill of exceptions worthy of serious consideration, and the testimony of the plaintiff Evensen shows that his conclusion as to the sufficiency of the work was based solely upon the opinion of his attorney. He said that he did not know whether or not the work would tend to develop the entire group. His testimony is worthless.

To permit a judgment to stand upon such evidence would be to make a farce of judicial proceedings; to substitute conclusions of interested parties for facts.

Defendant called eight or ten disinterested witnesses, some of whom were men of technical training and wide experience as mining operators in the Tonopah District, who gave testimony to the effect that the shaft in question was sunk in the proper place to develop the group of claims. In behalf of the defendant company, evidence was given that at a meeting of the officers and board of directors the question of doing the annual labor for all of the claims at the point at which it was done was considered, and the advantages thereof, and it was decided to adopt that plan for the development of the group of claims, and the work was done accordingly. In the face of the record, we are clearly of the opinion that the judgment of the lower court should have been in favor of the defendant company.

There is no substantial evidence in the record to sustain the judgment. The undisputed evidence shows that more than enough work was done for the entire group. If mining claims can be forfeited upon such testimony as that before us, development of mining ground when several claims are held in a group will be greatly retarded, to the disadvantage of the industry, of a mining district, and of the state. In this connection, we quote with approval the language of the Supreme Court of Wyoming in Sherlock v. Leighton, 9 Wyo. 297, 308, 63 Pac. 580, 583:

"With the single exception of the testimony of the adverse claimant, who expressed as his opinion that the tunnel in no way tended to the benefit of the claim, there is no support in the evidence of the allegations of forfeiture. To hold, upon the strength of his testimony alone, as against all the other facts in the case and the judgment of other experienced miners, that there had been an abandonment or forfeiture, although the locator had, in good faith, made the required expenditure, believing that the work done would inure to the advantage of his claim, and assist in its development, would shock our sense of justice. It would amount to substituting for the honest judgment of the locator the judgment, doubtless equally as honest, of his adversary, who has sought to get possession of the property by taking advantage of the supposed forfeiture. It seems to us that in determining the question as to the beneficial character of a tunnel such as was constructed in this case, where the opinions of expert witnesses differ upon the question, some force should be given to the honest intention and good faith of the locator, and in a doubtful case that might be sufficient to turn the scale. But, according to most of the witnesses in the case at bar, the work was of benefit, and that opinion appears to us to be supported by the facts in the case. The great weight of the evidence upon the proposition is clearly opposed to the theory of the defendant in error. We regard the conflict, so far as the facts are concerned, as so slight and unimportant that the case does not call for the application of the rule by which an appellate court is guided where a decision upon a question of fact is found to rest upon conflicting evidence. In our judgment, the evidence is insufficient to sustain the allegation of forfeiture of the Cleveland lode."

6. A point is sought to be made of the fact that the court viewed the premises in question. It is the rule in this state that a view cannot be considered as evidence, but only for the purpose of enabling the court to better understand and comprehend the evidence introduced, and to intelligently apply it. Albion M. Co. v. Richmond M. Co., 19 Nev. 225. But if the contrary rule existed, we do not think that, in the face of the record in this case, the view would justify the judgment. As we look upon the record, there is no substantial oral evidence therein in behalf of plaintiffs, and a mere view, considering the nature of the case, is not sufficient to sustain the judgment, and certainly not in the face of the evidence in behalf of appellant.

There being no evidence in the record to sustain the judgment, it is reversed.

[NOTE—SANDERS, J., having been counsel for the plaintiffs in the trial court, did not participate in the consideration of the case.]

[Nos. 2396, 2397, 2401]

COUNTY OF PERSHING, W. C. PITT, J. T. GOODIN,
H. J. MURRISH, JOHN A. JURGENSON, C. L.
YOUNG, AND J. H. CAUSTEN, PETITIONERS, *v.*
THE SIXTH JUDICIAL DISTRICT COURT OF
THE STATE OF NEVADA, IN AND FOR THE
COUNTY OF HUMBOLDT, AND HONORABLE
T. C. HART, DISTRICT JUDGE THEREOF, PRESIDING,
RESPONDENTS.

STATE OF NEVADA, EX REL. COUNTY OF PERSH-
ING, PETITIONER, *v.* T. P. EBERT, A. F. TROUS-
DALE, AND J. I. PETERSON, AS COUNTY COM-
MISSIONERS OF THE COUNTY OF HUMBOLDT, STATE
OF NEVADA, RESPONDENTS.

ZOE PALMER ODEN, RESPONDENT, *v.* JOHN I.
PETERSON, T. P. EBERT AND A. F. TROUS-
DALE, AS THE BOARD OF COUNTY COMMISSIONERS
OF HUMBOLDT COUNTY, STATE OF NEVADA; J. W.
DAVEY, AS COUNTY CLERK OF SAID HUMBOLDT
COUNTY; F. GERMAIN, AS COUNTY AUDITOR OF
SAID HUMBOLDT COUNTY; AND F. G. HOENSTEIN,
AS COUNTY TREASURER OF SAID HUMBOLDT COUNTY,
APPELLANTS.

[181 Pac. 960; 183 Pac. 314]

1. COUNTIES—CREATION. EXISTENCE, AND CHANGE—LEGISLATIVE
CONTROL.

Since a county is called into existence by the legislature,
and therefore is its creature, its territory may be cut up in
parcels by the legislature, and its common property and common burden apportioned in such manner as the legislature may
deem reasonable and equitable. or its existence as a county
may be blotted out, all even against the will of its inhabitants.

2. STATUTES—LAW TO TAKE EFFECT ON CONTINGENCY—POWER OF
LEGISLATURE.

The legislature has power to pass a law to take effect on a
contingency expressed in the body of the law; and may designate such contingency as a vote of the people of the territory
affected by the law.

3. COUNTIES—FORMATION OF NEW OUT OF OLD—REFERENDUM—CON-
STITUTION—"IN AND FOR."

Stats. 1919. p. 75, creating and organizing the county of
Pershing out of a portion of Humboldt County, is not a local

law "in and for" Humboldt County, making necessary referendum to the voters of such latter county under Const. art. 19, sec. 3, providing the referendum powers are reserved to the electors of each county as to all local legislation in and for the respective counties.

4. STATUTES — TITLE — ORGANIZATION OF COUNTY — CONSTITUTIONALITY.

Stats. 1919, p. 75, organizing the county of Pershing out of a portion of Humboldt County, and certain of its provisions, *held* not unconstitutional on the ground that such provisions are not embraced by the title, the disputed provisions being incident to the complete organization of the county, and germane to the main object of the act.

5. STATUTES—PARTIAL INVALIDITY—EFFECT.

Unless the validity of a whole statute depends on the constitutionality of one or more provisions not germane to the title, or are so blended with the scope and purpose of the act as a whole as to affect its validity or any other of its provisions, the invalidity of one or more of such provisions does not defeat the general scope and purpose of the act.

6. CONSTITUTIONAL LAW—DETERMINATION OF CONSTITUTIONAL QUESTIONS.

The constitutionality of statutory provisions should not be passed upon until some right dependent on the particular provision is brought before the court for adjudication.

7. CONSTITUTIONAL LAW—RIGHT TO QUESTION STATUTE.

One not prejudiced by the enforcement of a statute cannot question its constitutionality or obtain decision as to its validity on the ground it impairs the rights of others, so that a county from whose territory another is formed by the legislature cannot question the validity of the formative statute in its provisions designating officers of the new county, etc.

ON PETITION FOR REHEARING

1. APPEAL AND ERROR—REHEARINGS.

Rehearings in the supreme court are not granted as a matter of right, and are not allowed for the purpose of reargument, unless there is reasonable probability that the court may have arrived at an erroneous conclusion.

2. COUNTIES—CHANGE OF BOUNDARIES—CONSOLIDATION OR CREATION.

Unless a limitation exists in the constitution, the power of the legislature is absolute, by general or special statutes, to provide change of boundaries, division, addition, consolidation of existing counties, or the creation and organization of new counties.

3. CONSTITUTIONAL LAW—DIVISION OR CREATION OF NEW COUNTY.

The whole matter of the division of counties and the creation of new ones is in its nature political, and not judicial, and belongs wholly to the legislative department of the government.

4. STATUTES—REFERENDUM—CONSTRUCTION.

In construing the referendum as applied to legislation for counties, the usual rules of construction are applicable: the the thing to be sought being the thought expressed.

5. CONSTITUTIONAL LAW—COUNTIES—VESTED RIGHTS—BOUNDARIES OF COUNTIES—RIGHTS OF INHABITANTS.

The inhabitants of a county have no vested rights as far as the boundaries of the county or the extent of its territory are concerned, and the same may be changed without their consent.

APPEAL from Sixth Judicial District Court, Humboldt County; *E. F. Lunsford,* Judge.

Petition for writ of prohibition by the County of Pershing and others against the Sixth Judicial District Court and others, and petition for mandamus by the State of Nevada, on the relation, etc., against Tom P. Ebert and others and suit by Zoe Palmer Oden against John I. Peterson and others, resulting in an injunctive order, from which defendants appeal. **Alternative writ of prohibition made permanent and peremptory, writ of mandate directed to issue, and injunctive order affirmed.**

On petition for rehearing, **former opinion adhered to.**

Moore & McIntosh and *Norcross, Thatcher & Woodburn,* for Petitioners:

The district court of one county has no jurisdiction to enjoin the officers of another county from performing their official functions. Such an assumption of power would be an unlawful interference with both the legislative and executive branches of the government. Const. Nev. arts. 3, 6; State v. Dickerson, 33 Nev. 540; Wallace v. Reno, 27 Nev. 71; Gibson v. Mason, 5 Nev. 284; Osborn v. Bank, 22 U. S. 866; In Re Estate of Sticknoth, 7 Nev. 236; State v. Ormsby County, 7 Nev. 392; Ex Parte Blanchard, 9 Nev. 101; Ex Parte Darling, 16 Nev. 98; Esmeralda County v. District Court, 18 Nev. 438; State v. Wildes, 116 Pac. 595; State v. Arrington, 18 Nev. 412. A court cannot assume allegations of the unconstitutionality of a statute to be true. Rev. Laws, 5142. The right of public officials to perform the duties of their several offices cannot be attacked collaterally. 29 Cyc. 1416.

Only such laws or resolutions as pertain "to such county only" can be submitted to a referendum vote. The act in question pertains to Pershing County as well as to Humboldt County. Immediately upon the approval of the act creating the county of Pershing, it became a county as much as any other county in the state. Leake v. Blaisdel, 6 Nev. 43; Clark v. Irwin, 5 Nev. 111; Hooten v. McKinney, 5 Nev. 194. Such an act as the one in question can be submitted to the electors of the entire state only. State v. Brodigan, 37 Nev. 37. The legislature only has power to enact legislation authorizing the submission of "local, special and municipal legislation" to counties or municipalities. Const. Nev. sec. 3, art. 19.

A county is an integral part of the state for governmental purposes. Const. Nev. arts. 4, 8, 15, 18; 15 C. J. 388; 7 C. J. 923; Sacramento County v. Chambers, 164 Pac. 613; Hersey v. Milson, 47 Mont. 132; News Co. v. Grady County, 161 Pac. 207; Madden v. Lancaster County, 65 Fed. 188; People v. Johnson, 34 Colo. 143; Laramie County v. Albany County, 92 U. S. 307; Cons. Ice Co. v. City, 49 N. E. 713; Schweiss v. District Court, 23 Nev. 226. The creation of new counties is not among the powers of a board of county commissioners. Ann. Cas. 1916B, 820; Hopping v. Richmond, 150 Pac. 977.

R. M. Hardy, District Attorney of Pershing County, for Petitioners:

The power to create counties, to alter the boundaries of those in existence, to provide for their government and for the general regulation of their affairs, is inherently and exclusively in the legislature. Const. Nev. sec. 1, art. 4.

The creation of new counties, the changing of county boundaries, and the making of all provisions germane and pertinent thereto, by legislative enactment, is not

only by virtue of the authority of the constitution, but
it has become the established and recognized system.
This system should not be disturbed by the judiciary,
except upon the strongest showing of abuse or usurpa-
tion of power.   State v. Stoddard, 25 Nev. 452; Clarke
v. Irwin, 5 Nev. 111; Hooten v. McKinney, 5 Nev. 194;
Gibson v. Mason, 5 Nev. 284; Hess v. Pegg, 7 Nev. 23;
Evans v. Job, 8 Nev. 322; Youngs v. Hall, 9 Nev. 212;
State v. Swift, 11 Nev. 128; Tilden v. Esmeralda County,
32 Nev. 320; State v. Lytton, 31 Nev. 67.

Warren & Hawkins and *Thos. A. Brandon* (*Edward
F. Treadwell,* of Counsel), for Respondents:

The people of each county have a right to a referendum with respect to any local, special or municipal act of
the legislature applicable only to such county.   Const.
Nev. sec. 1, art. 9; State v. Brodigan, 37 Nev. 37; Rose
v. Port of Portland, 82 Or. 541.

While the constitutional provision granting the referendum to counties and municipalities in regard to local,
special and municipal legislation is not self-executing,
it was put into effect and operation by the act of 1915,
and the legislature, irrespective of any such provision
in the constitution, had power to confer the right of
referendum upon the people of the county affected with
respect to such legislation.   Stats. 1915, p. 157.

The legislature has power to pass a law to take effect
on a contingency, and it may designate that contingency
as a vote of the people of the certain territory affected.
26 Am. & Eng. Ency. 567; People v. McFadden, 81 Cal.
489;   In Re Pfahler, 150 Cal. 71; Van Dusen v. Fridley,
6 Dak. 622; People v. Raynolds, 10 Ill. 1; Jasper County
v. Spittler, 13 Ind. 235.   It is customary for the legislature to refer the question of county division to a vote ·
of the people of the county.   Trinity County v. Polk
County, 58 Tex. 321; Duncombe v. Prindle, 12 Iowa, 2;
Reynolds v. Holland, 35 Ark. 56; State v. Nelson, 34
Neb. 162; Wayne Co. v. Cobb, 35 Neb. 231.

The act in question is local, special and municipal, and

applies only to one county. Const. Nev. sec. 3, art. 19;
Stats. 1915, p. 157. Even after the act was passed Pershing County did not become an organized county until
all its officers were installed. State v. Blasdel, 6 Nev. 40;
People v. McGuire, 32 Cal. 140.

The act having been, by the constitution and the
statute, passed subject to the referendum, and the referendum having been duly invoked with reference thereto,
the operation of the act is suspended thereby. Rigdon
v. Common Council, 30 Cal. App. 107; Norris v. Cross,
25 Okl. 287; Stetson v. City of Seattle, 74 Wash. 606;
Sears v. Multnomah County, 49 Or. 42; State v. Moore,
103 Ark. 48; Kemper v. Carter, 165 S. W. 773; Commonwealth v. Day, 23 S. W. 193; Akin v. State, 14 Tex. Cr.
App. 142.

The act in question is unconstitutional, because it
attempts to consolidate the offices of clerk and treasurer
and the offices of sheriff and assessor. Const. Nev. sec.
32, art. 4; State v. Douglas, 33 Nev. 82.

Contrary to the constitution, the act embraces more
than one subject, and attempts to amend acts which are
not referred to in the title. Const. Nev. sec. 17, art. 4;
Philbin v. McCarty, 24 Kan. 393; Ballentyn v. Wickersham, 75 Ala. 533. The constitution is mandatory in
this particular. State v. Silver, 9 Nev. 226; State v.
Rogers, 10 Nev. 250; State ex rel. Drury v. Hallock, 19
Nev. 384.

Where constitutional and unconstitutional provisions
of a statute are so inseparably blended as to make it
clear that either would not have been enacted without
the other, the whole act is void. San Francisco v. S. V.
W. W., 48 Cal. 493; Read v. Railroad, 32 Cal. 212;
Orange County v. Harris, 97 Cal. 600; Lathrop v. Mills,
19 Cal. 513.

If the provisions of the act regarding the consolidation
of officers are unconstitutional, it results that the proper
officers of the county have never been appointed, the
county never organized, and that these proceedings must
be dismissed. State v. Blasdel, 6 Nev. 40; People v.

McGuire, 32 Cal. 140; Commissioners v. Perkins, 38 Pac. 915; Commissioners v. Woods, 106 Pac. 923; Mile v. Kent, 60 Ind. 231; Buckinghouse v. Gregg, 19 Ind. 401.

By the Court, SANDERS, J.:

These cases were argued and submitted as a single case. For convenience we will refer to it as the case of Pershing County against Humboldt County, since it appears that the latter declines to recognize Pershing County as being a legally created and established county of the state.

On March 18, 1919, an act of the legislature was approved entitled "An act creating and organizing the county of Pershing out of a portion of Humboldt County, and providing for its government, and to regulate the affairs of Humboldt County and Pershing County." Stats. 1919, p. 75. On the same day, to wit, March 18, 1919, the governor approved an act entitled "An act to amend sections 16 and 19 of an act entitled 'An act creating and organizing the county of Pershing out of a portion of Humboldt County, and providing for its government, and to regulate the affairs of Humboldt County and Pershing County.'" Stats. 1919, p. 82.

On the change from the territorial to a state government the several counties of the Territory of Nevada were recognized as legal subdivisions of the state. Since that time the legislature has, by special legislative enactments, changed the boundaries of some, consolidated and divided others, until there now exists seventeen organized counties in the state, including the alleged county of Pershing.

Subject in a state only to constitutional limitation, a county is the merest creature of the legislature. It is recognized by the fundamental law of this state as a body corporate. Const. Nev. art. 17, sec. 1.

1. From the legislature a county derives its name, its extent of territory, its mode and manner of government, its power and rights. It is a creature of the legislature. Called into existence by it, and subject to the restric-

tions named, its whole being may be changed by the same power which created it. Its territory may be cut up and parceled out to the other counties; its common property and common burden apportioned in such manner as to the legislature may seem reasonable and equitable; its existence as a county blotted out; and this all against the will of its inhabitants. Vincent v. County of Lincoln (C. C.) 30 Fed. 751; Comrs. of Laramie County v. Comrs. of Albany County, 92 U. S. 307, 23 L. Ed. 552; Board of Comrs. v. City of Osborne (Kan.) 180 Pac. 233; Cooley, Const. (2d ed.) 192; 11 Cyc. 341–345; 7 R. C. L. 923–926.

2, 3. But, if we clearly interpret the position taken by the learned counsel for Humboldt County in these original proceedings, it is their contention that since the enactment of the initiative and referendum by the legislature and its ratification by the people, the fundamental principle that a state through the legislative department of its government may divide the established territory of a county and give to a new county taken therefrom a corporate existence is "local legislation" within the meaning of the referendum clause of the constitution and the act passed in aid of its execution (Const. Nev. art. 19, sec. 3; Stats. 1915, p. 157), and therefore the act creating and organizing Pershing County out of a portion of Humboldt County is reserved by the referendum law to the people of Humboldt County to signify by their votes, at an election called for that purpose, their approval or rejection of the law, and that the referendum having been duly invoked with reference to the law in question, its operation is suspended until the qualified electors of Humboldt County have been given an opportunity to signify their approval of the law. We fully recognize the rule that the legislature has the power to pass a law to take effect on a contingency expressed in the body of the law, and that the legislature may designate that contingency as a vote of the people of the territory affected by the law. 26 Am. & Eng. Ency. Law, 567. This rule is recognized to ,a certain extent by this court in the case of Hess v. Pegg, 7 Nev. 28, and was expressly applied by the Supreme Court of California to the division of a county in the case of People v. McFadden, 81 Cal. 489, 22 Pac. 851. But it is manifest from section 20 of the act that it was the intention of the legislature that the act creating and organizing the county of Pershing out of a portion of Humboldt County should become effective immediately, without regard to the will of the inhabitants of Humboldt County. This is a matter for the legislature, and it is not for this court to oppose its judgment to that of the legislature in this important particular. Unless the law be in "clear, palpable and direct conflict with the written constitution," it must be sustained."

Sec. 3, art. 19, of the constitution provides, inter alia:

"The initiative and referendum powers in this article provided for are further reserved to the qualified electors of each county and municipality as to all local, special and municipal legislation of every character in or for said respective counties or municipalities."

We concede, or it must be conceded, that an act creating a new county out of territory of an established county relates to and necessarily affects the latter, but we are unable to bring ourselves to the conclusion that such legislation is a local law "in or for" the county out of which the new county is created. But on the contrary, if it be local legislation, as the term is used in section 3, article 19, of the constitution, it is legislation for the new county of Pershing, and not for the old county of Humboldt.

Counties are of purely a political character, constituting the machinery and essential agency by which free governments are upheld, and through which, for the most part, their powers are exercised. Their functions are purely of a public nature. 11 Cyc. 351.

Whatever may be the literal import of the initiative and referendum amendment to the constitution, it must be construed with others of the organic law. It cannot be construed that the legislature and the people intended by its enactment and adoption to surrender the sovereignty of the state over a particular portion of its territory to the people who inhabit it. Such interpretation would amount to a recognition of the state's independent right of dissolution. It would lead to sovereigntial suicide. It would result in the creation of states within the state, and eventually in the surrender of all state sovereignty. Hedges, "Where the People Rule," 15–16.

In view of the essential character and nature of a county as it relates to and is connected with the sovereignty of the state, we are of the opinion that the power which the legislature possesses to divide counties and apportion their common burdens is not abridged, limited, restricted or affected by the initiative and referendum, and the law in question is not thereby suspended.

4. It is next insisted and strenuously urged that the special provisions of the act, incident to the organization of the county of Pershing, are within the constitutional prohibition against the enactment of special and local laws and void; as in section 9 of the act it is attempted to consolidate the offices of clerk and treasurer, and the offices of sheriff and assessor; that section 19 of the act is contrary to the general law regarding the apportionment of senators and representatives; that the act purports to divide townships, school districts and election precincts, and makes no provision for township government in that portion of territory falling within Pershing County; that the act contains provisions not embraced by its title, and attempts to amend specific statutes not referred to in the title and which are not reenacted. To discuss these disputed provisions separately would extend this opinion to an unreasonable length. The law concerning them is well settled and has been applied in numerous cases arising out of just such cases as this.

By the very terms of the title of the act the disputed provisions are incident to the complete organization of Pershing County and are germane to the main object of the act.

5. Unless the validity of the whole act depends upon the constitutionality of one or more of these provisions, or that they are so blended with the general scope and purpose of the act as a whole as to affect the validity of the whole act, or any other of its provisions, its validity, if it should be invalid, does not defeat the general scope and purpose of the act. People v. McFadden, supra.

6, 7. Conceding, but not deciding, that one or more of the provisions is against the general law for a uniform system of government for the counties of the state, we ought not in this action to express any opinion as to its constitutionality. "It will be time enough to pass upon it when some right dependent thereon is brought before the court for adjudication." Furthermore, we are of the opinion that the parties respondent have not shown themselves to be in a position to attack the constitutionality of these separate provisions. The rule is well established that one who is not prejudiced by the enforcement of an act of the legislature cannot question its constitutionality, or obtain a decision as to its invalidity, on the ground that it impairs the rights of others. 6 R. C. L. 89. This rule applies to the position of Humboldt County in this case. We are unable to perceive in what manner the designation of officers of Pershing County and the manner of its organization affects Humboldt County.

Without regard to the constitutionality of the separate and distinct provisions of the act, we are clearly of the opinion that the act as a whole is constitutional. It is therefore ordered that the alternative writ of prohibition heretofore issued be and is hereby made permanent and peremptory; and it is further ordered that the writ of mandate, as demanded, do issue; and the injunctive order appealed from is affirmed.

ON PETITION FOR REHEARING

By the Court, SANDERS, J.:

1. Rehearings are not granted as a matter of right (Twaddle v. Winters, 29 Nev. 108, 85 Pac. 280, 89 Pac.

289), and are not allowed for the purpose of reargument, unless there is reasonable probability that the court may have arrived at an erroneous conclusion. State v. Woodbury, 17 Nev. 337, 30 Pac. 1006.

In this case we are satisfied that the opinion answers satisfactorily all the points raised in opposition to its conclusions, but, as some question of doubt is raised as to the extent to which the decision goes, we take the liberty of summarizing for the benefit of counsel what is actually decided:

First—A county is a political subdivision of a state, through which, for the most part, its sovereign powers are exercised.

Second—The law creating Pershing County out of a part of Humboldt County is, as a whole, constitutional.

Third—That the said law is not abridged, limited, or restricted by the initiative or referendum clause of our constitution, and that the taking effect of the said law is not thereby suspended.

Fourth—That the completed law is not local, special, and municipal legislation within the meaning of the referendum clause of the constitution that reserves to the qualified electors of a specified county the power to approve or reject at the polls legislation of every character in or for such specified county.

In arriving at these conclusions we applied long-established principles:

2. First—Unless a limitation exists in the constitution of a state, the power of the legislature is absolute, by general or special statute, to provide the change of the boundaries, the division, addition, consolidation of existing counties, or the creation and organization of new counties. This doctrine finds its reason in the "essential nature of counties as political subdivisions of the state and as the creatures of its sovereign will."

3. Second—The whole matter of the division of counties and the creation of new ones is in its nature political, and not judicial, and belongs wholly to the legislative department of the government. Riverside County v. San Bernardino County, 134 Cal. 520, 66 Pac. 788.

4. Third—In construing the referendum as applied to legislation for counties, we applied the usual rules of construction applicable to the construction of laws enacted in the usual way, keeping in mind that "the thing to be sought is the thought expressed" (State v. Doron, 5 Nev. 399), and that it was the duty of this court, if possible, to give to the language of the measure such a construction as to make effective the reservation of power on the part of the people, and not to presume anything from its language that would negative the material inferences that may be drawn from "the people's law." McClure v. Nye, 22 Cal. App. 248, 133 Pac. 1145; Hodges v. Dawdy, 104 Ark. 583, 149 S. W. 656.

From the application of these principles and rules of construction we concluded that the statute creating Pershing County out of the territory of Humboldt County was, as a whole, constitutional, and further held that such act was not of the class of legislation referred to and embraced by the referendum; hence the asserted right of the people of Humboldt County to veto the law creating Pershing County by their ballots became a political question, and this court was without authority to adjudge matters of this kind between the two counties.

Counsel insist that the broad and comprehensive language of the referendum reserves to the people of a county the right to determine whether the act creating a new out of the old should become operative. The principal argument so earnestly advanced in support of this proposition is that it is a "local law" within the meaning and contemplation of the provision of the referendum as applied to counties, and they further insist that the opinion so declared. We do not recede from the declaration that the law is "local" legislation, but not for Humboldt County within the meaning of the word "local" as used in the referendum. The act is "local" legislation, for the reason that a general law could not be made applicable to such cases. Evans v. Job, 8 Nev. 322.

"It is not denied that the legislature has power to erect

a county, that is, to define its territorial limits and boundaries by special act, and thereby to subdivide one or more old counties, because it is said such action is clearly a part of proper legislative power not prohibited, and no general law could in such case be made applicable." State v. Irwin, 5 Nev. 111.

5. Neither do we recede from the declaration that the creation of a new county necessarily affects the territory out of which it is carved; but it does not follow that such a law affects the corporate existence of the old, its government, or its status as a political subdivision of the state. Neither does it destroy or impair its usefulness as a component part of the scheme of state government. It retains all its powers, rights, duties, and privileges, and remains subject to all its duties and obligations to the state, and is in no sense affected, injured, or damaged, except that its dominion and control is reduced to a less area of territory than that formerly occupied, to which its inhabitants, it is conceded, or must be conceded, have no vested right.

Neither do we recede from the declaration made in the opinion (though not material to the issue) that, if any one be entitled to vote on the proposition whether the completed act should become operative, it should be the people of Pershing County. On them especially rest the privileges, responsibilities, and burdens of the new county. People v. Kennedy, 207 N. Y. 533, 101 N. E. 442, Ann. Cas. 1914C, 616. But counsel argue that this reasoning is illogical, because Pershing County at the time the officers of Humboldt County called an election had not been created. If this be so, then why do counsel importune us to protest the political rights of the people of Humboldt County to determine whether the law that created Pershing County should become operative? But they assert that, conceding it to be a completed law, it is a law for Humboldt County. If this be true, we apprehend that the people of Pershing County would be here protesting with equal earnestness and vigor against a judicial recognition of such a law.

We are impressed that the argument of the petitioner is but a play on words. The language of the referendum construes itself. "The thing to be sought is the thought expressed." The primary and culminating thought expressed in the referendum is to reserve to the people of a county the right of referendum of legislation of every character for a county; legislation for "each county of the state"—that is, an established and existing county. Its language clearly shows that the people regarded counties and municipalities as being distinct and independent entities, each performing its duty in the scheme of government to the people it serves. The words "in or for" indicate two sources of legislation for the government of counties—that originating through a law-making body within the county, and that originating in a law-making body without the county. Rose v. Port of Portland, 82 Or. 541, 162 Pac. 498.

The word "for" defines and limits the character of such legislation, whether it emanates from within or without the county. Clearly it must in either case be legislation "for" the county; that is, "with respect to," with "regard to," legislation for its government and exercise. This limitation of power furnishes a strong argument of its existence, and involves necessarily the exclusion of things not expressed. The people themselves having limited their power to affirm or reject legislation "for" a county, it is impossible for us to extend its meaning to include legislation of a strictly political nature and character that concerns the status of the county as a political subdivision of the state, through which the state, for the most part, exercises its governmental powers, legislation of an entirely different character from that of "local" legislation as used in the referendum. It is fair to presume that the people adopted this particular measure, in its limited form, with full knowledge of the inherent power of the state over its territory and the recognized mode and manner followed and pursued by the state with reference to the division and creation of counties from the date of its organization. It is also not unfair to presume that the people adopted the referendum as it relates to counties with full knowledge that the framers of the constitution did not delegate to the legislature or to the counties of the state its inherent power in the matter of the division and creation of new counties, and that the legislature derives its power and control over territory of the state, not through the organized law, but from the character and nature of our form of government,

In the absence of clear, explicit, and unmistakable language to show that the people reserved to themselves the power to divide counties and establish new ones, together with the power to veto such laws when duly enacted by the legislature, we decline to announce a principle that would tend to undermine what we consider to be a power inherent in a state.

In the case of Gibson v. Mason, 5 Nev. 283, there is an exhaustive and able discussion of the sovereignty of the state as against the sovereignty of the people. It is therein announced that an act of the legislature made dependent upon the people's votes or approval is utterly void. This doctrine has been superseded by the referendum clause of the constitution. It is now held, and the law is so familiar as to render any review unnecessary, that the legislature may delegate to municipalities and restricted localities the right to determine whether they will act under or take advantage of statutes pertaining to such subjects as municipal government and excise. People v. Kennedy, supra.

As stated in the opinion, we are not concerned with the wisdom or policy of the legislative act in question. The legislature had the power to give to electors of the entire county of Humboldt the right of referendum. And the people themselves, when they adopted the initiative and referendum, had they so desired, could have reserved to themselves the option to adopt or reject legislation of the character here in question. But these are matters for the legislature and the people to deal with, and not courts.

The petition for rehearing is denied.

COLEMAN, C. J., concurring:

I concur in the opinion of Mr. Justice SANDERS.

Two purposes were sought to be accomplished by the act attacked in these proceedings. The first was to create Pershing County, and the second to provide the necessary organization for the government thereof. Had an independent act been passed creating Pershing County, which might have been done, as was held in Leake v. Blasdel, 6 Nev. 40, and leaving to a separate and distinct bill the providing for its government, I am unable to see how it could be contended that such an act creating Pershing County would be such "local, special and municipal legislation * * * in and for" Humboldt County as was contemplated· by the constitutional amendment in question. In fact, the very argument made by counsel for respondent is inconsistent with any other conclusion. They insist that the act creating Pershing County is within itself a dismemberment of Humboldt County. How, then, can it be said on the other hand that it is an act "in and for" Humboldt County? Their argument is not only inconsistent with the conclusions they seek to have us arrive at, but shows conclusively the weakness of their position. There is a great difference between the creation of a new county and legislating for one already in existence, and such is the chief distinction between the case before us and the one contended for by counsel for Humboldt County. This being true, the mere fact that the act in question contains provisions creating Pershing County, and also provisions incident to the creation of that county and providing for the government thereof, does not change the situation in the least.

[No. 2358]

STATE OF NEVADA, Ex Rel. R. H. JONES, AND
JANE DOE JONES, HIS WIFE, PETITIONERS *v.*
WILLIAM BONNER, JUSTICE OF THE PEACE
OF SPRAGG TOWNSHIP, LYON COUNTY, NEVADA,
RESPONDENT.

[181 Pac. 586]

1. JUSTICES OF THE PEACE—CERTIORARI—REVIEW—JURISDICTION—
    RECORD—PRESUMPTIONS.
       Judgment of a justice of the peace against defendants will
    be held void on certiorari, record or files of the case not
    affirmatively showing summons was served or that defendants
    appeared, nothing being presumed in favor of jurisdiction of
    courts of limited jurisdiction, and it not being permissible to
    consider affidavits that summons was in fact served.

ORIGINAL PROCEEDING in certiorari by the State, on
the relation of R. H. Jones and another, against William
Bonner, Justice of the Peace. **Judgment set aside.
Rehearing denied.**

R. L. Waggoner, for Petitioners:

The justice of the peace had no jurisdiction at the
time to hear the case and enter the judgment. The
record fails to show that summons was served on either
of the defendants. The affidavit of service filed by the
officer is insufficient. Rev. Laws, 5022. "Nothing can
be presumed in favor of the jurisdiction of a justice of
the peace. The statutory provisions for acquiring jurisdiction must be strictly pursued." Victor M. & M. Co. v.
Justice Court, 18 Nev. 21. "There is no presumption in
favor of jurisdiction of justices of the peace. Little v.
Currie, 5 Nev. 90; Whitewell v. Barbier, 7 Cal. 54;
Keybers v. McComber, 7 Pac. 838.

It is not permissible to add to the return by parol evidence. "The general rule is well settled that parol evidence is ordinarily inadmissible to contradict or vary a
judgment, decree, or record of court expressed in plain
and unambiguous language." Elliott on Evidence, vol. 1,
par. 618; Bays v. Trulson, 35 Pac. 26; Underhill on Evidence, sec. 390; Jones on Evidence, sec. 343.

H. Pilkington, for Respondent.

By the Court, COLEMAN, C. J.:

This is an original proceeding in certiorari to inquire into the jurisdiction of the justice of the peace of Spragg Township, Lyon County, to render a certain judgment in favor of Mrs. J. Bean and against R. H. Jones and Jane Doe Jones, his wife. The record of the justice of the peace relative to the case, as certified to this court, is as follows:

"Complaint filed; summons issued; affidavit for attachment filed; undertaking for attachment filed; writ of attachment issued; affidavit for arrest filed; undertaking for arrest filed; order of arrest indorsed in summons; docketing case; judgment entered in the above-entitled case for plaintiff for amount prayed for in the sum of $30 and attorney fee of $15, and costs of this action taxed to defendant. E. A. Blanchard, Acting Judge."

Section 5732 of the Revised Laws of 1912, as amended (Stats. 1913, p. 360), provides how and by whom a summons may be served, and also makes provision for the return showing service thereof. It will be seen from a perusal of the record of the justice of the peace that, so far as appears therefrom, no service of summons had been made upon either of the defendants at the time the judgment was rendered, nor is there in the files sent up by the justice of the peace the original summons showing service thereof; nor does the record show that the defendants appeared in the action. It is an ancient rule that nothing is presumed in favor of the jurisdiction of courts of limited jurisdiction. That such a court has jurisdiction must affirmatively appear; and, unless it does so appear, judgment by such a court is void for want of jurisdiction. This is not a new question in this state. It was before the court in 1866, and the court then held that such a judgment as is here involved was void, as the court was without jurisdiction. McDonald v. Prescott & Clark, 2 Nev. 109, 90 Am. Dec. 517. It would be a waste of time to enlarge upon this point. See, also, 16 R. C. L. 367; 24 Cyc. 497.

We may say that there are different affidavits on file in this court to the effect that the summons was in fact served. These we cannot consider. This case shows the importance of attorneys giving their personal attention to the preparing of and superintending the making of returns in suits in justices' courts. In this proceeding counsel for petitioners admit the indebtedness. It may be that the officer who made the service of the summons —if in fact any was made—can now make his return showing service of summons, thereby giving the justice of the peace jurisdiction to proceed. But as to this we express no opinion.

It not appearing from the record and files of the case mentioned that the justice of the peace had jurisdiction to consider the same, it is ordered that the judgment rendered in said justice's court in favor of Mrs. J. Bean and against R. H. Jones and Jane Doe Jones, his wife, be, and the same is hereby, declared null and void, and is hereby set aside, and that relators have and recover their costs.

ON PETITION FOR REHEARING

Per Curiam:

Rehearing denied.

[No. 2364]

W. H. CAMPBELL, RESPONDENT *v.* JOE VANETTI AND ANGELO CAPURO, APPELLANTS.

[181 Pac. 963]

1. BROKERS—ACTION FOR COMMISSION.

> In a broker's action for commissions for the sale of land, a finding that the contract was one of general employment to find a purchaser at any price, defendant to pay 5 per cent commission, was not supported by proof of a contract that plaintiff was to find a buyer for the property at a stated price upon which a 5 per cent commission was to be paid.

APPEAL from Second Judicial District Court, Washoe County; *Thomas F. Moran,* Judge.

Action by W. H. Campbell against Joe Vanetti and another. Judgment for plaintiff, and from an order denying a new trial, defendants appeal. **Remanded, and new trial directed.**

Orvis Speciali and *Mack & Green,* for Appellants:

Where a broker undertakes to find a purchaser for specific property within a fixed time and at a fixed price, he is not entitled to any commission until he has performed the undertaking; and the loss, if any, occasioned by his failure to perform the undertaking, is his own. 9 C. J. 587, 611; 19 Cyc. 240; 4 C. J. 303; Sibbald v. Bethlehem Iron Co., 83 N. Y. 378; Fulz v. Wimer, 9 Pac. 316; Ernst v. Ganahl, 166 Cal. 493; Brown v. Mason, 155 Cal. 155; Holmes v. Silcox, 160 N. W. 465; Wylie v. Bank, 61 N. Y. 416. "Inasmuch as it is elementary law that where a contract is made on a certain named condition, a party seeking to recover under the contract must bring himself within the condition." 4 R. C. L. 322.

LeRoy F. Pike and *Roy W. Stoddard,* for Respondent:

"The universal rule is that, unless limited by express provisions of the contract, a broker is entitled to his compensation when he has done all his contract required of him." 9 C. J. 587, 589. "If property is placed in the hands of a broker for sale at a certain price, and a sale is brought about through the broker as a procuring cause, he is entitled to commissions on the sale, even though the final negotiations were conducted through the owner, who, in order to make the sale, accepts a price less than that stipulated to the broker." The law will not allow the owner of property sold to reap the fruits of the broker's labor and then deny him his just reward. Ann. Cas. 1913E, 784; Slotboom v. Simpson Lumber Co., 67 Or. 516; 4 R. C. L. 433; Ann. Cas. 1913D, 823; Ann. Cas. 1914C, 132.

By the Court, SANDERS, J.:

This action was brought by W. H. Campbell, plaintiff, to recover from the defendants a real estate brokerage commission, alleged to have been earned by the plaintiff in finding a purchaser for the defendants' ranch, and personal property thereon, situate in Pleasant Valley, Washoe County, Nevada.

The trial court conformed its findings to the facts alleged in the complaint, and found in the language of the complaint that the defendants were owners of the property; that in the latter part of February, 1917, the defendant, Joe Vanetti, for himself and his cotenant, Angelo Capuro, entered into a certain agreement and contract with the plaintiff, conditioned that, if the plaintiff would find a buyer for the property, the defendants would pay to the plaintiff 5 per cent commission on the sale price of the said property for and in consideration of his services; that thereafter, on or about the 8th day of May, 1917, the plaintiff took one L. A. L. Green to the property, where he introduced Green to the defendants, the said Green stating that he desired to purchase a ranch; that Green, in the presence of the defendants, inspected the ranch and entered into negotiations with the defendants to purchase the same; that thereafter, on the 24th of November, 1917, Green purchased the property for the price of $23,250; and that thereafter

the plaintiff demanded of the defendant Vanetti that
the defendants pay to him, under the terms of the contract, 5 per cent of the sale price of the ranch and
personal property, to wit, $1,162.50.

As a conclusion of law the court found that the plaintiff was entitled to recover from the defendants the said
sum and his costs of suit. Upon these findings the court
rendered judgment in favor of the plaintiff and against
defendants for said sum. From the judgment and an
order denying to the defendants a new trial the defendants prosecute this appeal.

This action is upon a special contract of employment,
oral it is true, but clear and definite in its terms, and the
respective rights and obligations of the parties should
have been decided by the terms of the agreement and
appropriate rules of law applied to the particular facts.

The finding that the defendant, Joe Vanetti, entered
into an agreement or contract with the plaintiff, conditioned that if the plaintiff would find a buyer for the
defendants' ranch and personal property thereon the
defendants would pay to the plaintiff, in consideration of
his services, 5 per cent commission on the sale price, is
not sustained by the evidence. The only evidence in support of this finding is the plaintiff's understanding of
his rights under or flowing from the contract and his
acts and conduct indicative of such understanding, but
the contract as proved furnishes no foundation for his
understanding. The evidence of the plaintiff, testifying
as a witness in his own behalf, shows that he was
employed to find a buyer for the property at a stated
price of $24,000, and it was agreed that for this service
he should be paid 5 per cent commission on the sale price
of the property. The court, in effect, found that the
contract was one of a general employment of the plaintiff to find a purchaser at any price and that the defendants promised to pay 5 per cent commission on the sale
price, whatever it might be. This was not the contract.

There being an essential difference between the
express contract declared on and that proved, the defen-

dants' exception to the refusal of their motion for a new trial is sustained, and the cause is remanded to the district court for a new trial.

COLEMAN, C. J., concurring:

I concur in the judgment of reversal, for the reason that it appears from the evidence that the defendant Capuro was not a party to the employment of the plaintiff. He was asked: "Did you ever have any conversation or make any contract with Mr. W. H. Campbell, the plaintiff, with regard to the sale of your ranch to Mr. Green or any one else?" To which he answered, "No." He was asked similar questions several times and his answer was invariably "No." His codefendant gave similar testimony. The plaintiff testified that he had no conversation with defendant Capuro concerning the deal, as they could not understand each other. There could have been no ratification by Capuro, as there is not a scintilla of evidence to the effect that the terms of the contract which Vanetti made were ever brought to his knowledge prior to the closing of the deal.

I am not in accord with the conclusions reached by my learned associates on the question discussed in their opinion. Where a broker is employed to sell real estate, it is a general rule that when he finds a person who is ready, willing and able to buy upon the terms named, he has earned his commission; and when the broker introduces a prospective purchaser to the seller, and the seller, without breaking off negotiations, thereafter sells the property at a reduced figure, the broker is entitled to his commission. See exhaustive note to Smith v. Preiss, Ann. Cas. 1913D, 823, 824, citing many cases; 19 Cyc. 249–251.

In the instant case, in my opinion, the court was justified from the evidence in concluding that the negotiations initiated in February were never broken off, and that plaintiff was the procuring cause of the sale which was consummated. Appellants have sought to make much of the fact that several months elapsed between the time of the introduction of Green to Vanetti and the date of the sale. In the light of the testimony, I fail to see the force of this contention. Furthermore, there is evidence that it was necessary to bring two suits to quiet title to certain portions of the ranch. What, if any, effect the defects in the title had in causing the delay is not apparent.

[No. 2365]

SOUTHERN PACIFIC COMPANY (A CORPORATION), APPELLANT, *v.* E. J. HAUG, RESPONDENT.

[182 Pac. 92]

1. CARRIERS—LIMITATION OF LIABILITY FOR NEGLIGENCE—LOSS.
   A common carrier cannot, by contract, avoid liability for loss or damage to freight caused by its own negligence or that of its servants.

2. CARRIERS—LIABILITY FOR LOSS OR DAMAGE—LIMITATION—VALUATION.
   A railroad's contract fixing a valuation on intrastate shipment negligently destroyed *held* void, where property's actual value was greater.

3. CARRIERS—LOSS OF GOODS—DAMAGES—MEASURE.
   Irrespective of statute, it is a general rule that measure of damages where goods intrusted to a carrier are destroyed is their value with interest from the date delivery should have been made.

APPEAL from Second Judicial District Court, Washoe County; *George A. Bartlett*, Judge.

Action by E. J. Haug against the Southern Pacific Company. Judgment for plaintiff, and defendant appeals. Affirmed, COLEMAN, C. J. dissenting.

Brown & Belford, for Appellant:

While a common carrier cannot by contract avoid its liability for negligence, its liability can be fixed and limited where, in view of a consideration such as a lower freight rate, a valuation is placed by the shipper on the goods, such valuation being placed for the purpose of securing such lower rate. Hart v. Railroad, 112 U. S. 331; Donlon v. S. P. Co., 90 Pac. 603; 12 Ann.

Cas. 118, 1124, 1130; Pacific Express Co. v. Foley, 26 Pac. 665; Bernard v. Adams Express Co., 176 Mass. 280; Durgen v. Atlantic Express Co., 20 Atl. 328; Zimmer v. Railroad, 137 N. Y. 460; Tewes v. S. S. Co., 186 N. Y. 151; Hill v. Railroad, 74 Pac. 1054; Loesser v. Railroad, 69 N. W. 372; 10 C. J. 165; 1 Hutchinson on Carriers (3d ed.) sec. 426; 4 Elliott on Railroads (2d ed.) sec. 1510.

The ruling of the Supreme Court of Nevada in Zetler v. T. & G. R. R. Co., 35 Nev. 381, 37 Nev. 486, should not be extended to the case at bar. It should be strictly limited to cases like the Zetler case, or frankly overruled. Clarke-Lawrence Co. v. Railway Co. 61 S. E. 365; Henry v. Canadian Pac. Ry. Co., 1 Man. 210; 10 C. J., sec. 237.

The public generally, and particularly all persons in any way interested in any shipment over a railroad within this state, must be presumed to have notice of the schedules of rates filed with the state railroad commission and the classifications of freight in force, which must also be filed, and all the rules and regulations that in any manner affect the rates charged, which must be published with, and as a part of, such schedules. Rev. Laws, 4552; American Sugar R. Co. v. Railroad, 207 Fed. 33; Armour Packing Co. v. U. S., 209 U. S. 56; Smith v. Railway, 107 N. W. 56; Enderstein v. Railway, 157 Pac. 670.

Withers & Withers, for Respondent:

Public policy will not permit a common carrier to escape liability for negligence by any contract or any conditions placed upon a bill of lading. A common carrier may limit its liability as an insurer by reasonable and fair contracts or regulations. 10 C. J., secs. 168, 218. There is a distinction between liability for negligence and as an insurer. Zetler v. Railroad, 35 Nev. 381, 27 Nev. 486.

Plaintiff is entitled to recover the full value of the goods destroyed. He had never seen the bills of lading until after the goods had been destroyed. 1 Ann. Cas. 672; 12 Ann. Cas. 1125.

The court cannot overrule the Zetler case. "It is also a well-known rule that the courts have nothing to do with the general policy of the law." Vineyard L. & S. Co. v. District Court, 171 Pac. 166, 168. "Courts are justified in· overruling former decisions only where the same are deemed to be clearly erroneous." Ex Parte Woodburn, 32 Nev. 136.

By the Court, DUCKER, J.:

This is an appeal from a judgment in favor of the respondent for the sum of $2,365.90 for damages for the destruction of certain personal property, consisting of wedding presents, furniture, and other household goods, belonging to respondent.

The appellant is a railroad company and a common carrier. The said personal property was received by it at Reno, Nevada, for shipment to Mina, Nevada, en route to its final destination at Manhattan, Nevada. A collision occurred between two of the railroad company's trains a short distance from Reno, and the car in which the said personal property was being carried was wrecked and burned and the property totally consumed by fire. Appellant admitted negligence and sought to make a partial defense. In the appellant's answer the following partial defense was pleaded:

"That on or about August 14, 1917, said Nevada Transfer Company delivered to defendant at its depot in Reno, Nevada, for shipment and transportation over defendant's line of railroad from Reno, Nevada, and thence to Tonopah, Nevada, over the railroad of the Tonopah and Goldfield Company, a connecting carrier, en route to its final destination which was Manhattan, Nevada, certain personal property which defendant alleges, on information and belief, to have been the property of the plaintiff and the property mentioned and intended to be described by the complaint herein, as having been delivered to defendant for shipment by said

Nevada Transportation Company, which said property was contained in boxes and other packages, the contents of which were unknown to defendant except one cook-stove, and all of which property except said cook-stove was represented by the Nevada Transfer Company to be household goods. That the said personal property was then and there delivered to defendant and by it received for shipment over its said line of railroad as aforesaid and a bill of lading made out and executed by and in behalf of said Nevada Transfer Company as shipper and by and in behalf of the said defendant, the said goods being consigned to the plaintiff, with destination indicated as Manhattan, Nevada. And defendant further alleges upon information and belief that, prior to the delivery of said personal property to defendant, said Nevada Transfer Company had by the person in possession and in control of the said property, and from whom said Nevada Transfer Company received it, and who was acting for and in behalf of the owner thereof, been hired and employed, authorized and directed to haul and carry the said personal property to the defendant at its depot in Reno, and to deliver said personal property to the defendant for shipment and consigned as aforesaid, and to make and enter into any necessary and proper contract or arrangement with defendant for the transportation of such property, including the making of a declaration of the value of said goods for the purpose of obtaining the lowest freight rates thereon under the schedules and classifications hereinafter alleged.

"II· That on the said 14th day of August, 1917, and long prior thereto, the defendant and said Tonopah and Goldfield Railroad Company, its connecting carrier, had certain schedules of joint rates in force between Reno, Nevada, and Tonopah, Nevada, which said schedules had as parts thereof and attached thereto, the rules and regulations in force, including the classifications upon which said rates were made and based, and including a certain classification known as and called the Western Classification, and which schedules and classifications provided for two different freight rates classified as household goods and shipped in less-than-carload lots. That the joint rate from Reno, Nevada, to Tonopah, Nevada, over the railroad of defendant and over the Tonopah and Goldfield Railroad on said 14th day of August, 1917, upon household goods, where the actual value of each article shipped did not exceed $10 per hundred pounds, or the proportionate amount thereof, if the weight was less than 100 pounds, subject to rule 2 of the Western Classification, was $1.55 per hundred-weight, and that the freight rate upon household goods shipped in less-than-carload lots, whose actual valuation exceeded $10 per 100 pounds, subject to rule 2 of said Western Classification, was $2.32¼ per hundred pounds. That rule 2 of said Western Classification was and is as follows:

" 'Rule 2. Ratings for various articles are conditioned upon actual valuations declared by the shipper at time and place of shipment; and the following stipulation must be entered in full on shipping order and bill of lading and signed by the shipper:

" 'I. We hereby declare the value of the property herein described to be .... per ....

....[Shipper's signature.]

" 'Where shipper refuses to declare value at time and place of shipment, goods will not be accepted for transportation.'

"That the said Western Classification and schedules of freight rates and tariffs were on the said 14th day of August, 1917, and long prior thereto, contained in printed schedules filed by and in behalf of the defendant and said Tonopah and Goldfield Railroad Company and on file with the Railroad Commission of Nevada, and that two copies of said schedules for the use of the public were then on file and kept on file in each of the depots, stations and offices of the defendant and of the Tonopah and Goldfield Railroad Company within the State of Nevada where passengers or freight were received for transportation, including the depots, stations and offices at said Reno and Tonopah, and in such form and place as to be accessible to the public and where said schedules could be conveniently inspected, and that the rates and charges hereinbefore in this answer specified, were named in such schedules and were then in force.

"III. That said personal property so delivered by said Nevada Transfer Company to defendant as aforesaid on August 14, 1917, and represented by it as aforesaid to be household goods and which defendant, according to its information and belief, alleges to have been of the kind of goods classified and described in said schedules of freight rates as household goods, was shipped in less than a carload lot, and that the total weight of the articles so delivered to defendant and received for transportation by it as household goods was 3,655 pounds. That the said cook-stove was shipped separately and weighed 225 pounds, and took a freight rate from Reno to Tonopah, in accordance with said tariff schedules of $1.28 per hundredweight. And defendant alleges on information and belief. that said Nevada Transfer Company, the shipper of said personal property, knowing the classification of household goods, and that there were two freight rates thereon depending upon whether the value of said goods did or did not exceed $10 per 100 pounds and knowing the requirement of said rule 2 of said Western Classification that, where the rating of goods shipped was conditioned upon actual valuation, such valuation must be declared, and, desiring and intending thereby that only the lower of said freight rates should be charged and collected thereon, did declare, at the time and place of shipment, that the value of the property shipped (other than said cook-stove) did not exceed $10 per 100 pounds for each article, or the proportionate amount thereof if the weight was less than 100 pounds, and that the following stipulation was on said August 14, 1917, entered in full in writing on each shipping order and bill of lading covering the shipment of said property and was signed by the Nevada Transfer Company as shipper:

" 'I. We hereby declare the value of property herein described to be not to exceed $10 per 100 pounds for each article or proportionate amount thereof if weight is less than 100 pounds.'

"IV. That the bills of lading upon which said goods were received for transportation and transported by the defendant, and which were signed by said Nevada Transfer Company and by the defendant, expressly provided that every service to be performed thereunder should be subject to all the conditions, whether printed or written, therein contained, including the conditions on the back thereof, which said conditions were agreed to by the shipper and accepted for the shipper and his or its assigns, and that among the conditions printed upon the back of said bills of lading, was the following:

" 'The amount of any loss or damage for which any carrier is liable shall be computed on the basis of the value of the property at the time and place of shipment under the bill of lading.' "

Then follows a statement in the pleading to the effect that, by reason of the facts alleged, plaintiff (respondent herein) should be estopped from proving or attempting to prove that the actual value of the property, excepting said cook-stove, was more than the agreed valuation.

Respondent demurred to this partial defense. The court below sustained the demurrer and, after a trial of the case, rendered judgment for the actual value of the property with interest thereon at the rate of 7 per cent from the date of judgment.

The principal error assigned is the action of the court in sustaining respondent's demurrer which deprived appellant of the partial defense pleaded. As previously stated, the loss of the property through the negligence of the railroad company's employees was admitted. The shipment was an intrastate transaction.

It will be observed that the contract in the bills of lading does not exempt the company from liability for loss or damage, but limits such liability to an agreed valuation of the property, based on the lower of two freight rates for transportation.

1. That a common carrier cannot by contract exempt itself from liability for loss or damage of freight occasioned by its own negligence, or that of its servants, is so elementary as to require no citation of authority.

2. But on the precise question presented in this case concerning its liability under a contract obviously made to obtain a cheaper rate of transportation, by a declared valuation, there are two well-recognized rules regulating a common carrier's liability.

The rule declared by the Supreme Court of the United States concerning interstate shipments as announced in Hart v. Pennsylvania Railroad Co., 112 U. S. 331, 5 Sup. Ct. 151, 28 L. Ed. 717, and reaffirmed in Adams Express Co. v. Croniger, 226 U. S. 491, 33 Sup. Ct. 148, 57 L. Ed. 314, 44 L. R. A. (N.S.) 257, and later decisions of that court, is that—

"Such a carrier may, by a fair, open, just, and reasonable agreement, limit the amount recoverable by a shipper in case of loss or damage to an agreed value made for the purpose of obtaining the lower of two or more rates of charges proportioned to the amount of the risk." Adams Express Co. v. Croniger, supra.

This is the federal rule and is adhered to in a $number$ of the states in cases involving interstate shipments, and in some jurisdictions is applied by the state courts to intrastate transactions.

In a number of states, prior to the Carmack amendment (Act June 29, 1906, c. 3591, sec. 7, pars. 11, 12, 34 Stat. 595) of the interstate commerce act (Act Feb. 4, 1887, c. 104, sec. 20, 24 Stat. 386, U. S. Comp. St. secs. 8604a, 8604aa) and the interpretation of that amendment in Adams Express Co. v. Croniger, supra, the rule was declared, that—

"When loss or damage results from a violation of the contract of shipment, growing out of the negligence of of the carrier or its servants, any limitation as to the amount recoverable for loss or injury contained in the contract of shipment is inoperative, although a reduced rate is charged." 10 C. J., p. 171, and cases cited.

Of course, it cannot be said that the federal rule applicable to limited liability contracts in interstate carriage is necessarily operative as regards intrastate shipments, but appellant asks that it be applied here. We are of the opinion that the question is not one of first impression in this court, and that it was determined in Zetler v. T. & G. R. R. Co., 35 Nev. 381, 129 Pac. 299, L. R. A. 1916A, 1270, adversely to appellant's contention, and the rule there declared for this state that a common carrier is liable for the actual value of property lost through negligence, notwithstanding a contract for a lesser valuation. The case was affirmed on a rehearing. Zetler v. T. & G. R. R. Co., 37 Nev. 486, 143 Pac. 119. In that case the action against the railroad company was for damages for the loss of a passenger's trunk delivered from the baggage-room to some person not entitled to receive it.

The court said in the original opinion, and in substantially the same language in the decision on rehearing, that—

The delivery of the trunk "was such negligence on the part of the company as to render it liable for the value of the articles lost, nothwithstanding the contract."

Appellant earnestly insists that the case of Zetler v. T. & G. R. R. Co. is not controlling in the case before us, and that we should confine it within its particular facts, and thus distinguish it from the instant case, or else overrule it as erroneous, for the reason that it involved an interstate carriage, and the court was therefore bound to apply the federal rule concerning limited liability contracts.

Aside from its being a case involving an interstate shipment, we can discern no substantial difference in the facts of the former case and the one at bar. In each case there was a contract for carriage at an agreed valuation. In the one case the contract was printed on the ticket of the passenger, and in the other was contained in the bill of lading.

From the affirmative defense in the answer in the instant case it appears that the valuation.was made to obtain the lesser of two freight rates for carriage, and from the facts of the case of Zetler v. T. & G. R. R. Co. it appears that the baggage, which was valued in the contract at $100, was carried free in consideration of the ticket, but that a higher valuation could have been obtained upon the payment of additional proportionate rates.

That it was baggage lost by negligence in the case of Zetler v. T. & G. R. R. Co., and freight destroyed in the instant case, makes no distinction in facts that calls for the application of a different rule of liability. Saunders v. Southern Ry. Co., 128 Fed. 20, 62 C. C. A. 523.

In Hutchinson on Carriers, vol. 3, sec. 1297, the author says:

"In general, it may be stated that there is no distinction between the baggage of a passenger and ordinary goods, in respect to rights of parties to enter into contracts limiting the liability of the carrier."

We see nothing in the language of the court in Zetler v. T. & G. R. R. Co., either in the original opinion or in the opinion on rehearing, from which a conclusion can be reasonably drawn that the court intended to limit the rule announced to more than ordinary negligence.

But assuming that such a construction might be placed on the language of the court, it cannot be said that there is a greater degree of negligence in the act of a servant of a common carrier in delivering a passenger's trunk to a person not entitled to receive it, than in the acts of employees of such a carrier which occasion a head-on collision between trains by which property is lost in the one instance and destroyed in the other.

That the court, in Zetler v. T. & G. R. R. Co., intended to and did announce a rule of liability in this state as to

common carriers for ordinary negligence in the transportation of property in this state notwithstanding a
special contract limiting the amount of recovery to an
agreed valuation, is further apparent from the fact that
the court clearly recognized the well-settled right of such
carrier to protect itself from liability as an insurer, by
a proper contract. Upon this point the court said:

"Under the contentions made, it may be conceded for
the purposes of this case that 'it is competent for passenger carriers by specific regulations which are reasonable and not inconsistent with any statute or its duties
to the public, and which are distinctly brought to the
knowledge of the passenger, to protect themselves
against liability as insurers of baggage exceeding a fixed
amount in value, except upon additional compensation.' "

And added:

"Even if so, it has been held, where such is acknowledged to be the law by decision or even by statute, that
the carrier is liable for the baggage lost through his
negligence, notwithstanding a valid contract limiting
the amount of the liability." (Citing cases.)

The language quoted above, as well as that employed
by the court in its opinion on rehearing, convinces us
that appellant's contention, that the court intended to
limit the case to an exception of the federal rule heretofore stated, is not inferable, except by a most constrained construction of the language used.

We deem it unnecessary to decide in this case, which
involves an intrastate transaction, whether or not this
court, in Zetler v. T. & G. R. R. Co., which involved an
interstate carriage, should have been governed by the
interstate commerce act as amended by the Carmack
amendment, and construed in Adams Express Co. v.
Croniger, supra. Adams Express Company v. Croniger
was decided by the United States Supreme Court after
the original opinion was rendered in Zetler v. T. & G.
R. R. Co. and before the rehearing in the latter case. It
was cited to this court in that case on the rehearing, and
the court adhered to its original opinion in the decision

on rehearing. Regardless of the interstate feature of the case, we think Zetler v. T. & G. R. R. Co. is ruling in this action for the reasons given.

By reason of the view we have taken, it is unnecessary to determine whether or not the respondent was bound by the declaration of value made by the Nevada Transfer Company, from which appellant received the goods for shipment.

3. There was no error committed in including, in the judgment, interest on the actual value of the property destroyed.

Where the matter is not regulated by statute, it is well settled as a general rule that the measure of damages in a case of a common carrier is the value of the goods intrusted to it for transportation, with interest from the time they ought to have been delivered. New York, Lake Erie and Western Ry. Co. v. Estill, 147 U. S. 591, 13 Sup. Ct. 444, 37 L. Ed. 292; Fell v. Union Pac. Ry. Co., 32 Utah, 101, 88 Pac. 1003, 28 L. R. A. (N.S.) 1, 13 Ann. Cas. 1137; 10 C. J. 400.

The judgment of the lower court is affirmed.

COLEMAN, C. J.: I dissent.

[No. 2375]

IN THE MATTER OF THE ESTATE OF STEWART McKAY, DECEASED.

[184 Pac. 305]

1. APPEAL AND ERROR—DETERMINATION OF RIGHT TO APPEAL BEFORE HEARING ON MERITS.

    Ordinarily questions not pertaining to the regularity and efficacy of an appeal, but affecting its merit, should not be determined on motion to dismiss; but a party's right to be heard on the merits is statutory, depending entirely on whether he or she is within the general class designated by the statute, and the question should be determined in advance of hearing on the merits.

2. DESCENT AND DISTRIBUTION—GRANDNIECE EXCLUDED FROM INHERITANCE BY NEPHEWS AND NIECES.

    Stats. 1897, c. 106, regulating descent, as amended by Stats. 1915, c. 130, sec. 259, providing as to nephews and nieces in the third degree of kinship, excludes a grandniece from any inheritance, so that such grandniece was not an "heir" of testatrix, and section 272, defining the right of representation, does not bear on the former section, except as a statutory rule of interpretation.

3. CONSTITUTIONAL LAW—POLICY OF LAW MATTER FOR LEGISLATURE.

    The policy or expediency of a law is within the exclusive domain of legislative action, and is a forbidden sphere for the judiciary.

APPEAL from Second Judicial District Court, Washoe County; *George A. Bartlett*, Judge.

In the Matter of the Estate of Stewart McKay. Petition for distribution by James A. Fraser and others, executors, was opposed by Bertha Laughton, and from an adverse judgment she appeals. **Appeal dismissed. Rehearing denied.**

H. V. Morehouse and *Percy & Smith*, for Appellant:

Cases may be found where the court has properly held that an appeal may be dismissed on motion when the appellant is not a party aggrieved, but those are cases in which the record on appeal does not make the very point, as one of the questions raised by the appeal, and material to the appeal itself. The lower court ·on demurrer declared appellant not a party to the proceeding, because not interested in the estate of the decedent. From that ruling she appeals; and being a party in the lower court against whom the ruling was made, she has by law the right to test that very ruling in this court. Whether or not she was a party aggrieved was the very point passed upon by the lower court, and it becomes one of the material questions for this court on appeal. "The question is one going to the merits of the controversy, and not involving the regularity and efficiency of the appeal from the circuit court." In Re Mendenhall's Will, 72 Pac. 318. The appeal has been duly perfected, all technical matters have been duly compiled with, and the appeal is regularly and properly before this court. "Questions, therefore, which affect the merits will not be considered by the appellate court on such motion, as they are grounds for reversal or affirmance of the judgment." 2 Pl. & Pr. 346; Barnhart v. Fulkerth, 28 Pac. 221; Oregon Timber v. Seton, 111 Pac. 376; Hayne, New Trial & Appeal, sec. 272.

Appellant is entitled to share with respondents in the distribution of the estate, not as an heir of decedent, but by "right of representation," as heir of her deceased mother, who was sister of the respondents. Rev. Laws, 5857, 6116, 6129. "Courts must give effect to all the provisions of a statute relative to one subject-matter, though found in different sections." Hoffman v. Lewis, 87 Pac. 167; Trapp v. Wells Fargo & Co., 97 Pac. 1003; Lawson v. Tripp, 95 Pac. 520; Dutro v. Cudd, 91 Pac. 460; Norcker v. Norcker, 71 Pac. 816; City of Denver v. Campbell, 80 Pac. 142; Harrington v. Smith, 28 Wis. 59; Cooley, Const. Lim. 58; Cory v. Carter, 48 Ind. 327; Cleveland v. Bockus, 33 N. E. 421. "No part of a statute should be rendered nugatory." Torreyson v. Board, 7 Nev. 19.

Fred C. Peterson, C. F. McGlashan, and *Hennessy & Peterson,* for Respondents:

Motion to dismiss is the proper remedy. Appellant is not an heir at law of decedent, and therefore not interested in the settlement of the final account and distribution of the estate. She is not a party aggrieved by the decree of the district court, and therefore cannot be

heard on this appeal. Motion to dismiss appeal should
be granted. Rev. Laws, 5327; C. C. P. Cal., sec. 938;
In Re Antoldi Estate, 81 Pac. 278. "The objection that
one who has appealed has not right to appeal because
not aggrieved by the decision may, in some jurisdictions,
be taken by motion to dismiss the appeal." Smith v.
Stillwell, 80 Pac. 333; Deiter v. Kiser, 162 Cal. 315;
Hadfield v. Cushing, 35 R. I. 306; Amory v. Amory, 26
Wis. 157.

"The estate shall go to the next of kin in equal
degrees." Rev. Laws, 6116. "The degrees of kindred
shall be computed according to the rules of the civil
law * * *." Rev. Laws, 6119.

"Representation in America was never presumed, but
was applied only where the statute affirmatively provided therefor." Knapp v. Windsor, 6 Cush. 156. "Next
of kin of equal degree" excludes a grandniece. Conradt
v. Kent, 130 Mass. 287; Douglas v. Cameron, 47 Neb.
358; Van Cleve v. Van Fossen, 73 Mich. 342; Schenck
v. Vail, 24 N. J. Eq. 538; Quinby v. Higgins, 14 Me. 309;
In Re Ellen Nigro, 172 Cal. 474.

By the Court, DUCKER, J.:

The appellant, Bertha Laughton, is a grandniece of the
deceased, Stewart McKay, and claims that he died intestate as to certain lands located in Washoe County,
Nevada.

Stewart McKay died in the State of California on the
3d day of February, 1917, and left no wife, or issue, or
father, or mother, or brother, or sister surviving him.
His nearest of kin are James A. Fraser, Addie Fraser
Gunnarson, Tillie Fraser, and Jessie Fraser, surviving
children of a deceased sister. The appellant's mother,
Hughena Sapp, was a sister of said children, and died
prior to the death of Stewart McKay.

The deceased, Stewart McKay, was possessed of certain property in California and lands situated in Nevada
at the time of his death. He left a will in which said
James A. Fraser, Addie Fraser Gunnarson, and Tillie

Fraser, were named executor and executrices of said estate.

The administration of said estate in the Second district court of Washoe County, Nevada, is ancillary to the probate of said will in the State of California. The said executor and executrices filed a petition for distribution in the Second judicial district court, to which appellant filed her objections, and a petition praying that it be adjudged and decreed by the court that the said Stewart McKay died intestate as to said real property, and that she be decreed to be an heir of said decedent by representation through her deceased mother, Hughena Sapp, and entitled to an undivided one-fifth interest in said real estate. A demurrer to her petition was filed by the executor and executrices, which was sustained by the court, and her petition denied. It was further ordered and adjudged that the said Stewart McKay, deceased, died testate as to the real property involved herein, situate in the county of Washoe, State of Nevada. Hence this appeal.

The respondent heirs, the nephew and nieces of Stewart McKay, deceased, moved to dismiss the appeal, on the ground that appellant is not an heir at law and is therefore not a person entitled to appeal, under section 5327 of the Revised Laws of Nevada. This section provides that "any party aggrieved may appeal in the cases prescribed in this title." If appellant is not an heir at law of the deceased, Stewart McKay, she is not a party aggrieved by the ruling of the court below, and not authorized to appeal.

1. Ordinarily questions which do not pertain to the regularity and efficacy of an appeal, but affect its merit, ought not to be determined on a motion to dismiss the appeal. But a party's right to be heard upon the merits of an appeal is a statutory right, which depends entirely upon whether such party is within the general class designated by the statute. It is obviously a preliminary question, which should be determined in advance of a hearing on the merits and at the earliest opportunity.

In Amory v. Amory, 26 Wis. 157, under a statute providing that "any person aggrieved by any order, sentence, judgment or denial of a judge of the county court, may appeal therefrom to the circuit court for the same county," the court said:

"The question whether the party appealing in any case is a person thus designated by the statute, and to whom the right of appeal is given, is essentially a preliminary one. The objection being raised that the appellant is not such person, but a stranger to the order or sentence appealed from, it is clearly in the nature of matter in abatement, which, like any other, should be brought forward before further steps are taken, though not waived, perhaps, if not so brought forward. If sustained, it goes to show that the party appealing, or attempting to do so, cannot prosecute that appeal, nor any other, and that the merits of the order or sentence appealed from should never be tried at his instance or suggestion. It follows, therefore, that his appeal should be dismissed, and that, too, at the earliest possible moment when the fact can be judicially ascertained. The reason and propriety of this rule or mode of proceeding are obvious to require comment or explanation."

The appellant in the case, supra, claimed to be the widow of the testator, James Amory, and had attempted to contest the probate of the will.

So in Hadfield v. Cushing, 35 R. I. 306, 86 Atl. 897, it was held, on a motion to dismiss an appeal, that an expectant heir of a grandfather then living was not aggrieved by a decree of the probate court appointing a guardian for such grandparent, so as to entitle her to appeal therefrom. The motion to dismiss the appeal in the preceding case was made under a statute of the State of Rhode Island which provides:

"Any person aggrieved by an order or decree of a court of probate may, unless provision be made to the contrary, appeal therefrom to the superior court for the county in which such probate court is established," etc.

Appellant herein expresses a willingness that the

question of her heirship be determined on the motion, if it can be done, but questions the right of this court to decide it in this manner, for the reason that her heirship was the very point passed upon by the court below, and thus becomes a material question for this court to decide upon appeal. Her counsel cite In Re Mendenhall's Will, 43 Or. 542, 72 Pac. 318, 73 Pac. 1033; Barnhart v. Fulkerth, 92 Cal. 155, 28 Pac. 221, Oregon Timber and Cruising Co. v. Seton et al., 59 Or. 64, 111 Pac. 376, 115 Pac. 1121, and Hayne, New Trial & App. (Rev. Ed.) sec. 272, and 2 Pl. & Prac. 346, in support of her contention. These authorities sustain the general rule that on a motion to dismiss an appeal the court will not consider the merits of the controversy. In none of these, and in no other cases, so far as we have been able to ascertain, was the question decided, under a statute similar to ours, that where the point on appeal involved the right of appeal it could not be determined on a motion to dismiss.

2. On the motion before us we are confronted with the query: Was the appeal properly taken? If in solving this question it appears that the appellant is not a party aggrieved, the appeal must be dismissed.

Assuming, for the purpose of this decision, that Stewart McKay died intestate as to the real estate in question, the estate is cast into the fourth subdivision of section 259 of the act to regulate the settlement of estates of deceased persons (Stats. 1897, c. 106), as amended in 1915 (Stats. 1915, c. 130), for the intestate left no issue, nor wife, nor father, nor mother, and no brother or sister living at his death. But, as our decision must rest upon a construction of the entire section, we will set it forth. The section reads:

"SEC. 259. When any person having title to any estate, not otherwise limited by marriage contract, shall die intestate as to such estate, it shall descend and be distributed subject to the payment of his or her debts, in the following manner:

"First—If there be a surviving husband or wife, and

only one child, or the lawful issue of one child, one-half
to the surviving husband or wife, and one-half to such
child or issue of such child. If there be a surviving
husband or wife and more than one child living, or one
child living and the lawful issue of one or more deceased
children, one-third to the surviving husband or wife, and
the remainder in equal shares to his or her children, and
to the lawful issue of any deceased child by right of
representation. If there be no child of the intestate
living at his or her death, the remainder shall go to all
of his or her lineal descendants, and if all of the said
descendants are in the same degree of kindred to the
intestate, they shall share equally, otherwise they shall
take according to the right of representation.

"Second—If he or she shall leave no issue, the estate
shall go, one-half to the surviving husband or wife,
one-fourth to the intestate's father and one-fourth to
the intestate's mother, if both are living; if not, one-
half to either the father or mother then living. If he
or she shall have no issue, nor father, nor mother, the
whole community property of the intestate shall go
to the surviving husband or wife, and one-half of the
separate property of the intestate shall go to the surviving husband or wife, and the other half thereof shall
go in equal shares to the brothers and sisters of the
intestate, and to the children of any deceased brother or
sister by right or representation. If he or she shall
leave no issue, or husband, or wife, the estate shall go,
one-half to the intestate's father and one-half to the
intestate's mother, if both are living; if not, the whole
estate shall go to either the father or mother then living.
If he or she shall leave no issue, father, mother, brother,
or sister, or children of any issue, brother or sister, all
of the property * * * shall go to the surviving
husband or wife.

"Third—If there be no issue, nor husband, or wife,
nor father, nor mother, then in equal shares to the
brothers and sisters of the intestate, and to the

children of any deceased brother or sister by right of representation.

"Fourth—If the intestate shall leave no issue, nor husband, nor wife, nor father, nor mother, and no brother or sister living at his or her death, the estate shall go to the next of kin in equal degree, excepting that when there are two or more collateral kindred in equal degree, but claiming through different ancestors, those who claim through the nearest ancestors shall be preferred to those who claim through ancestors more remote; provided, however, if any person shall die leaving several children, or leaving one child and issue of one or more children, and any such surviving child shall die under age and not having been married, all of the estate that came to such deceased parent shall descend in equal shares to the other children of the same parent, and to the issue of any such other children who may have died, by right of representation.

"Fifth—If at the death of such child, who shall die under age and not having been married, all the other children of this said parent being also dead, and any of them shall have left issue, the estate that came to such child by inheritance from his or her said parent shall descend to all the issue of the other children of the same parent, and if all the said issue are in the same degree of kindred to said child they shall share the said estate equally; otherwise they shall take according to the right of representation.

"Sixth—If there be no surviving husband, or wife, or kindred, except a child or children, the estate shall, if there be only one child, all go to that child; and if there be more than one child, the estate shall descend and be distributed to all the intestate's children, share and share alike.

"Seventh—If there be no surviving husband, or wife, or kindred, except a child or children and the lawful issue of a child or children, the estate shall descend and be distributed to such child or children and lawful issue

of such child or children by right of representation, as
follows: To such child or children each a child's part,
and to the lawful issue of each deceased child, by right
of representation, the same part and proportion that its
parent would have received in case such parent had been
living at the time of the intestate's death; that is, the
lawful issue of any deceased child shall receive the part
and proportion that its parent would have received had
such parent been living at the time of the intestate's
death.

"Eighth—If there be no surviving husband, or wife,
or kindred, except the lawful issue of a child or children,
all of the estate shall descend and be distributed to the
lawful issue of such child or children by right of representation, and this rule shall apply to the lawful issue of
all such children and to their lawful issue ad infinitum.

"Ninth—If the intestate shall leave no husband, nor
wife, nor kindred, the estate shall escheat to the state for
the support of the common schools."

Computing their degrees of kinship to the intestate
according to the rules of the civil law, the nephew and
nieces, James A. Fraser, Addie Fraser Gunnarson, Tillie
Fraser, and Jessie Fraser are in the third degree, and the
the grandniece, Bertha Laughton, in the fourth degree.
It is thus seen that the nephew and nieces are in the
class designated by the first part of the fourth subdivision of the section, as "next of kin in equal degree," and
must inherit to the exclusion of the grandniece, unless
the proviso in this subdivision providing for representation shows a contrary legislative intent in this kind of
a case. It is purely a question of statutory construction.

The first inquiry is as to the scope of the proviso.
Does it limit the fourth subdivision of the section alone,
or has it a wider application?

"The natural and appropriate office of the proviso
being to restrain or qualify some preceding matter, it
should be confined to what precedes it unless it clearly
appears to have been intended for some other matter. It
is to be construed in connection with the section of which

it forms a part, and is substantially an exception. If it be a proviso to a particular section, it does not apply to others unless plainly intended. It should be construed with reference to the immediately preceding parts of the clause to which it is attached." Sutherland on Statutory Construction, 296.

The preceding quotation states the general rule and its exception. We think the proviso in this case falls within the exception to the general rule stated. It will be observed that the proviso is confined to an estate of inheritance descending from a deceased parent to a child who subsequently dies under age and not having been married.

It deals exclusively with this single source of title, while the other subdivisions provide for the descent of the property of the intestate, however the title may have been acquired. The words in the proviso, "all the estate that came to such deceased parent," plainly mean an inheritance which, under the conditions named, descends to the deceased minor's brothers and sisters, or their issue, as the case may be.

It is thus seen that the proviso announces an exception to the general scheme of descent embraced in the section; and so construing it in this light it clearly appears that it was not intended to qualify or limit the preceding parts of the clause or section only, but to operate, under the given circumstances, independently, and to each subdivision of the section.

"The proviso may qualify the whole or any part of the act, or it may stand as an independent proposition or rule, if such is clearly seen to be the meaning of the legislature as disclosed by an examination of the entire enactment." Black on Interpretation of Laws, 273.

In United States v. Babbit, 1 Black, 55, 17 L. Ed. 94, the question was as to the fees a register of a land office was entitled to receive, and turned on the scope of the proviso. The court said:

"We are of opinion that the proviso referred to is not limited in its effect to the section where it is found, but that it was affirmed by Congress as an independent proposition, and applies alike to all officers of this class."

These latter authorities illustrate the exception to the general rule governing the construction and effect of a proviso. We are of the opinion that the term "next of kin in equal degree," in the fourth subdivision, excludes from the inheritance all kindred not in that degree of kinship to the intestate. This is the established law in all jurisdicitions where the statute of descent is the same or substantially the same as the statute under consideration. Douglas et al. v. Cameron et al., 47 Neb. 358, 66 N. W. 430; Conant v. Kent, 130 Mass. 178; Van Cleve v. Van Fossen, 73 Mich. 342, 41 N. W. 258; Estate of Nigro, 172 Cal. 474, 156 Pac. 1019; Schenck v. Vail, 24 N. J. Eq. 538.

The reasons for the rule are stated in Douglas v. Cameron, supra. The subdivision of the statute construed is identical with the fourth subdivision of our statute, and the matter corresponding to the proviso is more distinctly set forth in a separate subdivision of the Nebraska statute. One of the questions decided was that the grandchildren of a deceased sister did not inherit, when there were living nieces and nephews of the intestate. The question is the same here. The court said:

"It seems to be the policy of all the statutes at some point more or less remote to cut off representation entirely among collaterals, and where, because of unequal degrees of kinship, representation would otherwise be necessary, to defeat it by making a per capita distribution among those nearest in degree and excluding the more remote. Our law seems to reach that period where, at any point among collaterals beyond the children of brothers and sisters, the surviving kindred fall into unequal degrees. This is the construction given elsewhere to statutes resembling ours [citing cases]. Cases holding a different rule, so far as we have found any, have been under statutes which by their clear language required a different construction."

In Schenck v. Vail, supra, the New Jersey statute provided:

"When any person shall die seized of any lands," etc., "and without lawful issue, and without leaving a brother or sister of the whole or half blood, or the issue of any such brother or sister, and without leaving a father or mother capable of inheriting by this act the said lands," etc., "and shall leave several persons, all of equal degree of consanguinity to the person so seized, the said lands shall then descend and go to the said several persons of equal degree of consanguinity to the person so seized, as tenants in common, in equal parts, however remote from the person so seized the common degree of consanguinity may be."

In construing the language the court said:

"The legislative endeavor in this passage is plain. It is to designate the class of persons who are to take the land on the contingency specified. The terms used, considered intrinsically, are explicit and perfectly intelligible. Accepting them in their ordinary and natural meaning, the expression 'several persons, all of equal degree of consanguinity' to a deceased person, admits of but a single interpretation; the words, ex vi terminorum, exclude all those who do not stand in the same degree of blood, and in their usual import they utterly refuse to comprehend, in the same category, both first and second cousins."

And again is reference made to this policy of exclusion of collaterals not in equal degree:

"Such exclusion of the rule in this connection tends, I think, very decidedly in the direction of a sound policy. It harmonizes with the rule of law which circumscribes, within reasonable bounds, the right of representation in the distribution of personalty. It prevents titles to realty from becoming uncertain and intricate, by reason of the vast multiplication of owners."

The Michigan statute construed in Van Cleve et al. v. Van Fossen et al., supra, is similar to the statute under consideration here. The fifth subdivision of the Michi-

gan statute and the fourth subdivision of the Nevada
statute are alike, and the sixth subdivision of the statute
of the former state is substantially the same as the proviso of the Nevada statute, and is connected to said
fifth subdivision by the words "Provided, however."
In Van Cleve v. Van Fossen the question decided was
that grandnieces did not inherit with the nieces of the
intestate.

"It is plain, therefore," said the court, "that these
[grandnieces] do not stand in an equal degree as next
of kin to the deceased. The term 'next of kin' in the
statute signifies those who stand in the nearest relationship to the intestate, according to the rules of the civil
law for computing degrees of kinship. In this subdivision of the statute there are no words suggesting that
any one is to take by the right of representation. But
the idea is excluded by the words that the estate shall
descend to his 'next of kin in equal degree.' We must
so construe this statute as to give each word and sentence force and effect, and the words 'in equal degree'
exclude all others than those who stand in the same
degree of kinship to the intestate."

In Conant v. Kent and Estate of Nigro, supra, grandnieces and grandnephews were held to be excluded from
a share of the inheritance by reason of the term in the
respective statutes, "next of kin in equal degree."

There is, in fact, little room for construction. The
plain language of the fourth subdivision designates a
particular class of collateral kindred that shall inherit
under certain conditions, and the body of the section
reveals nothing to indicate that the rule in this subdivision was not intended as a rule of exclusion. Appellant is not in an equal degree of kinship with the nephew
and nieces of the intestate, and by the express prohibition of the statute cannot inherit.

An estate descending to a deceased minor, who had
never been married, is not involved here, and it is therefore apparent that the proviso, upon which her counsel

so much rely, cannot help appellant. She is not within the special case necessary to invoke its application.

Counsel for appellant insist that succession by right of representation is carried into the fourth subdivision by reason of section 272, which is a section of the same statute. Section 272 reads:

"Inheritance or succession 'by right of representation' takes place when the descendants of any deceased heir take the same share or right in the estate of another person that their parents would have taken if living. * * *"

This section is what it purports to be, a definition of the term "by right of representation," and is not intended as a rule of distribution. It has no bearing on section 259, except as a statutory rule of interpretation of the term wherever employed therein. This construction is apparent from the face of section 272, and the care observed by the legislature to provide for representation in the first, second, third, fifth, seventh, and eighth subdivisions of section 259, and in the special instance in the fourth subdivision, tends strongly to negative the idea of an intention to provide for it throughout the section by a separate and general provision.

3. Much has been said by counsel for appellant of the injustice of a rule that will deprive appellant of her inheritance. Even so, we cannot amend the statute. The policy, wisdom, or expediency of a law is within the exclusive theater of legislative action. It is a forbidden sphere for the judiciary, which courts cannot invade, even under pressure of constant importunity.

As appellant is not an heir at law of the intestate, and therefore not a party aggrieved by the ruling of the lower court, the appeal is dismissed.

ON PETITION FOR REHEARING

Per Curiam:

Rehearing denied.

[No. 2387]

ALBERT B. HILTON, Petitioner, v. THE SECOND
JUDICIAL DISTRICT COURT OF THE STATE
OF NEVADA, IN AND FOR THE COUNTY OF
WASHOE, AND THOMAS F. MORAN, JUDGE OF
SAID COURT, RESPONDENTS.

[183 Pac. 317]

1. PLEADING—CROSS-COMPLAINT—MATTERS ALLEGED IN COMPLAINT.
    If an averment of marriage and residence are necessary
    and indispensable facts to be stated in a complaint for support
    and maintenance, they are equally so in a cross-complaint in
    a divorce action, regardless of the fact that the plaintiff has
    alleged that there was a marriage and that the parties resided
    in the state.

2. HUSBAND AND WIFE—SUPPORT AND MAINTENANCE.
    A wife may maintain an action against her husband for
    support and maintenance without applying for divorce, under
    Stats. 1913, c. 97.

3. HUSBAND AND WIFE—MAINTENANCE.
    To entitle a wife to recover in an action under Stats. 1913,
    p. 120, for support and maintenance, without applying for
    divorce, it is incumbent upon her to make a showing of the
    marriage relation, her needs, and the ability of her husband,
    as in a suit for divorce.

4. HUSBAND AND WIFE—SUPPORT AND MAINTENANCE—STATUTE.
    The object of Stats. 1913, c. 97, giving wife right of action
    against husband for support and maintenance without apply-
    ing for a divorce, is to give the wife a sure and speedy remedy
    through an independent action when she has any cause of
    action for divorce against her husband, or when he has
    deserted her for a period of ninety days, and, being remedial,
    must be liberally construed with a view to promote its object,
    the jurisdiction of the court being neither limited nor
    restricted.

5. HUSBAND AND WIFE—SUPPORT AND MAINTENANCE—RESIDENCE.
    The requirement as to residence in section 7 of Stats. 1913,
    c. 97, giving wife right of action against husband for support
    and maintenance without applying for a divorce, relates to the
    venue of the action and not to jurisdiction of the parties, and
    such residence need be such only that an ordinary action
    could be maintained by her according to the statute regulating
    the venue of civil action, so enlarged as to permit her to sue
    in the county where the husband may be found.

6. CERTIORARI—GROUNDS—ERRORS.
    A claim that a court erred in determining that a wife's
    cause of action for support and maintenance was brought
    within Stats. 1913, c. 97, was not a claim that the court
    exceeded its jurisdiction, so as to be reviewable on certiorari.

7. CERTIORARI—WHEN ISSUES—NECESSARY PARTIES.

    In the exercise of its discretion the supreme court may issue, under Rev. Laws, 5685, a writ of certiorari to review an action of a district court without notice to the adverse party, but the supreme court should not be asked, in such a proceeding, to annul a judgment granting support and maintenance to a wife, where the adverse party is not made a party to the application for the writ.

8. CERTIORARI—ACTION OF COURT—DUTY TO AID APPELLATE COURT.

    On certiorari to review the action of the district court, the latter should not place itself in the position of adverse party, as if it had some personal interest in sustaining its judgment, or throw obstacles in the way to prevent a review of its proceedings, as by failing to give notice to adverse party of proceedings.

APPLICATION by Albert B. Hilton for certiorari to review an action of the Second Judicial District Court of the State of Nevada, in and for the County of Washoe, and Thomas F. Moran, Judge thereof. **Writ dismissed. Rehearing denied.** COLEMAN, C. J., dissenting.

Platt & Sanford, for Petitioner:

An amended pleading supersedes the original and renders it functus officio. McFadden v. Ellsworth, 8 Nev. 57; Reihl v. Likowski, 33 Kan. 515. "Where pleadings are amended, they take the place of the original, and all subsequent proceedings in the case are based upon the amended pleadings." Armstrong v. Henderson, 102 Pac. 361; Evinger v. Moran, 14 Cal. App. 328; Barber v. Reynolds, 33 Cal. 497; Lane v. Choctaw O. & G. R. Co., 19 Okl. 324; People v. Hunt, 12 Or. 208; Raymond v. Thexton, 7 Mont. 299; Bray v. Lawrey, 163 Cal. 256; Dibble v. Reliance L. I. Co., 149 Pac. 171.

A defendant claiming affirmative relief must plead as fully as if he were plaintiff. Rose v. Treadway, 4 Nev. 455; Gulling v. Bank, 28 Nev. 486. "The cross-demand must be pleaded as fully and distinctly, and with the same substantial requisites as an original cause of action; it must be sufficient in itself without recourse to other parts of the pleading, unless by express reference." 31 Cyc. 227; White v. Regan, 32 Ark. 381; Coulthurst v. Coulthurst, 58 Cal. 239. The cross-complaint contains no

allegation of marriage, residence, or of a cause of action
for desertion upon which the judgment and decree was
based. A cross-complaint in a divorce action which fails
to allege jurisdictional facts confers no jurisdiction upon
a court to render judgment upon it.

There is no defect of parties, and the defendant in
the action below is not a necessary party to this proceeding. Inquiry may be made into the jurisdiction
of the inferior tribunal. State v. Breen, 41 Nev. 516;
McKibbin v. District Court, 41 Nev. 431; Conway v.
District Court, 40 Nev. 395; Yowell v. District Court,
39 Nev. 423; McLeod v. District Court, 39 Nev. 337;
National M. Co. v. District Court, 34 Nev. 67; Jumbo M.
Co. v. District Court, 28 Nev. 253; Fitchett v. Henley,
31 Nev. 326.

Likewise, this court has many times taken jurisdiction
over mandamus proceedings in the absence of any reference by title or otherwise to the original party defendant in the court below. Jensen v. District Court, 41
Nev. 135; State v. District Court, 40 Nev. 163; Worthington v. District Court, 37 Nev. 212; Floyd v. District
Court, 36 Nev. 349; McKim v. District Court, 33 Nev.
44; Silver Peak v. District Court, 33 Nev. 97; Bell v.
District Court, 28 Nev. 280.

Except through the discretion of the court or judge
issuing the writ, the statute does not contemplate making a defendant in the court below a necessary party to
the writ. Rev. Laws, 5685. The writ may be directed
to the inferior tribunal, board or officer, or to any other
person having the custody of the record. Rev. Laws,
5686. The only inquiry upon a writ of certiorari is as to
whether the inferior tribunal had jurisdiction to make
the order in question. Rev. Laws, 5687; Kapp v. District Court, 31 Nev. 444; Baker v. Superior Court, 71
Cal. 583.

Extraordinary writs will issue in cases in which there
is no plain, speedy or adequate remedy by appeal. State
v. District Court, 38 Nev. 323.

Norcross, Thatcher & Woodburn, for Respondent:

There is a defect of parties. The defendant in the court below should be made a party, as she has a substantial interest in the proceedings. State v. Commissioners, 23 Nev. 247.

The petition does not state facts sufficient to authorize the issuance of the writ. The petitioner invoked the jurisdiction of the respondent court. The defendant appeared and answered and the cause was tried. The court had jurisdiction of the subject-matter of the action and to hear and determine the controversy, and having had such jurisdiction, it is immaterial for the purpose of this proceeding whether its decision was correct or erroneous. Const. Nev. sec. 6, art. 6; Stats. 1915, pp. 26, 120; Phillips v. Welch, 12 Nev. 158; In Re Wixom, 12 Nev. 219; State v. District Court, 16 Nev. 76; Wilson v. Morse, 25 Nev. 375.

The writ of certiorari cannot be invoked to serve the purpose of an appeal or writ of error. Phillips v. Welch, supra; Fall v. Commissioners, 6 Nev. 100; Rev. Laws, 5684. Certiorari does not lie where there is an appeal. Leonard v. Peacock, 8 Nev. 157; Nevada Central R. R. Co. v. District Court, 21 Nev. 409.

Allegation of residence on behalf of a cross-complainant is unnecessary. Newman v. Newman, 112 Pac. 1007; Sterl v. Sterl, 2 Ill. App. 223; Charlton v. Charlton, 141 S. W. 290; Clutton v. Clutton, 31 L. R. A. 160; Pine v. Pine, 100 N. W. 938; Von Bernuth v. Von Bernuth, 74 Atl. 700; 9 R. C. L. sec. 201. Allegations of the answer may be taken in aid of the complaint. The same rule applies in case of a cross-complaint, the allegations of the complaint aiding the cross-complaint. Cavender v. Cavender, 114 U. S. 164; Richardson v. Green, 61 Fed. 423; McManus v. Ophir M. Co., 4 Nev. 15; Waples v. Hays, 118 U. S. 6; Hagan v. Walker, 14 How. 29; Meadow Valley Co. v. Dodds, 6 Nev. 251; Riverside Fixture Co. v. Quigley, 35 Nev. 17; Hawthorne v. Smith, 3 Nev. 182.

The allegation of desertion in the cross-complaint is plain and unequivocal; and even if it be by way of recital, objection should have been taken by demurrer; and if not so taken, it is waived. Winter v. Winter, 8 Nev. 129.

After issue has been joined and a decision rendered upon the merits, it is the duty of the appellate court to support the pleadings by every legal intendment, if there is nothing material in the record to prevent it. Meadow Valley Co. v. Dodd, supra; Skyrme v. Occidental M. M. Co., 8 Nev. 228. Pleadings shall be liberally construed, with a view to substantial justice between the parties. Rev. Laws, 5065, 5066.

Objection to the jurisdiction, when dependent not upon the power of the court under the constitution and laws or the jurisdiction over the parties, but upon the so-called insufficiency of the cross-complaint, must be timely. The petitioner by his conduct is now estopped from raising the question. Grant v. Grant, 38 Nev. 185; Phillips v. Snowden, 40 Nev. 66.

By the Court, SANDERS, J.:

Upon the application of Albert B. Hilton, in the form of a verified petition, this court, without requiring notice of the application to be given the adverse party or an order to show cause, issued a writ of certiorari.

The facts in brief are as follows:

Albert B. Hilton commenced an action for an absolute divorce against his wife, Katherine C. Hilton, in the above-named respondent court, upon the grounds of cruelty and desertion. The defendant wife, after denying all the allegations of the complaint, except the averment of the residence of the plaintiff and the marriage relation of the parties, proceeded as follows: "For a further answer and defense and for a cross-complaint defendant alleges," and then proceeds to charge the plaintiff with specific acts of cruelty, in violation of his marital obligation, and that for a period of more than twelve months prior to the filing of her cross-complaint the plaintiff wilfully and without cause and against the will of the defendant deserted the defendant, and that such desertion has ever since so wilfully continued and is now continuing. It then goes on to state the plaintiff's ability, his spendthrift habits, and alleges that if the plaintiff is not compelled to make a reasonable settlement upon defendant she will be left without adequate means of support, and particularly means of support in the way in which the defendant has been accustomed, and concludes with the prayer that plaintiff take nothing by reason of his action for divorce; that the defendant have a judgment and decree against plaintiff for her permanent support and maintenance, and other relief. Upon the trial of these issues before the court, and without objection to the pleadings on the part of either of the parties to their legal sufficiency, the court rendered its decree in favor of the defendant wife and against the plaintiff husband, and adjudged and ordered that he pay to the defendant, until the further order of the court, as and for her permanent support and maintenance, the sum of $600 per month. No appeal was taken from this judgment and decree.

1. The petitioner asks by this proceeding that the decree rendered against him be annulled, upon the ground that the court was without jurisdiction of the subject-matter and of the parties, in that the cross-complaint contains no averment of marriage or residence, or that the defendant was a resident within the county in which her cross-action was filed. Counsel for respondent, who are in fact attorneys for defendant, insist that as the defendant was brought within the jurisdiction of the court by the plaintiff's action for divorce, and having gone to trial upon the issues joined without objection to the pleading, he is in no position to complain or to say that the court was without jurisdiction of the subject-matter and of the parties. Ordinarily this is true, but if the averment of marriage and residence are necessary and indispensable facts to be stated in a complaint for support and maintenance, they are

equally so in a cross-complaint in a divorce action. The rule is elementary that a defendant claiming affirmative relief must plead as fully as if he were plaintiff. Dixon v. Pruett, 42 Nev. 345, 177 Pac. 11; Rose v. Treadway, 4 Nev. 455, 97 Am. Dec. 546.

2. Whatever be the rule, in the absence of a statute, district courts are, by statute in this state, given jurisdiction over the subject-matter and of the parties to an action brought by the wife against her husband for support and maintenance without her applying for a divorce. Stats. 1913, p. 120.

3. There is no doubt that to entitle the plaintiff to recover in such action it is incumbent upon her to make a showing of the marriage relation, her needs, and the ability of her husband, as in a suit for divorce. Nelson on Divorce, sec. 1003.

The cross-complaint shows satisfactorily these facts without reference to the other pleadings in the case. Furthermore, it is obvious from the record that the objection to the pleading on this ground is more technical than real or meritorious, but the point—that the cross-complaint contains no averment of the residence of the parties within the jurisdiction of the court— is one of first impression and is worthy of further discussion.

Coulthurst v. Coulthurst, 58 Cal. 239, is cited by counsel for petitioner in support of the proposition that in this state the cross-complainant in a divorce suit must plead residence. The case is not in point. The defendant's case is not a cross-action for divorce, as in the case cited, but is a cross-action for support and maintenance without divorce.

In the case of Hardy v. Hardy, 97 Cal. 125, 31 Pac. 906, it is held that the right of the wife to maintain an action for support and maintenance is independent of the right to maintain an action for divorce, and, being based upon the obligation of the husband to support the wife, may be instituted at any time after his desertion of her when he fails to give such support. This is true of our statute.

Section 1 of the act provides:

"When the wife has any cause of action for divorce against her husband, or when she has been deserted by him and such desertion has continued for the space of ninety days, she may, without applying for a divorce, maintain in the district court, an action against her husband for permanent support and maintenance of herself or of herself and of her child or children."

4. The object of the statute is to give to the wife a sure and speedy remedy through an independent action when she has any cause of action for divorce against her husband, or when he has deserted her for a period of ninety days. The jurisdiction of the court is neither limited nor restricted. The statute is remedial, and must be liberally construed with a view to promote its object. It affords a remedy not heretofore given a wife to enforce the performance of a duty without resorting to a divorce action.

Section 7 of the act provides:

"In all cases commenced hereunder, the proceedings and practice shall be the same, as nearly as may be, as is now or hereafter may be provided in actions for divorce; and suit may be brought, at the option of the wife, either in the county in which the wife shall reside, at the time the suit is commneced, or in the county in which the husband may be found."

5. If we clearly interpret the position taken by counsel for the petitioner, it is their contention that before the wife may exercise the option granted her by the statute she must allege in her complaint that she was a resident within the county in which her action was commenced. We are of the opinion that the requirement as to residence relates to the venue of the action, and not to jurisdiction of the parties. The section provides that she can bring her suit either in the county in which she shall reside or in the county in which the husband may be

found. If the word "residence," as here used, be intended as a prerequisite condition to her right to maintain her action, we apprehend that the legislature would have manifested its intent in more direct terms. It cannot be successfully urged, though it is strongly intimated by counsel for petitioner, that "residence," as employed in the section, must be extended to mean the period of residence as is required in divorce actions. If this be true, a derelict husband could defeat the object of the statute by placing himself and his property beyond the jurisdiction of the court before the statutory period of residence of six months had run. The statute places no such limitation upon the wife's right to maintain her suit. The statute was designed to incorporate such action into the system of remedies in use in this state. Her residence need be such only that an ordinary action could be maintained by her according to the statute regulating the venue of civil actions, so enlarged as to permit her to sue in the county where the husband may be found. The record shows affirmatively that the plaintiff husband was found within the jurisdiction of the court when her cross-action was filed, and that he was an actual bona-fide resident in the county where found. This being true, the court acquired jurisdiction of the parties, and having jurisdiction of the subject-matter of the action, the judgment sought to be annulled by this proceeding will not be disturbed.

Whether or not a nonresident wife may maintain an action against a nonresident husband for support and maintenance under the statute, is a question concerning which we do not express an opinion.

6. It is further insisted by counsel for petitioner that the court erred in determining that the defendant's cause of action for support and maintenance was brought within the statute. Stats. 1913, p. 120. If this be error, it was not an excess of jurisdiction, and may be corrected by the usual mode for the correction of errors. Wilson v. Morse, 25 Nev. 376, 60 Pac. 832.

7. We do not commend the practice adopted in this case by either of the parties. The writ issued is irregular in form; it is directed to both the court and the judge thereof; the latter is commanded by the writ to show cause why the relief prayed for by the petitioner should not be granted. The relief demanded is that the judgment be annulled. The parties to the judgment are the only persons interested in the question of its validity. We concede that in this case the writ should not have issued without notice to the adverse party, for the reason, not as contended by counsel for respondent that she is a necessary party, but because should this court annul the judgment rendered by the respondent it would not bind the defendant unless she had her day in court on the hearing of the certiorari. Wilson v. Morse, supra; Pollock v. Cummings, 38 Cal. 685; Fraser v. Freelon, 58 Cal. 645. But the failure of the petitioner to make the defendant in the action a party to the application for the writ, or the failure of this court to give to her notice of the application, furnishes no ground under our statute for quashing the writ. The respondent tribunal is the real party respondent to a writ of certiorari (Rev. Laws, 5686), although other parties might appear to maintain or object to the proceedings and be subject to costs (Bailey on Juris., sec. 434a). This, however, is a matter entirely within the discretion of the court. In the exercise of our discretion we are empowered to issue the writ even without notice to the adverse party. Rev. Laws, 5685.

8. The procedure adopted by counsel for respondent places the respondent court in the position of an adverse party as if it had some personal interest in sustaining its judgment. It is commendable in respondent tribunals to at all times protect their jurisdiction, but in so doing they are not authorized to challenge the jurisdiction of their superior, or throw obstacles in the way to prevent a review of their proceedings. The respondent is truly interested in seeing that it may not be shorn

of its power, if not by collusion, yet by the failure to have the question of its jurisdiction presented as forcibly as it might be presented. Sharp v. Miller, 54 Cal. 329 (concurring opinion). We welcome this practice, but do not sanction its being used to defeat the purpose of the writ. Entertaining the views as hereinabove expressed, we conclude that the writ should be dismissed.

It is so ordered.

COLEMAN, C. J., dissenting:

I dissent from the conclusion reached by my learned associates as to the sufficiency of the cross-complaint. The only allusion in the cross-complaint to a marriage between plaintiff and defendant is found in a paragraph which reads:

"That since the marriage of plaintiff and defendant, plaintiff has treated defendant with extreme cruelty, and defendant cites the following specific instances of such cruelty.   *   *   * "

Whatever may be the practice in other states, section 110 of our civil practice act (Rev. Laws, 5052) provides for the filing of a cross-complaint. The facts must be stated in the cross-complaint as fully as in the complaint. The general rule as to the requirements of a cross-complaint is stated in 5 Ency. Pl. & Pr. at page 680, as follows:

"A cross-complaint, like an original complaint, must state facts sufficient to entitle the pleader to affirmative relief, and it cannot be helped out by the averments of any of the other pleadings in the action; it must itself contain all the required facts" (citing numerous authorities).

In Collins v. Bartlett, 44 Cal. 371, it is said:

"In considering the cross-complaint, we have accepted as true all its allegations, but the agreed statement of facts and the finding have not been considered in connection with the cross-complaint, for they cannot be regarded as adding thereto any further fact. The cross-complaint must fall unless it is sustainable on its own allegations of fact."

In Conger v. Miller, 104 Ind. 592, 4 N. E. 300, it is said:

"A cross-complaint, like a complaint, must be good within and of itself, without aid from other pleadings in the cause" (citing Campbell v. Routt, 42 Ind. 410; Masters v. Beckett, 83 Ind. 595; Ewing v. Patterson, 35 Ind. 326).

In Coulthurst v. Coulthurst, 58 Cal. 239, which was an action for a divorce, wherein the defendant filed a cross-complaint praying for divorce, in which there was no allegation of marriage or residence, the court said:

"It is claimed on this appeal that the defendant's cross-complaint was totally defective, for the reason that it contained no averment of marriage, or residence for the period of six months within the state. It is well settled that both of these facts are necessary and indispensable in a complaint for a divorce, and the only question is: Are they equally essential in a cross-complaint? [The court here quotes as above from Collins v. Bartlett, 44 Cal. 371.] * * * And in the case of Kreichbaum v. Melton, 49 Cal. 55, the court holds that: 'A cross-complaint must state facts sufficient to entitle the pleader to affirmative relief; and it cannot be helped out by the averments of any of the other pleadings in the action. Like a complaint, it must itself contain all the requisite facts.' See, also, Haskell v. Haskell, 54 Cal. 262.

"Applying the principles laid down in the above cases to the defendant's cross-complaint, it is very obvious that it was materially defective as a pleading, and did not entitle defendant to the relief granted by the court."

I am unable to find any case laying down a different rule, where the civil practice act of the state provides for a cross-complaint, as does ours. It matters not what the reason for such a rule may be, so long as it exists, and of its existence there can be no doubt. In the prevailing opinion, Nelson on Divorce is cited as sustaining the doctrine that the marriage relation must be shown in an action growing out of the relationship. If it must be shown, it must also be pleaded. The allegation quoted from the cross-complaint is a statement based upon a mere assumption of marriage. It does not suffice.

I express no opinion as to other questions discussed.

ON PETITION FOR REHEARING

Per Curiam:

Rehearing denied.

[No. 2319]

STATE OF NEVADA, Ex Rel. ANTHONY JURICH, PETITIONER, *v.* C. J. McFADDEN, JUDGE OF THE NINTH JUDICIAL DISTRICT COURT OF THE STATE OF NEVADA, IN AND FOR WHITE PINE COUNTY, RESPONDENT.

[182 Pac. 745]

1. MOTIONS—TRIAL—RESETTING OF CASE—NOTICE.

If considered as a motion, within the meaning of civil practice act, sec. 5362, and rule 10 (Rev. Laws, 4942) of the district courts, an application to reset a case for trial on an earlier date than that fixed should be denied, where the five days' notice required in case of motions was not given, and the action of the court in granting the motion, of which no notice at all was given, although defendant was present in court at the time the application was made, cannot be sustained on the ground that the courts have inherent power to regulate their own docket and control their own business.

2. TRIAL — SETTING OF CASE FOR TRIAL — RESETTING — WAIVER OF ERRORS.

Where defendant was present in court at the time plaintiff's counsel applied to reset the case for trial on an earlier date than that originally fixed, and defendant resisted the application solely on the ground that the court was without authority to order the case, which was on the jury calendar, to be tried before a special venire, and that he was entitled to trial before the regular panel, there was a waiver of the failure of the applicant to give the five days' notice required in case of motions.

3. CERTIORARI—REVIEW—HARMLESS ERROR—JURY.

Where trial court directed a verdict, that defendant was erroneously compelled to go to trial before a special venire was harmless.

4. JURY—JURY TRIAL—SPECIAL VENIRE.
   Under Rev. Laws, 4940, declaring that it shall be in the
   discretion of the court, with the consent of all parties litigant,
   either to draw the names of the jurors from the box, as provided in the act, or to issue an open venire directed to the
   sheriff, etc., the court is without authority to order a special
   venire, which is unknown to the statute law, to try a case
   over the exceptions of one of the parties.

5. CERTIORARI—TRIAL—PROVINCE OF COURT—DIRECTION OF VERDICT.
   The trial judge, in the exercise of sound discretion, may in
   a proper case direct a verdict, and, though the direction of
   verdict be improper, it is not within the jurisdiction of the
   court so as to be reviewable on certiorari: and this is so,
   though there was no mode of review in particular case.

ORIGINAL PROCEEDING in certiorari by the State of
Nevada, on the relation of Anthony Jurich, against C. J.
McFadden, Judge of the Ninth Judicial District Court
of the State of Nevada, in and for White Pine County.
On motion to quash writ. **Motion sustained, and pro-
ceeding dismissed. Rehearing denied.**

A. Jurich and *H. W. Edwards,* for Petitioner:

The judgment of the lower court is in excess of jurisdiction and a proper subject for the writ of certiorari.
Radovich v. W. U. T. Co., 36 Nev. 343; Floyd v. District
Court, 36 Nev. 349; State v. District Court, 147 Pac.
612; Miller v. Superior Court, 144 Pac. 978.

The case having been regularly set, the court had no
power to act further in the matter, unless properly
brought before it. A motion, which must be in proper
form and supported by affidavit or other proof, is necessary. Rev. Laws, 5362; Rule 10, Dist. Court. Failure
to comply with the rule makes it the duty of the court
to deny a motion. Symons-Kraussman v. Liquor Co., 32
Nev. 242; Lightle v. Ivancovich, 10 Nev. 41; Haley v.
Bank, 20 Nev. 410.

The mode of selection and formation of a regular jury
is prescribed by statute. A special jury may be had
only with the consent of all parties to the action. Rev.
Laws, 4940. Where consent is not given, the regular
jury should try the case. 24 Cyc. 258. In the selection
of a special jury the law must be strictly complied with.
Railroad v. Shane, 157 U. S. 348.

Respondent directed the jury to bring in a verdict against relator, which was equivalent to a denial of a jury trial, and the deciding of a question of fact by the court. Rev. Laws, 5199; Const. Nev. art. 7; Treadway v. Wilder, 12 Nev. 108.

Chandler & Quayle, for Respondent:

The inquiry is restricted to the question of jurisdiction. Rev. Laws, 5684, 5690; Maynard v. Bailey, 2 Nev. 313; In Re Wixom, 12 Nev. 219. The district courts have final appellate jurisdiction in cases arising in justice courts. Const. Nev. sec. 6, art. 6. On certiorari the inquiry is limited to determining whether the inferior tribunal has exceeded its jurisdiction. Paul v. Armstrong, 1 Nev. 82; Maynard v. Bailey, 2 Nev. 313; State v. Washoe County, 5 Nev. 317; Maxwell v. Rives, 11 Nev. 213; Phillips v. Welch, 12 Nev. 158; State v. District Court, 16 Nev. 76; Chapman v. Justice Court, 29 Nev. 154; Fitchett v. Henley, 31 Nev. 326; State v. Breen, 173 Pac. 555. "An erroneous judgment rendered by a court having jurisdiction to render it cannot, merely because it is erroneous, operate as the basis for a writ of review." Cam v. District Court, 170 Pac. 409.

The trial court has inherent power to take such steps and make such orders as may be necessary to the dispatch of its business, and the disposition of causes pending on its docket, and to that end may, of its own motion, set or reset a case for trial. Cochrane v. Parker, 12 Colo. App. 170; Union Brewing Co. v. Cooper, 60 Pac. 946. The fixing of a time for trial is necessarily within the discretion of the court. McLeod v. District Court, 157 Pac. 649; Ranson v. Leggett, 90 S. W. 668; Bonney v. McClelland, 85 N. E. 242; Linderman v. Nolan, 83 Pac. 796. The court has inherent right to control its own calendar. Smith v. Keepers, 66 How. Pr. 474.

If notice of motion to reset the case was necessary, petitioner waived such notice by his presence in court. 19 R. C. L. 674; McLeran v. Shartzer, 5 Cal. 70; Reynolds v. Harris, 14 Cal. 668; Curtis v. Walling, 18 Pac.

54; Acock v. Halsey, 27 Pac. 193; Herman v. Santer, 37 Pac. 509; Woodward v. Brown, 51 Pac. 2; Lellman v. Mills, 87 Pac. 985; Bohn v. Bohn, 129 Pac. 981.

If the court exceeded its jurisdiction in ordering the open venire, and if relator had any real objection to trying the case before such a jury, he could have prevented the trial by securing a writ of prohibition. Rev. Laws, 5708, 5710. A party is not entitled to the writ if he fails to exercise diligence in protecting his interests. 11 C. J. 111; Kootenai County v. Board, 169 Pac. 935; Palmer v. Railroad Commission, 138 Pac. 997.

The court had jurisdiction of the parties and of the subject-matter, and had the power to hear and determine a motion for a directed verdict. 38 Cyc. 1563; Oscanyan v. Winchester, 103 U. S. 261. The power in no way infringes the constitutional right of trial by jury. 24 Cyc. 193.

By the Court, SANDERS, J.:

This is an original proceeding in certiorari, growing out of the following facts:

Bill Margeas brought an action in the justice's court of Ely Township No. 1, White Pine County, Nevada, against Anthony Jurich, to recover the sum of $100. Anthony Jurich, who is an attorney at law, answered in proper person, and, in addition to resisting the demand of the complaint, set up a counter-claim for $55. The justice of the peace rendered judgment for costs in favor of Jurich, but denied recovery on his alleged counter-claim. Margeas appealed to the district court, where Jurich demanded a jury trial. On September 8, 1917, the cause was set for trial on October 16, 1917, at which time a regular jury panel was to be in attendance. On September 18, 1917, Jurich and one of the firm of attorneys for Margeas being present in court in connection with other matters, the following proceedings were had in connection with the case of Margeas v. Jurich:

"Mr. Quayle (attorney for Margeas)—I wish to ask with reference to the case of Bill Margeas against

Anthony Jurich—I wish to ask if it is possible, in view of
Mr. Margeas having qualified and being subject to call
at any time to the draft, if we cannot in that case agree
upon a special venire so that that can be tried. Mr.
Jurich has demanded a jury trial and it is very doubtful
if Mr. Margeas will be here in October, when the regular
venire will be in attendance, and if that case can be tried
early next week we will be able to have a conclusion
before Mr. Margeas goes away to war.

"Mr. Jurich—The case has been set regularly before
the regular jury, and I insist on it being tried in the
regular way.

"The Court—Well, he has been drafted and he is going
to answer the call of his country, and he has a right to
have this civil business disposed of. I will set it for
next Wednesday morning for a special venire at 10
o'clock, September 24.

"Mr. Jurich—Let the record show that I object to the
court resetting the case, and having demanded a jury
trial and the case having been set in the regular way
that I want to try the case before the regular jury; and
at this time I do not consent, but object, to the special
venire.

"The Court—The objection will be overruled and the
venire will be issued.

"Mr. Jurich—Take an exception."

The case was tried before the district court with a
jury on September 24, 1917, and at the conclusion of
the testimony counsel for Margeas moved the court to
direct the jury to find a verdict in favor of the plaintiff
for $95. Upon the conclusion of the argument the court
granted the motion, and the defendant excepted. The
jury were then recalled into the jury box, whereupon
the court stated:

"Gentlemen of the jury, during the recess of the
court a motion was made by the plaintiff for a directed
verdict, and the court has the power and control over
the verdicts in civil cases. That motion is granted, and
you are instructed to bring in the following verdict:

'We, the jury duly sworn and impaneled to try the issues in this case, find for the plaintiff in the sum of $95. Dated September 24, 1917.' Have your foreman sign that and return it into court."

Mr. Jurich excepted to the instruction and the verdict, on the ground and for the reason that under the law and the evidence in the case the court had no such power.

"The Court—You may raise that by motion to set aside the verdict.

"Mr. Jurich—Well, at this time I ask the court for my right under the constitution to argue this case to the jury.

"The Court—It will be denied.

"Mr. Jurich—Take an exception to that. Then I ask the court at this time to give the case to the jury to decide.

"The Court—I have overruled that already, so that it will be the same ruling.

"Mr. Jurich—Take an exception."

Thereupon the officers were sworn and took charge of the jury, who retired to deliberate on their verdict. Thereafter the jury returned into court.

"The Court—Gentlemen, have you the verdict that I handed you signed by your foreman?

"Foreman—Your honor, the jury wishes to know if it is compulsory on their part to render their verdict, or can they make another verdict?

"The Court—No, you have to render the verdict the court instructs you under instructions; you have to follow the instructions.

"Mr. Jurich—I take an exception to the court instructing the jury.

"The Court—The exception may be noted. You may retire again and return signed that verdict that I have directed."

Thereupon the jury again retired to deliberate, thereafter returning into court.

"The Court—Have you a verdict, gentlemen of the jury?

"Foreman—Yes, sir.

"The Court—The clerk may read the verdict."

The verdict as read was in the words and figures as that directed by the court. Thereupon, at the request of defendant, the clerk polled the jury on said verdict, eleven jurors answering that the foregoing was their verdict, and one juror answering no, that it was not his verdict.

"Mr. Jurich—I would like thirty days' stay.

"The Court—I will give you thirty days. Gentlemen, you will be excused from any further deliberation of the case."

Judgment was entered on the verdict rendered. Subsequently, defendant, having no remedy by appeal, filed in this court his petition for a writ of certiorari, claiming that the respondent exceeded his jurisdiction and refused to regularly pursue his authority. The writ was issued, and in response thereto the record is now before this court for review.

Respondent, in addition to his answer and return, has moved to quash and dismiss the writ, on the ground that the petition does not state facts sufficient to warrant its issuance. By stipulation both the motion to quash and the hearing on the merits are to be considered together and the case submitted on briefs.

The relator contends that the district court exceeded its jurisdiction in three particulars: (1) In resetting the case for trial; (2) in ordering a special venire; (3) in directing a verdict for plaintiff. These will be discussed in their order.

1, 2. (1) If the application to reset the case for trial on an earlier date than as originally fixed by the court, out of favor to the plaintiff, is to be regarded or considered as a motion, within the meaning of the civil practice act relative to motions, and rule 10 of district courts (sections 5362 and 4942 of the Revised Laws), confessedly the application was not in accordance with the statute or the said rule as to the requirement that

such motion must be noticed at least five days before
the date specified for a hearing. Attempt is made to
maintain the action of the court upon the ground that
courts have inherent power to regulate their own docket
and control their own business. This position is not
tenable in face of the explicit and unconditional direction of the statute and said rule of court. But, as
the record shows that the defendant was present and
resisted the application, on the ground only that the
court was without authority to order the case to be tried
before a special venire and his right to a trial before
the regular panel, this constituted a waiver of the formal
defects of the application. Granger v. Sherriff, 133 Cal.
419, 65 Pac. 873; Garrett v. Wood, 24 App. Div. 620, 48
N. Y. Supp. 1002. That such defects could be waived
is amply supported by authority. · 19 R. C. L. 674.

3, 4. (2) Conceding that the district court, out of
favor to the plaintiff, arbitrarily reset the case for an
earlier date before a "special venire," without the consent of the defendant and over his objection, we cannot
see the relevancy of the defendant's exception to the act
of the court; for, since the court directed a verdict for
the plaintiff, it was not the voluntary act of the jury, and
the irregularity complained of seems wholly immaterial.
The jury was bound to comply with the direction of the
court, apart from their personal views on the questions
before them. Cook v. White, 43 App. Div. 388, 60 N. Y.
Supp. 153. The relator could in no sense be said to be
prejudiced or injured by the trial of his case before a
"special venire" that did not and could not act on his
case.

For the benefit of future cases we deem it essential to
announce that there is no such thing in this state as a
"special venire," and that the statute (Rev. Laws, 4940),
which in explicit and unconditional terms provides:

" * * * And it shall at all times be in the discretion
of the court, with the consent of all parties litigant to
the action or actions to be tried thereby, either to draw

the names of the jurors from the box, as in this act provided, or to issue an open venire directed to the sheriff, requiring him to summon * * * "
—is mandatory.

The court had neither jurisdiction, power, nor authority to order an open venire to try the case without the consent of the defendant, notwithstanding the exigency of the plaintiff's situation. To hold otherwise would defeat the purpose of the statute and operate to deprive a litigant of the benefit of a trial of his cause before a regular panel of jurors. This may not be done without his consent.

5. (3) It is conceded, or must be conceded, that by the weight of authority the trial judge, in the exercise of sound discretion, may in a proper case direct the verdict. 38 Cyc. 1563. The principle is also well settled that certiorari will not lie to review the exercise of discretion on the part of courts or officers. 2 Bailey on Jur., sec. 436a. And in this jurisdiction, where the writ only issues to review jurisdictional defects in proceedings by organized courts or other tribunals acting judicially, the question of discretion or its abuse does not arise. In Re Wixom, 12 Nev. 219. The court in this instance, in directing the verdict it did, may have abused its discretion, its action may have afforded good grounds for a new trial, but there is nothing in the return to the writ to show that the trial court departed from any express provision of law or some prescribed rule of procedure, or that it exceeded its jurisdiction in directing the verdict.

But the argument is earnestly advanced that as the case is nonappealable this court will review the evidence to determine whether the directed verdict should be sustained. The fact that the case is nonappealable is convincingly answered by Chief Justice Hawley in the case of Phillips v. Welch, 12 Nev. 175. This case also holds that the hardship of the case, even if conceded to exist, cannot be considered, and quotes in this connection from the Supreme Court of the United States (Ex Parte Kearney, 7 Wheat. 45, 5 L. Ed. 391) :

"Where the law is clear, this argument can be of no avail. * * * Wherever power is lodged, it may be abused. But this forms no solid objection against its exercise. Confidence must be reposed somewhere; and if there should be an abuse, it will be a public grievance, for which a remedy may be applied by the legislature, and is not to be devised by courts of justice."

The cases of Radovich v. W. U. Tel. Co., 36 Nev. 344, 135 Pac. 920, 136 Pac. 704, Floyd v. District Court, 36 Nev. 349, 135 Pac. 922, Wong Kee v. Lillis, 37 Nev. 5, 138 Pac. 900, are cited by the relator in support of the proposition that this court, on certiorari in a nonappealable case, will examine and weigh the evidence to determine whether a ruling on an essential question of law that goes to the right of the defendant to maintain his defense is sustainable from the evidence. While certain sweeping expressions are found in the reasoning of those cases that open the door to such argument, we do not think any one of the cases goes to the extent as contended for by the relator. The irregularities discussed and ruled upon in those cases showed an obvious departure from some prescribed rule of procedure, and consisted of the omission on the part of the trial judge to do something that was necessary for the orderly conduct of the case, or doing it at an unreasonable time and in an improper manner. But here we are asked to review and weigh evidence, not to determine whether the court departed from some express rule 'of procedure or exceeded its jurisdiction, but to say that the court committed palpable error and a moral wrong in arbitrarily directing a verdict against the relator. This cannot be done in a proceeding of this character.

It is earnestly insisted that as the issue was one purely of fact the effect of the directed verdict deprived the relator of his statutory and fundamental right to have that issue tried before a jury. The authorities do not sustain this proposition. 38 Cyc. 1563; 24 Cyc. note 40, 193; Hawke v. Hawke, 82 Hun, 439, 31 N. Y. Supp. 968.

The motion to quash the writ must be sustained, and the proceeding dismissed.

It is so ordered.

ON PETITION FOR REHEARING

Per Curiam:

Rehearing denied.

[No. 2372]

THE STATE OF NEVADA, EX REL. LESTER D. SUMMERFIELD, AS DISTRICT ATTORNEY OF WASHOE COUNTY, NEVADA, PETITIONER, *v.* THOMAS F. MORAN, AS ONE OF THE JUDGES OF THE SECOND JUDICIAL DISTRICT COURT OF THE STATE OF NEVADA, IN AND FOR THE COUNTY OF WASHOE, RESPONDENT.

[182 Pac. 927]

1. CRIMINAL LAW—SUSPENSION OF SENTENCE—CONSTITUTIONALITY OF STATUTE.

Rev. Laws, 7259, authorizing the court to suspend sentence except in specified cases, is unconstitutional; there being no constitutional authority therefor, and method of suspending sentence provided for by Const. art. 5, secs. 13, 14, being exclusive.

2. CRIMINAL LAW—LIMITATION ON POWER—SUSPENSION OF SENTENCE.

Where the constitution enumerates certain cases in which the collection of a fine may be suspended, or certain methods whereby it may be done, or confers such power upon certain official or officials, the power so conferred is exclusive.

ORIGINAL PROCEEDING in mandamus by the State of Nevada, on the relation of Lester D. Summerfield, as District Attorney of Washoe County, Nevada, against Thomas F. Moran, as one of the Judges of the Second Judicial District Court of the State of Nevada, in and for the County of Washoe. **Writ issued.**

Lester D. Summerfield, District Attorney (in pro. per.), and *W. M. Kearney,* Deputy District Attorney, for· Petitioner:

The court was without authority to suspend sentence. The court acted under and by virtue of section 7259 of Revised Laws of 1912. Said statute is unconstitutional and void, as under it the court exercises the pardoning power, which is by the state constitution vested in the board of pardons. Const. Nev. art. 3, sec. 1, art. 5, sec. 14. The pardoning power being vested in the board of pardons, the courts are excluded from exercising, directly or indirectly, the same power. People v. Brown, 19 N. W. 571; Neal v. State, 30 S. E. 858; U. S. v. Wilson, 46 Fed. 748; People v. Barrett, 63 L. R. A. 82; In Re Flint, 71 Pac. 531; In Re Webb, 62 N. W. 177.

The pardoning power being vested in the board of pardons, it cannot under the constitution be exercised by any other branch of the government, except "in the cases herein expressly directed or permitted." There has been no such express direction or permission. Ex Parte Shelor, 33 Nev. 361.

W. M. Kennedy, E. W. Cheney, and *LeRoy F. Pike,* Amici Curiæ, for Respondent:

The Constitution of Nevada (art. 5, sec. 14) provides that the governor and certain other officials may remit fines and forfeitures, commute punishments, and grant pardons "after conviction." The word "conviction," as used in this section, means not only the verdict or plea of guilty, but the judgment of the court imposing sentence. Smith v. Commonwealth, 14 Serg. & R. 69; Commonwealth v. Gorham, 99 Mass. 420; Marion v. State, 20 N. W. 389; State v. Townley, 48 S. W. 833; Gallagher v. State, 10 Tex. App. 469; Commonwealth v. Kiley, 23 N. E. 55; State v. Barnes, 4 South. 560; Gilmore v. State, 108 Pac. 416. "A conviction in a clause of the constitution giving the governor power to grant pardons after convictions for all offenses means conviction by the verdict and the judgment of the court." State v. Alexander, 76 N. C. 231.

It was the intention of the legislature to make ,the suspension of sentence not an exercise of the court's leniency or to confer upon the court the pardoning power, but to make the suspension a part of the judgment. The suspension of the sentence is a part of the sentence. Ex Parte Mitchell, 126 Pac. 856; In Re Wadleigh, 23 Pac. 191; In Re Hart, 149 N. E. 568; People v. Stickle, 121 N. W. 497; State v. Smith, 90 N. E. 607; Gray v. State, 8 N. E. 16; State v. Mallshan, 118 Pac. 42.

By the Court, COLEMAN, C. J.:

This is an original proceeding in mandamus.

The facts out of which the proceeding grows are these: In the year 1915 one Adrian C. Wheeler was convicted of a crime in the district court of Washoe County, Nevada; the respondent presiding. Thereafter the respondent, as such judge, pronounced judgment and sentence upon said Wheeler, whereby it was ordered, adjudged, and decreed that he pay a fine, and that upon default in the payment of said fine he be confined in the county jail; and as a part of said judgment it was ordered that such sentence and judgment be stayed and suspended during good behavior, and until a further order of the court. The said Wheeler has paid no part of said fine nor served any part of said sentence. The purpose of this proceeding is to compel the respondent judge to enforce the payment of the fine, and in default of such payment to commit the said Wheeler to jail in pursuance of the sentence and judgment of the court.

The court in suspending the judgment and sentence acted in pursuance of section 7259 of the Revised Laws of 1912, which provides:

"Whenever any person shall be convicted of any crime except murder, burglary in the first degree, arson in the first degree, robbery, carnal knowledge of a female child under the age of ten years, or rape, the court may in its discretion, at the time of imposing sentence upon such person, direct that such sentence be stayed and suspended and that the defendant be released from custody on such conditions as the court may impose until otherwise ordered by such court."

It is the contention of the petitioner that the court was without authority to suspend the sentence and judgment of the court, for the reason that the statute in question is unconstitutional, null, and void.

1. The writer of this opinion, while district judge, on several occasions suspended sentence, no objection having been raised as to the constitutionality of the statute in question; but on careful examination of the question here presented he is convinced that such action was without authority of law. Article 5, section 13, of the Constitution of Nevada, authorizes the governor "to suspend the collection of fines and forfeitures, and grant reprieves for a period of sixty days"; and section 14 of the same article of our constitution provides:

"The governor, justices of the supreme court and attorney-general, or a major part of them, of whom the governor shall be one, may upon such conditions and with such limitations and restrictions as they may think proper, remit fines and forfeitures, commute punishments and grant pardons after convictions, in all cases, except treason and impeachments, subject to such regulations as may be provided by law, relative to the manner of applying for pardons."

2. We see no way to escape the conclusion that the authority to suspend the collection of a fine can be exercised only in the manner provided in the constitution. To hold, in the face of the provisions mentioned, that the courts also can suspend the collection of a fine would be to override our constitution; for, while there is nothing in the constitution which expressly provides that the legislature may not confer this authority upon the courts, it must necessarily follow that where the constitution enumerates certain cases in which the collection of a fine may be suspended, or certain methods

whereby it may be done, or confers upon a certain official or officials such power, the power so conferred must be held to be exclusive. This view is not open to debate. In State v. Arrington, 18 Nev. 412, 4 Pac. 735, the court said:

"We admit also that the legislature can perform any act not prohibited by the constitution; that, outside of constitutional limitations and restrictions, its power is 'as absolute, omnipotent, and uncontrollable as parliament.' But in seeking for limitations and restrictions, we must not confine ourselves to express prohibitions. Negative words are not indispensable in the creation of limitations to legislative power, and if the constitution prescribes one method of filling an office, the legislature cannot adopt another."

If this view is correct, of which there can be no doubt, the legislature cannot confer upon the courts authority to suspend a sentence. Under our constitution the governor can suspend the collection of a fine for only sixty days, and it would certainly be a remarkable thing if a judge should have the authority to suspend indefinitely the collection of a fine. To confer such authority upon a trial court would be to give it, though subject to local influences and environment, greater power than that possessed by the chief executive of the state. It is very clear that our constitution contemplated no such authority. But it would seem that this court has substantially determined this very question. In Ex Parte Shelor, 33 Nev. 361, 111 Pac. 291, it was held that the indefinite suspension of a fine is in effect substantially a remission thereof, and that the board of pardons alone could exercise that authority. To take any other view would enable the trial courts in an indirect manner to accomplish that which they cannot do directly. To do so would result in a dual system of paroling persons convicted of crime—something repugnant to the spirit of our organic law.

The question of the authority of the trial courts of the country to suspend sentences has been considered in

many cases, and the overwhelming weight of authority
is against it. In the case of People v. Brown, 54 Mich.
15, 19 N. W. 571, the court, speaking through that eminent authority on constitutional law, Judge Cooley, in
considering the authority of a trial judge to suspend a
sentence, said:

"That there may be no misapprehension on this point,
it is only necessary to understand exactly what it was
the judge was requested to do. In terms, it was to suspend sentence. Now, it is no doubt competent for a
criminal court, after conviction, to stay for a time its
sentence, and many good reasons may be suggested for
doing so, such as to give opportunity for a motion for a
new trial or in arrest, or to enable the judge to better
satisfy his own mind what the punishment ought to be
(Com. v. Dowdican's Bail, 115 Mass. 133); but it was
not a suspension of judgment of this sort that was
requested or desired in this case; it was not a mere
postponement; it was not delay for any purpose of
better advising the judicial mind what ought to be done;
but it was an entire and absolute remission of all penalty,
and the excusing of all guilt. In other words, what was
requested of the judge was that he should take advantage of the fact that he alone was empowered to pass
sentence, and, by postponing indefinitely the performance of this duty, indirectly, but to complete effect, grant
to the respondent a pardon for his crime.

"Now, it cannot for a moment be supposed that any
thirty-five intelligent citizens of this state are ignorant
of the fact that the power to pardon is an executive
power, expressly vested by the constitution of the state
in the governor, and exclusively belonging to his office.
And knowing that fact, as these petitioners must have
done, they could scarcely fail to understand that this
judge would be usurping the functions of the executive
were he to assume to give total immunity from punishment. No doubt judges have done this sometimes, under
the pressure of such influences as appear here; but this
is no reason for asking a repetition of the wrong; it is

rather a reason for being especially careful and particular not to invite it, lest by and by it comes to be understood that the power to pardon, instead of being limited to one tribunal, is confided to many, and that the pressure of influence and respectability may be. as properly employed with a judge to prevent sentence as many seem to think it may be with a governor to procure a formal pardon."

In Neal v. State, 104 Ga. 509, 30 S. E. 858, 42 L. R. A. 190, 69 Am. St. Rep. 175, being a case growing out of the suspension of sentence by the trial court, it is said:

"The plaintiff in error contends that 'the action of the court, after passing sentence, in suspending the execution of the same,' was 'an unwarranted interference with the powers, duties and functions of the executive.' We think that this contention is sound. The constitution of the state expressly provides that the governor 'shall have power to grant reprieves and pardons, to commute penalties, remove disabilities imposed by law, and to remit any part of a sentence for offenses against the state, after conviction, except in cases of treason and impeachment, subject to such regulations as may be provided by law relative to the manner of applying for pardons. * * *' If the execution of a sentence, which has been imposed in accordance with law, can be suspended, either in whole or in part, as the judge may see fit, during the pleasure of the court, then the court may in this way indirectly grant a reprieve, commute a penalty, or remit any part of a sentence, and thus practically exercise powers which the constitution confers exclusively upon the governor of the state. For a sentence, the execution of which is suspended during the pleasure of the court may never be enforced, as it may never be the pleasure of the court to revoke the order of suspension and enforce its execution. If a court can indefinitely suspend the execution of a sentence, it may even indirectly exercise all the pardoning power conferred upon the chief executive of the state, except that portion of it which embraces the removal of disabilities imposed by the law, in certain criminal cases, as a consequence of conviction. The fundamental law provides that when the governor exercises any of these functions he shall report his action and the reasons therefor to the legislature. Surely the judges of courts having criminal jurisdiction cannot, unhampered by such a requirement, exercise any of these powers."

Judge Beatty, in United States v. Wilson (C. C.) 46 Fed. 748, in passing upon this question, said:

"There can be no doubt of the right of a court to temporarily suspend its judgment, and continue to do so from time to time, in a criminal cause, for the purpose of hearing and determining motions and other proceedings which may occur after verdict, and which may properly be considered before judgment, or for other good cause. In this cause, however, the record does not show that the suspension was for any such reason, or for a certain or short time, but, on the contrary, it appears it was for such uncertain time as the defendant should continue to remain favorably impressed with the laws of the land as to obey them. Instead of this being a mere suspension of sentence, it operated as a condonation of the offense, and an exercise of a pardoning power which was never conferred upon the court. In this I think the court clearly transcended its authority."

The Supreme Court of Illinois, speaking through Mr. Justice Carter, after reviewing many cases, in People v. Barrett, 202 Ill. 287, 67 N. E. 23, 63 L. R. A. 82, 95 Am. St. Rep. 230, says:

"Whatever may have been the practice at common law, or whatever may be the practice in other states of this country, in regard to the suspending of sentence for the purpose of giving the accused a chance to reform, and thus virtually reprieving him, the legislature of this state has adopted a different method to give persons convicted of crimes the opportunity to reform, by providing a system of parole, and boards to administer the same; and, in view of the expressed policy of the legislation of this state, we are disposed to hold that the trial courts do not have the power to suspend the imposition of the sentence indefinitely after conviction, or to do such acts that virtually amount to an indefinite suspension of sentence, or to release the prisoner on parole."

The language just quoted applies with greater force to Nevada, because of the fact that our constitution provides the method of giving persons convicted of crime an opportunity to reform. See, also, Snodgrass v. State, 67 Tex. Cr. R. 615, 150 S. W. 162, 41 L. R. A. (N.S.) 1144.

It appearing that the statute in question is in violation of the express provisions of the constitution, it follows that the action of the court in suspending the sentence passed was and is without force and effect, and the writ will issue as demanded in the petition; but in order that the said Wheeler may make application to the governor or the board of pardons for a suspension of the collection of said fine, or such other clemency as he may see fit to seek, the service and execution of the order will be stayed for a period of twenty days.

[No. 2370]

J. B. DIXON, Petitioner, v. THE SECOND JUDICIAL DISTRICT COURT OF THE STATE OF NEVADA, IN AND FOR THE COUNTY OF WASHOE. Respondent.

[183 Pac. 312]

1. CERTIORARI—DILIGENCE IN PROCURING RECORD.

Though Rev. Laws, 5686, requires clerk of court to return transcript with writ of certiorari where writ is directed to the court, prosecutor of writ is required to use due diligence in having complete record made out, and on his failure so to do proceedings will be dismissed.

2. CERTIORARI—DILIGENCE OF PETITIONER—DISMISSAL OF PROCEEDINGS.

In certiorari proceedings in supreme court against lower court, where clerk refused to annex transcript to writ because of petitioner's failure to pay fees, court will not dismiss proceedings on ground that petitioner failed to exercise due diligence in having record made out, where petitioner acted in good faith, believing that his duty ended upon issuance of writ, and that it was then the supreme court's duty to require lower court and clerk to return writ with transcript under Rev. Laws, 5686, 5687.

3. CERTIORARI—TRANSCRIPT—COSTS.

Clerk of court is not required under Rev. Laws, 5686, to annex transcript in returning writ of certiorari directed to the court, unless petitioner in serving writ upon clerk pays the fees prescribed by law for the making of the transcript.

4. CERTIORARI—NATURE OF PROCEEDINGS.

Proceedings on certiorari are of appellate nature, though not pursued in ordinary and technical form of appeal.

ORIGINAL PROCEEDING in certiorari by J. B. Dixon against the Second Judicial District Court of the State of Nevada, in and for the County of Washoe. **Application denied.**

J. B. Dixon (in pro. per.), for Petitioner:

In certiorari there are no formal pleadings on the part of respondent. In some jurisdictions the respondent is termed the defendant. The return takes the place of an answer in the ordinary action, and is sometimes designated as such. 2 Spelling, Extr. Rem., sec. 2005.

When the writ is directed to a tribunal, the clerk shall return the writ with the transcript required. There is no provision in the statute requiring the payment of fees of any kind to the clerk, or that he shall make return on the payment of his fees. Rev. Laws, 5686, 5687.

If the clerk is entitled to payment of fees in advance, he must make demand for some specific amount, and it must be the correct amount. A general demand for payment is not sufficient. People v. Board, 20 N. Y. Supp. 280. He may not refuse a return because his fees are not paid. Ex Parte Davies, 3 Q. B. 425, 3 L. C. 60. The court will compel a respondent to make a return. Talbot v. White, 1 Wis. 444; Pittman v. Haggins, 91 Ga. 107; McManus v. McDonough, 4 Ill. App. 180; People v. Brooklyn, 5 How. Pr. 314.

A return may be waived by the parties. By stipulation the record may be submitted with the same effect as though a return had been made. Muldoon v. Pawtucket, 22 R. I. 191; McKay v. Jones, 30 Ark. 148; Deans v. Wilcoxin, 18 Fla. 531; Cushwa v. Lamar, 45 W. Va. 326.

Anthony M. Turano, for Respondent:

The writ should be dismissed. Petitioner has failed to perfect his proceeding upon the writ. There is no transcript before the court, petitioner having failed, neglected and refused to pay the legal fees due and payable to the respondent court, or any fees whatsoever. Stats. 1917, p. 11; Rev. Laws, 1699.

By the Court, SANDERS, J.:

A writ of certiorari issued out of this court, directed to the Second judicial district court of the State of Nevada, in and for the county of Washoe, upon the verified petition, duly filed herein, of J. B. Dixon, the petitioner, commanding said district court to certify and annex to the said writ a transcript of the record and proceedings in that certain action therein pending, wherein Miller & Mashburn are plaintiffs, and J. B. Dixon is defendant, and to desist from further proceedings in said action until the further order of this court.

E. H. Beemer, the clerk of the respondent court, being the officer upon whom the law imposes the duty to return with the writ the transcript required (Rev. Laws, 5686) in response to the writ, filed his affidavit, from which it appears that at the time the petitioner served upon affiant the said writ he demanded of the petitioner certain fees prescribed by law for making the transcript; that the petitioner declined and refused to pay any fees, and for that reason alone the affiant states he did not return with the writ the transcript required. There is also appended to the writ the affidavit of Thomas F. Moran, judge of the respondent court, stating that he directed E. H. Beemer, the clerk of his court, to comply with the provisions of said writ upon the prepayment by the petitioner of the fees prescribed by law for making and certifying the transcript required. Thereafter, upon the application of the petitioner, supported by his affidavit setting forth the steps taken by him to have a full and complete return made to the writ, this court made an order, directed to the respondent court, to show cause, on a day certain, why the writ should not be returned as directed. The respondent has not complied with the order to show cause, but it appears that E. H. Beemer, clerk, on the day fixed for the return of the order to show cause, filed a supplemental affidavit, stating therein that the petitioner had refused, and continues to refuse to pay the fees which he, the said clerk, claims he was compelled by law to charge and collect for the performance of the service required. Prior to the issuance of the said show-cause order, the respondent and the plaintiffs in the action filed a motion to dismiss the writ, upon the ground that the petitioner had not used due diligence in having a transcript of the proceeding sought to be reviewed made out and returned with the writ.

1. The statute requires that, when a writ of certiorari is directed to a tribunal, the clerk, if there be one, shall return the writ with the transcript required. Rev. Laws, 5686. Such officer may be compelled summarily

to make a return, yet it is incumbent upon the prosecutor of the writ to use due diligence in having a complete record made out, and that his proceeding will be dismissed if he fails to use due diligence in the prosecution thereof. I. X. L. Lime Co. v. Superior Court, 143 Cal. 170, 76 Pac. 973.

2. We think the record shows satisfactorily that the petitioner in good faith was of the opinion that his duty ended when the writ issued, and that it then became a matter for this court to see that the respondent and the said clerk performed the express and unconditional duty enjoined upon them by the statute. Rev. Laws, 5686, 5687. We therefore decline to dismiss the writ upon the grounds stated in the motion.

On the other theory of the case, it is the contention of the petitioner that the affidavits annexed to the writ are no answer to the writ, and that the respondent court, through its clerk, should be compelled by an order of this court to make return of the writ as required by law without prepayment of the official fees or any charge demanded of him by the clerk for making the transcript required.

3. The frequency of applications to this court to hear and correct all sorts of grievances held against inferior courts in the trial of civil actions through the instrumentality of extraordinary writs has grown burdensome. We now are asked to declare that on certiorari official fees for necessary services to be performed in connection with the remedy are entirely dispensed with, from the fact that the statute is silent as to the matter of fees, and to hold that the party invoking the remedy is exempt from payment of fees for such services as must be performed in order that the record to be reviewed may be placed before the reviewing tribunal. We are of the opinion that a proceeding on certiorari occupies no different position in the system of remedies as provided by law in the matter of official fees from that of any other civil proceeding. Certiorari is designed for the benefit of the party or parties in interest in having the

record of the action reviewed. By invoking the remedy such persons seek to maintain a private right or privilege in which the state, the county, the people, or their officials have no interest. Our legislature has seen fit to provide for and to establish by general and special laws a system of fixed fees to be charged and collected by salaried officials for their services, and such officials are held accountable for their refusal or neglect to charge and collect such fees except where they are waived by statute. These fees are the property of the state, county or municipality, as the case may be, and must be paid into the public treasury. No reason is apparent why the charges imposed by law for the services of state and county officers, rendered for the benefit of private parties on certiorari, should be waived, or such party be exempt from their prepayment. Had such been the intention of the legislature, it should have been so expressed, and not left to favor. The fact that a court is the only real party respondent does not call for any different conclusion. Such court is not a party defendant to the writ, and is in no sense an adverse party to the action. It is not in accordance with our sense of "propriety or expediency" that a trial court acts under the peril of being charged with the prepayment of official fees if it errs in its judgment of the rules of law, and it would be unreasonable to say that to review an issue of law the party in interest is exempt from the payment of official fees because it is an issue of law that is to be reviewed.

4. Proceedings upon certiorari are of appellate nature, though not pursued in ordinary and technical form of appeal (Peacock v. Leonard, 8 Nev. 250), and no cogent reason is suggested why a different rule as to cost should be applied.

The question here presented has been considered in all its phases in the case of I. X. L. Lime Co. v. Superior Court, supra. As the statute in California with reference to writs of certiorari is the same as that of ours, and as the case cited was decided upon identically the same state of facts and the same question involved, we adopt the reasoning of that decision and apply it to the case at bar. But the petitioner insists that case is not in point because of the proviso contained in section 2 of an act regulating the fees and compensation of the county clerk of Washoe County, wherein it is provided:

"That said clerk shall neither charge, nor collect any fees for services by him rendered to the State of Nevada or the county of Washoe, or any city or town within said * * * county, or any officer thereof, in his official capacity." Stats. 1917, c. 10.

It is argued that, as the respondent court is a part of the state government and also a part of the government of Washoe County, the services to be performed by the clerk are for the benefit of said county. There is nothing in this contention.

We hold that the affidavits annexed to the writ show a legitimate excuse for the noncompliance with the writ, and that the application of the petitioner for process compelling the making and certification of the transcript required without the payment of legal fees of the clerk must be denied.

It is so ordered.

[No. 2382]

IN THE MATTER OF THE APPLICATION OF WILLIAM H. BRENNEN, FOR A WRIT OF HABEAS CORPUS.

[183 Pac. 310]

1. HUSBAND AND WIFE—DESERTION—NONSUPPORT—PROSECUTION— VENUE.

 Prosecution of husband for desertion and nonsupport of wife and child under Act Pa. March 13, 1903 (P. L. 26), need not be instituted at place of his residence, or county in which offense is alleged to have been committed, but may be instituted wherever relief may be needed; such statute, in view of section 2, and in view of act April 13, 1867 (P. L. 78), to which it is supplementary, being remedial as well as penal. with purpose of affording relief to dependent wives and children.

ORIGINAL PROCEEDING. Application of William H. Brennen for a writ of habeas corpus. Petitioner directed to surrender himself to sheriff.

Wm. McKnight, Moore & McIntosh, and *Edna C. Plummer,* for Petitioner:

 The court of Clearfield County, Pa., the county out of which the indictment issued, was and is devoid of jurisdiction to try petitioner on the indictment so filed, he never having been a resident of or domiciled in said county. One who commits a crime is answerable therefor only in the jurisdiction where the crime was committed; and in all criminal prosecutions, in the absence of statutory provision to the contrary, venue must be laid as in the county of the offense, and it must be proved as laid. State v. Dangler, 74 Ohio St. 49, 77 N. E. 271.

 The offense charged is not a continuing offense, nor one which might be termed transitory or ambulatory in its nature. In Re Roberson, 38 Nev. 326, 149 Pac. 182.

Leonard B. Fowler, Attorney-General, for Respondent.

By the Court, DUCKER, J.:

This is an original proceeding in habeas corpus.

 The return to the writ shows that the petitioner was held in custody of the relators, Joseph Stern, sheriff of Ormsby County, State of Nevada, and A. M. Gorman, as agent of the State of Pennsylvania, under a warrant of arrest issued by the authority of the governor of Nevada pursuant to a requisition from the governor of the State of Pennsylvania, demanding the extradition of the petitioner as a fugitive from justice.

The crime charged is desertion and failure to support wife and child, alleged to have been committed by petitioner in the county of Clearfield, State of Pennsylvania, on or about the 1st day of July, 1917.

Upon the issuance of the writ petitioner was admitted to bail by this court.

It is conceded that the indictment found in said Clearfield County substantially charges an offense under the laws of Pennsylvania, and that petitioner was in that state at the time alleged. The evidence adduced upon the hearing of the return to the writ in this court was taken by deposition under stipulation, and petitioner testified in his own behalf at the hearing. He asserts that the evidence shows that he was never a resident of Clearfield County, but, on the contrary, shows that he was a resident of and domiciled in Jefferson County, and when the actual separation from his wife occurred he was residing in Indiana County, Pa. He insists, therefore, that as a matter of law the court of Clearfield County has no jurisdiction of the offense charged, and that he is entitled to his release. This is the sole question for determination.

We think the jurisdiction of the court of Clearfield County, under the laws of the State of Pennsylvania, to try petitioner for the offense charged and render judgment, does not rest upon the ground of his residence or home in that county, but upon the fact that he was in that state at the time the offense is alleged to have been committed by him.

Petitioner was indicted in Clearfield County under a statute of the State of Pennsylvania which provides:

"If any husband or father, being within the limits of this commonwealth, shall hereafter separate himself from his wife or from his children, or from wife and children, without reasonable cause, and shall wilfully neglect to maintain his wife or children, such wife or children being destitute, or being dependent wholly or in part on their earnings for adequate support, he shall be guilty of a misdemeanor; and on conviction thereof be sentenced to imprisonment not exceeding one year, and to pay a fine not exceeding $100, or either, or both, at the discretion of the court; such fine, if any, to be paid or applied in whole or in part to the wife or children, as the court may direct." Act of March 13, 1903, P. L. 26.

This enactment is clearly supplementary to an act of the legislature of the State of Pennsylvania passed in 1867 (P. L. 1867, p. 78), and was so considered by this court in Ex Parte Hose, 34 Nev. 87, 116 Pac. 417. The act of 1867 provides:

"If any husband, or father, being within the limits of this commonwealth, has, or hereafter shall, separate himself from his wife, or from his children, or from wife and children, without reasonable cause, or shall neglect to maintain his wife, or children, it shall be lawful for any alderman, justice of the peace, or magistrate, of this commonwealth, upon information made before him under oath, or affirmation, by his wife, or children, or either of them, or by any other person, or persons, to issue his warrant to the sheriff, or to any constable, for the arrest of the person against whom the information shall be made, as aforesaid, and bind him over, with one sufficient surety, to appear at the next court of quarter sessions, there to answer said charge of desertion."

In subsequent sections of this act provisions are made authorizing the court of quarter sessions to make proper orders compelling the person against whom complaint is made to pay such sums as the court may deem reasonable and proper for the support of the wife and children, or either, and to commit him to prison until he comply with such order or give security therefor. It has been decided by the courts of last resort in Pennsylvania, construing the act of 1867, that any court of quarter sessions within the commonwealth has jurisdiction to try a person complained of under this act, without reference to where the original desertion may have been. Barnes v. Commonwealth, 2 Pennypacker (Pa.) 506; Demott v. Commonwealth, 64 Pa. 302; Commonwealth v. Tragle, 4 Pa. Super. Ct. 159.

Aside from its penal nature and the combination of the acts of desertion and failure to provide into one offense, the later act is a virtual reenactment of the earlier act.

While there is no decision of the courts of Pennsylvania construing the act of 1903 as to the proper venue of an action instituted under it, still an examination of the two acts leads us to the conclusion that there was no intention in the later act to restrict the jurisdiction of the courts with reference to the residence of the offender within the state.

The purpose of the act of 1867 is not to punish criminals, but to relieve dependent wives and children by providing for their maintenance. Commonwealth v. Tragle, supra. But it is equally certain that while the act of 1903 makes desertion and nonsupport a misdemeanor and punishable, its purpose is also to relieve dependent wives and children by providing for their maintenance, both independently of the act of 1867, and in aid thereof.

This is apparent from that part of section 2 of the act of 1903 which provides:

"That upon conviction, the court may suspend sentence, upon and during compliance by the defendant with any order for support thereafter made against him, as already made or as may thereafter be modified, in the manner now provided by law; and if no such order shall have been made, then the court trying the defendant may make such order for the support by the defendant of his wife and children, or either of them, which order shall be subject to modification by the court on cause shown, and may suspend sentence, upon and during the compliance by defendant with such order then made or as thereafter modified and entry of bond by defendant, with surety approved by the court, conditioned on compliance with such order,"

Provision is also made in this act empowering the court to order any fine that may be levied to be applied in whole or in part to the maintenance of the wife or children of the delinquent. It is plain that the act of 1903 was intended by the legislature of Pennsylvania to be supplementary to the act of 1867 in its purpose, and to furnish an additional remedy for dependent wives and children against delinquent husbands and fathers by invoking the strong arm of the criminal law in their behalf. Such being its scope and purpose as revealed by the entire structure of the act, it would contravene the plain spirit of the statute to assume that the legislature intended it to be less effective in its purpose than the act of 1867 by restricting the venue to the residence of the offending husband or father.

The statute of 1903 is both penal and remedial, and in our judgment constitutes an exception to the general rule of criminal procedure that the venue must be laid in the county where the offense is alleged to have been committed.

Counsel for petitioner cite the opinion of this court in the case of In Re Roberson, 38 Nev. 326, 149 Pac. 182, L. R. A. 1915E, 691, and insist that it is ruling on the question of jurisdiction here presented. It is a sufficient answer to this contention to state that in that case the petitioner was indicted under a statute of the State of North Carolina substantially different in its structure and purpose from the statute before us in this case. The statute of the State of North Carolina, and which is a section of the criminal code, provides:

"If any husband shall wilfully abandon his wife without providing adequate support for such wife, and the children which he may have begotten upon her, he shall be guilty of a misdemeanor." Code, sec. 970.

The part of the opinion in which the jurisdictional

power of the court of one county to control the trial of a case where the desertion takes place in another county of the state is discussed in the case of In Re Roberson is based upon a decision of the superior court of North Carolina holding that under the laws of that state the superior court of one county has no jurisdiction of criminal offenses committed in another county, and also rests upon the decisions of the court of other states upon statutes different from the statute under consideration here.

Moreover, it appears that it was unnecessary to determine this question in the case of In Re Roberson, for the reason that the court held that the petitioner was not within the State of North Carolina when he formed the intention to abandon his wife, and was therefore not a fugitive from justice subject to interstate extradition.

In Re Roberson is not ruling in the case at bar. There are few questions more uncertain in the whole scope of the law than the question of fact as to the proper venue in cases of abandonment of wife and children. The books reveal a long and melancholy train of instances where justice has been defeated by misplaced venue, due to the transitory nature of the husband's abode, or to his action in causing his wife to live in places apart from his own residence. We are therefore not indulging an unfair inference to believe that the legislature of the State of Pennsylvania was probably moved by these considerations, in the enactment of the statutes of 1867 and 1903, to give the courts of that state jurisdiction in this class of cases without reference to the residence or domicile of the parties within the state. The power of the legislature to do this, in the absence of constitutional restrictions, is unquestioned.

The wisdom of the legislature is apparent in this particular case. It appears from the evidence that the petitioner and his wife were married in Clearfield County, the home of the wife; that they went from there to Armstrong County and thence into Jefferson County, from whence, at the direction of petitioner, the

wife returned to live in Clearfield County. He then
moved into Indiana County, and finally went from that
county to Eureka, Nevada. It also satisfactorily appears
that before leaving Pennsylvania he visited her at Clearfield County on several occasions, and they stopped
together at a hotel in that county and cohabited as husband and wife. Having directed her to go into Clearfield
County, and cohabiting with her there, it may be justly
remarked, as was said in Commonwealth v. Tragle,
supra, under a similar state of facts, that his argument
here against the jurisdiction of the court of that county
comes with bad grace, and well illustrates the wisdom
of the statute in allowing the proceedings to be instituted
wherever the relief may be needed.

It is ordered that petitioner forthwith surrender himself to the sheriff of Ormsby County, State of Nevada,
to be delivered into the custody of the duly appointed
agent of the State of Pennsylvania for return to that
state, and that upon compliance with this order his bail
may be exonerated.

[No. 2385]

PETER ESCALLE, RESPONDENT, *v.* FRANK MARK, ALSO KNOWN AS FRANKS MARKS, APPELLANT.

[183 Pac. 387]

1. STATUTES—CONSTRUCTION—PURPOSE—INTENT.
   In construing a statute the legislative intent controls, and in seeking the intent the evil sought to be remedied should be ascertained.

2. FRAUDULENT CONVEYANCES—BULK-SALES LAW—PURPOSE.
   The main purpose of the bulk-sales law is to protect wholesalers.

3. FRAUDULENT CONVEYANCES—BULK-SALES LAW—CONSTRUCTION—"VOID."
   Bulk-sales law, declaring certain sales "void," does not preclude the seller from recovering the purchase price of a sale made in violation of its terms; "void," as used in the statute, meaning "voidable."

APPEAL from Second Judicial District Court, Washoe County; *George A. Bartlett*, Judge.

Action by Peter Escalle against Frank Mark, also known as Frank Marks. From a judgment for plaintiff and an order denying a new trial, defendant appeals. **Affirmed.**

Platt & Sanford, for Appellant:

The agreement violates the bulk-sales law (Rev. Laws, 3908, 3909, 3911), is in direct violation of its provisions, and unenforceable either in law or equity.

The statute has been strictly enforced, and an agreement under it based upon the sale of a stock of goods in a partnership arrangement has been held invalid and void. Marlow v. Ringer, 91 S. E. 386; Daly v. Sumpter Drug Co., 127 Tenn. 421; Ann. Cas. 1914B, 1101.

The contract being expressly declared void by the statute, the court is without jurisdiction to enforce it. 9 Cyc. 475; 13 C. J. 492–497, 507.

Robert Richards, for Respondent:

The sole purpose of bulk-sales laws is the protection of creditors at the time and place of the transfer of merchandise in bulk. Such is the intent, and when that

object and intent are satisfied the statutes cannot be
further extended. When the "reason of the rule ceases,
the rule itself ought to cease." 1 Blackstone's Commen-
taries; 12 R. C. L. 525.

The phrase, "such sale or transfer shall be fraudulent
and void," means "such sale or transfer shall be fraudulent and voidable as to creditors," and nothing more.
"The invalidity in any case applies only to where the
rights of creditors are involved, and sales in violation of
the statutes are perfectly valid between the immediate
parties or those claiming under them. Though the word
'void' is used in the statute, in legal effect it means
'voidable at the instance of an attaching creditor.'"
12 R. C. L. 525; MacGreenery v. Murphy, 76 N. H. 338,
82 Atl. 720, 39 L. R. A. 374; Dickinson v. Harbison, 78
N. J. Law, 97; Kelly-Buckley Co. v. Cohen, 195 Mass. 585;
Squire v. Tellier, 185 Mass. 18; Brown v. Brown, 50
N. H. 552; Columbia Co. v. Braillard, 12 Wash. 22;
Woodcock v. Bolster, 38 Vt. 632; Van Shaack v. Robbins,
36 Iowa, 201. "The term 'void' is equivocal. It may
import absolutely null or merely voidable." Southern
Co. v. Barr, 148 S. W. 845.

Bulk sales are absolutely valid and binding between
the parties themselves. 12 R. C. L. 525; Newman v.
Garfield, 104 Atl. 882; Oregon Co. v. Hyde, 169 Pac.
791; Benson v. Johnson, 165 Pac. 1001.

By the Court, COLEMAN, C. J.:

This action was instituted by plaintiff, who is respondent here, to recover from the defendant (appellant)
the balance of the purchase price of a one-half interest
in and to a hotel and saloon business conducted by the
plaintiff in Reno, and a like interest in the stock, fix-
tures, furnishings, furniture, and appurtenances thereof.
Judgment was rendered in favor of the plaintiff, and
from an order denying defendant's motion for a new
trial, and the judgment, an appeal has been taken.

1-3. The only point urged upon our consideration as
a reason why the judgment and order appealed from

should be reversed is that prior to the making of the sale section 2 of the "Bulk-Sales Act" (Stats. 1907, p. 209; Rev. Laws, 3909) was not complied with. That section reads:

"Whenever any person shall bargain for or purchase any portion of a stock of merchandise otherwise than in the ordinary course of trade and in the regular and usual prosecution of the seller's business, or an entire stock of merchandise in bulk, for cash or on credit, and shall pay any part of the price, or execute and deliver to the vendor thereof or to his order, or to any person for his use, any promissory note or other evidence of indebtedness, to give credit, whether or not evidenced by promissory note or other evidence of indebtedness, for said purchase price or any part thereof, without at least five days previously thereto having demanded and received from the said vendor or his agent the statement provided for in section 1 of this act, and verified as there provided, and without notifying also at least five days previously thereto, personally or by registered mail, every creditor as shown upon said verified statement when said proposed sale or transfer is to be made, and the time and conditions of payment, and without paying or seeing to it that the purchase money of said property is applied to the payment of bona-fide claims of the creditors of the vendor as shown upon said verified statement, share and share alike, such sale or transfer shall be fraudulent and void."

Section 1 of the act provides:

"It shall be the duty of every person who shall bargain for or purchase any portion of a stock of merchandise, otherwise than in the ordinary course of trade and in the regular and usual prosecution of the seller's business, or an entire stock of merchandise in bulk, for cash or on credit, before paying to the vendor or his agent or representative, or delivering to the vendor or his agent or representative, any part of the purchase price thereof or any promissory note or evidence therefor, to demand of and receive from such vendor or agent, or if the vendor or agent be a corporation, then from the president, vice-president, secretary, or managing agent of such corporation, a written statement, sworn to substantially as hereinafter provided, of the names and addresses of all the creditors of said vendor to whom said vendor may be indebted, together with the amount of the indebtedness due or owing or to become due or owing by said vendor, to each of the said creditors, and it shall be the duty of the said vendor or agent to furnish such statement, which shall be verified."

To be more specific, it is contended that because of the failure of the defendant to demand and receive from the plaintiff, five days previous to the consummation of the sale, the sworn statement provided for in section 1 of the act in question, and give five days' notice of such proposed sale to the creditors of the vendor, the sale was and is absolutely null and void, and that for this reason the plaintiff cannot recover the unpaid amount of the purchase price.

It is true that the statute says that when there is a failure to comply with section 1 of the act the sale shall be "fraudulent and void"; but did the legislature mean that a sale should be absolutely "void" as between the parties, regardless of the fact that no creditor was prejudiced thereby? We think not. It is a cardinal rule of statutory construction that the legislative intent controls (Worthington v. District Court, 37 Nev. 212, 142 Pac. 230, L. R. A. 1916A, 696, Ann. Cas. 1916E, 1097), and in seeking the intention of the legislature in enacting a certain law we must ascertain the evils sought to be remedied. This court, speaking through Hawley, J., in Ex Parte Siebenhauer, 14 Nev. 365, said:

"The meaning of words used in a statute may be sought by examining the context and by considering the reason or spirit of the law or the causes which induced the legislature to enact it. The entire subject-matter and the policy of the law may also be invoked to aid in its interpretation, and it should always be construed so as to avoid absurd results"—citing Roney v. Buckland, 4 Nev. 45; State v. Dayton and Virginia T. R. Co., 10 Nev. 155; Silver v. Ladd, 7 Wall. 219, 19 L. Ed. 138; State v. Judge, 12 La. Ann. 777; State v. Mayor, 35 N. J. Law, 196.

It was said in Columbia & P. S. Co. v. Braillard, 12 Wash. 22, 40 Pac. 382:

"It is doubtless true that the word 'void,' when used in a statute, does not mean absolutely void for every purpose, and in determining its meaning in a given case regard must be had to the subject-matter of the statute, its scope, purpose and effect."

See, also, Colburn v. Wilson, 24 Idaho, 94, 132 Pac. 579; Thompson v. Esty, 69 N. H. 55, 45 Atl. 566.

It is said:

"Every statute must be construed with reference to the object intended to be accomplished by it. In order to ascertain this object it is proper to consider the occasion and necessity of its enactment, the defects or evils in the former law, and the remedy provided by the new one; and the statute should be given that construction which is best calculated to advance its object." 36 Cyc. 1110.

It was also said by this court in Ex Parte Siebenhauer, supra, 14 Nev. 369:

"In order to reach the intention of the legislature, courts are not bound to always take the words of a statute either in their literal or ordinary sense, if by so doing it would lead to any absurdity or manifest injustice, but may in such cases modify, restrict, or extend the meaning of the words, so as to meet the plain, evident policy and purview of the act, and bring it within the intention which the legislature had in view at the time it was enacted. Gibson v. Mason, 5 Nev. 285; Reiche v. Smythe, 13 Wall. 164, 20 L. Ed. 566; Burgett v. Burgett, 1 Ohio, 480, 13 Am. Dec. 634; McIntyre v. Ingraham, 35 Miss. 52; Camp v. Rogers, 44 Conn. 291; Castner v. Walrod, 83 Ill. 178, 25 Am. Rep. 369; Fisher

v. Patterson, 13 Pa. St. 338; Bishop on Statutory
Crimes, sec. 212."

See, also, 36 Cyc. 1111.

In Goldfield Con. M. Co. v. State, 35 Nev. 178, 127 Pac.
77, it was said:

"All laws should receive a sensible construction.
General terms should be so limited in their application
as not to lead to injustice, oppression, or an absurd consequence. It will always, therefore, be presumed that
the legislature intended exceptions to its language which
would avoid results of this character. United States v.
Kirby, 7 Wall. 482, 19 L. Ed. 278. And see State v.
McKenney, 18 Nev. 189, 2 Pac. 171; State v. Krutt-
schnitt, 4 Nev. 178."

In the light of these rules of construction, let us
ascertain what evil the legislature sought to remedy by
enacting the bulk-sales law. In 12 Ruling Case Law, sec.
54, page 525, it is stated that the bulk-sales law has but
one aim, namely, "to prevent a sale of goods in bulk until
the creditors of the seller have been paid in full." It is
common knowledge that the main purpose of the law is
to protect the wholesaler. Prior to the passage of the
law, it was a common practice for retailers to sell their
stock of goods in bulk, pay no one, and leave the man
who sold them the goods without recourse. Such practices became so distastrous to the wholesalers that they
were driven to the necessity of procuring legislation
which would afford them protection against unscrupu-
lous retail merchants. The bulk-sales law is the result.

"The object of this act was, no doubt, to protect whole-
sale merchants particularly against fraudulent sales by
retailers; but the act by its terms protects all creditors
of merchants alike." McDaniels v. Connelly Shoe Co.,
30 Wash. 549, 71 Pac. 37, 60 L. R. A. 947, 94 Am. St.
Rep. 889; Eklund et al. v. Hopkins et al., 36 Wash. 179,
78 Pac. 787.

This being the purpose of the law, how can it be
successfully urged, as contended by appellant, that we
should hold that such a sale as here in question was

absolutely void? It is true that the statute says a sale shall be void when the terms of the act are not complied with; but to our minds, when construed in the light of the purpose of the statute, it was clearly the intention of the legislature that the sale should be voidable only. It is not pointed out what protection would or could be afforded any one by placing any other construction upon the law.

But all rules of construction aside, it seems to us that no other conclusion can be reached, from a reading of the entire act itself, especially section 4 thereof (Rev. Laws, 3911). This section provides that, if the vendor produces and delivers a written waiver of the requirements of the act as to notice to creditors, from at least a majority in number and amount of his creditors, the provisions of the act shall not apply. If it was the purpose of the legislature in enacting the law to protect any but creditors, the section just referred to is a most remarkable one. In fact, we cannot escape the conclusion, from a consideration of this very section, that the sole purpose of the law is to protect creditors. If such was not the intention, the legislature would never have embodied section 4 in the law, because it would manifestly have made the act inconsistent in its operation. Such seems to have been the conclusion reached by the Supreme Court of New Jersey, in considering the effect of a similar provision in the bulk-sales law of that state, in the case of Dickinson v. Harbison, 78 N. J. Law, 97, 72 Atl. 941. The court in that case said:

"The body of the act, as will be observed, declared that a sale should be void as to creditors unless certain things were done by the purchaser. The proviso, however, speaks of the sale as 'such voidable sale.' The word 'void' was used in the sense of voidable. The proviso itself shows that the sale was a nullity only when attacked by creditors within a certain period."

So in our statute the "body of the act" provides that a sale which is made without first complying with certain terms thereof shall be "fraudulent and void," while section 4 says such requirements may be waived by creditors.

Many cases may be found growing out of the bulk-sales statutes of various states, wherein the word "void" is construed to mean "voidable"; such construction invariably being reached upon the theory that such was the evident intention of the law-making bodies. To quote from all of them would unnecessarily lengthen this opinion, and we content ourselves with the following extracts:

"The phrase 'fraudulent and void as to creditors' relates to attaching creditors who seek to set aside the vendee's title, which, until set aside, is a valid title. As between the parties to the sale, the title passed to the vendee, and it remains in him until it is vacated by a creditor of the vendor upon proceedings instituted for that purpose, or until the vendee disposes of the property. Though the word 'void' is used in the statute, in legal effect, it means voidable at the instance of an attaching creditor." McGreenery v. Murphy, 76 N. H. 338, 82 Atl. 720, 39 L. R. A. (N.S.) 374.

"The question whether in a statute the term 'void' is used with entire technical accuracy, or only in its less strict meaning as 'voidable,' is frequently one of difficulty. In many statutes the word is used in its strict technical sense, and in many it is used in the sense of voidable. In view of the subject-matter of this statute, the conditions of the law prior to its passage, the abuse which it aims to correct, and the manifest difficulty of any other view, we are of the opinion that the legislature intended to place the kind of sale named in the statute into the class of sales theretofore existing as fraudulent and for that reason voidable by creditors, unless the conditions therein prescribed were complied with; or, in other words, it is intended to create another instance of a sale which the creditors might avoid as being fraudulent and for that reason against their rights. But it was not the intention of the statute that this kind of sale should stand upon any different footing from that of the general class to which it was added. The sale is voidable like the other kinds of sales which are commonly called void as against creditors, and the right of the creditor in this sale is similar in its nature to the right of the creditor in such other sales. Such an interpretation of the statute seems to us reasonable, and in accordance with the general principle of law applicable to the subject-matter. See, in this connection, the language used by Knowlton, C. J., in giving the opinion of the court in Squire v. Tellier, 185 Mass. 18, 69 N. E. 312, 102 Am. St. Rep. 322." Kelly-Buckley Co. v. Cohen, 195 Mass. 585, 81 N. E. 297:

"Knowlton, C. J. * * * A sale made in violation of the statute is void only as against creditors, and, if the vendor's debts are paid, the sale cannot be interfered with. A purchaser, to be safe, has only to see that the vendor's creditors are provided for. The vendor may sell freely, without regard to the statutes, if he pays his debts." Squire v. Tellier, 185 Mass. 18, 69 N. E. 312, 102 Am. St. Rep. 322.

"But since the decision in State v. Richmond, 26 N. H. 232, this term 'void' is perhaps seldom, unless in a very clear case, to be regarded as implying a complete nullity, but is to be taken in a legal sense, subject to large qualifications in view of all the circumstances calling for its application and the rights and interests to be affected in a given case." Brown v. Brown, 50 N. H. 552.

"It is doubtless true that the word 'void,' when used in a statute, does not always means absolutely void for every purpose; and in determining its meaning in a given case regard must be had to the subject-matter of the statute, its scope, purpose, and effect." Columbia Co. v. Braillard, 12 Wash. 22, 40 Pac. 382.

"The question involves the construction of a clause of our revenue law: * * * 'Provided further, that in all cases where the owner of land sold for taxes shall resist the validity of such tax title, such owner may show and prove fraud committed by the officer selling the same, or the purchaser to defeat the same; and if

fraud is so established such sale and title shall be void.'
This controversy involves the construction of the
* * * clause just quoted. * * * The word 'void'
has, with lexicographers, a well-defined meaning: 'Of
no legal force or effect whatsoever; null and incapable of
ratification.' Webster's Dict. But it is sometimes, and
not infrequently, used in enactments by the legislature,
in opinions by courts, in contracts by parties and in
arguments by counsel, in the sense of 'voidable'; that
is, capable of being avoided or confirmed. Idem. The
word 'void,' when used in any of these instruments, will
therefore be construed in one sense or the other, as shall
best effectuate the intent in its use, which will be determined from the whole of the language of the instrument
and the manifest purpose it was framed to accomplish.
Or, as the same rule has been more extendedly stated:
'It is the duty of the court to ascertain the meaning of
the legislature from the words used in the statute and
the subject-matter to which it relates, and to restrain its
operation within narrower limits than its words import,
if the courts are satisfied that the literal meaning of
its words would extend to cases which the legislature
never designed to include in it.' Leeses, etc. v. Blougher,
14 Pet. 178, 10 L. Ed. 408. This rule is broader than
the one first stated, for it would justify restraining the
meaning of a word to narrower limits than its import;
whereas, to restrain the word 'void' to the meaning of
'voidable' is to give it one of its not unfrequent accepted
significations." Van Shaack v. Robbins, 36 Iowa, 201.

See, also, Southern Co. v. Barr (Tex. Civ. App.) 148
S. W. 845; 12 R. C. L. 525; Newman v. Garfield (Vt.)
104 Atl. 882; Oregon Co. v. Hyde, 87 Or. 163, 169 Pac.
791; Benson v. Johnson, 85 Or. 677, 165 Pac. 1001, 167
Pac. 1014.

For the reasons given, it follows that the order and
judgment appealed from must be affirmed.

It is so ordered.

[No. 2383]

JOHN CONNOLLY, RESPONDENT, *v.* JOHN SALSBERRY AND KAWICH CATTLE COMPANY (A CORPORATION), APPELLANTS.

[183 Pac. 391]

1. VENUE—CHANGE—STATUTE.
   Rev. Laws, 5015, relating to change of venue, is mandatory, and a proper application for a change must be granted.

2. VENUE—CHANGE—TIME.
   Under Rev. Laws, 5015, providing for change of venue upon application made before the time for answering has expired, a stipulation made by attorneys, pursuant to district court rule No. 27, extending defendants' time to answer, did not extend the time to apply for a change of venue.

3. VENUE—STIPULATION—CONSTRUCTION—"MOVE."
   A stipulation extending defendants' time to appear, demur, answer, or "move" did not extend the time to move for a change of venue as a matter of right.

4. VENUE—CHANGE—STATUTE.
   Rev. Laws, 5015, subd. 1, authorizing court on motion to change place of trial in certain cases, does not authorize court to change the venue at any time before trial, in a case where defendant has filed no seasonable written application.

APPEAL from Seventh Judicial District Court, Esmeralda County; *J. Emmett Walsh*, Judge.

Action by John Connolly against John Salsberry and the Kawich Cattle Company. From an order denying change of venue, defendants appeal. **Affirmed.**

Hugh H. Brown, for Appellants:

The lower court was in error in refusing to remove the case to the county where the partnership realty was situated, and where both defendants resided at the commencement of the action. Rev. Laws, 5011, 5014, 5015; Falls Co. v. Brower, 11 S. E. 313.

The time to file demand for change of venue was enlarged by the stipulation extending the time to answer. The statute should be liberally construed. Change of venue is a common-law right. 4 Ency. Pl. & Pr. 375. The right is now generally regulated by statute. Such statutes are ordinarily construed liberally. Bush v. Eureka, 97 Cal. 135; State v. Spokane, 82 Pac. 875; 4

Ency. Pl. & Pr. 389. An extension of time to answer does not waive the right to demand change of venue. Donisthorpe v. Lutz, 136 N. W. 233.

Stiplation was authorized, made and filed pursuant to court rule (Rule 27, Sup. Ct.), which is of the same dignity as the statute itself. "Time to answer," as fixed by the stipulation, is in legal effect the same as if fixed by statute. Haley v. Bank, 20 Nev. 410.

The statute does not prescribe any fixed period for filing a motion for change of venue. It may be filed at any time, provided the moving party is not guilty of unreasonable delay. Clark v. Campbell, 54 How. Prac. 166; Palmer v. Schwarzemback, 136 N. Y. Supp. 85; Barkley v. Supreme Lodge, 167 Pac. 701; Allen v. Riley, 15 Nev. 452.

Hoyt, Gibbons, French & Henley, for Respondent:

The action does not involve the determination of a right or interest in real property. In a suit to dissolve a partnership, the venue is determined by the residence of the parties, and not by the locality of the firm assets, even when such assets include real estate; and hence the initial proceedings for the dissolution of a partnership and appointment of a receiver should be had in the place of the partners' domicile. Williams v. Williams, 145 N. Y. Supp. 564; Cox v. Manning, 79 S. E. 484; Goodfrey v. White, 5 N. W. 243; Clark v. Brown, 23 Pac. 299.

The time to file a demand for change of venue was not enlarged by the stipulation extending the time to answer. The language of the statute is peremptory. Rev. Laws, 5015; Clarke v. Lyon County, 8 Nev. 181; Wadleigh v. Phelps, 82 Pac. 200; State v. District Court, 97 N. W. 112; Peter v. Carlson, 149 N. W. 536; Irwin v. Taubman, 128 N. W. 617.

By the Court, DUCKER, J.:

This is an appeal from an order of the district court in and for the county of Esmeralda, denying appellants' demand and motion for a change of venue. The action is for a dissolution of partnership and an accounting, and the complaint was filed in the district court of said county on July 16, 1918. On the same day the complaint and summons was served on the defendants in the county, and on July 26, 1918, the following stipulation, signed by the respective attorneys, was filed:

"It is hereby stipulated, by and between the parties hereto, that the defendants shall have, and are hereby given, to and including Wednesday, July 31, 1918, in which to appear, demur, answer, or move in the above-entitled cause."

On July 31, 1918, the defendants served and filed a demand and a motion for a change of venue to Nye County, Nevada, supported by an affidavit of the defendant John Salsberry. The change of venue was sought upon the ground that the action seeks the recovery of an interest in real property located entirely in Nye County, and that at the time the action was commenced both of the defendants resided in Nye County. The application was made under that part of the provisions of section 5015 of the Revised Laws of Nevada which reads as follows:

"If the county designated for that purpose in the complaint be not the proper county, the action may, notwithstanding, be tried therein, unless the defendant, before the time for answering expires, demands in writing that the trial be had in the proper county, and the place of trial be thereupon changed by consent of the parties, or by order of the court, as provided in this section. The court may, on motion, change the place of trial in the following cases:

"1. When the county designated in the complaint is not the proper county."

Section 5011 of the Revised Laws provides:

"Actions for the following causes shall be tried in the county in which the subject of the action, or some part thereof, is situated, subject to the power of the court to change the place of trial, as provided in this act:

"1. For the recovery of real property, or an estate, or

interest therein, or for the determination in any form
of such right or interest, and for injuries to real property."

Section 5014 provides, in part:

"In all other cases [cases designated in preceding
sections] the action shall be tried in the county in which
the defendants, or any of them, may reside at the commencement of the action."

1. When the facts are shown to exist as to the locus
of the real of the real estate and the purpose of the
action, or the residence of the defendant as designated
in either of the two preceding sections, and the demand
for a change of venue to the proper county is seasonably
and properly made in accordance with section 5015, the
court in which the action is commenced is compelled
to grant the application. The statute is peremptory.
Williams v. Keller, 6 Nev. 144; Clarke v. Lyon County,
8 Nev. 181.

We need not examine that phase of the case wherein
the contention lies that Nye County is the proper county
for trial by reason of the situation of the real estate
claimed to be involved in the action, for it appears by
the affidavit of the defendant Salsberry, made in support
of the demand and motion, which is uncontradicted, that
the residence of the defendants was in that county when
the action was commenced. This, under the statute, is
sufficient ground for the application for a change of the
place of trial.

In ruling on the application the trial court held that
the time given defendants by stipulation to appear,
demur, answer, or move did not extend their time to
demand or move for a change of venue, and that the
same was not filed within the statutory time fixed by
said section 5015. The ruling and order of court are
assigned as error by the appellant, and he contends:

(1) That the time to file a demand for a change of
venue was enlarged by the stipulation extending the
time to answer.

(2) That the statute does not prescribe any fixed

period for filing a motion for a change of venue, and it may be filed at any time, provided the moving party is not guilty of unreasonable delay.

(3) That if the statute does prescribe a fixed period for filing a motion for a change of venue, then the time to file the motion was enlarged by the stipulation extending the time to move.

2. The statute, by the term "before the time for answering expires," fixed a definite time in which the defendants could make a demand for a change of the place of trial, and that time, by reason of the service of summons upon them in the county in which the action was commenced, was within ten days from such service. No other construction can be placed upon the language used. The written stipulation, made by the attorneys under the authority of rule 27 of the district court rules, extended the time for defendants to answer the complaint, to and including July 31, 1918, but did not, in this regard, likewise change the time for them to make a demand for a change of venue.

Counsel for appellants contends that the statute fixing the time for a demand for a change and the stipulation must be read together, and, when we so read, the legal effect is to extend the time for making a demand as well as the time to answer, and relies largely for the force of this contention upon the rule adopted by a majority of the federal courts in cases of removal of causes pending in the state courts. The federal statute (Act Aug. 13, 1888, c. 866, sec. 3, 25 Stat. 435) provides that, whenever any party is entitled to remove any suit "from a state court to the Circuit Court of the United States, he may make and file a petition in such suit in such state court at the time, or any time before the defendant is required by the laws of the state or the rule of the state court in which such suit is brought to answer or plead to the declaration or complaint of the plaintiff." That a stipulation extending the time to answer extends the time for removal, is held by a majority of the federal courts, but there is ample and well-reasoned authority to the contrary in those courts. See Velie v. Manufacturers' Accident Indemnity Co. of the United States (C. C.) 40 Fed. 545; Foster on Fed. Prac. (5th ed.) p. 1817.

There is no diversity of opinion among the state courts which have had occasion to pass upon the effect of a stipulation extending time to answer. They hold that it does not extend the time to make a demand for a change of venue. In Peterson v. Carlson, 127 Minn. 324, 149 N. W. 536, the court, in passing on the question, said:

"It is contended that the stipulation extending the time for answering ipso facto extended also the time for making a demand for a change of venue. We cannot so hold. There is simply no connection between the making of an answer and the making of a demand for a change of venue, and a stipulation extending the time for one could not by any permissible construction extend the time for the other."

In the case of Irwin v. Taubman, 26 S. D. 450, 128 N. W. 617, the court, in construing a statute the same as the one under consideration in connection with a written stipulation for extension of time to answer, held that it did not extend the time within which the defendant could demand a change of venue. The court said:

"In our opinion the legislature did not intend, by the use of the term 'before the time for answering expires,' to include such time as might be stipulated by the parties for answering. * * * To give the language of the statute the construction contended for by the appellant leaves it too vague and uncertain as to the time when the application should be made. We cannot presume that this change in the phraseology, made in 1909, was not intentional and not for a purpose. The reason that may have suggested itself to the legislature for this change, substituting the words 'before the time for answering expires' for the words 'before answer,' was to limit the time definitely, in order that no misunderstanding might arise as to when the motion for the change should be made, in analogy to the ruling in the federal courts."

In the Iowa case (Donisthorpe v. Lutz, 155 Iowa, 379, 136 N. W. 233), cited by appellants, the statute fixing the time for a motion for a change of venue is entirely different from the Nevada statute, and prescribes that the defendant shall file his motion for a change before any pleading is filed by him.

To consider the statute and rule 27 of the district court with the stipulation made by its authority in pari materia, as appellant does, would cause the statute in effect to read "before the time for answering expires or within which it may be extended," a meaning inconsistent with its plain and positive terms. The rules adopted by the supreme court for its own government and the government of the district court have the force and effect of statutory provision, as declared by this court, but they cannot be "inconsistent with the constitution or laws of the state." If found so, they must give way to the constitution or laws, as the case may be. The statute simply measures the time within which the demand may be made by a certain standard, for the purpose of requiring the application to be made at an early and definite period of the proceedings, to the ultimate end that the parties may, with reasonable certainty, be speedily informed of the place of trial. This salutary purpose ought not to be frustrated by any constrained construction of the statute or of rules and stipulations.

3. It is urged that, if the words "to answer" in the stipulation had not the effect to extend the time for the demand, that part stipulating time to move did; but we do not so view it. If the term "move" can be construed to include more than ordinary motions to pleadings and the like, and to extend to motions for change of venue, generally regarded as dilatory motions, it certainly cannot be held to include a demand for a change of venue as a matter of right. We are of the opinion that the term was intended to include neither a motion nor demand for a change of venue, and that the defendants, failing to.

make a demand for a change within the time prescribed by statute, waived their right to do so.

We are asked by counsel for appellant to apply the principle of estoppel. If respondent's counsel had entered into a written stipulation in terms giving appellant an extension of time in which to make a demand for a change, this contention would receive consideration; but, as no such stipulation is before us, the question of estoppel is not involved.

4. Can a motion for a change of venue, on the ground that the county in which the action is commenced is not the proper county, be made effectively at any time, and without making a seasonable written demand, if there has been no unreasonable delay? It seems that this question has been decided adversely to appellant's contention by this court in Elam v. Griffin, 19 Nev. 442, 14 Pac. 582. The court said:

"The defendants are residents of Eureka County, and are sued in an action of debt in the district court of Lincoln County. Upon their motion, the place of trial of the action was changed to the county of their residence, but no demand in writing therefor was made, as contemplated by section 3043, Gen. Stats. The object of the demand is to allow the plaintiff an opportunity of voluntarily correcting his error by amendment, stipulation, or otherwise, without the expense and delay of a motion. [Citation.] By omitting to make the demand, respondents waived the right to have the case heard in Eureka County and the action became triable in Lincoln County. [Citations.] Order reversed and cause remanded."

Section 3043 of the General Statutes, referred to in the opinion, has been reenacted in identical language in section 5015 of the Revised Laws. No demand in writing was made in Elam v. Griffin, supra, but there can be no difference in effect between a failure to make the demand and the failure to make it within the time prescribed by law, as in the present case.

It is obvious that the legislature intended to require a

written demand as a prerequisite to a motion for a change of venue, upon the ground that the action is not commenced in the proper county. We must construe the statute so as to give effect, if possible, to all of its parts; and to allow another construction would nullify the provision requiring a demand, and attribute to the legislature the performance of an idle ceremony in enacting it.

The right of a defendant to have a cause tried in the county of his residence is an absolute right, which he may exercise within a given time. A defendant is at once informed by the service of summons whether the county in which the action is instituted is the county of his residence, and it is the policy of the law to require him to make his election within the definite time prescribed, and in default thereof the right to a change of venue on this ground is waived.

If he were permitted by motion, under subdivision 1 of the section, to exercise this statutory privilege at any time before the trial of the cause, a demand in writing would serve no purpose whatever. Subdivision 1 is designed only to enable a defendant to obtain an order of the court removing the action after a proper and seasonable demand has been made. Bohn v. Bohn, 164 Cal. 532, 129 Pac. 981.

The New York authorities cited by appellant, construing a statute somewhat similar, hold generally that the demand may be dispensed with in a proper case; but we are not inclined to this view, both from our construction of the statute and the former decision of this court. In the case of Barclay v. Supreme Lodge, 34 Cal. App. 426, 167 Pac. 701, also cited, the application was granted solely upon the conveniences of witnesses. It is therefore not in point.

The order of the district court is affirmed.

[No. 2376]

RENO ELECTRICAL WORKS (A CORPORATION), RESPONDENT, *v.* UNITED STATES FIDELITY & GUARANTY COMPANY (A CORPORATION), APPELLANT.

[183 Pac. 386]

1. PLEADING — VARIANCE BETWEEN PLEADING AND INSTRUMENT REFERRED TO.

In an action by subcontractor against the surety on contractor's bond, the fact that the bond denominated the subcontractor as the electric works, while the complaint named it as the electrical works, is immaterial under Rev. Laws, 5080, 5081, the variance probably being due to a mere clerical error.

2. CONTRACTS—ADOPTION—EXECUTION.

Parties may adopt a written contract, and thus make it as binding as though formally executed by both, without signing it; and hence in an action by subcontractor against the surety on the contractor's bond, brought after complete performance by subcontractor, the fact that the written subcontract was not executed is no defense.

3. JUDGMENT—DEFAULT—NOTICE OF SUBSEQUENT PROCEEDING.

Where defendant was in default, the fact that the court made findings and entered judgment without notice is no ground of objection, for after default it would be a useless thing to require service of notice on defendant.

APPEAL from Second Judicial District Court, Washoe County; *Thomas F. Moran,* Judge.

Action by the Reno Electrical Works against the U. S. Fidelity & Guaranty Company. From a judgment for plaintiff, defendant appeals. Affirmed.

Harwood & Tippett, for Appellant:

The findings and judgment are not sustained by the pleadings.

It is affirmatively shown by the complaint that the alleged contract purports to be between Reno Electric Works and Caldwell & Son, while plaintiff sues under the name of Reno Electrical Works. There is no allegation that the two corporations are one and the same, if such be indeed the case.

The alleged contract is not signed, and there is not any allegation covering this omission and defect.

The judgment must be sustained by the complaint. If

there is any variance of parties or of proof, as shown by the judgment roll, the judgment cannot be sustained.

The court erred in entering judgment without notice to the defendant. Even though the defendant failed to answer, it was entitled to notice of all proceedings after the entering of its appearance.

LeRoy F. Pike, for Respondent:

The pleadings show that the Reno Electrical Works and the Reno Electric Works are one and the same corporation. Even if there is a variance, it is not a material variance. A variance is not material unless it has actually misled the adverse party. Rev. Laws, 5080, 5081; 31 Cyc. 703; 22 Ency. Pl. & Pr. 569, 571; State v. White, 34 S. C. 59; People v. Phillips, 70 Cal. 61; People v. Chretien, 137 Cal. 454; Dudley v. Duvel, 70 Pac. 68. It is not the policy of the law to prevent justice by trivial defenses, but on the contrary to see that substantial justice is done. Jones v. S. F. Sulphur Co., 14 Nev. 172.

Appellant's objection that the contract was not signed by plaintiff is frivolous. It is necessary to prove the signing of a contract only by the party to be charged. 6 Cyc. 11; 9 Cyc. 299; Esmay v. Gorton, 18 Ill. 483; Waltz v. Waltz, 84 Ind. 403; Railroad v. Orendorff, 37 Md. 328; Johnson v. Dodge, 17 Ill. 433. "When a contract is signed by one of the parties only, but is accepted and acted upon by the other party, it is just as binding as if it were signed by both of the parties." 9 Cyc. 300; Bloom v. Hazzard, 104 Cal. 310; Reedy v. Smith, 42 Cal. 245; Luckhart v. Ogden, 30 Cal. 543.

Plaintiff had the legal right to have the clerk enter judgment by default, without notice thereafter to defendant. Stats. 1913, p. 110; 23 Cyc. 759. If default was improperly taken, it was the proper practice to move to set it aside. Kidd v. Mining Co., 3 Nev. 381.

By the Court, DUCKER, J.:

This is an action upon a bond executed by defendant surety company, the appellant here, to secure subcontractors, laborers, and materialmen for labor performed and material furnished in the erection, construction, alteration, or repair of a public building or structure.

The second amended complaint alleges substantially that a contract was entered into for the construction of a public building; that thereafter the contractors entered into a contract with plaintiff as subcontractor for the furnishing of material and labor, and for certain construction in connection with said public building; that the plaintiff has performed the conditions of this contract, and there is nothing owing to plaintiff from the contractors on said contract, except the sum of $509.50, still unpaid, though demand has been made of the said contractors, who refuse to pay the same.

The complaint further alleges the completion of said public building, and its acceptance within ninety days of the commencement of this action; that a joint and several bond was executed to the trustees of the public building by appellant, conditioned that the contractors would satisfy all claims and demands incurred in the construction of said building, whereby a cause of action accrued to the benefit of plaintiff against defendant under the laws of this state. It is also alleged that plaintiff has been compelled to employ counsel to prosecute the action, and that the sum of $250 is a reasonable sum to allow plaintiff as counsel fees in the action. A copy of the contract with plaintiff and a copy of said bond are attached to and made a part of the complaint, marked "A" and "B," respectively.

Defendants demurred to the second amended complaint on the ground that it failed to state a cause of action. It was overruled by the court, and, the defendant having failed to answer within ten days limited by the order, its default was entered and judgment rendered in favor of plaintiff, according to the prayer of the complaint.

Defendant appeals from the judgment, and assigns as error: (1) That judgment is contrary to law; and (2) that the court erred in making its findings of fact and

conclusions of law and in entering judgment, because the
same were made and entered without notice to defendant.

It is claimed that the findings and judgment are not
sustained by the pleadings, and are therefore contrary
to law. This alleged error lies in the fact that the plaintiff is named in the complaint as the Reno Electrical
Works, whereas in the attached copy of the contract the
subcontractor is named Reno Electric Works; and also
in the fact that the copy of the contract is not signed,
and does not purport to be signed, by either Reno
Electrical Works or Reno Electric Works.

1. In respect to the first phase of the question, the
difference in the names, at the most, is an immaterial
variance. The references in the complaint to the contract show that Reno Electrical Works, Reno Electric
Works, and subcontractor are the same entity. The
indorsement on the copy of the contract "Reno Electrical Works" tends strongly to indicate that the word
"Electric" in the body thereof is a clerical error. Appellant could not possibly have been misled in this respect,
and the court was authorized, not only by the general
rule of law concerning immaterial variances, but by the
the liberal statutory rule, in finding the fact in conformity with the pleadings. Rev. Laws, 5080, 5081.
The contention that the judgment is contrary to law
because the copy of the contract annexed to the complaint is not signed by respondent is untenable.

2. Parties may adopt a written contract, and thus
make it binding as though formally executed by both,
without signing it. The copy of the contract is signed
by the contractor, and respondent's assent to it is shown
by a full performance of its conditions. "If a person
accepts and adopts a written contract, even though it is
not signed by him, he is deemed to have assented to its
terms and conditions and to be bound by them." 6 R. C.
L. p. 642; Bloom v. Hazzard, 104 Cal. 313, 37 Pac. 1037;
Memory v. Niepert, 131 Ill. 623, 23 N. E. 431; Story on
Contracts (5th ed.) sec. 509.

It appears from the allegations of the complaint that the contract alleged therein was acted upon by the parties—by the respondent in finishing the work required by the contract, and by appellant in paying more than two-thirds of the contract price for such work. The contractual relation is evidenced by these mutual acts, and makes the contract binding on each of the parties, if neither had signed it.

3. The court did not err in making findings and in entering judgment without notice to appellant.

Appellant was in default, and notice of subsequent proceedings is nowhere required by statute or rule of court. After default a defendant cannot be heard to contest the subsequent proceedings, and certainly it would be a useless thing to require notice of any to be served upon him. Norris v. Campbell, 27 Wash. 654, 68 Pac. 339.

Judgment affirmed.

[No. 2386]

IN THE MATTER OF THE APPLICATION OF J. B. DIXON FOR A WRIT OF HABEAS CORPUS.

[183 Pac. 642]

1. LICENSES—CITY OCCUPATION TAX.

   An admission to the bar of a state is a vested and valuable right, but subject to taxation, including a city occupation tax.

2. LICENSES—OCCUPATION TAX—UNIFORMITY—ATTORNEYS.

   A city ordinance, imposing a tax upon the occupation of attorney at law, *held* not in violation of Const. art. 10, sec. 1, providing for an equal and uniform rate of taxation.

3. LICENSES—LICENSE TAX ON OCCUPATION—CONSTITUTIONALITY.

   The imposition of a license tax upon an occupation is not illegal, because not expressly authorized by the state constitution, but is permissible, unless prohibited thereby.

4. HABEAS CORPUS—HEARING ON PETITION.

   On an original petition for habeas corpus by an attorney at law, convicted on failure to pay occupation tax, petitioner cannot be permitted to show that the facts proven on the trial at which he was convicted were not sufficient to constitute the crime charged.

5. HABEAS CORPUS—ORIGINAL PETITION—HEARING.

   In an original application for habeas corpus by one convicted of violation of an occupation-tax law, the court cannot consider the abuse of the lower court's discretion in refusing to grant a continuance of the trial in which the petitioner was convicted, or an objection to evidence as incompetent or the exclusion of evidence offered in petitioner's behalf.

ORIGINAL PROCEEDING in habeas corpus upon petition of J. B. Dixon. **Petition dismissed and petitioner remanded to custody.**

J. M. Frame and *J. B. Dixon* (in pro. per.), for Petitioner:

The right to practice law in the State of Nevada, under a license duly issued by the supreme court, is a vested right. The license is a contract in the highest sense, the obligations of which the legislature cannot impair by making additional requirements or by delegating to a municipality the right to impose a license tax. The license is imposed merely for the sake of the revenue to be derived from the tax. In the case at bar, the penal part of the ordinance is essentially an interference with vested rights, is in its nature prohibitive and in its operation ex post facto. "No state shall pass any law impairing the obligation of contracts." U. S. Const. art. 1, sec. 10. "The office which the party acquires is one of value." Bradley v. Fisher, 13 Wall. 354; In Re Garland, 18 U. S. 370; Pierce v. Carskadon, 16 Wall. 234, 21 L. Ed. 276; Cummins v. Missouri, 4 Wall. 277; Dartmouth College Case, 4 Wheat. 518, 4 L. Ed. 629; Fletcher v. Peck, 6 Cranch, 87.

The ordinance in question is unconstitutional, in that the tax sought to be imposed is not uniform and equal. (Const. Nev. art. 10, sec. 1.) Even in states where occupation licenses for revenue are allowed, it is necessary that they be uniform and graduated. Ala. Com. C. & I. Co. v. Roysburg, 59 South. 305; Braman v. Alameda, 124 Pac. 243; People v. Wilson, 94 N.'W. 141; State v. Doran, 134 N. W. 53; City v. Donoker, 108 Pac. 1086; Sacramento v. Crocker, 16 Cal. 119.

Neither the state nor the city of Reno has any right to levy an occupation tax, unless such right is specifically set forth in the constitution. Const. Nev. art. 10, sec. 1; 6 Am. & Eng. Ency. Law, 925, 931.

The petitioner is entitled to produce evidence to show that the facts proven on the trial were not sufficient to constitute the alleged crime. Eureka Bank Cases, 35 Nev. 80; 1 Bailey, Hab. Corp., p. 87, et seq.

Petitioner was entitled to a continuance, on account of the unavoidable absence of his counsel at the time the case was called for trial. State v. MacKinnon, 41 Nev. 182; Brown v. State, 47 S. E. 543; Boott v. State, 68 S. W. 171; Cornelius v. Commonwealth, 64 S. W. 412.

L. D. Summerfield, District Attorney, for Respondent:

"In the absence of any constitutional prohibition or restriction, it is within the undoubted power of the legislature to impose a tax upon employments, occupations, or vocations, or to authorize municipal authorities so to do." 4 Dillon, Mun. Corp. (5th ed.), sec. 1410; 25 Cyc. 599; 3 McQuillin, Mun. Corp. 986; City of Newton v. Atchison, 1 Pac. 288; Pollock v. Farmers' L. & T. Co., 39 L. Ed. 1108; Ex Parte Cohn, 13 Nev. 424.

The right to practice law may be taxed. 6 C. J. 570;
4 Cyc. 898; 4 Dillon, Mun. Corp., sec. 1408. A municipal license tax may be imposed, notwithstanding that a
state license also is required. Ex Parte Siebenhauer, 14
Nev. 365. The ordinances are constitutional. Gold-
thwaite v. City Council, 50 Ala. 486.

The ordinance does not impair the obligation of contracts nor take a vested right without due process of
law. Ex Parte Williams, 31 Tex. Crim. 262; 8 Cyc. 938;
Blanchard v. State, 18 L. R. A. 409. Neither does it
violate the constitutional provision as to uniformity of
taxation. 4 Dillon, Mun. Corp., sec. 1410; 3 McQuillin,
Mun. Corp., sec. 1001; Ex Parte Robinson, 12 Nev. 263.

The writ of habeas corpus is not intended to have the
force and effect of an appeal, writ of error, or certiorari,
nor is it designated as a substitute for either. Ex Parte
Smith, 2 Nev. 338; Ex Parte Winston, 9 Nev. 71; Ex
Parte Maxwell, 11 Nev. 428; Ex Parte Davis, 33 Nev.
309; Ex Parte Breckenridge, 34 Nev. 275. There is a
well-defined distinction between writs sued out before
and after a final judgment. 21 Cyc. 325, 326.

By the Court, COLEMAN, C. J.:

This is an original proceeding in habeas corpus.

Petitioner was proceeded against before the judge of
the municipal court of the city of Reno, charging him
with violating the ordinance of that city making it a
misdemeanor for attorneys to practice law without paying a license fee. Petitioner having been convicted as
charged, it was adjudged that he pay a fine, and in
default thereof that he be confined in jail. Failing to
pay the fine, petitioner was incarcerated as adjudged.
He now seeks to be discharged upon this writ, alleging
numerous reasons as grounds therefor.

1. The chief reasons urged upon our consideration are
that the ordinance is unconstitutional, in that it is in
violation of a vested right, that it is ex post facto, and
that it deprives petitioner of his property without due
process of law.

Counsel for petitioner cite authorities to the effect that an admission to the bar is a vested property right, and call our attention to what is known as the Lawyers' Tax Cases, 8 Heisk. (Tenn.) 565, as sustaining the contention that a license tax upon an attorney, such as here questioned, is in violation of the constitutional rights of a member of the bar, and is null and void. While counsel for petitioner has filed a very elaborate brief, citing many authorities, and by a process of reasoning satisfactory and convincing to himself of the soundness of his conclusion, the only case cited which sustains the view contended for by him is the Lawyers' Tax Cases, supra. But that case stands alone, and is by a divided court. In a note to Blanchard v. State of Florida, 18 L. R. A. 409, it is said:

"In Lawyers' Tax Cases, 8 Heisk. 565, decided by the Supreme Court of Tennessee in 1875, which case was also reported as Cardwell v. State, in 17 S. W. 109, in advance sheets only and left out of the permanent bound volume, a statute making it unlawful to practice law without payment of a license tax was held unconstitutional; two judges holding that the right to practice law could not be taxed, and two others holding that the practice of law by a duly admitted attorney without payment of the tax could not be made unlawful, while two judges held that the statute was constitutional. The serious division of opinion among the judges of the court much impairs the effect of the decision as an authority, and it is at any rate in conflict with all other cases on the subject."

In Stewart v. Potts, 49 Miss. 749, the Supreme Court of Mississippi disposes of the question, without citing an authority, in the following words:

"The only question made * * * is as to the constitutionality of the tax. This question is considered too well settled to require discussion. This right has been directly exercised by the federal government, and its equivalent has been practiced by this state ever since its organization. The same may be said of every state in the Union. If the tax is inexpedient, or excessive, the remedy is at the ballot-box."

In Young v. Thomas, 17 Fla. 169, 35 Am. Rep. 93, the court, passing upon the question, observed:

"The plaintiff in this case insists in his bill that the levy of this tax is in derogation of his vested rights as an attorney. In the language of the Court of Appeals of Virginia (Ould & Carrington v. City of Richmond, 23 Grat. [Va.] 469, 470, 14 Am. Rep. 139), 'a lawyer's license authorizes him to practice law in any court of the commonwealth. It is a vested civil right, yet it is as properly a legitimate subject of taxation as property to which a man has a vested right. I cannot perceive that there would not be as much reason for saying that a man's property was not taxable because he has a vested right to it, as for saying that a lawyer's license is not taxable because he has a vested right to it.' The matter of regulating the admission of persons to practice law is the subject of legislative action and control. At common law the courts had no power to admit attorneys or counselors. State ex rel. Wolfe v. Kirke, 12 Fla. 281, 95 Am. Dec. 314. Their duties are of such character that in order to secure proper qualification for their discharge the legislature imposes the duty of examination and determination upon the courts. The only difference between this pursuit and that of any other for which a license is not required is that a qualification looking to competency is required in one, and the right independent of qualification is in the other. Because the law prescribes certain methods by which the existence of the qualification to follow a pursuit is determined, and after determining their existence a general authority to follow such pursuit is granted, gives no greater right to follow that pursuit than exists in any citizen to follow any other legitimate calling or vocation. There is a general right in every citizen to acquire, possess and protect property, and yet in the absence of such constitutional limitation upon the power of taxation, it extends, as is said by Mr. Justice Cooley, 'to every trade or occupation, to every object of industry, use or enjoyment, and to every species of possession.' The power of the legislature to impose a license tax upon lawyers is affirmed in the following cases: State v. King, 21 La. Ann. 201; Simmons v. State, 12 Mo. 268, 49 Am. Dec. 131; Stewart v. Potts, 49 Miss. 749; Ould & Carrington v. City of Richmond, 23 Grat. (Va.) 464, 14 Am. Rep. 139; Jones v. Page & Stallworth, 44 Ala. 658."

In Cousins v. State, 50 Ala. 113, 20 Am. Rep. 290, the Supreme Court of Alabama, in sustaining a license tax on attorneys, used the following language:

"But it is contended that the lawyer alone is exempted from this power of regulation by the general assembly. This exemption he derives from the privilege to practice his profession at all, dependent upon his license as an attorney at law. In the technical sense of the word, the sense in which it is used in the statute, he is no lawyer without a lawyer's license to confer that privilege upon him. The license of an attorney at law creates his occupation simply. If he does not engage in its practice, he is not bound to pay the license demanded by the statute. If he does, then he must do so under the law which prescribed the conditions upon which the occupation may be engaged in or carried on. There is nothing particularly sacred in the profession or business of a lawyer, which puts him above the legislative power to place on his shoulders his just share of the necessary burdens of the state. If his share of this particular burden is unequal, and he complains of it for this reason, it will be removed; but, without this, he has no more right to avoid his duty than the tobacco dealer, the peddler, or the citizen who publishes a newspaper or bakes bread. The right to regulate the property and the vocations of its citizens by the state is sovereign, and it should neither be abrogated nor abandoned."

The court of last resort of Virginia, in disposing of the question presented in Ould & Carrington v. City of Richmond, 23 Grat. (Va.) 464, 14 Am. Rep. 139, said:

"Yet, whilst a lawyer's license authorizes him to practice law in any court of the commonwealth, and it is not in the power of any municipality to deprive him of that right, or to take away his license, it is a civil right and privilege, to which are attached valuable immunities and pecuniary advantages, and is a fair subject of taxation by the state, or by a municipal corporation where he resides and enjoys the privilege. It is a vested civil right; yet it is as properly a legitimate subject of taxation as property to which a man has a vested right. I cannot perceive that there would not be as much reason for saying that a man's property is not taxable, because he has a vested right to it, as for saying that a lawyer's license is not taxable, because he has a vested right to it."

That great constitutional lawyer and jurist, Judge Cooley, whose word is accepted as of persuasive force in considering such questions, states the rule in the following words:

"Lawyers are subject to such license taxes for practicing their profession as may be imposed by the state and by municipal authorities. The license authorizing them in the first instance to pursue their calling, is an evidence of character and capacity, and carries with it no exemption from taxation by license tax. The profession has no special privilege from that of other occupations. It is true that the right to impose an occupation tax on practitioners of law has been much contested, as depriving the attorney of a vested right, or as impairing the obligation of a contract, or as being, in effect, a tax on the privilege of seeking justice in the courts; but it has, nevertheless, been sustained with only faint dissent."

In Ex Parte Williams, 31 Tex. Cr. R. 262, 20 S. W. 580, 21 L. R. A. 783, it is said:

"But to tax the employment of a vested right has never been held to impair it, or interfere with its exercise. The question before us, then, is not whether defendant shall

be deprived of the right to practice law by forbidding the
exercise of the right, or by annexing conditions impossible of performance, as in the Garland case (4 Wall. 333,
18 L. Ed. 366), but whether, having been licensed and
permitted to practice, he may be taxed for the privilege
granted by the state; for, though a license be a vested
right, yet, unless there is something in the privilege by
which the state has relinquished the right of taxation,
it is presumed to be accepted subject to the power of the
state to impose upon its exercise a share of the public
burdens by way of taxation. Providence Bank v. Bill-
ings, 29 U. S. (4 Pet.) 553, 7 L. Ed. 953. This question
has been repeatedly before the courts of the country,
and, with but a single qualified exception, they have
declared that the practice of the legal profession is subject to an occupation tax, like any other occupation. In
the leading case of Ould v. Richmond, 23 Grat. 464, 14
Am. Rep. 139, the court says that, while the lawyer could
not be deprived of his right, except by the judgment of
a court, it was also a valuable civil right and privilege,
to which were attached valuable immunities and pecuniary advantages, and is a fair subject of taxation by
the state. Weeks, Attorneys at Law, sec. 41; Tiedeman,
Pol. Powers, 101; State v. Haynes, 4 S. C. 410; Jones
v. Page, 44 Ala. 658; Cousins v. State, 50 Ala. 113, 20
Am. Rep. 290; In Re Knox, 64 Ala. 465; Savannah v.
Hines, 53 Ga. 616; Wright v. Atlanta, 54 Ga. 645; Holland v. Isler, 77 N. C. 1; Wilmington v. Macks, 86 N. C.
88, 41 Am. Rep. 443; State v. King, 21 La. Ann. 201;
State v. Waples, 12 La. Ann. 343; Young v. Thomas, 17
Fla. 170, 35 Am. Rep. 93; State v. Gazley, 5 Ohio, 22;
State v. Hibbard and State v. Proudfit, 3 Ohio, 63; St.
Louis v. Laughlin, 49 Mo. 559."

See, also, Lent v. City of Portland, 42 Or. 488, 71 Pac.
645; City of Sonora v. Curtin, 137 Cal. 583, 70 Pac. 674.

The authorities all agree with one contention of petitioner, and that is that an admission to the bar of a
state is a vested and valuable right; but they go a step

further than petitioner, and hold that such vested right should be taxable, and rightly so. Why should a member of the bar who is engaged in the practice of his profession be free from taxation? Should he, merely because he has been adjudged qualified to pursue a certain calling and has acquired a vested right in consequence thereof, be more sacred than the peddler or the merchant? If there should be any preference, we can see no reason why the lawyer should be the privileged one. In his admission to the bar he is favored over the average citizen. He is protected. He is protected, in that no one else can invade the realm until designated by some authority as qualified to do so. But because he is thus favored for life, during good behavior, should that be pleaded as such a vested right as sets him apart from the rest of the world as one immune from sharing the burdens of the government which gives him protection? The man who acquires a right or privilege not enjoyed by all humanity ought to be willing to bear his share of taxation. The courts of the land, with a peculiar unanimity, have held, in no uncertain terms, that he should, and we are in accord with both the conclusions reached and the reasons given therefor.

2. It is next contended that the ordinance is in violation of article 10, section 1, of the Constitution of Nevada, which provides for an equal and uniform rate of taxation. It is not pointed out in just what way the taxation under this ordinance is not uniform. It provides for a graduated rate of taxation, based upon the individual income; and, as said in some of the cases in which this question is considered, it is impossible to attain uniformity to a mathematical exactness. In Ould & Carrington v. City of Richmond, supra, it was observed:

" * * * The tax ought to be proportioned, as nearly as practicable, to the value of that right and privilege. But exact justice and equality are not attainable, and consequently not required." [Citing authorities.]

In Ex Parte Robinson, 12 Nev. 263, 28 Am. Rep. 794,

the court, speaking through Hawley, J., held that the section of the constitution in question did not apply to licenses imposed for conducting any business or profession. To the same effect: Ex Parte Cohn, 13 Nev. 424; City of Ogden v. Crossman, 17 Utah, 66, 53 Pac. 985; Dillon, Municipal Corporations, vol. 4 (5th ed.) sec. 1410; McQuillin, Muncipal Corporations, sec. 1001.

3. It is also insisted that the imposition of a license tax is illegal, because not expressly authorized by the state constitution. Such is not the law. Dillon, Mun. Corp. ·(5th ed.) sec. 410, says:

"In the absence of any constitutional prohibition or restriction, it is within the undoubted power of the legislature to impose a tax upon employments, occupations, or vocations, or to authorize municipal authorities so to do."

Cyc. states the rule in the following language:

"In the absence of any inhibition, express or implied, in the state constitution, the legislature may, either in the exercise of the police power or for the purposes of revenue, levy license taxes on occupations or privileges within the limits of the state." 25 Cyc. 599.

The same rule is declared in 3 McQuillin, Municipal Corporations, sec. 986.

The Supreme Court of Kansas, speaking through Brewer, J., later one of the great justices of the Supreme Court of the United States, in considering this and other questions raised in this case, said:

"In the absence of any prohibition, express or implied, in the constitution, the legislature has power, either directly to levy and collect license taxes on any business or occupation, or to delegate like authority to a municipal corporation. This seems to be the concurrent voice of all the authorities. In 1 Dillon, Mun. Corp. (3d ed.) sec. 357, note, the author says: 'Unless specially restrained by the constitution, the legislature may provide for the taxing of any occupation or trade, and may confer this power upon municipal corporations.' In Burroughs, Taxation, 148, is this language: 'Where the

constitution is silent on the subject, the right of the state
to exact from its citizens a tax regulated by the vocations they pursue cannot be questioned.' In Savings
Society v. Coite, 6 Wall. 606, 18 L. Ed. 897, the Supreme
Court of the United States thus states the law: 'Nothing
can be more certain in legal decision than that the privileges and franchises of a private corporation, and all
trades and vocations by which the citizens acquire a
livelihood, may be taxed by a state for the support of
the state government.' Hamilton Co. v. Massachusetts,
6 Wall. 638, 18 L. Ed. 907; Cooley, Taxation, 384–392,
410. On page 394 the author observes: 'The same is
true of occupations; government may tax one, or it may
tax all. There is no restriction upon its power in this
regard, unless one is expressly imposed by the constitution.' In State Tax on Foreign-Held Bonds, 15 Wall.
300, 21 L. Ed. 179, Field, J., among other things, speaking of the power of taxation, says: 'It may touch property in every shape—in its natural condition, in its
manufactured form, and in its various transmutations;
and the amount of taxation may be determined by the
value of the property, or its use, or its capacity, or its
productiveness. It may touch business in the almost
infinite forms in which it is conducted—in professions,
in commerce, in manufactures, and in transportation.
Unless restrained by the constitution, the power as to
the mode, forms, and extent of taxation is unlimited.'
See, also, the authorities collected in Fretwell v. City of
Troy, 18 Kan. 274. Nor does this rest alone upon a mere
matter of authority. Full legislative power is, save as
specially restricted by the constitution, vested in the
legislature. Taxation is a legislative power. Full discretion and control, therefore, in reference to it, is
vested in the legislature, save when specially restricted.
There is no inherent vice in the taxation of vocations.
On the contrary, business is as legitimate an object of
the taxing power as property. Oftentimes a tax on the
former results in a more even and exact justice than one
on the latter. Indeed, the taxing power is not limited to

either property or vocations. It may, as was in fact
done during the late war and the years immediately
succeeding, be cast upon incomes, or placed upon deeds
or other instruments. We know there is quite a prejudice
against occupation taxes. It is thought to be really
double taxation. Judge Dillon well says that 'such taxes
are apt to be inequitable, and the principle not free from
great abuse.' Yet, wisely imposed, they will go far
towards equalizing public burdens. A lawyer and a
merchant may out of their respective vocations obtain
the same income. Each receives the same protection
and enjoys the same benefits of society and government.
Yet the one having tangible property pays taxes; the
other, whose property is all in legal learning and skill,
wholly intangible, pays nothing. A wisely adjusted
occupation tax equalizes these inequalities." City of
Newton v. Atchison, 31 Kan. 151, 1 Pac. 288.

4. It is urged that petitioner should be permitted to
produce evidence for the purpose of showing that the
facts proven on the trial at which he was convicted were
not sufficient to constitute the crime charged. To support this contention our attention is called to the Eureka
Bank Cases, 35 Nev. 80, 126 Pac. 655, 129 Pac. 308.
Those cases do not justify any such contention; and
this court, speaking through Hawley, C. J., in Phillips v.
Welch, 12 Nev. 158, squarely disapproved of such a
practice. The court said:

"No court can discharge on habeas corpus a person
that is in execution by the judgment of any other court
having jurisdiction of the subject-matter. * * *"

This statement is reasonable and unanswerable. If
any other position be taken, it will lead to interminable
litigation, and establish a rule that, in its consequences,
if carried to its logical conclusion, will destroy the force
of every judgment, until, perchance, the court of final
resort has put its stamp of approval upon it.

5. It is also contended that petitioner should be discharged because the trial court abused its discretion in
refusing to grant a continuance of the trial of petitioner,

and for the further reason that the trial court admitted, over objection, incompetent evidence, and refused to admit in evidence competent and material testimony offered in behalf of petitioner, "and in various ways prevented petitioner from having a fair and impartial trial." These are matters which a court cannot consider in a proceeding of this character.

Petitioner's brief presents some other points, but they are either disposed of by what we have said, or are so utterly without merit as not to justify specific consideration. The petition should be dismissed, and petitioner remanded to custody.

It is so ordered.

[No. 2339]

PIETRO CASSINELLI, Appellant, *v.* HUMPHREY SUPPLY COMPANY (a Corporation), Respondent.

[183 Pac. 523]

1. APPEAL AND ERROR—FINDINGS—CONCLUSIVENESS.
   A finding of fact based on a substantial conflict in material evidence is conclusive upon appeal.

2. APPEAL AND ERROR—FINDINGS—CONCLUSIVENESS.
   A finding based upon undisputed facts or the construction of a written instrument is not binding upon appeal.

3. SALES—ACTION FOR PURCHASE PRICE—ADMISSIBILITY OF EVIDENCE.
   In action for purchase price of hay destroyed by fire, evidence that a stick was placed in the hay to indicate amount covered by the sales agreement *held* immaterial on question whether hay subject to agreement was ascertained so as to pass title, where a subsequent written agreement fixed exact amount of hay sold.

4. SALES—PASSING OF TITLE—"SPECIFIC OR ASCERTAINED GOODS."
   Where all the hay in certain stacks was sold except thirty tons retained by the seller, the hay sold was "specific or ascertained goods" within uniform sales act, sec. 18, providing that the property in such goods is transferred at time the parties intend.

5. SALES—UNIFORM SALES ACT—CONSTRUCTION.
   Uniform sales act, sec. 19, prescribing several rules for ascertaining the intent of the parties as to when title passes, merely creates presumptions which give way if a contrary intent appears.

6. SALES—PASSING OF TITLE—UNIFORM SALES ACT.

Uniform sales act, sec. 19, rule 5, creating a presumption that title does not pass until the goods have been delivered, *held* inapplicable to an agreement under which certain hay was to be constructively delivered immediately after it had been measured.

7. SALES—PASSING OF TITLE—UNIFORM SALES ACT.

Uniform sales act, sec. 19, rule 1, creating a presumption that title is intended to pass where there is an unconditional contract to sell certain specific goods in a deliverable state, etc., *held* inapplicable to an agreement to sell all the hay in certain stacks except thirty tons to be retained by the seller.

8. SALES—PASSING OF TITLE—CONSTRUCTION OF CONTRACT.

A contract under which all hay in certain stacks was sold, excepting thirty tons to be retained by the seller, etc., *held* to make measurement of the hay a condition precedent to the passing of title despite the use of the words "bought" and "sold" in the contract.

9. SALES—DESTRUCTION OF GOODS—SELLER'S LIABILITY.

Under the direct provisions of uniform sales act. secs. 8, 22, the seller must bear the loss of hay covered by a sales agreement, but to which title had not passed, when it burned without the fault of either party.

10. SALES—EVIDENCE—ADMISSIBILITY.

In seller's action to recover purchase price of hay which defendant claimed had not been measured so as to pass title before it was accidentally burned, evidence that plaintiff's sons measured the hay after sales contract was executed, but before date agreed upon for measurement, *held* inadmissible to show compliance with contract.

APPEAL from Second Judicial District Court, Washoe County; *R. C. Stoddard,* Judge.

Action by Pietro Cassinelli against the Humphrey Supply Company. Judgment for defendant, and plaintiff appeals. **Affirmed.**

Mack & Green (*A. F. Lasher,* of Counsel), for Appellant:

There was a bona-fide sale of specified and ascertained property, though the quantity by which the whole purchase price was to be ascertained was not determined.

It can scarcely be denied that hay stacked in a deliverable condition, all raised and grown upon the same farm, is "fungible goods." The term "fungible" has been applied to grain, oil, and wine. Williston on Sales, sec.

159. It has also been applied to barrels of flour. Pleasants v. Pendleton, 6 Rand. 473, 18 Am. Dec. 726. So likewise to bales of cotton. Aderholt v. Embry, 78 Ala. 185; Phillips v. Acmulgee, 55 Ga. 633. It has been applied even to cattle and sheep. Walts v. Hindry, 13 Fla. 523.

Whether the transaction constituted a sale which passed the title from the seller to the buyer is simply a matter of intention of the parties. It is obvious that the intention disclosed by the record was that the buyer became the owner of the hay, leaving appellant no longer any right or title to dispose of the property to another, and no other interest in the property than a lien of an unpaid seller. Neither delivery nor the ascertainment of quantity were necessary prerequisites to the passage of title to the buyer. Williston on Sales, sec. 267.

Neither delivering, weighing, counting nor measuring of personal property is essential to the transfer of title. De Fonclear v. Shottenkirk, 3 Johns. (N. Y.) 1808; Graff v. Fitch, 58 Ill. 373. "Where the parties to a contract of sale intend a present vesting of title, the title passes at once though delivery is not to be made until later. Kneeland v. Renner, 2 Kan. App. 451; Byles v. Colier, 54 Mich. 1; Boswell v. Green, 25 N. J. Law, 390; Burt v. Dutcher, 34 N. Y. 493. When such is the intention of the parties, the sales become complete before the article sold has been weighed or measured or the price ascertained. Boswell v. Green, 25 N. J. Law, 390; Shealy v. Edwards, 73 Ala. 175; Chamblee v. McKenzie, 31 Ark. 155; Graff v. Fitch, 58 Ill. 373; Hagins v. Combs, 43 S. W. 222; Allen v. Elmore, 121 Iowa, 241.

The court erred in excluding evidence which tended to show what the intentions of the parties were with reference to the immediate transfer of title. "For the purpose of ascertaining the intention of the parties, regard shall be had to the terms of the contract, the conduct of the parties, usages of trade, and the circumstances of the case." Uniform Sales Act, Stats. 1915,

p. 199; 17 Cyc. 472, 670; 9 Ency. Ev. 377, 378, 381; Jones on Ev., sec. 455.

The court erred in refusing to admit evidence which was relevant, material and competent, and in ordering other proper evidence to be stricken from the record. The evidence offered and rejected bore directly upon the object which the parties had in view when they executed the written contract. It had a strong tendency to show that the parties intended to effect a present transfer of title by the agreement in the case. "The rule does not forbid an inquiry into the object of the parties in executing and receiving the instrument." Brick v. Brick, 98 U. S. 514; 2 Elliott on Contracts, secs. 1641, 1655.

Cheney, Downer, Price & Hawkins, for Respondent:

The issues raised in the case are whether at the time of the contract the hay was in a deliverable condition, whether it was delivered, whether anything remained to be done in reference thereto to pass the title from the plaintiff to the defendant, and whether it was the intention of the parties to so pass the title. The finding of the lower court was adverse to appellant. The questions of fact are not reviewable on this appeal. The only questions to be considered are, first, upon the fact as found by the court, did the title to the property and the risk of its loss pass from the seller to the buyer before it was destroyed by fire; and, second, did the court err in its rulings upon the admission of testimony and the motion to strike?

"If the terms of the bargain were not sufficient to enable a competent person to determine to what portion of the mass the bargain related, it would seem impossible, however, for the property to pass until the separation was made." Williston on Sales, secs. 158, 258.

The agreement provided that the hay was to be delivered. There had been no delivery. Delivery is a question of fact. Engemann v. Delaware L. & W. R. Co., 97 Atl. 152. "Delivery means voluntary transfer of

possession from one person to another." Uniform Sales
Act, sec. 76. The contract is wholly in writing. It is to
be considered by the court, and the intention of the parties is to be ascertained therefrom. Williston on Sales,
sec. 262; Foster v. Rope, 111 Mass. 10; Berney v. Alexander, 178 Pac. 979. "If the contract to sell requires the
seller to deliver the goods to the buyer, * * * the
property does not pass until the goods have been delivered to the buyer or reached the place agreed upon."
Under this section of the uniform sales act, where the
contract required the goods to be delivered, the courts
uniformly hold that title does not pass until there has
been delivery. Conroy v. Barrett, 158 N. Y. Supp. 549;
Hauptman v. Miller, 157 N. Y. Supp. 1104. This was the
established principle of law before the uniform sales act
was adopted. Atlanta B. S. Co. v. Vulcanite P. C. Co.,
203 N. Y. 133, 96 N. E. 370; Chandler G. & M. Co. v.
Shea, 213 Mass. 398, 100 N. E. 663. The hay in question never passed from the seller to the buyer. Conroy
v. Barrett, 158 N. Y. Supp. 549; Hauptman v. Miller,
157 N. Y. Supp. 1104; Bondy v. Hardina, 102 N. E. 935;
Barnard v. Tidrick, 152 N. W. 692.

The words "bought" and "sold" are frequently used
to express a mere agreement to sell. Walti v. Gaba, 116
Pac. 963. "Not too much stress must be laid upon the
use of the words 'sell' or 'buy' by the parties. These
words are constantly used as meaning or including contract to sell or contract to buy." Williston on Sales,
sec. 262.

The evidence objected to and stricken out was wholly
immaterial. Had it been admitted, the decision would
have been the same.

By the Court, DUCKER, J.:

The appellant, who was plaintiff in the court below,
brought his action against the Humphrey Supply Company to recover the unpaid purchase price of 296⅛ tons
of hay. The complaint alleges that at the time of the
sale the hay was in a deliverable condition, and was

agreed to be delivered and was delivered in the stack at and where the same was then stacked, and nothing remained to be done with reference thereto to pass the title to defendant, and it was the intention of plaintiff and defendant to pass the title to the hay by agreement, and that the title did thereby pass from plaintiff to defendant. It is also alleged that no part of the purchase price of said hay has been paid except the sum of $500, and the remainder of the purchase price of the hay, the sum of $2,468.33 is due, owing, and unpaid. All of these allegations are denied in the answer except the payment of the sum of $500, and in the counter-claim the return of this sum is demanded.

The answer also alleged the following agreement in writing.

"Humphrey Supply Company.   "No. 964.

"Dec. 1st, 1916.

"Bought of Peter Cassinelli the following. I have sold all of my hay to Humphrey Supply Co., except about thirty tons at Ten Dollars per ton to be measured by same rule as sold to Nevada Packing one year ago, to be fed by P. Cassinelli free or we can feed ourselves, Cassinelli to furnish team and wagons.

"The above hay to be delivered at once when measured and I hereby acknowledge receipt of $500.

"His mark X   Peter Cassinelli,
                                      "Seller.
"H. L. Nichols,
                                      "Buyer.
"W. E. Fuhrman."

On the issues thus made the trial court found that on December 2, 1916, all the hay referred to in this action was consumed by fire and destroyed; that at the time the hay was so burned and destroyed all of said hay was owned and in the possession of the plaintiff herein; that the hay in the stacks was not in a deliverable condition at the time it was burned, and had not been delivered to, or accepted by, the defendant; that the terms of said written agreement had not been complied with at the time the hay was burned; that the title to the hay or any of the hay referred to did not pass from the plaintiff to the defendant.

From the judgment rendered in favor of defendant and an order denying a motion for a new trial this appeal is taken.

A number of errors are assigned by appellant, and the principal one is that the court erred in finding that the hay in the stacks was not in a deliverable condition at the time it was sold, and had not been accepted by the defendant, and that the title had not passed from the plaintiff to defendant. It is insisted that such finding is not sustained by the evidence. On the other hand, respondent contends that the facts found are not reviewable here because they were found on a conflict of the evidence; and the only question we can consider in reference thereto is whether the conclusion that the title to the hay did not pass is a correct conclusion of law to be drawn from the facts found by the trial court.

1, 2. If there is a substantial conflict of the material evidence upon which the finding rests, this contention may be admitted. The question of whether the title passed depends entirely upon the intention of the parties, if the goods were specific and ascertained goods.

"If the intention is to be determined mainly from a construction of written instruments, the legal effect of which is for the court, and uncontradicted evidence, it is one for the courts." 24 R. C. L. sec. 275.

"The question is essentially one of fact; and though if the whole contract of the parties is reduced to writing this question is determined by the court, as also if the facts are so clear as to justify but one conclusion." Williston on Sales, sec. 262.

If the question is one for the court, either by reason of the construction of a written instrument or undisputed facts, this court is not bound by the findings or conclusions of the lower court, but may draw its own conclusion as to the legal effect of the written instrument or other evidence. 3 Cyc. p. 347.

The inquiry arises, therefore, as to how far the finding

of the court is based upon conflicting evidence, and necessitates a brief summary thereof.

On November 30, 1916, appellant was the owner of and in possession of two stacks of hay, situated upon his ranch near Reno, and on that day Mr. Small, representing the Humphrey Supply Company, went to appellant's ranch and entered into negotiations with him for the purchase of the hay for the compnay. The next day, Friday, December 1, appellant went to the office of respondent in Reno, and the agreement set out in the answer was executed by appellant and respondent. At the time of the execution of the agreement respondent gave appellant its check for $500. Mr. Small was present, and it was agreed between appellant and Mr. Small that they would measure the hay on the following Monday. At some time between the day the agreement was executed and the Monday following all the hay was burned through no fault of either party. This summary comprises all of the uncontradicted evidence that has any bearing upon the intention of the parties. There is also in the record the undisputed testimony of the two sons of the appellant that on December 1, at their father's instance, they measured the hay claimed to have been sold to respondent; but this evidence was retained in the record, by the ruling of the court, only for the purpose of showing the quantity of the hay, in case the court found that there had been a completed sale. The only evidence in which there is a conflict of a substantial nature is as to whether Mr. Small and appellant, when negotiating at the latter's ranch on November 30, segregated or identified the hay which respondent desired to purchase from the thirty tons which the appellant wished to retain. Appellant testified that on this occasion Small drove a stick in the stack on the east side to indicate the amount of hay he desired and the quantity reserved by appellant. Mr. Small testified that he did not put any stick in the stack and did nothing to designate the portion of the hay appellant was to keep for himself.

3. From the aforesaid ruling of the lower court on the

evidence of appellant's sons, and its judgment in favor of respondent, it is apparent that the court did not consider their testimony that they found a stick in the stack and measured from it when they measured the hay on December 1.

There is no intimation of a finding on this conflicting evidence in the findings of the trial court, nor is it mentioned in the brief oral opinion of the court incorporated in the record. Even if the stick was placed in the stack by respondents' agent, the act was, at the most, a mere estimation of the amount of hay desired, and was superseded by the written agreement which fixed the amount of hay to be taken by respondent and the amount to be retained by appellant to a definite number of tons, to be ascertained by actual measurement. The testimony of appellant and Mr. Small on this question was therefore immaterial, and a finding upon it, if made, would have been ineffective.

A consideration of the provisions of the sales act (Stats. 1915, c. 159) is necessary to a determination of the principal question involved.

We are admonished by the statute to so interpret and construe its provisions as to effectuate its general purpose to make uniform the laws of those states which enact it. Uniform Sales Act, sec. 74. Consequently a large number of the authorities cited by the appellant, having no reference to the uniform sales act, will not be considered as aids to our construction.

"It is apparent that, if these uniform acts are construed in the several states adopting them according to former local views upon analogous subjects, we shall miss the desired uniformity, and we shall erect upon the foundation of uniform language separate legal structures as distinct as were the former varying laws." Commercial Bank v. Canal Bank, 239 U. S. 520, 36 Sup. Ct. 194, 60 L. Ed. 417, Ann. Cas. 1917E, 25.

Section 76 of the act defines "goods" to "include all chattels personal other than things in action and money." By sections 17 and 18 of the act, goods are divided into two classes—"unascertained goods" and "specific or ascertained goods."

"SEC. 17.   Where there is a contract to sell unascertained goods, no property in the goods is transferred to the buyer unless and until the goods are ascertained, but property in an undivided share of ascertained goods may be transferred as provided in section 6.

"SEC. 18. (1) Where there is a contract to sell specific or ascertained goods, the property in them is transferred to the buyer at such time as the parties to the contract intend it to be transferred.   (2) For the purpose of ascertaining the intention of the parties, regard shall be had to the terms of the contract, the conduct of the parties, usages of trade, and the circumstances of the case."

It thus becomes important to ascertain which one of the classifications of the statute embraces the subject-matter of the controversy, for clearly, by the express prohibition of section 17, no property in the hay which was burned could have passed unless the property which respondent desired to purchase had been previously ascertained.   If the hay was specific or ascertained goods, the property could pass only at the time the parties intended it to be transferred, as provided in section 18.

4. Counsel for respondent contend that the hay was not "specific or ascertained goods," but we are of the opinion that it was.   It was in a specified mass of two two stacks of hay which had been examined by Mr. Small on November 30, and it does not appear from the agreement or circumstances attending it that any selection as to quality or other character was to be made. From the written agreement it appears that all of the hay was included in the arrangement, except about thirty tons reserved by appellant, and its terms exclude any legitimate inference that it was the intention of the parties that either allotment was to come from any portion or section of the stacks.   We need not determine whether the hay in the stacks was fungible goods or not, within the meaning of that section of the act which

defines fungible goods to be "goods of which any unit is from its nature or by mercantile usage treated as the equivalent of any other unit." It is sufficient that the parties in their agreement treated the hay as fungible goods by making no reservation for selection from any part of the mass. Conceding for the purposes of this decision that the hay was fungible goods, it was still specific and ascertained goods, for it was all in a specified mass, and considered the same in quality and value. If appellant had sold an undivided share of it to respondent, segregation would be necessary to give each his property in severalty; but before such severance the property of each in a proportionate share of the entire mass would be no less definite and ascertained. \ Kimberly v. Patchin, 19 N. Y. 330, 75 Am. Dec. 334; Kingman v. Holmquist, 36 Kan. 735, 14 Pac. 168, 59 Am. Rep. 604.

Section 6 of the uniform sales act provides for the transfer of fungible goods, and as we conclude that the subject-matter of the agreement comprehends specific or ascertained goods, as designated by section 18, we must look to the intention of the parties for the residence of title when the hay was burned.

5, 6. The uniform sales act, in section 19, prescribes several rules for ascertaining the intention of parties, and counsel for respondent contend that if the goods were specific rule 5 applies.

Of course these rules are mere rules of presumption, and by the terms of the act must give way if a contrary intention appears. Rule 5 reads:

"If the contract * * * requires the seller to deliver the goods to the buyer, or at a particular place, or to pay the freight or cost of transportation to the buyer, or to a particular place, the property does not pass until the goods have been delivered to the buyer or reached the place agreed upon."

This rule is declaratory of the common law. It is based upon a theory analogous to that supporting rule 2 of section 19—something further remains to be done, not, indeed, to put the goods in a deliverable state, but in order to carry out the bargain. Williston on Sales, par. 280.

Counsel base their contention in this respect upon the theory that the agreement obligates the appellant to deliver the goods as a condition precedent to the transfer of the property, and there was no delivery.

But it is not clear that the agreement effects such an obligation. The agreement contemplates delivery after measurement. This is plain from the language, "The above hay to be delivered at once when measured." And it is likewise clear that the delivery was intended to be made at the stack grounds, for it is apparent from the language used in the agreement, "to be fed by P. Cassinelli free or we can feed ourselves, Cassinelli to furnish the teams and wagons," that the respondent intended to feed the hay to stock directly from the stack grounds. The weakness, therefore, of respondent's contention that rule 5 applies lies in the fact that the agreement for delivery in no way changes the rule of law that in the absence of a contract, express or implied, or usage of trade to the contrary, the place of delivery is the seller's place of business, if he have one, and, if not, his residence. Uniform Sales Act, sec. 43. In the case before us the agreement merely provides for delivery at once after measurement at the stack grounds, which, under the facts of this case, constituted the appellant's place of business. The effect of the agreement in this regard is the same as if delivery had not been mentioned, but left to the implication of the law. To construe a contract of sale as vesting title to specific and identified property only on delivery to the buyer, or to a particular place, its terms evidencing such intention must be clear and explicit. "Slight evidence is, however, accepted as sufficient to show that title passes immediately on the sale, though the seller is to make a delivery." Benjamin on Sales, sec. 325.

The cases cited by counsel for respondent (Hauptman v. Miller et al., 94 Misc. Rep. 266, 157 N. Y. Supp. 1104, and Conroy v. Barrett, 95 Misc. Rep. 247, 158 N. Y. Supp. 549), wherein rule 5 is construed, and the contract involved held to be within the terms of that rule, and which they contend support their theory that the parties intended the transfer of the property to be dependent upon delivery, do not, in our opinion, sustain it. In the former case there was no contention that the rule did not apply. This was conceded by the plaintiff, who sought to show compliance with the contract by delivery to the defendant at their place of business, and the court held on appeal that he had failed to prove such delivery. In the latter case, of the facts and the law the court said:

"The contract not only required the sellers to deliver the goods to the buyer, but it also required the sellers to deliver the articles at a particular place. The sellers having agreed to make the delivery, they were bound to see that delivery was properly made, and the title to the article remained in them until the agreement of sale and delivery had been completed."

In the instant case it is apparent that only a constructive delivery was contemplated. No physical act on the part of appellant was necessary to accomplish delivery. The hay was to be fed from the stacks to respondent's stock. Delivery under these circumstances would necessarily have been incidental to and effectuated by the measurement made by the parties. An act so inconsequential would hardly justify the inference that it was intended as the event that was to transfer the property. We think the intention of the parties as to delivery was merely to postpone it until immediately after measurement, and therefore that rule 5 has no application.

7. Counsel for appellant insist that the true rule for ascertaining the intention in this case is formulated by rule 1, which provides:

"Where there is an unconditional contract to sell specific goods, in a deliverable state, the property in the goods passes to the buyer when the contract is made, and it is immaterial whether the time of payment, or the time of delivery, or both, be postponed."

This rule is also declaratory of a common-law rule, that if the buyer or seller makes a proposition of purchase or sale, and either accepts, and the goods are in possession of the seller, and nothing remains to be done to identify them, or in any way prepare them for delivery, the sale is completed, and the property in the goods passes at once. Time of payment or delivery is immaterial. This rule establishes a presumption that the title passes when the contract is made if the goods are identified, and nothing remains to be done other than delivery of the goods and payment of the price. Williston on Sales, sec. 264.

We think that this rule is also inapplicable.

8. The private matter in the transaction is the condition as to measurement, and, on the whole, it is fairly collectible that the parties intended this requirement as essential to consummate the sale In the written contract it is stipulated that the hay should be measured prior to delivery and by an agreed standard of measurement, "by same rule as sold to Nevada Packing one year ago."

The written contract is silent as to the time and by whom the measurement was to be made, but these factors are supplied by the understanding between Mr. Small and appellant at the time of the execution of the contract. Mr..Small testified, and it was uncontradicted by appellant, and corroborated by Mr. Nichols, that at that time appellant agreed that the hay should be measured the following Monday. It appears that Mr. Small and appellant were to participate in the measurement. Neither of the parties had waived the stipulations concerning measurement when the hay was burned. Both had the right to participate in the measurement of the hay. Delivery had been postponed by the express terms of the contract until after measurement. There was something more to be accomplished by the measurement than the mere ascertainment of the price to be paid for the hay.

It was a necessary act under the contract to separate appellant's thirty tons from the larger mass which respondent proposed to purchase, so that the latter could be fed from the stacks to its stock without incurring the danger of feeding any portion of the hay reserved by appellant.

If respondent had contracted for all of appellant's hay in the two stacks, then it would be certain that measurement could serve no purpose except to ascertain the price to be paid.

If such was the case here, then the rule contended for by appellant, and to sustain which he has cited numerous authorities, that property in goods will pass to the buyer though the goods sold are afterwards to be weighed, measured, or counted, might apply. This rule, however, has its most frequent application when there has been a delivery, and the quantity of goods sold is yet to be ascertained to fix the price. Benjamin on Sales, secs. 418–423. In this case, however, delivery having been specially postponed until after measurement, and the former being necessary, not only to ascertain the price, but to distinguish into severalty the subject-matter of the contract so that the acts of possession and ownership mentioned in the contract might be properly exercised over it, the circumstances strongly indicate that the parties regarded measurement as essential to complete the sale. The effect of the agreement and understanding concerning measurement was to make it impossible for the buyer to take possession of the property until that had been done. The measurement was "something further to be done," as stated in Williston on Sales, supra, "not, indeed, to put the goods in a deliverable state, but in order to carry out the bargain," and to put the buyer in possession of the property.

Considerable stress is laid by counsel for appellant upon the words "bought" and "sold," used in the contract, as indicating a present sale. These terms are frequently used in executory contracts, consequently their literal meaning is not necessarily evidence of a present sale.

In Elgee Cotton Cases, 22 Wall. (U. S.) 180, 22 L. Ed. 863, the contract of sale contained this expression: "We have, this 31st of July, 1863, sold unto Mr. C. S. Lobdell our crops of cotton," etc. The contract was held executory only:

"Not too much stress must be laid upon the use of the words 'sell' or 'buy' by the parties. These words are constantly used as meaning or including contract to sell or contract to buy." Williston on Sales, sec. 262.

We see no reason for attributing any particular significance to the buying and selling clauses of the contract.

The case of Welch v. Spies, 103 Iowa, 389, 72 N. W. 548, illustrates the distinction which may be drawn as to intention between the sale of an entire mass and a part of a larger mass from which reservations are made by the vendor. Plaintiff sold defendant not less than 1,600 nor more than 2,300 bushels of corn at so much a bushel, and received $50 of the purchase money. The corn was in two cribs, one containing 1,600 bushels intact, and the other, which had been opened, about 700 bushels. Plaintiff reserved a right to retain 200 or 300 bushels, if he needed them, and a third party was entitled to 50 bushels. The jury by its verdict found that the agreement was effectual to transfer the title to the 1,600 bushels only of corn in the crib which had not been opened. The court said the evidence to sustain the finding was ample.

In Kimberly v. Patchin, supra, 19 N. Y. 338, 75 Am. Dec. 334, the leading American case holding that, upon a sale of a specified quantity of grain, its separation from a mass indistinguishable in quality or value, in which it is included, is not necessary to pass title when the intention to do so is otherwise clearly manifested, the court recognized that in such a case it was quite possible and competent for parties to intend measurement as a condition to be performed before title vests in the purchaser. Upon this point the court said:

"Upon a simple bill of sale of gallons of oil or bushels of wheat, mixed with an ascertained and defined larger quantity, it may or may not be considered that the parties intend that the portion sold shall be measured before the purchaser becomes invested with the title. That may be regarded as an act remaining to be done, in which both parties have a right to participate. But it is surely competent for the vendor to say in terms that he waives that right, and that the purchaser shall become at once the legal owner of the number of gallons or bushels embraced in the sale."

We hold that, under the particular facts of this case, measurement was a condition precedent in the contract to the transfer of property in the hay, and that the title had not passed to the buyer when the hay was burned.

9. When the hay was burned the risk of the loss was with the seller, for there is nothing in the agreement to place the risk on the buyer. This proposition is made a positive rule of law by the terms of the uniform sales act.

With certain exceptions not presented by the facts of this case, section 22 of the act provides:

"Unless otherwise agreed, the goods remain at the seller's risk until the property therein is transferred to the buyer; but when the property therein is transferred to the buyer, the goods are at the buyer's risk, whether delivery has been made or not."

In the absence of agreement to the contrary, the risk is with the seller, though the goods are identified, till the moment when the property is transferred. If the goods are destroyed or injured before that time, the buyer cannot be compelled to pay the price, and, if he has paid the price in advance, it may be recovered. Williston on Sales, sec. 301.

The risk not having passed to the buyer when the hay was burned without the fault of either party, the contract was avoided. This is the effect of section 8 of the uniform sales act:

"When there is a contract to sell specific goods, and subsequently, but before the risk passes to the buyer, * * * the goods wholly perish, the contract is thereby avoided."

10. We find no error in the rulings of the court excluding and striking out certain testimony. The principal

objection in this regard is to the ruling of the court in striking out the testimony of plaintiff's sons respecting measurements which they made of the hay after the contract was executed and before the date agreed for measurement. This testimony was immaterial as tending to show compliance with the contract. It was pertinent only for the purpose of tending to establish the quantity of hay in the stacks in case the court found that there was a completed sale, and it appears that the court by its ruling retained the testimony in the record for this purpose.

In view of our opinion on the merits of the case, we have deemed it unnecessary to consider respondent's motion to dismiss the appeal.

The judgment of the district court is affirmed.

SANDERS, J.: I concur.

COLEMAN, C. J.: I concur in the order.

REPORTS OF CASES

DETERMINED BY

THE SUPREME COURT.

OF THE

STATE OF NEVADA

OCTOBER TERM, 1919

[No. 2394]

IN THE MATTER OF THE ESTATE OF CHARLES F. FORNEY, DECEASED.

[184 Pac. 206; 186 Pac. 678]

1. BASTARDS—LEGITIMATION MUST BE VALID IN STATE WHERE BASTARD AND FATHER LIVED.

   Legitimation of a bastard must be according to the law of the state in which she and her father had lived during their joint lives, to entitle her to take as his heir personal property which he left in another state.

2. BASTARDS—FOR LEGITIMATION FATHER MUST HAVE FAMILY INTO WHICH CHILD IS RECEIVED.

   Under Civ. Code Cal. sec. 230, for legitimation of a bastard, the father must have a family into which the child can be received.

ON PETITION FOR REHEARING

1. BASTARDS—LEGITIMATION, ONCE MADE, CANNOT BE REPUDIATED.

   Once a child born illegitimate has been legitimated, from such moment it acquires every legal right which a child born in wedlock can enjoy, its right of inheritance becomes fixed, and the father cannot repudiate his act in legitimating it.

2. BASTARDS—WHAT LAW GOVERNS LEGITIMATION.

   There can be only one proper state for the legitimation of a child born illegitimate; and, if it is not legitimated according to the laws of such state, it is not legitimated anywhere.

3. BASTARDS—LEGITIMATION CONTROLLED BY LAW OF STATE OF
   DOMICILE OF FATHER.

   Where a bastard child was born in California to a father
   there resident, and subsequently the father died leaving personalty in Nevada, the child cannot claim such personalty on
   any theory of legitimation under Nevada law, not having been
   legitimated in California, whose laws controlled.

4. APPEAL AND ERROR—NO CONSIDERATION ON REHEARING OF QUES-
   TION NOT URGED ON ORIGINAL HEARING.

   A question not urged in the supreme court on original hearing of the appeal cannot be considered on rehearing.

APPEAL from Second Judicial District Court, Washoe
County; *George A. Barlett*, Judge.

In the Matter of the Estate of Charles F. Forney,
Deceased. From the decree of distribution, and an order
denying a motion for a new trial, the administrator and
the State appeal. **Reversed. Petition for rehearing
denied.** SANDERS, J., dissenting.

Sardis Summerfield, for Appellant:

Under the law of California, decedent at no time occupied the legal status which enabled him by mere declarations and conduct to adopt claimant. Decedent was not
a man of family, and had no wife nor family home. In
order to prevail, claimant must bring herself squarely
within the provisions of the California statute. Cal.
C. C., sec. 230.

Legal adoption is purely a creation of statute law, and
was and is unknown to the common law. Blythe v.
Ayres, 96 Cal. 575; Estate of De Laveaga, 142 Cal. 169.

Adoption properly applies only to persons who are .
unrelated by blood to the adopting party. 1 Cyc. 917;
Morris v. Estate of Sessions, 70 Mich. 297; Russell v.
Russell, 84 Ala. 48; Vidal v. Commagere, 13 La. Ann.
516; People v. Norton, 59 Barb. 169; Brady v. Miles,
23 Ind. App. 432. Legitimation applies only to bastards
upon whom the parent confers the status of legitimacy.
5 Cyc. 632; Blythe v. Ayres, 96 Cal. 559.

The laws of California must control in the distribution
of the estate. Ross v. Ross, 129 Mass. 243; White v.
Tennant, 31 W. Va. 790; Smith v. Howard, 86 Me. 203;

Higgins v. Eaton, 188 Fed. 958; Hayes v. Pratt, 147 U. S. 570; Metcalf v. Lowther, 56 Ala. 318; Gibson v. Dowell, 42 Ark. 133. "The law of the domicile governs the distribution of personal property." Woerner's Law Amer. Admin., par. 565. "The law of the domicile of the parties is generally the rule which governs the creation of the status of an adopted child. 1 Cyc. 931. Even if the law of Nevada controls, respondent has failed to establish her heirship.

L. B. Fowler, Attorney-General, and *Robert Richards,* Deputy Attorney-General, for the State:

The decree and order appealed from should be reversed, with the direction to the lower court to enter its order and decree of escheat of the residue of the estate on the record as provided by law.

To entitle respondent to the residue of the estate, the record must bring her clearly within the provisions of law. The statutes of succession and distribution in all jurisdictions are not predicated on inherent right, since there is no natural right subsisting in any one to succeed to an ancestor's property at the time of his demise. 14 Cyc. 225; 8 Cyc. 894.

As the domicile of an illegitimate child is that of the mother, the laws of California are applicable to the facts of this case. "It is the rule of the American cases that the domicile of an illegitimate child is that of the mother." Louisville & N. R. Co. v. Kimbrough, 115 Ky. 512; McNicoll v. Ives, 3 Ohio N. P. 6, 4 Ohio S. & C. P. Dec. 75; Blythe v. Ayres, 96 Cal. 532; Cal. C. C., sec. 230; Garner v. Judd, 136 Cal. 395; Estate of De Laveaga, 142 Cal. 158. The existence of a family into which the child can be received is essential to an adoption under the statute. Estate of Gird, 157 Cal. 538; Estate of Jones, 166 Cal. 108.

Questions arising on similar statutes in other jurisdictions have been decided in accordance with the California decisions. Watson v. Richardson, 110 Iowa, 673; Morton v. Morton, 62 Neb. 427.

James T. Boyd and *Harlan L. Heward,* for Respondent:

Our courts have jurisdiction where property is situated in the state. When its status is established, the law gives the child a right of succession and a right to inherit whatever property the father might be possessed of in this state. The law of California is not the same as ours. It establishes a right of succession to property in that state and what acts are necessary upon the part of the father of an illegitimate child to give the child the right to inherit property in that state. Such statutes have no extraterritorial force. Hood v. McGehee, 189 Fed. 205; Brown v. Finley, 21 L. R. A. 679; Blythe v. Ayres, 96 Cal. 532; In Re Loyd's Estate, 148 Pac. 522.

The respondent claims the property by virtue of the statute of Nevada. Rev. Laws, 5833; Van Horn v. Van Horn, 45 L. R. A. 93; Brown v. Finley, 21 L. R. A. 679.

By the Court, COLEMAN, C. J.:

Charles F. Forney, long a resident of Truckee, Cal., died leaving on deposit in certain banks in Reno, Nevada, the sum of $4,500. The public administrator of Washoe County, Nevada, qualified as administrator of the estate, and in due time filed his final report and petition for distribution, which alleges:

"That the whole of said estate is the separate property of said decedent, and that your petitioner is informed and believes, and therefore alleges the fact to be, said decedent at the time of his death left him surviving no wife, nor father, nor mother, nor sister, nor brother, nor any children, nor ancestors, nor descendants, whomsoever, and left him surviving no heir or heirs at law or next of kin whatsoever, and, according to the best information and belief of your petitioner, all the rest, residue, and remainder of said estate should escheat herein and be distributed to the State of Nevada pursuant to the provisions of law."

On the 10th day of April, 1915, one Gladys Pohl, by and through her guardian ad litem, filed in the matter of said estate her petition, reciting that she was the daughter of the deceased and one Minnie Pohl; that she was born at the town of Truckee, Cal., on the 6th day of April, 1908, and that ever since her birth she had continued to reside with her mother in said town; that the said Forney, on various and divers occasions, publicly acknowledged the said Gladys Pohl to be his daughter; that he provided her with the common necessaries of life, and informed various and divers persons that the said Gladys Pohl was his daughter, and that he intended to care and provide for her as a father should; that said Gladys Pohl is the only child of deceased, and that there are no other heirs. Said petition concludes with a prayer that the estate of the deceased be distributed to her after the payment of all charges of administration.

Upon the hearing, the court found the facts to be as alleged in the petition of said guardian, and entered a decree accordingly. From the decree, and from an order denying a motion for a new trial, the administrator and the state have appealed.

1. Counsel for appellants contend that the statute of California controls in determining whether or not Gladys Pohl was legitimated by Forney during his lifetime, while counsel for respondent argue that the statute of Nevada controls. The petition filed in behalf of the minor does not allege facts sufficient to make out a claim under the California law, in that it fails to allege that Forney received the child into his family.

A child's right to inherit depends upon its status. There must be some fixed place where the status of the child can be established. What better place than the residence of both parties? Common sense and reason both so dictate. The status of a child is not an ambulatory thing, which can be shifted from place to place to suit any condition that may arise. If any other rule prevailed, and Forney had left money on deposit in several states, the minor might be permitted to lay claim to the deposits in all of them except the state in which she and Forney had lived during their joint lives, which would be, it seems to us, a reflection upon the law. It was to avoid such absurd results that led to the establishing of the rule recognized in Ross v. Ross, 129 Mass. 243, 37 Am. Rep. 322, and therein expressed in the following language:

"It is a general principle that the status or condition of a person, the relation in which he stands to another person, and by which he is qualified or made capable to take certain rights in the other's property, is fixed by the law of the domicile, and that this status and capacity are to be recognized and upheld in every other state, so far as they are not inconsistent with its own laws and policy. Subject to this limitation, upon the death of any man, the status of those who claim succession or inheritance in his estate is to be ascertained by the law under which that status was acquired; his personal property is indeed to be distributed according to the law of his domicile at the time of his death, and his real estate descends according to the law of the place in which it is situated; but, in either case, it is according to those provisions of that law which regulate the succession or inheritance of persons having such a status."

This rule is recognized by and stated in Woerner's American Law of Administration (2d ed.) at section 565, as follows:

"It has been repeatedly stated that the law of the domicile governs the distribution of personal property, so that it is unnecessary to cite authorities here in support of this principle."

It is said in 1 Cyc., p. 931:

"The law of the domicile of the parties is generally the rule which governs the creation of the status of an adopted child."

There may be some exceptions to the general rule laid down, but these exceptions are made in favor of persons domiciled in the state in which the property is situated. 22 R. C. L., p. 42, sec. 8.

In opposition to the rule laid down, counsel for respondent rely upon the cases of Hood v. McGehee (C. C.) 189

Fed. 205, Brown v. Finley, 157 Ala. 424, 47 South. 577, 21 L. R. A. (N.S.) 679, 131 Am. St. Rep. 68, 16 Ann. Cas. 778; Blythe v. Ayres, 96 Cal. 532, 31 Pac. 915, 19 L. R. A. 40, and In Re Loyd's Estate, 170 Cal. 85, 148 Pac. 522. We do not think any of the cases cited sustains the contention. In the first case mentioned, real estate was involved, and question as to the adoption of the plaintiffs was not in controversy. It was purely a question as to whether or not adoptive children by proceedings under the laws of Louisiana, or the defendants, the next of kin, should inherit under the laws of Alabama. The court said:

"Each state has exclusive jurisdiction of the regulation of the transfer and descent of real estate within its limits. It would be competent for the legislature of Alabama to deny the right to inherit real property to children adopted in its own courts by its own procedure. It would be competent for it to confer such rights on children of its own adoption and deny it to those of the adoption of foreign states. This is what Alabama legislation, as construed by its court of last resort, has accomplished."

In the Loyd case the question here presented was not considered nor disposed of. In the case of Blythe v. Ayres the child sought to recover under the laws of California, the state in which the father had lived, and where all the declarations and acts relied upon to establish legitimation had taken place. In the opinion we find nothing repugnant to the rule stated. Brown v. Finley seems to sustain the contention made for it, but it is not in accord with the general rule, and does not appeal to our sense of what the law ought to be.

.2. Having reached the conclusion that the law of California controls, let us inquire what the law of that state is as to the legitimating of a child born out of wedlock. Section 230 of the Civil Code of California reads as follows:

"The father of an illegitimate child, by publicly acknowledging it as his own, receiving it as such, with the consent of his wife, if he is married, into his family, and otherwise treating it as if it were a legitimate child, thereby adopts it as such; and such child is thereupon deemed for all purposes legitimate from the time of its birth. The foregoing provisions of this chapter do not apply to such an adoption."

This statute has been construed by the Supreme Court of California in several cases, and in the matter of the Estate of De Laveaga, 142 Cal. 158, 75 Pac. 790, it was held that the existence of a family into which a child could be received was essential to an adoption, and in Estate of Gird, 157 Cal. 534, 108 Pac. 499, 137 Am. St. Rep. 131, the court, in speaking of this question, said:

"Different views have been entertained by justices of this court whether the existence of a family into which the child can be received is essential to an adoption under this section, but that question has been finally determined in the affirmative by this court in Estate of De Laveaga."

In addition to the California cases cited in the briefs of counsel, we call attention to In Re Walker's Estate (Cal.) 181 Pac. 792; In Re McNamara's Estate (Cal.) 183 Pac. 552, decided August 25, 1919. There is now pending and undecided before the Supreme Court of California the case of In Re Estate of Baird (No. S. F. 8995), in which the same question is involved. What constitutes a "family" has been a question of much concern before the Supreme Court of California.

But it not being contended that Forney had a family into which he could have taken the child, or that he did take her into his family, we are compelled to direct a reversal of the order and judgment appealed from, and that a new trial be granted; respondent to have leave to amend his petition, as he may be advised.

The judgment and order appealed from are reversed.

SANDERS, J., dissenting:

The State of Nevada and the public administrator of Washoe County, Nevada, through their joint and several notices of appeal, have appealed to this court from a decree and order adjudging and decreeing Gladys Pohl, a resident of the State of California, to be the lawful heir and distributee of the estate of Charles F. Forney, deceased, who died intestate (living and domiciled in the State of California, at Truckee, Cal.), on or about the 25th of October, 1913, and by their appeal have succeeded in having it authoritatively determined that, in this jurisdiction, the rule of comity or private international law must be applied to the succession and distribution of said estate, the case not being within the exceptions to either rule. From this, in my opinion, it follows that both justice and comity demand that the appellants before proceeding further should voluntarily move the lower court to remit the fund involved in this controversy to the place of the decedent's domicile to be distributed according to the foreign law. There are no creditors, either local or domiciliary, or any citizen or citizens of this state to be affected by such an order. That it is competent for the lower court to make an order transferring the residue of an estate in this situation, to be handed over to some person authorized by proper authority to receive it at the domicile of the deceased, I consider undoubted. Gravillon v. Richard's Exr., 13 La. 293, 33 Am. Dec. 563. Should the appellants oppose an application for such an order, on the ground that Gladys Pohl is an illegitimate child of the deceased and not capable of inheriting under the foreign law, it would bring to the attention of the lower court a matter overlooked by the experienced and able counsel for the appellants and respondent, which I deem to be pertinent and controlling in so far as the State of Nevada is concerned in the succession or escheat of said estate. The State of Nevada does not come in by way of succession, but by an action or information of escheat to vest title to the residue of the estate in the hands of the public administrator in the State of Nevada. Escheat is not succession. It is the very opposite of succession. It is what happens when there is no succession. Estate of Miners, 143 Cal. 194 (dissenting opinion), 76 Pac. 968.

Before the State of Nevada can successfully assert its

claim of escheat, it must affirmatively appear that the person seized of the estate, real or personal, died within this state. Rev. Laws, 6130. The information filed by the state in the district court, alleging the state to be escheatable, does not contain such an allegation, but it is conceded, or must be conceded, that Forney died without and not within the State of Nevada. It is true, the statute provides that if the intestate shall leave no husband or wife, nor kindred, the estate shall escheat to the state for the support of the common schools. As amended, Stats. 1917, p. 37. It is also true that every citizen dying is presumed to leave some one entitled to claim as his heir, however remote, unless one or the other of the two exceptions known to the law—alienage or illegitimacy—should intervene. People v. Fulton Fire Ins. Co., 25 Wend. (N. Y.) 205.

Escheat in this jurisdiction depends upon positive statute. Like forfeiture, it is not favored. 10 R. C. L. 613.

Our statute provides:

"If any person shall die, or any person who may have died, within this state, seized of any real or personal estate, and leaving no heirs, representatives, devisees or legatees capable of inheriting or holding the same, and in all cases where there is no owner of such estate capable of holding the same, such estate shall escheat to and be vested in the State of Nevada." Rev. Laws, 6130.

This statute dates back to territorial days. It was the territorial law (Stats. 1861, p. 240), which was carried into the state law, and has remained on our statute books unchanged by amendment or supplement down to the present time.

The case as made by the state clearly falls within the purview of the first clause of the section that deals expressly with heirs capable of inheriting or holding the estate of a person who dies or died within the state. It is useless for me to enter upon an exhaustive discussion of this legislation. Its reason and purpose are obvious.

The motives and conduct of these high officers—the

attorney-general and the public administrator of Washoe County—are not questioned. They have sought with great zeal and ability, in the performance of their duty, to reach beyond the limits of the local law to enrich the State of Nevada at the expense of an unfortunate child, recognized by the local law to be an heir and entitled to the distribution to her of the fund here litigated. The question is one of strict legal right, and unless the right of the state can be maintained under its own law, which, in my view, cannot be successfully done, it follows that the information filed in the district court by the attorney-general, alleging that the residue of the fund in the hands of the public administrator of the estate of Charles F. Forney, deceased, is escheatable, should be dismissed.

Entertaining these views, it is not necessary for me to discuss the motion to dismiss the appeal of the public administrator. I have, however, a strong impression that he is in a much better position to appeal from the judgment and decree than the State of Nevada.

ON PETITION FOR REHEARING

By the Court, COLEMAN, C. J.:

Counsel have filed a petition for a rehearing. It is an earnest plea in behalf of the unfortunate child; and, were it our duty to yield to the impulses of humanity. rather than to be controlled by cold principles of law, we would likely heed the same. But while all law is bottomed upon the theory that it works justice, there is no delusion that any abstract rule of law can in all cases work out results which satisfy our humanitarian instincts. The Creator, in establishing the laws of nature, well knew that the rain would fall upon the just and the unjust alike, and that, while the operation of every law of nature would injure some, the great masses of humanity would benefit thereby. So, in this case, we must lay down a rule which will be disastrous to the petitioner, but which, in the course of years, will effectuate justice in the great majority of cases. In fact, we are laying down no new rule; we are simply adhering to well-established principles.

Counsel, after conceding the necessity of determining the status of Gladys Pohl, say that it must be determined under the law of this state. That is the sole question before the court. Upon our first consideration of the case, we were convinced as to the law which controls in establishing the status of the child. It seemed so clear to us at that time that we were, perhaps, somewhat lax in reasoning out the question. In response to the contention urged upon us, let us ask: Why should the question of the child's status be determined under the law of Nevada? This leads us to ask: What is a status? Is it an imaginary thing? Is it something which comes into existence to meet a temporary need, and which, when it has served the temporary purpose, may be abandoned? Or is it something which is permanent and enduring and which continues to exist to meet changing conditions and new situations in life, defying the will of the adopting parent himself, and even a change of the law? A child's status is nothing more nor less than its relationship to some other person, or to the state. We are aware that some courts seem to have had trouble in disposing of the question before us, but it seems clear that the trouble was due to a superficial, rather than to a careful, consideration of the underlying reasons which led up to the passage of statutes permitting the legitimation of bastards by the father, such as exist in California and Nevada.

1-2. It being established that a child is once legitimated, from that moment it acquires every legal right which a child born in wedlock can enjoy. Its right of inheritance becomes fixed. Could its father, after once legitimating a child, repudiate that act? Could he then, through pique, disappointment, the conduct of the mother, the adherence of the child to its mother's cause in a controversy between the father and mother, a new liaison, or an imaginary grievance against the child itself, denounce the child as an illegitimate, recall his former acts of adoption, and make illegitimate one whom he had solemnly made legitimate? We say no; that the status of legitimacy once established is established for all times, conditions, purposes, and states. Conversely, we say that there can be only one proper state for the legitimation of a child, and, if it is not legitimated according to the laws of that state, it is not legitimated anywhere. When and where, then, does legitimation take place? Does it take place in the state of the legitimating parent, and at the time and place of the performing of the act of legitimating, or does it take place in a foreign state, and at some time other than the performing of the act?

3. As of what time can it be said that Forney legitimated the child in Nevada? Had he left no property in Nevada, would any one say the child was legitimated in this state? We think not. But the fact that he left money in this state is sought to be made the turning-point of the case. A child's status cannot be made to turn upon the existence or nonexistence of an estate. There are things more sacred to most of us than property, and one of them should be a person's status as to legitimacy.

The logic of counsel's argument is to make the status of the child turn upon the fact that Forney left personal property in this state. It seems to us that they have put the cart before the horse. The right to inherit depends upon the child's status, and not its status upon the existence of an estate in Nevada. If counsel's theory is correct and were carried to its logical conclusion, a situation might present itself wherein a child would be legitimate in Nevada and enjoy all the rights and privileges thereof, and be illegitimate in California, for the reason that the California statute pertaining to the legitimating of an illegitimate requires things not required in Nevada, while it is the policy of the law to hold legitimate everywhere a child once legitimated. 5 R. C. L. 920.

And, further, if counsel's theory is correct, a father,

having once legitimated a child in Nevada, where the law as to legitimating a bastard is not so rigid as in California, and being unable to obviate the force and effect of such legitimation in this state, but being desirous of accomplishing the same result, and of depriving such child of its right to inherit, and to make sure of doing it, and the facts not being such as would constitute a legitimating in California, would simply have to transfer his property from Nevada to California. What court would sanction such an act? Status does not depend upon the existence of inheritable property, but the right to inherit does depend upon the child's status. And we might say, parenthetically, that since realty is distributed according to the lex loci rei sitæ and personalty according to the lex domicilii, the question in this instance is whether or not the child was legitimated under the laws of California. In view of the fact that both the deceased and the child were at all times domiciled in California, and of the fact that personalty is distributed according to the law of the domicile, we have never considered the question a debatable one. Nor is it. The Blythe case, 96 Cal. 532, 31 Pac. 915, 19 L. R. A. 40, mentioned in our former opinion, really decides the question. That was a case in which Blythe, domiciled in San Francisco, while on a visit to England, begot the child in question. After its birth, and while it was living in England, he performed acts in California which were held sufficient to legitimate the child under the California law, and the court held that, in determining the status of the child, the law of the parent's domicile controlled.

Professor Minor, in his Conflict of Laws, in discussing the question as to what law governs in fixing the status of a child, says, at section 100:

"Two points should be noticed in this connection, which will aid us in determining the proper law in this case. The first is that the legitimation of a bastard is the creation of a status which is beneficial to him, and it should be presumed in his favor whenever adequate reason exists for such a course. The second is that this beneficial status cannot be accorded the infant at the expense of a change of status on the part of the father not warranted by his domiciliary law.

"Applying these two principles, it follows that the law of the father's domicile at the time of the legitimating act will be the proper law to determine the status of both parties. If by that law the act in question legitimates the bastard, the beneficial status thus created will in general be recognized everywhere, including the bastard's domicile, though by the law of the latter state the act would not suffice to create a legitimation. On the other hand, if by the law of the father's domicile legitimation is not the result of the act claimed to have that effect, though under the bastard's domiciliary law legitimation would result therefrom, the status of legitimation should not be conferred upon the bastard, for that would be to subject the status of the father to a law to which it is not properly subject."

The Supreme Court of Massachusetts, in Irving v. Ford, 183 Mass. 448, 67 N. E. 366, 65 L. R. A. 177, 97 Am. St. Rep. 447, quotes the above language approvingly; and adopts the rule therein stated. And it was said in Richmond v. Taylor, 151 Wis. 633, 139 N. W. 435:

"So, also, the law of the domicile of the person making the written acknowledgment, and not that of the domicile of the child or the mother, governs the question of legitimation."

See, also, 7 C. J. 951.

As to the case of Wolf v. Gall, 32 Cal. App. 286, 163 Pac. 347, we simply wish to say that we have never attached any weight to it, so far as the question in this case is concerned; for, no matter what significance might be given it under ordinary circumstances, the Supreme Court of California, on appeal (32 Cal. App. 286, 163 Pac. 351), held that it was not entirely in accord with its reasoning. In any event, we would hardly be justified in assuming that an inferior court can reverse a superior one; and, so far as we are advised, the law as laid down in the Blythe case is still good in California.

But counsel say that it has been repeatedly announced that the courts of California will decide such questions as this according to the laws of that state, regardless of international law, or any other law, and hence there can be no law of comity between this state and California upon the question. No decision of the California court so holding has been called to our attention. The Blythe case, in our opinion, refutes the statement, if anything. In that case the court awarded the estate to a child which had been born in England and had never seen America until after the death of its father, and the opinion turned upon the proposition that the law of the domicile of the father controlled a rule which we know to be supported by practically all of the authorities in the United States, and as well, we believe, by sound reason. Had the child in that case been domiciled in Nevada, the same rule would have governed.

4. Counsel insist that the state cannot claim the money in question by escheat. This question was not urged upon us nor considered upon the original hearing; and, as said on rehearing in Nelson v. Smith, 42 Nev. 302, 176 Pac. 261, 178 Pac. 625, it cannot be now considered. But it seems to us that the point is out of the case. Petitioner must stand or fall upon her rights as a legitimated child. If she was not legitimated, she cannot take the property, and it matters not to her what becomes of the etsate.

The petition for rehearing is denied.

SANDERS, J.: I dissent.

[No. 2404]

IN THE MATTER OF THE APPLICATION OF LOUIS PIEROTTI FOR A WRIT OF HABEAS CORPUS.

[184 Pac. 209]

1. GAMING—NICKEL-IN-THE-SLOT MACHINE GAMBLING DEVICE.
   Nickel-in-the-slot machines, by which a player has a chance of losing the amount he plays or receiving a larger amount. are well-known gambling devices.

2. GAMING—NUISANCE—GAMING-HOUSES NUISANCES AT COMMON LAW.
   While at common law gaming or gambling was not itself unlawful, and is not now a crime unless so made by statute, yet at common law public gaming-houses were nuisances, not only because they were deemed great temptations to idleness, but because they were apt to draw together numbers of disorderly persons.

3. LOTTERIES—NICKEL-IN-THE-SLOT MACHINES, THOUGH GAMBLING DEVICES, NOT LOTTERIES.
   A nickel-in-the-slot machine, although a gambling device and expressly brought within the purview of the earlier gambling statutes, is not a lottery. within Const. art. 4, sec. 24, declaring that no lotteries shall be authorized in the state; and hence the state legislature may, as it did in Stats. 1915, except slot machines for the sale of cigars and drinks and no backplay allowed.

4. CONSTITUTIONAL LAW—WHETHER ALLOWING NICKEL-IN-THE-SLOT MACHINES INJUDICIOUS QUESTION FOR LEGISLATURE.
   Whether a law allowing nickel-in-the-slot machines to a limited extent is unwholesome is a question for the legislature or the people, and not the courts.

ORIGINAL PROCEEDING. Application of Louis Pierotti for a writ of habeas corpus. Writ issued.

Norcross, Thatcher & Woodburn, for Petitioner:

Sections 6494 and 6495 of the Revised Laws do not embrace or include the device or slot machine mentioned in the complaint. The acts and things which petitioner is charged with having committed are not prohibited under the laws of the State of Nevada, but are specifically excluded from the operation of the law denouncing and making criminal the use of slot machines. Stats. 1915, p. 462.

The word "lottery," as used in section 24, article 4,

Constitution of Nevada, and section 6494 of the Revised Laws, does not contemplate a slot machine.

Legislative and executive construction has been adopted and acted on with the acquiescence of the people for many years, which, in the absence of any imperative reason for the contrary, should be accepted as a correct interpretation of the constitutional provision. Bruce v. Schuyler, 4 Gilman, 221; Comstock v. Cover, 35 Ill. 470; People v. Loewenthal, 93 Ill. 191; People v. Board, 100 Ill. 495; People v. Fidelity & Casualty Co., 153 Ill. 25; People v. Olson, 92 N. E. 157; Worthington v. District Court, 37 Nev. 244; State v. Cole, 38 Nev. 215; State v. Brodigan, 35 Nev. 38; State v. Glenn, 18 Nev. 34; State v. Grey, 21 Nev. 378.

"Questions relating to the policy, wisdom and expediency of the law * * * are not for the courts to determine." Ex Parte Boyce, 27 Nev. 299, 65 L. R. A. 47, 1 Ann. Cas. 66; Gibson v. Mason, 5 Nev. 283.

Criminal statutes must be strictly construed. In their interpretation, words in common use are to be construed in their natural, plain and ordinary signification. 36 Cyc. 1114; Shulthis v. MacDougal, 162 Fed. 331; Austin v. Cahill, 88 S. W. 542; Ex Parte Deidesheimer, 14 Nev. 311; Ex Parte Davis, 33 Nev. 316.

L. B. Fowler, Attorney-General; *Robert Richards*, Deputy Attorney-General; *L. D. Summerfield*, District Attorney, and *W. M. Kearney*, Deputy District Attorney, for Respondent:

The writ should be discharged and the petitioner remanded the custody of the law. Slot machines are "lotteries" within the meaning of the constitution and the statutes. All questions involved in this proceeding have been finally settled by the decisions of this court. Ex Parte Blanchard, 9 Nev. 104; State v. Overton, 16 Nev. 136.

The statute has enlarged upon the term "lottery," and kindred schemes and devices. Rev. Laws, 6494, 6495.

"Calling it, by name, a 'slot machine,' instead of a

'lottery machine,' does not vary its character." Loiseau v. State, 22 South. 138; Paulk v. Jasper Land Co., 22 South. 495; City of New Orleans v. Collins, 27 South. 532; Johnson v. State, 34 South. 1018; Meyer v. State, 37 S. E. 96.

No city ordinance or legislative statute can make lawful the use of any lottery device, in the face of the constitutional inhibition against lotteries. Barry v. State, 45 S. W. 571.

By the Court, SANDERS, J.:

The thing or device denominated in the complaint "a lottery" is a "nickel-in-the-slot machine." The act complained of is that the petitioner wilfully and unlawfully set up a nickel-in-the-slot machine in his place of business at 128 Commercial Row, in the city of Reno, Nevada.

The offense charged, with the word "lottery" entirely removed therefrom, would be a public nuisance.

Every place wherein any gambling game or device is kept, or any article, apparatus, or device useful therefor is kept, "shall be a public nuisance." Rev. Laws, 6561.

1. Nickel-in-the-slot machines have a well-defined meaning in criminal law.

"Slot machine by which the player has a chance of losing the amount he plays is a * * * gambling device." Territory v. Jones, 14 N. M. 579, 99 Pac. 338, 20 L. R. A. (N.S.) 239, and note, 20 Ann. Cas. 128, and note; 12 R. C. L. pp. 721, 726, 728, 729.

It would be idle for us to deny that chance is the material element in the operation of such machines. The player hopes to get cigars or drinks for nothing. The dealer hopes chance will save him from giving something for nothing. If it were not for the chance to win cigars or drinks, the customers of the dealer would not use the machine. Lang v. Merwin, 99 Me. 486, 59 Atl. 1021, 105 Am. St. Rep. 293.

Since the year 1901, in this jurisdiction, nickel-in-the-slot machines played for cigars and drinks (now, perforce of the statute, nonintoxicating drinks, Stats. 1919, p. 1) are expressly brought within the purview of gambling statutes. Stats. 1901, c. 13, 1905, c. 52, 1907, c. 212, 1908–1909, c. 210, 1913, c. 149, and 1915, cc. 30, 284.

2. At common law "gaming" or the synonymous term "gambling," was not in itself unlawful, and is not now eo nomine a crime, unless so made by statute. 12 R. C. L. 708. "But at common law all public gaminghouses were nuisances, not only because they were deemed great temptations to idleness, but also because they were apt to draw together great numbers of disorderly persons." Scott v. Courtney, 7 Nev. 419.

3. Our legislature, in the exercise of its powers over the policy and morals of the people, found it desirable to declare every place wherein any gambling game or device is kept, or any article, apparatus, or device useful therefor is kept, to be a public nuisance. But in 1915 the legislature (Stats. 1915, c. 284), in legislating upon the subject of gambling, found it desirable and expedient to modify the stringent provisions of the antigambling law by inserting therein a proviso:

"Provided, however, that nothing in this paragraph shall be construed as prohibiting social games played, only for drinks and cigars served individually, or for prizes of a value not to exceed two dollars, nor nickel-in-the-slot machines for the sale of cigars and drinks and no playback allowed."

The paragraph referred to in the proviso reads:

"Every person who shall play at any game whatsoever, other than those hereinabove excepted, for money, property, or gain, with cards, dice or any other device which may be adapted to or used in playing any game of chance, or in which chance is a material element, or who shall bet or wager on the hands or cards or sides of such as do play as aforesaid, shall be deemed guilty of a felony."

It is obvious that the purpose of the proviso was to exempt players at such machines from prosecutions for a felony, and also to declare places wherein such gambling devices are kept to be unlawful places. If it was competent for the legislative body to pass the act declaring every place wherein a gambling device which is adapted and used for the purpose of gambling to be a public nuisance, it must be conceded that it was competent for that body by the adoption of the proviso to make the place, which but for the statute would be a public nuisance, a lawful place. It is true as a general proposition that courts will not hold conduct to constitute a nuisance where authority therefor exists by virtue of legislative enactment. This rule is supported by abundant authority. 20 R. C. L. 500 and note. But it must be observed that this rule is subject to the limitation above indicated, that it must be competent for the legislative body in the first instance to declare the thing or place a nuisance. This is a matter for judicial determination and brings us to the real and only point to be determined in this proceeding. Has the legislature, by the adoption of the proviso above quoted, sanctioned a lottery?

Unless gambling devices, such as nickel-in-the-slot machines, may be said to be brought within the constitutional inhibition (art. 4, sec. 24)—"No lotteries shall be authorized by this state"—the legislature has not exceeded its power in adopting the proviso in question. A lottery is defined by statute to be any scheme for the disposal or distribution of property, by chance, among persons who have paid or promised to pay any valuable consideration for the chance of obtaining such property, or any portion of it, * * * whether called a lottery, raffle or gift enterprise, or by whatever name the same may be known. Rev. Laws, 6494. It would seem from this comprehensive language to have been the intention of the legislature to prevent every pecuniary transaction in which chance is a material element. In this connection it may be said that we are entirely in accord with what is said in the case of State v. Overton, 16 Nev. 136, an able and exhaustive discussion of the subject of lotteries.

There is no doubt that nickel-in-the-slot machines amount to the disposal of property by chance, but whether or not they amount to setting up, proposing or drawing a lottery as the word "lottery" is used in the constitution—"No lottery shall be authorized by this state" (Const. art. 4, sec. 24)—is an entirely different question. There can be no doubt of what was meant by this language of the constitution, and it clearly referred to the class of enterprises which had formerly been lawful if authorized by law, and criminal if unauthorized. People v. Reilly, 50 Mich. 384, 45 Am. Rep. 47.

It is contended by the state that the word lottery, as defined by the statute, expresses both the intention of the framers of the constitution and the legislature to prohibit the enactment of any law that sanctions the disposal of property by chance, "by whatever name the same may be known."

"It is a safe and necessary rule to construe criminal statutes so as to include what is fairly and reasonably within the legitimate scope of the language, but not to include what is not within the language merely because it partakes of similar mischievous qualities." People v. Reilly, supra.

It is true that in common parlance, in a dictionary sense and the statutory definition, the word "lottery" may be a game. But the legislature of this state, since the date of its organization as a state, has plainly drawn a distinction between lotteries and unlawful gaming. This distinction is universally recognized as being within the power of such bodies to make in the absence of any constitutional inhibition. Both are offenses against the law, and both are offenses against public policy. Temple v. Commonwealth, 75 Va. 901. The reason for the distinction is not difficult to find. A lottery is prohibited by the constitution as a public nuisance—a crime against the good order and the economy of the state. Rev. Laws, 6561. It is a crime that goes to the destruction of the morals of the people and paralyzes the industrial energy of society. From the language employed in the constitution it is evident that this was the understanding of its framers. Ex Parte Blanchard, 9 Nev. 104. "It is this extensive reach, and not merely its speculative purposes, which makes lottery gambling so dangerous" as to be a proper subject for constitutional prohibition. The reason for the distinction is forcibly expressed by the highest court of the land in this language:

"The suppression of nuisances injurious to public health or morality is among the most important duties of government. Experience has shown that the common forms of gambling are comparatively innocuous when placed in contrast with the widespread pestilence of lotteries. The former are confined to a few persons and places, but the latter infests the whole community; it enters every dwelling; it reaches every class; it preys upon the hard earnings of the poor; it plunders the ignorant and simple." Phalen v. Commonwealth, 8 How. 163, 12 L. Ed. 1030.

It is true that lotteries and unlawful gaming partake of the same mischief. They belong to the same family. Chance is the material element in both. The legislature is prohibited from legislating upon one and permitted by virtue· of its inherent powers to legislate upon the other as the occasion arises. This for the reason of the wide distinction or contrast between the vice of lotteries which infests the whole community and the mischief or nuisance of gambling which is generally confined to a few persons and places. To say that the legislature is without power to legislate upon the subject of gaming is to set at naught the basic power of the legislative branch of the government.

But it is urged that a nickel-in-the-slot machine for the sale of cigars and drinks is a gambling scheme or device for the disposal or distribution of particular classes of property, and is therefore brought within the statutory definition of lotteries, regardless of gambling statutes. Conceding this to be true, the question here is: Had the legislature the power to make such devices the subject of separate and distinct legislation because of their gambling qualities? The legislature derives its power to legislate upon such gambling devices from its inherent authority over the morals and policy of the people, and not from the statutory definition of lotteries.

The fact that the legislature had, by the proviso in question, sanctioned the adaptation and use of nickel-in-the-slot machines to stimulate the disposal of cigars and drinks by appealing to and arousing the gambling propensities of visitors to places where such devices are set up, does not change the character of the device from a gambling to a commercial transaction. But for its being a "gamble" customers would not use it. Gambling is the same yesterday, today, and forever. It is for the legislature, and not courts, to draw the line of demarcation between the varied kinds. It is not the province of courts to confound by construction what the legislature has made clear.

It is further argued that it is "automatic gambling," and easily distinguished from other forms of gambling, such as those games excepted from the operation of the antigambling law — poker, stud-horse poker, five hundred, whist, and solo, where the deal alternates. This we regard as being a distinction without a difference, and an admission that such machines are gambling devices and not lotteries, unless it be said that the excepted games are different from automatic gambling devices, in that skill is the material element in such games and not chance. This is absurd. Any game played with cards in which the hand at cards depends on a dealing with the face down is a game of chance. 12 R. C. L. 717.

It is argued that the language of the proviso, "for the sale of cigars and drinks," means "sales" as defined by law. There is no such thing as a "sale" by chance. To say that the restriction placed on the player in the proviso, "no playback allowed," applies to "sales" or to "lotteries," is impracticable, if not unreasonable.

It is insisted by counsel for the state that calling the scheme by name a slot machine instead of a lottery machine does not change its character. Neither does the fact that the proviso limits its operation and restricts the player exert any influence in determining its character. In support of this contention counsel quote extensively from the opinion of this court in the case of State v. Overton, supra. In that case the court had under review a special statute that clearly sanctioned a lottery; but the court, in addressing itself to the point that all schemes or devices in which chance is a material element are lotteries, did not see fit to include in its illustrations automatic gambling games, which we assume to have been then in operation in this state, such as faro, roulette, keno, and such gambling devices. It is fair to presume that had the court been of the opinion that the word "lottery" included these devices it may have properly brought them within the purview of the constitutional inhibition against lotteries. If these devices are lotteries, so are slot machines.

We are also referred to the case of Loiseau v. State, 114 Ala. 34, 22 South. 138, 62 Am. St. Rep. 84. In that case the indictment contained three counts: First, that defendant did unlawfully set up, carry on, or operate a device of chance, to wit, a slot machine; second, that he did unlawfully sell chances in a device of chance, to wit, a slot machine; and third, that defendant did set up, or was concerned in setting up or carrying on, a lottery, to wit, a slot machine. The defendant was convicted upon the first two counts. It will be observed that the indictment itself makes a distinction between gambling and lotteries, and the court in its opinion plainly recognizes the distinction by the use of this language:

"The evidence is the case authorized a conviction under either the first or second count of the indictment, and we are not prepared to say that he might not have been properly convicted under the third count."

The other cases cited by the state are taken from those jurisdictions where the word "lottery," as used in the organic law or statute, is extended by construction to all the various forms of gambling. The effect of these decisions is to say that gambling is per se a public nuisance, and therefore is brought within the constitutional and statutory prohibitions against lotteries.

4. It is useless to continue this discussion. The law in question may be considered unreasonable and unwholesome, but the motive that prompted the legislature in exempting from the operation of the antigambling law slot machines of the character here discussed is no concern of ours. It is a matter for the people or their representatives.

The criminal complaint in this case charges the petitioner with the crime of contriving, operating, setting up, proposing, and drawing a lottery, to wit, a nickel-in-the-slot machine for the sale of cigars and drinks, and no playback allowed.

Entertaining the views hereinabove expressed, we are clearly of the opinion that the complaint does not state a public offense, and the petitioner is entitled to be discharged from arrest on habeas corpus.

Let the writ issue.

[No. 2381]

OSCAR NEHLS AND FAY STANLEY, RESPONDENTS, *v.* WILLIAM STOCK FARMING COMPANY, APPELLANT.

[184 Pac. 212; 185 Pac. 563]

1. FRAUDS, STATUTE OF—PART PERFORMANCE HAS NO APPLICATION TO CONTRACT NOT TO BE PERFORMED WITHIN A YEAR.

    A contract not to be performed within one year is void (Rev. Laws, 1075), notwithstanding part performance; the doctrine of part performance having no application to such contract, and the statute being aimed exclusively at the time of performance, and not the subject-matter.

2. FRAUDS, STATUTE OF—PART PERFORMANCE TAKES LAND CONTRACTS OUT OF THE STATUTE.

    Part performance takes land contract out of statute of frauds when not to enforce the contract would result in a fraud being perpetrated upon a party who has partially performed.

3. FRAUDS, STATUTE OF — LESSOR OF HORSES AND TEAMS NOT ESTOPPED TO SHOW INVALIDITY OF CONTRACT.

    Where lessees hired horses to plow and seed land, after lessor had refused to furnish horses, and without being misled by any act or acts on part of lessor, lessor is not estopped from setting up invalidity of its parol contract to furnish horses under statute of frauds in lessees' action for damages for breach thereof.

ON PETITION FOR REHEARING

1. FRAUDS, STATUTE OF—ESTOPPEL TO SET UP STATUTE TO PREVENT PERPETRATION OF A FRAUD.

    In an action for a breach of an oral contract by which lessor was to furnish lessee with horses for seeding and harvesting a crop, whatever sum the plaintiffs spent in securing horses and operating the farm did not induce a change of position of plaintiffs, but was the result of a change of position, so that the doctrine of estoppel would not apply to prevent the defendant lessor from setting up the invalidity of the agreement under the statute of frauds, on the ground that the plea of the statute would work a fraud.

2. APPEAL AND ERROR—RAISING DEFENSES NOT MADE IN TRIAL COURT.

    Where, in an action for breach by lessor of his oral contract to furnish horses for making a crop, the matter of estoppel to set up the invalidity of the oral agreement under the statute of frauds because of the changed position of plaintiff was not a matter of evidence or contest at the trial, it cannot be relied on, on appeal.

3. FRAUDS, STATUTE OF—CHANGED POSITION OF PLAINTIFF INSUFFI-
CIENT TO ESTOP DEFENDANT FROM PLEADING STATUTE.

In lessees' action against lessor for breach of an oral contract to furnish horses to plant and harvest a crop, evidence
of lessees' changed position in accepting lease and oral agreement is insufficient to show the working of a fraud, and
thereby estop lessor from setting up the invalidity of the oral
contract under the statute of frauds, where there was no evidence that the plaintiffs could not obtain the identical employment they left to accept the lease and oral contract.

APPEAL from Sixth Judicial District Court, Humboldt
County; *Edward A. Ducker,* Judge.

Action by Oscar Nehls and another against the
William Stock Farming Company. Judgment for plaintiffs, and defendant appeals. **Reversed. Petition for
rehearing denied.**

Cheney, Downer, Price & Hawkins, for Appellant:

Respondents base their right to recover damages upon
an alleged violation of an alleged oral agreement, upon
the part of appellant, to furnish respondents, for the
entire term of five years, sufficient work horses. Therefore the alleged right to a money judgment is founded
upon an oral "agreement that, by the terms, is not to be
performed within one year from the making thereof,"
which said agreement is, by the statute of frauds,
declared to be void.

A contract partly in writing and partly oral is, in legal
effect, an oral contract. Snow v. Nelson, 113 Fed. 353.

Respondents admitted upon the trial that their cause
of action, the alleged oral agreement to furnish necessary horses for the five-year term, was within the
statute of frauds, but contend that by part performance
the case was taken out of the statute. Part performance
is not available in any case, except where the doctrine
of equity is invoked, as in an action for specific performance; but this is not an action for specific performance.
Rev. Laws, 1073, 1075; Pomeroy, Contracts (2d ed.) p.
141, Sheldon v. Preya, 57 Vt. 263; Osborne v. Kimball,
21 Pac. 153; Conoly v. Harrell, 62 South. 511; Johnson

v. Upper, 80 Pac. 801; Union S. & T. Co. v. Krumm, 152 Pac. 681; 20 Cyc. 284; 29 Am. & Eng. Ency. Law (2d ed.), p. 831; Thisler v. Mackey, 47 Pac. 175. "It is settled by a long series of authorities that a part execution of a verbal contract within the statute of frauds has no effect at law to take the case out of its provisions." Browne, Stat. Frauds (5th ed.), sec. 451; Long v. Long, 122 Pac. 1077; Fuller v. Read, 38 Cal. 99.

Salter & Robins, for Respondents:

No demurrer was interposed to the complaint on the ground of uncertainty or ambiguity. After verdict and judgment the court will look to the complaint only to see whether it attempts to set forth the cause of action, even though the allegations are contained only by way of recital. The defect, if any, is cured by verdict. Treadway v. Wilder, 8 Nev. 91; Winter v. Winter, 8 Nev. 129; Branson v. I. W. W., 30 Nev. 289.

By partial performance, the case is taken out of the statute of frauds. Jones on Ev., par. 432. In addition, the respondents have spent two years in carrying out their contract, and have materially changed their situation, to their financial loss, in their endeavor to carry out their part of the contract, the subject of the action. Seymour v. Oelrichs, 106 Cal. 88. "Contracts within the statute are not void, and, if performed or partly performed, they are, to the extent of such performance, taken out of the statute. When executed, or so far as executed, such contracts are valid, and as binding as if they had been in writing." Murphy v. DeHaan, 89 N. W. 100.

"The general rule under discussion is not violated by allowing parol evidence to be given of the contents of a distinct, valid, contemporaneous agreement between the parties which was not reduced to writing, when the same is not in conflict with the provisions of the written agreement." Jones on Ev., sec. 439; New York L. I. Co. v. Thomas, 104 S. W. 1074; Locke v. Murdock, 151 Pac. 298.

By the Court, COLEMAN, C. J.:

This is an action to recover damages for an alleged breach of contract. The complaint as amended pleads a written lease of certain lands for a period of five years, of date August 23, 1915, and also an oral contract whereby it is alleged the defendant agreed, as an inducement to the making of the lease, to furnish to plaintiffs, for a period of five years (during the term of the lease), without charge, sufficient horses to cultivate the land so leased and to harvest the crops. It is alleged in the complaint that plaintiffs entered into possession of the lands leased on November 14, 1915, and during the year 1916 cultivated and harvested a crop and surrendered one-third thereof to defendant as rental; that plaintiffs requested defendant to furnish them horses to plow and prepare lands for the crop of 1917, but that defendant refused to furnish the necessary horses, to wit, forty head; that because of such refusal plaintiffs rented fourteen head of horses at an outlay of $893; that they were damaged in the sum of $7,339 because of the failure to get the balance of the horses; and it contains certain other matters not necessary to state. An answer was filed denying the execution of the verbal contract; denying all other material allegations of the complaint, except execution of the written lease; pleading the statute of frauds, and setting up two causes of action as counter-claims. The reply admits the indebtedness pleaded in the counter-claims.

Upon the trial of the case, before a jury, plaintiffs offered evidence tending to prove that the defednant company orally stipulated and agreed with the plaintiffs to furnish sufficient horses to plow the ground leased; that in June, 1916, they demanded of defendant horses to prepare the land for the crop of 1917; that forty head of horses were necessary for the seeding and harvesting of the crop of 1917; that defendant refused to furnish the same, or any part thereof; that the plaintiffs hired fourteen head at an expense of $893, and that, because of defendant's refusal to furnish said forty head of horses, plaintiffs had been damaged in a large sum of money.

The defendant objected. to the testimony so offered, for the reason that such agreement relative to the furnishing of horses, not being in writing and not to be performed within one year, was within the statute of frauds (Rev. Laws, 1075), and null and void. The trial judge overruled the objections, to which ruling exceptions were taken. From a judgment in favor of plaintiffs, defendant has taken this appeal.

It is the contention of appellant that the judgment must be reversed, because the oral contract relied upon being for five years was within the statute of frauds, and null and void. It is not contended by respondents that the contract was one which was to be completed within a year, but it is asserted that it is taken out of the operation of the statute of frauds by partial performance.

1-2. Learned counsel have made in this court, as they no doubt did in the trial court, a very ingenious argument in support of their contention, and one which would appeal to and sway a trial judge who, in the bustle and rush incident to a jury trial, has not the time to give mature consideration to such arguments. After much reflection and investigation, we are convinced that the contention of the learned counsel cannot be sustained. The doctrine of part performance does not apply to contracts of the character here in question, but to contracts relating to land, when not to enforce the same would result in a fraud being perpetrated upon a party who has partially performed. The statute in question is aimed exclusively to the time of performance, and not to the character or subject-matter of the contract. The rule applicable to the situation here presented is enunciated in Pomeroy on Contracts (2d ed.) p. 141, as follows:

"The clause relating to contracts not to be performed within a year from the making thereof seems, by its very terms, to prevent any validating effect of part performance on all agreements embraced within it. As the prohibition relates not to the subject-matter, nor to the nature of the undertaking, but to the time of the performance itself, it seems impossible for any part performance to alter the relations of the parties, by rendering the contract one which, by its terms, may be performed within the year. It has, indeed, been held in some cases that, if all the stipulations on the part of the plaintiff are to be performed within a year, an action will lie for a breach of the defendant's promise, although it was not to be performed within the year and was not in writing. In all these cases, however, the promise of the defendant was simply for the payment of the money consideration, which might, in every instance, have been sued for and recovered upon his implied promise; and the doctrine itself has been expressly and emphatically repudiated by numerous other decisions."

This rule is recognized by ample authority. In Osborne v. Kimball, 41 Kan. 187, 21 Pac. 163, in considering just such a contention as is here made, the court says:

"The doctrine of partial performance is not applicable to this class of contracts. It is confined only to those relating to lands, the nonexecution of which would operate as a fraud upon the party who had made partial performance to such an extent that he cannot be reasonably compensated in damages. It is an equitable principle, frequently invoked in actions for the specific performance of parol contracts for the purchase of land, under which possession had been taken, improvements made, and where there has been payment or partial payment of the purchase price. The courts are slow to introduce additional exceptions, or to depart further from the strict letter of the statute of frauds, and even in the contracts of the class mentioned full payment of the purchase money is not a sufficient performance to take them out of the statute. Nay v. Mograin, 24 Kan. 80. We have heretofore had occasion to deny the enforcement of contracts other than those relating to land, and which were not to be performed within one year, where they had been partially performed, and we see no reason to extend the doctrine of enforcing such oral contracts upon the ground of part performance."

In another case in which the question arose the court used the following language:

"The respondent insists that there was such part performance both of the logging contract and of the hauling contract as to take them out of the statute of frauds. The doctrine of part performance, however, has no application to this clause of the statute of frauds. In the nature of the case, where the statute is directed solely to the time of performance and not to the character or subject-matter of the contract, part performance could not remove the ban of the statute without in effect repealing the statute." Union S. & T. Co. v. Krumm, 88 Wash. 20, 152 Pac. 681.

The case of Conoly v. Harrell, 182 Ala. 243, 62 South. 511, is also in point. Plaintiff and defendant entered into an oral agreement for the employment of plaintiff for a period exceeding one year, wherein it was agreed that in addition to a monthly salary the plaintiff should receive one-fourth of the net profits of the business. The court said:

"It appears from the bill that the monthly salary of complainant was paid to him up to November 1, 1907, for twelve months after the service began November 1, 1906. The contract alleged was an entirety. It was indivisible. Martin v. Massie, 127 Ala. 504, 29 South. 31. The partial (not complete) performance of the contract did not take it out of the statute of frauds. Scoggin v. Blackwell, 36 Ala. 351; Treadway v. Smith, 56 Ala. 345. The ground of the demurrer asserting that the agreement relied on was obnoxious to the statute of frauds should have been sustained."

In a note to Diamond v. Jacquith, L. R. A. 1916D, 880, the editor says:

"The rule that part performance will prevent the operation of the statute so far as performance has

gone, can, by the nature of things, have no application
to actions for the breach of contract. In such actions
recovery is based not upon what has been done under
the contract but upon the loss accruing from what has
not been done. Therefore, even in jurisdictions which
have adopted that rule, there can be found no ground
upon which to base a right of recovery for the breach of
a contract not to be performed within a year. It may
consequently be stated as a rule without exception that
the part performance of services under a parol contract
not to be performed within a year does not remove the
contract from the operation of the statute of frauds, so
that an action may be maintained for its breach, either
by the master or servant."

But counsel for respondent strenuously contend that
the defendant should be estopped from pleading and
urging the statute of frauds, and rely upon the case of
Seymour v. Oelrichs, 156 Cal. 782, 106 Pac. 88, 134 Am.
St. Rep. 154. That was a case in which Seymour, who
had a life position as captain of detectives in San Francisco, at a monthly salary of $250, entered into an oral
agreement with the defendants whereby he was to
resign as captain of detectives and accept a position
with them for ten years at a monthly salary of $300.
The defendants repudiating the contract, Seymour
brought suit. The defendants pleaded the statute of
frauds. The court held that because of the fact that
Seymour had been induced to give up his life position,
to which he could not be reinstated, defendants' refusal
to comply with the verbal agreement operated as a fraud
upon the plaintiff, and sustained the plea of estoppel.
The court said:

"The claim of plaintiff is not that mere part performance of a contract for personal services which by its
terms is not to be performed within a year, 'invalid'
under our statute because not evidenced by writing,
renders the same valid and enforceable. Such a claim
would, of course, find no support in the authorities.
Browne on Statute of Frauds, sec. 448. He necessarily

is compelled to rely solely on the claim that defendants by their conduct and promises, upon which he was entitled to and did rely, having induced him to give up his life position in the police department in order to enter their employ for a term of years at $300 a month, on the assurance from them that they would give him a written contract for such time and amount, and it being impossible for him to be placed in statu quo, are estopped from now setting up the statute of frauds as a defense to his action on the contract. Under this claim, the fact of part performance by plaintiff plays no part whatever. It was the change of position caused by his resignation from the police department upon which his claim wholly rests, and this resignation was, of course, no part of the performance of the contract of service, but was something that must be done by plaintiff before he could begin to perform, as was known to the defendants. Plaintiff's case, in this regard, would be just as strong if after his resignation he had been prevented by defendants from beginning to perform.

"The right of courts of equity to hold a person estopped to assert the statute of frauds, where such assertion would amount to practicing a fraud, cannot be disputed. It is based upon the principle 'thoroughly established in equity, and applying in every transaction where the statute is invoked, that the statute of frauds, having been enacted for the purpose of preventing fraud, shall not be made the instrument of shielding, protecting or aiding the party who relies upon it in the perpetration of a fraud or in the consummation of a fraudulent scheme.' 2 Pom. Eq. Jur., sec. 921. It was said in Glass v. Hulburt, 102 Mass. 24, 35, 3 Am. Rep. 418: 'The fraud most commonly treated as taking an agreement out of the statute of frauds is that which consists in setting up the statute against its enforcement, after the other party has been induced to make expenditures, or a change of situation in regard to the subject-matter of the agreement, or upon the supposition that it was to be carried into execution, and the assumption of rights thereby to be acquired; so that the refusal to complete the execution of the agreement is not merely a denial of rights which it was intended to confer, but the infliction of an unjust and unconscientious injury and loss. In such case, the party is held, by force of his acts or silent acquiescence, which have misled the other to his harm, to be estopped from setting up the statute of frauds.'"

3. Accepting the rule laid down in the Seymour case for our guidance in this case (and we know of no case more favorable to the plaintiffs), without expressing any view as to its correctness, still the plea of estoppel is not available. The Seymour case turned upon the proposition that it was the change of position caused by Seymour's resignation. No change of position on the part of the plaintiffs is alleged in the complaint, or proven, nor is there any allegation or proof of any act or acts or silent acquiescence of defendant which misled the plaintiffs. They had notice as early as June, 1916, that the defendant refused to furnish horses to seed the crop of 1917. They hired the fourteen horses mentioned with knowledge of defendant's refusal to furnish horses. It certainly cannot be said that they were misled in hiring the horses, by the conduct or silent acquiescence of the defendant, nor were they led to believe by such silent acquiescence that they would get any horses whatever for the seeding and harvesting of the 1917 crop, which is the big item of damage sought to be recovered. We think the court erred in admitting the evidence, for which reason the judgment must be reversed.

It is so ordered.

ON PETITION FOR REHEARING

By the Court, COLEMAN, C. J.:

A very urgent petition for a rehearing has been filed. It must be borne in mind that plaintiffs sought to maintain their position upon two theories only. The case was tried upon those two theories, and none other was suggested to the lower court, or to this court upon the original hearing. Those two theories were: First, because of part performance, the plaintiffs could not recover; and, secondly, that the defendant should be estopped from setting up the statute of frauds.

The basis of the plea of part performance was the labor expended by the plaintiffs, which was of value in dollars and cents. With our view as expressed in the opinion as to the inapplicability of the plea of part performance, it does not appear from the petition for rehearing that there is any dissatisfaction; but, relative to the position taken as to the claim of estoppel, plaintiffs apparently feel greatly wronged. Their reliance upon estoppel, both in the district court and before this court was based upon the expenditures made by them in conducting their operations under their lease and the loss incident to defendant's refusal to furnish horses. It involved the identical outlay relied upon in support of the plea of "part performance." In other words, it is contended that, if this outlay in question will not support the plea of part performance, it should estop the defendant company from urging the statute of frauds. After all, it is merely part performance which is relied upon as a basis for estoppel. It is said that our former opinion does not state all the facts. It is true that we did not state just how much money plaintiffs expended in their operations under their lease; but we did not think then, nor do we think now, that such a statement was vital. We stated facts from which it must necessarily be gathered that there were certain expenditures by plaintiffs for labor, etc., in conducting their operations and we do not think it material whether they spent $500 or $2,431.

1-3. It was our view upon the original hearing, as it is now, that whatever sum they may have spent in conducting those operations did not induce a change of position by plaintiffs, but was the result of the change of position. As we said in the original opinion, the doctrine of estoppel was held to apply in the Seymour case, 156 Cal. 782, 106 Pac. 88, 134 Am. St. Rep. 154, because of the changed position of Seymour, induced by the defendants. We held that the Seymour case was no authority in the instant case, because plaintiffs in this case did not rely upon a change in their position or prove such facts as brought them within the rule.

Though the trial court was very indulgent toward plaintiffs and permitted them to amend their complaint four or five times, there is no language in it which can, under the wildest stretch of imagination, be said to even verge upon an allegation or statement of facts tending to charge that the plaintiffs were induced to change their position because of anything done or said by the defendant; nor, if we can correctly interpret a record and briefs, did that theory ever occur to plaintiffs or their counsel until after the original opinion had been filed in this case. On petition for rehearing it is contended that each of the plaintiffs gave up positions, which meant at least $1,200 a year to them, to take the lease on the ranch. This is the first suggestion of this kind made in the case, and is not borne out by the evidence. The fact is that in making out their case no testimony was given by either of the plaintiffs concerning what they were doing or how much they were earning at the time the lease in question was entered into. This shows conclusively that the theory of changed position was not relied upon.

On cross-examination it was shown that the plaintiff Nehls had a position as a cook and was earning $45 a month, except during the haying season, when he earned $50. On cross-examination it was shown that Stanley had no permanent pursuit; that during a period covering a year prior to the execution of the lease he had been engaged in numerous employments, ranging from catching wild mustangs on his own account to breaking colts for others. It was not shown how much he earned; nor does it appear from the record that plaintiffs could not obtain the identical employment that they had when the lease was taken. Such are the facts relied upon to bring the instant case within the Seymour case. In the latter case it appears that Seymour was induced to give up a life position paying $250 per month—one to which he could not be restored. The feature of that case distinguishing it from this one was the giving up of a life position without being able to be restored to it. No such circumstances appear in the instant case. The court says in the Seymour case:

·   "While the question is by no means free from doubt, we believe that it should be held that there were sufficient facts in this case to support * * * the application of the doctrine of equitable estoppel."

Though the court entertained doubt in that case as to the correctness of its conclusions, yet it is insisted that the facts in this case (which is lacking in the elements which led the court to reach the conclusion it did in that case) should impel us to hold the defendants estopped from pleading the statute of frauds. There being no similarity between the two cases, the authority relied upon does not justify the position of respondents.

The petition is denied.

DUCKER, J., having presided in the lower court, did not participate.

[No. 2389]

MAY A. ADAMS, ALICE E. LUHRS, LULU M. HARRIS, AND WILLIAM T. BIRMINGHAM, RESPONDENTS, *v.* ELLA E. WAGONER AND ERNEST WAGONER (HER HUSBAND), AND H. BELLE WAGONER AND IRA WAGONER (HER HUSBAND), APPELLANTS.

[184 Pac. 814]

1. DEEDS—EVIDENCE SHOWING INCAPACITY OF GRANTOR.
   In action to cancel mother's deed to daughter, executed by mother while in her last illness and a few hours before her death, evidence *held* to show that mother, at the time of execution of deed, was not possessed of sufficient intelligence to understand fully the nature and effect of the transaction.

2. TRUSTS—EVIDENCE OF CONSULTATION BETWEEN CHILDREN INSUFFICIENT TO ESTABLISH TRUST.
   Evidence of consultation between children, without the knowledge or consent of the mother, whereby children agreed that mother, who was lying on deathbed, should convey property to one of the children, who agreed with the other children to pay the debts of the estate and distribute the residue by proper conveyance equally between other heirs, was not admissible as proof that child to whom property was so conveyed held land in trust for the other children.

3. DEEDS—SUFFICIENCY OF EVIDENCE TO SHOW UNDUE INFLUENCE.
   Evidence *held* to show that mother's deed to daughter, with whom mother was living at time of her death, executed while mother was in her last illness and a few hours before her death, was procured by undue influence of daughter.

4. APPEAL AND ERROR—REJECTION OF TESTIMONY HARMLESS ERROR.
   In suit to cancel mother's deed to daughter, refusal to permit another daughter, who had been joined with grantee daughter as defendant, to testify to transaction between her and mother with respect to mother's disposition of her property, if error, was harmless, where court permitted her statement that deed had been prepared in accordance with mother's directions to stand, and where it was such fact that was sought to be elicited by the rejected testimony.

5. DEEDS—DEED OF INCOMPETENT GRANTOR HELD VOID.
   Mother's deed to daughter, executed while mother was in her last illness, and at a time when she was not capable of comprehending fully and fairly the nature and effect of the transaction, *held* void.

APPEAL from Eighth Judicial District Court, Lyon County; *T. C. Hart,* Judge.

Suit by May A. Adams and others against Ella E.

Wagoner and others. From a judgment for plaintiffs, and from an order denying a motion for new trial, defendants appeal. **Affirmed.**

LeRoy F. Pike and *Walter M. Kennedy,* for Appellants:

In an attempt to defeat a deed with parol evidence, or to establish a trust with parol evidence, the evidence must be clear and attended with no uncertainties, and even then must be received with great caution. Dalton v. Dalton, 14 Nev. 419.

. The mental capacity of a person sufficient to execute a deed is the same as that of a person competent to execute a will. Boudin College v. Merritt, 75 Fed. 480.

The burden of proving fraud or undue influence rests upon the contestants of a will. In this case we may consider the deed the same as a will, and therefore the burden of proof rests upon the contestants. In Re Hess's Will, 31 Am. St. Rep. 665.

There is no presumption of fraud or undue influence from the mere fact that the will contains provisions beneficial to the scrivener. Jones on Ev., sec. 191; Carter v. Dixon, 69 Ga. 82; Horah v. Knox, 87 N. C. 483; Critz v. Pierce, 106 Ill. 167.

J. C. Campbell, for Respondents:

Where there is a substantial conflict in the evidence on material issues, it is well settled that the decision of the lower court will not be disturbed, if there is substantial evidence to support it. Palmer v. Culverwell, 24 Nev. 114; Welland v. Williams, 21 Nev. 390; Crawford v. Crawford, 24 Nev. 410; Barnes v. W. U. T. Co., 27 Nev. 438; Ford v. Campbell, 29 Nev. 578; Abel v. Hitt, 30 Nev. 93; Tonopah L. Co. v. Nevada A. Co., 30 Nev. 445; Turley v. Thomas, 31 Nev. 181.

Findings supported by any substantial evidence cannot be disturbed on appeal. Burns v. Loftus, 32 Nev. 55.

The trial court is the exclusive judge of the credibility of the witnesses. Anderson v. Feutsch, 31 Nev. 501.

"In some instances, the relation of the parties is such,
as where an attorney receives a gift from a client, or a
guardian from a ward, that the law itself takes notice
of the inequality of their situations, and demands of the
donee of a gift affirmative proof of the fairness and
good faith of the transaction." Whitely v. Whitely, 78
N. W. 1009. "Clear evidence is required that the transaction was understood, and that there was no fraud,
mistake, or undue influence." Ten Eyck v. Whitback,
50 N. E. 963; Gibson v. Hammang, 88 N. W. 500;
Brummond v. Krause, 80 N. W. 686; Todd v. Sykes,
33 S. E. 517; Cole v. Getsinger, 71 N. W. 75.

The striking out of the testimony of one of the defendants was not error; but even if it was, it was harmless
and not prejudicial to the defendants. Jones on Ev.,
sec. 773.

"When the evidence shows that a judgment is so
clearly right that it should not be reversed for error in
admitting or excluding evidence or giving instructions,
such error will not be considered on appeal." Yori v.
Cohn, 26 Nev. 206.

By the Court, SANDERS, J.:

This suit was brought by certain heirs of Annie
Hofheins, late of Yerington, Nevada, against other heirs
of said Annie Hofheins (all being her children), to cancel a conveyance of lands and personal property alleged
to have been obtained from her a few hours before her
death by the defendant children, when, from her condition, she was incapacitated of understanding the nature
and effect of the transaction, or, in case such should not
be found to be the fact, that the grantee in said conveyance, Ella E. Wagoner, be declared to hold all the property described in said conveyance in trust for all of the
children of Annie Hofheins; that she be required to
account, and that she be enjoined from disposing of any
of the property specified in the alleged conveyance.

With the exception of certain admissions, all the allegations of the complaint were denied by the answer, and

for an affirmative defense the defendants allege: For many years prior to the death of Annie Hofheins, the defendant Ella E. Wagoner lived with her mother at her home in Yerington, Nevada, nursed and cared for her mother, and in consideration of the services rendered and to be rendered by said Ella E. Wagoner, and the agreement on the part of her, the said Ella E. Wagoner, to pay the debts of said Annie Hofheins, the latter sold and delivered to Ella E. Wagoner all of the property described in the deed exhibited with the complaint and sought by the plaintiffs' action to be canceled and annulled; that Annie Hofheins, at the time of the execution and delivery of said deed was of clear and sound mind; that she freely and voluntarily acknowledged the conveyance to be her act and deed; that no trust was created or intended by her to be created by said instrument. The plaintiffs replied, and for reply denied the new matter contained in the answer.

The action being purely equitable in its nature, the issues were tried by the court without a jury. The court found, in part, as follows:

"That at the time Annie Hofheins's name was signed to said purported deed she was in her last illness, from which her death was then imminently impending, and from which she died on the day following the signing of said purported deed; that owing to said illness her mind was weakened and was lacking in understanding; that she was not at the time of signing said deed, nor thereafter, and for several hours prior thereto had not been, in mental condition competent to transact business, or to discuss understandingly any business transaction whatever; that because of her said illness and her consequent mental condition, as aforesaid, and her impending death from said illness, when her name was signed to said purported deed, she was not in mental condition to know or understand its contents, and did not then and there, nor thereafter, know or understand its contents nor apparent legal affect; that the said conveyance was not signed by any person for her, acting under her conscious direction and authority, while she, the said Annie Hofheins, understood the meaning of said purported deed, or comprehended the amount or nature of the property mentioned therein."

As a conclusion of law the court found that said purported deed should be by judgment and decree canceled and declared to be wholly null and void and of no legal force nor effect whatever. Upon this finding and conclusion the court rendered and caused to be entered its judgment. From the judgment and order denying their motion for a new trial the defendants have appealed.

1. The principle upon which courts of equity act in cases such as that disclosed by the court's finding is clearly stated in the early case of Harding v. Wheaton, 2 Mason, 378, Fed. Cas. No. 6051, affirmed by the supreme court, in Harding v. Handy, 11 Wheat. 125, 6 L. Ed. 429, and followed in Allore v. Jewell, 94 U. S. 511, 24 L. Ed. 260; Turner v. Insurance Co., 10 Utah, 74, 37 Pac. 94, and adjudicated cases without number. From a careful analysis of the conflicting testimony, the undisputed facts, and the attending circumstances surrounding the execution of the conveyance, we are irresistibly led by their combined effect to the conclusion that the deceased, if not disqualified, was, at the time of the conveyance, unfit to attend to business of such importance as the disposition of her entire property, and was not possessed of sufficient intelligence to understand fully the nature and effect of the transaction.

Counsel for the appellants insist, even conceding the physical and mental weakness of the grantor, that the formal execution, acknowledgment, and delivery of the instrument is convincing proof that grantor at the time acted upon her own independent, deliberate judgment, with full knowledge of the legal effect of the instrument, and insist that the case falls within that long line of authorities holding that it did not appear that the grantor was incapable of exercising a discriminating judgment. We are impressed that the conclusion of counsel is refuted by the undisputed testimony of the parties in interest present, aside from the independent evidence clearly tending to support the court's finding in this particular. It is obvious from the record that those who assumed to act for the grantor and to prepare a deed for her to execute were impressed at the time with the consciousness of the grantor's extreme weakness. The grantor was sick, dying, at the point of death, and within a few hours after the formal execution of the deed she lapsed into a state of coma, until overcome by death on the following day. The grantor took no part in the formation of the deed. No one counseled with or advised her of the purport of the deed, its contents, or its legal effect. She was not advised of her rights, and no one offered to her an explanation of its contents. It sufficiently appears from the evidence that May Adams, Ella E. Wagoner, and H. Belle Wagoner, children of the deceased present and parties to this suit, together with their attorney, held a consultation shortly before the execution of the deed, and without the presence and hearing of the deceased, concerning the disposition of the deceased's property, having in mind that the deceased, some time prior to the execution of the deed and before her condition had become serious, had expressed a desire that her interest in a certain tract of land be mortgaged to a sister of the deceased for the purpose of obtaining sufficient funds to defray the expenses of her illness.

As a result of the consultation between the children present and said attorney, it was agreed and understood between them that to save costs of administration, in the event of the death of their mother, a bargain-and-sale deed should be prepared for her to execute, conveying to Ella E. Wagoner, one of her children (appellant), all of her estate, with the understanding between themselves that the grantee would, upon the death of the grantor, pay the debts of the estate and distribute the residue by proper conveyance equally between all of the heirs of the deceased. This is the deed in question. It appears that H. Belle Wagoner was delegated to present the deed thus prepared to the grantor for her to execute, and it was understood that, in the event the grantor should raise any objection as to its contents, H. Belle Wagoner would explain to her the purport of the deed. No objection was made by the deceased, and it appears that because of her weakness her signature thereto was effected by H. Belle Wagoner guiding the hand of the deceased, and the deceased acknowledged the deed then and there before a notary.

2-3. While the evidence of the consultation between the children named and their attorney respecting the propriety of disposing of the property of the deceased without her knowledge or consent was not admissible as proof of a trust, as is urged by counsel for appellants in opposition to its admission as evidence for any purpose, it is strong evidence of a conviction that the grantor was at the time unfit to manage or incapable of making disposition of her property, or that she did not possess sufficient intelligence to understand fully the nature and effect of the transaction. Harding v. Wheaton, supra. We use the fact of the arrangement between the children present for the purpose of corroborating the observations already made as to the capacity of Annie Hofheins; for, if such an arrangement was made, it demonstrates in the most forcible manner the opinion of the family as to her incapacity, at least in a judicious manner, to dispose of her property. Assuming she might have been capable in law of executing a deed, it is impossible for us to ignore the fact that she was at the mercy of those immediately about her. We do not impute to any of the children present meditated fraud, or that one was any more responsible than the other for obtaining the deed under such circumstances, but we are constrained to hold that the deed was obtained by undue influence exerted over weakness, upon one whose mind had ceased to be the safe guide of her actions. It is, therefore, against conscience for Ella E. Wagoner to derive any advantage from the deceased's act.

The whole difficulty in this case arises from the conduct of Ella E. Wagoner after the procurement of the
deed. Since the death of the grantor she represents the
transaction as being an absolute sale to her of all the
property of the deceased. To prove this important
averment alleged in her answer to the complaint Ella E.
Wagoner undertook to prove by H. Belle Wagoner, her
codefendant, that Annie Hofheins had stated to her
that she intended all her property to go to Ella E.
Wagoner and to make her the object of her bounty.
The court sustained the objections interposed to all
questions designed to elicit from the witness the details
of any transaction between the deceased and the witness
with respect to the disposition of her property. We are
impressed that this course of examination was an
attempt to prove a consideration for the conveyance
different from that stated in the answer, as well as that
expressed in the deed itself.

4. But passing this, counsel for the respondents insist
that the witness, being a codefendant and a party in
interest, and the other party to the transaction being
dead, should not be permitted to testify. On the other
hand, counsel for appellants insist that since the witness
was made a party to the action against her will, and
that she, in her testimony, had disclaimed any interest
whatsoever in the result of the litigation, the testimony
was competent. Not deciding that the position of either
counsel is correct, the evidence of this witness shows (in
giving her version of the arrangement between the
parties as to the preparation of the deed) that she told
the attorney who prepared the instrument to make the
conveyance to Ella E. Wagoner, and in response to the
question: "Why did you tell Mr. Pilkington to make that
deed to Ella Wagoner to all of that property?" she
replied: "My mother told me to." For all intents and
purposes this was the evidence sought to be elicited. It
was known to the court that Ella E. Wagoner had for
many years lived with the deceased, shared with her the
responsibilities and conduct of her home, and that she

had cared for and nursed the deceased in her illness.
Since the court allowed the statement that the deed was
prepared in accordance with the deceased's direction to
stand, the court must have given the statement and the
existing relations between the grantor and the grantee
whatever weight they deserved, and the appellants were
not prejudiced.

· 5. We conclude to affirm the judgment and order, upon
the ground that, at the time of the execution of the
conveyance, Annie Hofheins was not capable of comprehending fully and fairly the nature and effect of the
transaction, its extent or its importance, and that her
mind had ceased to be a safe guide for her actions.

Let the judgment and order be affirmed.

[No. 2297]

FRED H. NIELSEN, RESPONDENT, v. NELLIE RICH-
ARDSON REBARD, AS ADMINISTRATRIX OF THE
ESTATE OF FRANK P. RICHARDSON, DECEASED,
APPELLANT.
[183 Pac. 984]

1. APPEAL AND ERROR—OBJECTION MADE FIRST TIME ON APPEAL.
   An objection that complaint utterly failed to state a cause
   of action may be raised for the first time on appeal.

2. PLEADING—FAILURE TO STATE CAUSE OF ACTION.
   An objection that the complaint utterly fails to state a cause
   of action may be raised at any time.

3. TROVER AND CONVERSION—OBJECT OF ACTION.
   Trover is an action, not to recover the specific thing, but to
   recover the value of the property wrongfully converted.

4. REPLEVIN—POSSESSION BY DEFENDANT NECESSARY.
   To enable a plaintiff to recover in replevin, the specific property must be in the possession of the defendant at the commencement of the action.

5. SPECIFIC PERFORMANCE—NOT APPLICABLE TO CORPORATE STOCK.
   Shares of corporate stock cannot be recovered in an action
   for specific performance, unless they possess peculiar and
   unusual value.

APPEAL from Seventh Judicial District Court, Esmeralda County; *J. Emmett Walsh*, Judge.

Action by Fred H. Nielsen against Nellie Richardson
Rebard, as administratrix of the estate of Frank P.

Richardson, deceased. From a judgment for plaintiff, and an order denying a new trial, defendant appeals. Reversed.

August Tilden, for Appellant:

The amended complaint does not state a cause of action, the decision is contrary to law and the evidence, and the pleadings and the findings do not justify or support the judgment.

The action is evidently not intended to be one of trover. Trover "is not to recover the thing converted, but damages for its conversion." 21 Ency. Pl. & Pr. 1012. It is not an action in replevin. There is no such description of any specific property as would enable an officer to identify it. Buckley v. Buckley, 9 Nev. 373.

The essential averment that defendant had possession at the time of the commencement of the action is not made. Gardner v. Brown, 22 Nev. 156.

There is no allegation of value, and hence no basis for the recovery of damages, which "is as much the primary object of the action of replevin as is the recovery of the property in specie." Buckley v. Buckley, 12 Nev. 423. There is no alternative tendered the defendant to deliver the property or pay its value, which is the defendant's privilege. Carson v. Appelgarth, 6 Nev. 187.

As a bill for equitable relief, the complaint is deficient in not averring any fact upon which the jurisdiction of equity depends. Oliver v. Little, 31 Nev. 476. An action to enforce redemption of pledged stock is to be governed by the rules applicable to the disposal of actions for specific performance. Krouse v. Woodward, 42 Pac. 1084. "The mere fact that the subject of the suit involves the estate of a deceased person will not justify the interference of equity when a legal remedy exists." 16 Cyc. 100.

Thompson & Thompson and *A. Grant Miller,* for Respondent:

Neither the notice of intention to move for a new trial nor the notice of appeal, nor any of the papers on file in

the case, outside of appellant's opening brief, makes any
charge that the complaint does not state a cause of
action. The ground of objection and appeal is first
mentioned in appellant's opening brief. It cannot be
urged as a ground of appeal. Appellant is estopped by
the proceedings and notices from now urging this
objection.

The judgment is in proper form, and conforms to the
pleadings, the evidence and the findings. 20 Ency. Pl. &
Pr. p. 504, et seq.

By the Court, COLEMAN, C. J.:

By this action plaintiff seeks to recover the possession
of specific stock, and of dividends earned thereon. Judgment was entered in the trial court as prayed, from
which, as well as from an order denying a new trial, an
appeal is taken.

1, 2. It is contended in this court that the amended
complaint does not state a cause of action, as to which it
is said, by counsel for respondent, that this point, not
having been made in the trial court, should not now
prevail. It is a well-recognized rule that, while courts
do not look with favor upon objections of this kind when
made for the first time in the appellate court (Omaha Nat.
Bank v. Kiper, 60 Neb. 37, 82 N. W. 102; Phoenix
v. Gardner, 13 Minn. 433 [Gil. 396]; Smith v. Dennett,
15 Minn. 86 [Gil. 59]; Donellan v. Hardy, 57 Ind. 399),
yet, if the complaint utterly fails to state a cause of
action, the point may be raised at any time (Stevenson
v. Lord, 15 Colo. 131, 25 Pac. 313; Van Doren v. Tjader,
1 Nev. 390, 90 Am. Dec. 498). In fact our code expressly
provides that all objections to a complaint may be
waived, except as to the lack of jurisdiction and the
failure of the complaint to state a cause of action. Rev.
Laws, 5045. It is incumbent upon us to determine the
question presented.

The amended complaint, in brief, alleges that on
November 23, 1914, and for a long time prior thereto,
Frank P. Richardson was engaged in the stock brokerage

business in Goldfield, and while so engaged acted in behalf of customers in buying and selling stock upon the Goldfield and San Francisco stock exchanges, and in so doing was governed by the rules of such exchanges and the customs of brokers of Goldfield; that on the date mentioned said Richardson died intestate in the town of Goldfield. It is further averred that long prior to the date of his death the deceased had established the custom with his patrons of buying mining stocks for them upon the payment of one-third or one-half of the purchase price thereof, and depositing the said stock in his safe, the balance of the purchase price to be paid at the date of the sale of such stock, or at such times as it might be withdrawn from said safe; that the deceased had established a custom in said business, with his customers, of buying mining stocks for them and paying therefor in full, and placing the same in his safe for such purchasers, the purchasers making no payment in cash at the time, but depositing an equal amount of stock in the same company as security for the amount due upon the purchases, permitting the customers to pay the amount due, with interest, at the time of such sale or withdrawal of the stock; that such customs were the ones prevailing among the stockbrokers of Goldfield at the time.

It is further alleged that on the 10th day of October, 1914, plaintiff purchased of the said Richardson 1,000 shares of the capital stock of the Jumbo Extension Mining Company, at the price of 39 cents per share, and paid in full therefor; that on October 22, 1914, pursuant to the established custom, as alleged, the deceased purchased for plaintiff 1,000 shares of the capital stock of the Jumbo Extension Mining Company at the price of 40 cents per share, on account of which plaintiff made no cash payment, but as security for the purchase price thereof deposited with the deceased the 1,000 shares purchased by plaintiff on October 10, 1914. It is further alleged that it was the custom of the deceased and other brokers in Goldfield, at the time of purchasing

stock for patrons, in cases in which it was not paid for,
to fix a limit for the payment of the balance due on such
contracts; that on November 22 it was agreed between
the plaintiff and deceased that the plaintiff should be
given until demand therefor in which to pay for the
stock, or until it should be sold, and that no demand had
been made.

It is further alleged in the complaint that on November
23, 1914, a special administrator was appointed as
administrator of said estate and that on December 21
regular letters of administration were issued to appellant,
who thereupon duly qualified, and that in pursuance
thereof she came into possession of 12,100 shares
of the capital stock of the Jumbo Extension Mining Company,
and all of the property and assets of the said
estate. It is further alleged that plaintiff filed with the
clerk of the court, within the time allowed by law, his
claim against said estate for the delivery of 2,000 shares
of the capital stock of the Jumbo Extension Mining
Company, and for a designated sum on account of
dividends earned on said stock. It is further alleged
that defendant, as such administratrix, refused to
deliver to plaintiff said stock; that the estate of
deceased is solvent; that plaintiff was served with
notice of the rejection by the administratrix of the said
claim, and that the time had not elapsed in which to
bring this action; that the said Jumbo Extension Mining
Company had declared certain dividends upon its
capital stock, and that plaintiff is entitled to recover the
dividends earned by said 2,000 shares of stock less the
sum due on the stock purchased October 22.

3, 4. In our opinion, the amended complaint does not
state a cause of action. It is not even claimed by respondent
that the action is one of replevin or trover. Trover
is an action not to recover the specific thing but to
recover the value of the property wrongfully converted.
21 Ency. Pl. & Pr. 1012. There is no attempt to recover
damages in the action; and it has been held that, to
enable a plaintiff to recover in replevin, the specific

property sought to be recovered must be in possession of the defendant at the time of the commencement of the action (Gardner v. Brown, 22 Nev. 156, 37 Pac. 240), and there is no allegation in the complaint to the effect that defendant had possession of such stock at the time the action was commenced.

5. The only theory upon which it is urged by the counsel for respondent that the complaint states a cause of action is that it is within the rule established by the case of Krouse v. Woodward, 110 Cal. 638, 42 Pac. 1084. From a reading of that case, it seems that it was one in the nature of specific performance, prosecuted under a provision of the civil code of that state. We have no such provision in our civil code, and it is a well-established rule in this jurisdiction that shares of stock cannot be recovered in an action for specific performance unless they possess peculiar and unusual value (State v. Jumbo Ex. M. Co., 30 Nev. 198, 94 Pac. 74; Oliver v. Little, 31 Nev. 476, 103 Pac. 240; Robinson M. Co. v. Riepe, 40 Nev. 121, 161 Pac. 304), of which there is no allegation in the complaint in this action.

It is clear that unless the complaint states. facts sufficient to entitle plaintiff to a decree compelling defendant to convey the stock claimed, there can be no sufficient allegation showing a right to dividends thereupon.

The complaint failing to state a cause of action, it is ordered that the judgment and order appealed from be reversed.

[No. 2377]

J. B. DIXON, Appellant, *v.* A. GRANT MILLER, Respondent.

[184 Pac. 926]

1. BILLS AND NOTES—WANT OF CONSIDERATION A DEFENSE AGAINST ORIGINAL PAYEE.

   As against the original payee who was not a holder of a note in due course, the maker may, under negotiable-instruments law, sec. 28, urge the absence or failure of consideration.

2. BILLS AND NOTES—ANSWER ALLEGING WANT OF CONSIDERATION SUFFICIENT.

   In an action on a note, the answer of the maker *held* sufficient to present as against the payee the defense of want of consideration.

3. EVIDENCE—PAROL EVIDENCE ADMISSIBLE TO SHOW WANT OF CONSIDERATION.

   The rule that parol evidence is not admissible to contradict or vary an absolute engagement to pay money on the face of a bill or note does not exclude evidence as between the immediate parties of a total failure or want of consideration, and the negotiable-instruments law, sec. 28, recognizes the right to urge want of consideration.

4. BILLS AND NOTES—EVIDENCE—WANT OF CONSIDERATION JURY QUESTION.

   Ordinarily a mere equality in the number of witnesses does not constitute a balance of evidence, and hence in an action on a note, where defendant urged want of consideration and testified to facts in support of his claim, which testimony was contradicted by plaintiff, the payee, the question is for the jury.

APPEAL from Second Judicial District Court, Washoe County; *Thomas F. Moran,* Judge.

Action by J. B. Dixon against A. Grant Miller, From a judgment for defendant, plaintiff appeals. **Affirmed. Rehearing denied.**

J. M. Frame and *J. B. Dixon* (in pro. per.), for Appellant:

The making of the note was presumptively within the knowledge of the defendant. 31 Cyc. 199; 1 Ency. Pl. & Pr. 811, et seq.; Spencer v. Levy, 173 S. W. 550; Brown v. Martin, 23 Cal. App. 736; Allen v. Surety Co., 129 N. Y. Supp. 228; Raymond v. Johnson, 17 Wash. 232; Howes v. Corti B. Co., 135 N. Y. Supp. 562.

Gray Mashburn and *A. Grant Miller* (in pro. per.), for Respondent:

Appellant seeks to make respondent liable for a deal that never was his own, and liable upon a note which was manifestly and certainly given in a representative capacity. This latter fact must have been known, and was known, to appellant at the time the note was signed.

The evidence clearly showed, beyond any dispute, a want of consideration. The lower court was the judge of the witnesses and their veracity, and of the weight to be given to their testimony. It is quite certain that the trial judge believed the defendant and disbelieved the plaintiff, and rendered his decision accordingly. We submit that under these circumstances the judgment will not be disturbed on appeal.

By the Court, DUCKER, J.:

The appellant and respondent are attorneys at law. The appellant, who was plaintiff in the court below, brought this action on a promissory note of which the following is a copy:

"$1,500.00   Reno, Nevada, June 14, 1910.

"Three months after date, for value received, I promise to pay to J. B. Dixon or order, the sum of fifteen hundred dollars with interest at the rate of eight per cent per annum until paid. In case this note is not paid at maturity and proceedings are taken to collect the same in court or otherwise, I agree to pay in addition to principal, interest and costs, reasonable attorney's fees. This note is secured by a chattel mortgage bearing even date herewith. [Signed] A. Grant Miller. A. Grant Miller, as Trustee for Union Printing and Publishing Company."

The defendant answered, and besides certain other matters, alleged as two separate defenses that the note and chattel mortgage referred to therein were executed by him in a representative capacity as the agent and trustee of the Union Printing and Publishing Company, a corporation; that the note and chattel mortgage were executed and delivered by respondent in said representative capacity to appellant to secure a certain contingent fee which appellant was to receive as an attorney in the event he successfully defended certain actions at law, in which one George W. Condon was plaintiff and the Forum Publishing Company, a corporation, Union Printing and Publishing Company, a corporation, A. Grant Miller as trustee for said last-mentioned corporation, and A. Grant Miller were defendants.

It is alleged in the reply that the chattel mortgage referred to was and is not a subsisting security for the payment of the promissory note at the time of the commencement of the action and for a long time prior thereto, for the reason that the property described therein had been taken out of the possession of appellant against his will by the sheriff of Washoe County and sold under a decree of court, thereby depriving appellant of his security. It is averred in the reply that there was a good, valid, and valuable consideration for said note, and denied therein that respondent acted merely as agent for said Union Printing and Publishing Company in the executing and delivering of said note. It is alleged that respondent, at appellant's request, made and executed the note sued upon and the chattel mortgage, both individually and as trustee for said Union Printing and Publishing Company, at appellant's request, and denied that appellant agreed to defend said actions for a contingent fee.

The lower court found that respondent made the note in a representative capacity only, as agent and trustee for the Union Printing and Publishing Company, and executed the chattel mortgage as such agent and trustee, as security for the payment of the contingent fee alleged in the answer; that judgments in said actions at law were rendered in favor of the plaintiff therein, and that appellant earned no fee under the contingent agreement; that there was no consideration passing from appellant for the note. Judgment was rendered in favor of respondent, and from the judgment and order of the

phase of the case. He testified that appellant did not earn and was not entitled to any fee. and that there was no consideration for the note, but these are conclusions, and without any probative force.

The appellant on rebuttal testified in detail as to the services he had rendered, and contradicted respondent as to any agreement to defend the cases for a contnigent fee. On this phase of the case he said, in substance:

"After several consultations with A. Grant Miller, late in March and early in April, 1910, I was retained and employed by him to conduct the defense of himself as an individual, the Union Printing and Publishing Company, and of himself as trustee for said last-named corporation. and also to act for E. H. Beemer, a stockholder of the Forum Publishing Company, as intervener, in actions Nos. 7114 and 7119. I did not agree or consent to take the cases on a contingent fee, or either of them, but the amount of my fee was not then fixed, for it was unknown what services would be required. As the trials of the two cases were approaching and it was possible then to determine approximately the value of the services already rendered and further probable services, I told Mr. Miller that the amount of my fees must be settled, and that if cash could not be paid I wanted some security. After some discussion it was agreed orally that $1,500 would be the reasonable value of my services, and Mr. Miller said that neither he nor the other defendants could pay cash, but that he would give me his promissory note for $1,500 and secure it by a mortgage on the personal property he had bought from the Forum Publishing Company. The note and mortgage were dated June 14, 1910, but were not executed and delivered to me until June 20 or 21, 1910. Neither at the time of the oral agreement made by me with Mr. Miller, nor at the time of the execution and delivery of the note and mortgage, was anything said by either Mr. Miller or myself that this note should be in any way contingent on the result of the suits or either of them."

It thus appears that there is a direct conflict in the

testimony between the parties as to the contingent fee
agreement. Neither is corroborated by any other testimony or circumstance in the case as to this phase of it.
The case made out by respondent, and upon which the
trial court based its findings, is therefore not strong. It
could not stand in some jurisdictions, where the rule prevails that where the claim of a party rests upon his
unsupported testimony, and is met by the positive denial
of the other, so that the case presented is merely oath
against oath, there is no preponderance, and the party
having the burden must fail. This, however, is not the
general rule.

"The general rule undoubtedly is that a mere equality
in number of witnesses does not constitute a balance of
evidence any more than disparity in number discloses a
preponderance, which it sometimes does. It cannot be
held as a proposition of law that, simply because an equal
number of witnesses testify in opposition to each other
upon a given question of fact, therefore the evidence is
equally balanced. The intelligence and integrity of the
witnesses, their means of information, as well as many
other things, are to be considered in determining upon
which side is the preponderance or greater weight of
evidence. Facts may exist which will turn the scale on
the one side—interest, motive, prejudice, manner of
testifying. These and other kindred things are to be
considered in determining which of the witnesses is
entitled to the greater credit." Moore on Facts, vol. 1,
p. 108; Howlett v. Dilts, 4 Ind. App. 23, 30 N. E. 313;
Johnson v. People, 140 Ill. 350, 29 N. E. 895; 10 R. C. L.
1007.

We are not inclined to disturb the finding of the lower
courts in this regard. The duty of judging the credibility and weighing the testimony of the two litigants
rested entirely upon the trial court. There is substantial
conflict in the evidence, which gives effect to the finding
of the trial court.

"If there is a substantial conflict in the evidence, then

the duty and responsibility of finding the facts from the evidence devolve upon the trial court, and constitute a question concerning which this court has nothing to do, even though we may feel that upon the whole evidence we should have come to a different conclusion." Bigelow, C. J., in Gardner v. Gardner, 23 Nev. 215, 45 Pac. 140.

See, also, Thompson v. Tonopah Lumber Co., 37 Nev. 183, 141 Pac. 71; Leete v. Southern Pacific Co., 37 Nev. 49, 139 Pac. 29; Robinson Mining Co. v. Riepe, 37 Nev. 27, 138 Pac. 910; Turley v. Thomas, 31 Nev. 181, 101 Pac. 568, 135 Am. St. Rep. 667.

From these views we are led to affirm the judgment, and deem it unnecessary to discuss the evidence bearing upon the question as to whether respondent acted in a representative capacity in executing and delivering the note to appellant.

Judgment affirmed.

ON PETITION FOR REHEARING

Per Curiam:

Petition for rehearing denied.

[No. 2412] ·

THE STATE OF NEVADA, Ex Rel. W. D. MOODY, Petitioner, *v.* W. H. WILLIAMS, J. D. AUSTIN, and L. L. ALLEN, as Members of the Board of County Commissioners of Churchill County, Nevada, Respondents.

[185 Pac. 459]

1. PROHIBITION—QUESTIONS OF PUBLIC IMPORT REVIEWABLE ON MERITS.

   On application for prohibition, the supreme court may consider the questions involved on their merits, where the public is vitally concerned and long and expensive litigation will thereby be avoided.

2. STATUTES—CONSTRUED IN LIGHT OF FACTS.

   A legislative enactment must be construed in the light of known facts suggested by the act itself.

3. TAXATION—TAX MUST BE FOR PUBLIC PURPOSE.

   There can be no lawful tax which is not laid for a public purpose.

4. COUNTIES—BONDS TO BE PAID BY TAXATION ILLEGAL UNLESS FOR PUBLIC PURPOSE.

   Where county and municipal bonds are issued whose payment is provided for solely by taxation, their validity depends upon the question whether the purposes to which the proceeds of the bonds are to be applied are public purposes.

5. COUNTIES—BONDS TO RAISE MONEY TO LOAN TO LAND OWNERS ILLEGAL.

   Stats. 1919, c. 204, authorizing the county of Churchill to issue bonds to establish a fund to loan to private land owners for the purpose of reclaiming arid lands, is invalid, in that the method provided is ineffective and would result in taxation for private purposes.

6. TAXATION—RESTRICTIONS ON POWER OF STATE TO TAX.

   The only restriction on the power of the state to tax property within its jurisdiction and to direct the purposes for which taxes shall be raised is that the assessment shall be uniform and equal and the purpose a public one.

7. STATUTES—LEGISLATIVE AND JUDICIAL POWERS.

   So long as the legislature acts within the powers given it, the courts cannot interfere.

8. TAXATION—TAX FOR PUBLIC IMPROVEMENT MUST BE EFFECTIVE.

   A tax for a public improvement to be legal must be effective, and a tax designed to accomplish a vast reclamation project must rest upon some safer hypothesis than the volition and individual energy of those upon whom is the duty to make the law authorizing the tax effective.

9. STATUTES—SCOPE OF POWERS.
    The courts cannot hold a statute valid because it is sanctioned by the legislature and public opinion, where the statute is not within scope of legitimate legislation.

PROCEEDING in prohibition by the State of Nevada, on the relation of W. D. Moody, against W. H. Williams, J. D. Austin, and L. L. Allen, as members of the Board of County Commissioners of Churchill County, Nevada. Writ ordered to issue. COLEMAN, C. J., dissenting.

G. J. Kenny, District Attorney, for Petitioner.

Leonard B. Fowler, Attorney-General; *Robert Richards,* Deputy Attorney-General, and *A. L. Haight,* for Respondents.

By the Court, SANDERS, J.:

The board of county commissioners of Churchill County, at its meeting in May, 1919, unanimously adopted this resolution:

"*Resolved,* That it is the intention of this board, under the authority of an Act of the Legislature of the State of Nevada, approved March 29, 1919, being chapter 204 of the Laws of Nevada, Twenty-Ninth Session, to proceed with the issuance of the bonds of this county, to the amount of $240,000, and to apply the moneys derived from the sale thereof towards the purposes specified in said Act."

1. An impression widely prevails that the legislature exceeded its authority in authorizing the board of county commissioners to issue the bonds provided for in the act (Stats. 1919, c. 204), and that the bonds would, if issued, be destitute of legal obligation. An early decision of the questions involved is important, because, if the act be legitimate legislation, the county may avail itself of its benefits and negotiate more easily and at higher figures the securities, and that, on the other hand, should the legislation be not legitimate, no steps may be taken under it, the evil of repudiation avoided,

as well as long-drawn-out and expensive litigation. We
deem these considerations sufficient to justify us in considering the question on its merits, without regard to
the method adopted (prohibition) to have the law
reviewed. State v. Osawkee Township, 14 Kan. 418, 19
Am. Rep. 99.

The board of county commissioners of Churchill
County is authorized, under the provisions of the act, to
prepare and issue bonds of said county, bearing interest
at the rate of 3 per cent per annum from date, in the sum
of $240,000. For a clear understanding of the nature of
the bonds and the legal questions involved, it is necessary
to give a summary of the provisions of the act. The sections that embody its principal features, in so far as
they relate to the bonds, are sections 6 and 7:

"SEC. 6. The board of county commissioners of said
county is hereby authorized to use the moneys derived
from the sale of said bonds, or such portion thereof as
they may deem advisable, in assisting bona-fide owners
and entrymen of agricultural lands in said county in
the leveling of such lands and in placing the same under
cultivation, under such regulations as said board may
adopt in conformity with the spirit of this act. Such
assistance shall be in the nature of loans made to such
owners and entrymen from said 'Reclamation Fund,'
and the said board is hereby authorized and required in
every case where such loan is made to secure the repay-
ment thereof by a first lien for the amount of such loan
upon the land embraced within the farm unit or legal
subdivision in which the land so to be leveled and placed
under cultivation, as specified in the application for such
loan, is situated. * * *

"SEC. 7. No loan shall be made from said 'Reclamation Fund' except for the purpose of placing under cultivation lands not leveled at the time of making application for such loan, nor shall any loan be made in an
amount exceeding the cost of leveling such lands, and
the amount which may be loaned for leveling any one
acre shall not exceed fifty dollars; provided, that upon
the unanimous vote of the members of the board of

county commissioners, in the case of lands unusually difficult to level and which, when leveled and placed under cultivation, will in the judgment of the board be of exceptional value, such loans may be made in an amount not to exceed seventy-five dollars per acre. No money shall be advanced upon any application for a loan hereunder until the land specified therein shall have been leveled and seeded nor until it shall have been demonstrated to the satisfaction of the board that it can be properly irrigated and that all work in connection with the land has been performed in conformity with the general scheme of reclamation, irrigation and drainage obtaining in the district in which such land is situated."

It is provided by section 8 that the money so loaned must be paid in annual installments, commencing at a time to be fixed by the board, but not later than July 1, 1923, and the whole amount thereof shall mature and be paid as the board may direct, but in any event prior to July 1, 1938.

The board is authorized by section 11 to charge and collect on said loans a rate of interest not in excess of 5 per cent per annum. The applicant for a loan is required to pay an application fee of not to exceed 2 per cent of the amount of the loan for which application is made.

By section 16 it is provided: The board of county commissioners shall annually levy and assess on all the taxable property of said county, including the net proceeds of mines, a special ad valorem tax for such amount as shall be necessary or sufficient to pay the interest semiannually as it shall accrue and also to pay the principal of such bonds as they severally become due, until all of said bonds with the interest shall have been fully paid.

2. To deal fairly with this legislation, it must be construed in the light of known facts suggested to us by the act itself. Whether the statements that follow are perfectly accurate or not is a matter of no great importance. The United States reclamation project referred to in

the act, known as the "Newlands Project," embraces within its scope the major portion of the area of lands within Churchill County. Approximately between 70,000 and 80,000 acres of land in said county are now under contract with the government to be irrigated from this source. It is fair to assume that such lands are covered with hills, mounds, gullies, and brush which render their irrigation and immediate production difficult—perhaps impossible—without a large expenditure of money. From the provisions of the act it is fair to assume that the owners and entrymen of these lands are not financially able to bring the same in their present condition up to their full measure of production, and if left to the individual efforts of their owners, without assistance, it would take time, possibly years of patient toil under adverse conditions and contingencies. It is evident that the legislative body considered the leveling and the placing of these lands under cultivation to be the proper subject of a public undertaking, and to accomplish this it has inaugurated a loaning enterprise. The loans authorized for the purposes stated are to be secured by a first lien upon the lands to be leveled, and also by special assessments to be annually levied and assessed sufficient to cover the annual installments of all outstanding loans as they become due and until fully paid. The conditions of the loans are that none shall be made except upon lands not leveled at the time of making application for such loans, and no money shall be advanced upon any application for a loan until the land specified therein shall have been leveled and seeded, nor until it shall have been demonstrated to the satisfaction of the board that the land is irrigable and that the applicant has done all the work in connection therewith in conformity with the general scheme of rereclamation obtaining in the district where the land is situated.

3, 4. If the legislation in question can be sustained at all, it must be so sustained under the general power of the state to direct and determine the objects to be provided for, fostered, or aided through the expenditure of public moneys. The exercise of such power necessarily involves a tax. It is in the power to direct the objects of taxation that the state finds its authority to organize irrigation, drainage, and assessment districts and to foster other public improvements equally as beneficial to the public. In order to speed up the cultivation of the lands specified in the act, it was the intention of the legislature to establish a tax or assessment district out of the entire county of Churchill. It is only in this view that the law can be vindicated, as it is fundamental that there can be no lawful tax which is not laid for a public purpose, and that, where county or municipal bonds are issued whose payment is provided for solely by taxation (as here), their validity depends upon the question whether the purposes to which the proceeds of said bonds are to be applied are public purposes. Gibson v. Mason, 5 Nev. 283; Gold Hill v. Caledonia S. & M. Co., 5 Sawy. 583, Fed. Cas. No. 5512, (9th Cir.) ; State v. Osawkee Township, supra; People v. Salem, 24 Mich. 452, 4 Am. Rep. 400; Citizens S. & L. Assn. v. Topeka, 20 Wall. 655, 22 L. Ed. 455.

5. As the proposed bonds involve the power of taxation, their validity must depend upon the legality of the tax. In so far as the result of the tax is to reclaim a large area of the agricultural lands of Churchill County, it may be said to be a tax for a public purpose. To this extent the legislation is legitimate, but the question to be determined is whether the plan adopted by the act for executing its purpose is equally legitimate. The plan adopted for the reclamation of the lands is to raise a fund by the sale of county bonds, the proceeds of which are to be applied in assisting owners and entrymen by way of loans from said fund to the amount of fifty to seventy-five dollars per acre for defraying the preliminary expense of leveling their lands and placing the same under cultivation. Our general objection to the tax is that it is a deviation from the usual and long course of usage of the taxing power. Our specific objection to the tax is that the board of county commissioners of

Churchill County is authorized to use the moneys derived from the sale of the bonds for private purposes. Under the plan adopted, a dozen or as many hundreds of acres of land may be placed under cultivation and the remainder left to go unreclaimed. One owner may be moved to take advantage of the proffered assistance, and others would not be so inclined. One owner or entryman might undertake, through the plan adopted, to reclaim all of his land, while others would be disposed to reclaim but a fraction of their holdings, or look to other sources for assistance than the public fund. It is clear that the operation of the law might result in the taxing of a citizen for the use of a private enterprise conducted by other citizens. Such result is an unauthorized invasion of a private right and contrary to the fundamental principle that no tax is a valid tax except it be laid for a public purpose.

6, 7. We concede that the only restriction on the power of this state to tax property within its jurisdiction and to direct the purposes for which taxes shall be raised is that the assessment shall be uniform and equal and the purpose a public one. So long as the legislature acts within these conceded powers, the courts may not interfere. Gibson v. Mason, supra; Gold Hill v. Caledonia S. & M. Co., supra.

8. We have above intimated that the primary scope and purpose of the act is legitimate legislation, in that it has for its object the reclamation of a vast area of irrigable agricultural lands in the county of Churchill. Our objection to the law is not directed to its object or its expediency. These are matters for the legislature and not for courts. Taxation is eminently practical, and for the purpose of deciding its validity a tax should be regarded in its actual practical results, rather than the reference to the beneficent purpose for which the tax is authorized. It is but just to assume that the legislature in adopting the loan plan was inspired with the belief or expectation that its operation would result in the reclamation of all the lands specified in the act. So far

so good, but when we come to analyze its provisions we find nothing in its terms or conditions that furnishes any assurance to the taxpayers of Churchill County that the plan adopted will accomplish the desired result. Under the plan adopted, it is reasonably probable and positively possible that the proceeds of the bonds will not be utilized for the purpose stated in the act. Before a citizen can be coerced to donate to a fund under the guise of a tax for a public improvement, it must be certain that the tax will result in its accomplishment. The obnoxious feature of the loaning enterprise that furnishes the consideration and inducement of the whole act is that it is ineffective and unenforceable. The whole scheme of the law seems to be based on the assumption that the loan fund, when once established from the sale of the bonds, will serve as an incentive or stimulus to the land owners or entrymen to bring all their holdings under cultivation in accordance with the terms and conditions of the act. We see in the law no rational ground for such assumption. It is not pretended that these farmers can be coerced to level and place their lands under cultivation, or that they will be impelled to patronize the loaning enterprise established directly for their benefit and indirectly for that of the public. Still, by the express terms of the act the taxpayers of said county are coerced to satisfy $240,000 worth of bonds by means of taxation without any assurance in advance that the purpose or the result of the tax will be accomplished. A tax for a public improvement to be legal must be effective. A tax designed to accomplish so vast an undertaking as the reclaiming of thousands of acres of lands to be legal must rest upon some safer hypothesis than the volition and individual energy of those upon whom it is the duty to make the law effective.

Entertaining these views, we conclude that the plan adopted for the execution of the law will not accomplish its purpose, and that the bonds in question, if issued, would be destitute of legal obligation.

9. A strong appeal is made to us to approve the loan

experiment to bring the lands specified in the act under cultivation because it is sanctioned by the legislature and public opinion, but these considerations do not supply the legal element necessary to bring the scheme to execute the law within the scope of legitimate legislation. "Ours is an unmixed duty, to declare the law as it is, and not as we might wish it to be."

Let the writ issue as prayed for.

COLEMAN, C. J.: I dissent.

[No. 2391]

PAUL GARSON, CHARLES DEGIOVANNI, L. PRO-SOLE, JOHN PECETTI, PIETRO QUILLICI, A. L. LAUGHTON, M. NORTENSEN, H. HANSEN, LOUIS GARDELLI, LASSARO CERVERI, A. PINCOLINI, S. GARAVENTA, H. BERSANI, JOHN PROSOLE, JOHN B. PECETTI, JULIUS LOMBARDI, DOMINIC CERFOGLIO, PETER CERFOGLIO, PICETTI LORENZO, MARTIN AGUERRELIARE, JERRY ZOLEZZI, GANDOLFO PIETRO, CHARLES DONDERO, J. II. SMITH, G. MARCHI, B. CAPURRO, RICK DE BERNARDI, AND C. ELGES, RESPONDENTS, *v.* STEAMBOAT CANAL COMPANY (A CORPORATION), APPELLANT.

[185 Pac. 801, 1119]

1. PUBLIC SERVICE COMMISSIONS—APPLICABILITY OF ACT OF 1919 TO APPEAL FROM JUDGMENT IN CASE BROUGHT UNDER ACT OF 1911.
   Where the facts involved in action to enjoin enforcement of rates fixed by public service commission under Stats. 1911, c. 162, transpired before the "act defining public utilities," etc. (Stats. 1919, c. 109), took effect, the appeal from the judgment was governed by former act, in view of section 44 of latter act.

2. APPEAL AND ERROR—CHANGE OF THEORY ON APPEAL.
   An act should not be alleged by a party in his pleading and denied by him on appeal.

3. WATERS AND WATERCOURSES—REGULATION—"PUBLIC UTILITY"—"PLANT."
   A canal company, engaged in the business of delivering water to a number of users for agricultural and other purposes, held a "public utility," within Stats. 1911, c. 162, sec. 3, making

a corporation, which owns, operates, or controls "any plant or equipment," or part thereof, for delivery of water to other persons a "public utility," and subject to control of public service commission; the word "plant" not having been used in its precise and technical meaning, requiring pumping station or other mechanical apparatus, and being sufficiently comprehensive to apply to the canal and business of such canal company.

4. PUBLIC SERVICE COMMISSIONS—RULES OF EVIDENCE.

Though the public service commission cannot dispense with the essential rules of evidence which conduce to a fair and impartial hearing on the question of rates, they are essentially empowered with liberal discretion in passing upon the competency of evidence.

5. WATERS AND WATERCOURSES—REGULATION OF RATES—HEARING OF PUBLIC SERVICE COMMISSION.

Public service commission's use, in hearing as to water rates, of testimony and data obtained at former hearings, after due notice that such testimony and data would be considered, and ample time for. examination thereof given all the parties to the proceeding, *held* not an abuse of discretion, where a full hearing was held, with full opportunity to all parties to introduce and cross-examine witnesses, and to test, explain, or refute such evidence; the use of such testimony and data not having deprived the parties of any substantial right.

6. CONSTITUTIONAL LAW—REGULATION OF RATES OF PUBLIC UTILITY A LEGISLATIVE FUNCTION.

The power to prescribe rates for a common carrier or a public utility company is a legislative function, as distinguished from judicial power, which the legislature has really exercised in the first instance, by prescribing that all rates shall be just and reasonable.

7. CORPORATIONS—RATES OF PUBLIC UTILITIES.

The right of public utilities to initiate their own rates is subject to the requirement that all rates shall be just and reasonable.

8. PUBLIC SERVICE COMMISSIONS—REVIEW OF ORDER ESTABLISHING RATES.

Under Stats. 1911, c. 162, sec. 26, and in view of Const. art. 4, sec. 20, district court's jurisdiction, on appeal from order of public service commission, is confined to the reasonableness of the rate change; the court having no right to assume administrative functions in establishing what in its judgment seems to be a reasonable rate.

9. PUBLIC SERVICE COMMISSIONS—RESTRAINING ENFORCEMENT OF RATES PENDENTE LITE.

Under Stats. 1911, c. 162, sec. 26, providing that all rates fixed by the public service commission shall be deemed in full force and effect until final determination, district court had no right to grant an injunction pendente lite restraining enforcement of the rate fixed by the commission.

10. CONSTITUTIONAL LAW—REGULATION OF CHARGES NOT A DENIAL
    OF DUE PROCESS OF LAW.

    Stats. 1911, c. 162, sec. 26, in so far as it provides that all
rates fixed by the public service commission "shall be deemed
reasonable and just and shall remain in full force and effect
until final determination by the courts having jurisdiction," is
not violative of Const. art. 1, sec. 8, guaranteeing that no person shall be deprived of property without due process of law.

11. PUBLIC SERVICE COMMISSIONS—RATES TO REMAIN IN FORCE PEND-
    ING JUDICIAL DETERMINATION.

    Stats. 1911, c. 162, sec. 26, providing that all rates fixed by
the public service commission "shall be deemed reasonable
and just and shall remain in full force and effect until final
determination by the courts having jurisdiction," does not
require that rates remain in full force and effect until final
determination in the supreme court, but only pending final
determination by district courts.

12. STATUTES—CONSTRUCTION TO GIVE EFFECT TO ENTIRE ACT.

    A statute should be construed so as to give effect, if possible,
to all its parts.

13. STATUTES—CONSTRUCTION TO AVOID ABSURD MEANING.

    Any reasonable construction which the phraseology of a
statute, or a part of a statute, will bear, must be drawn to
avoid an absurd meaning.

14. PUBLIC SERVICE COMMISSIONS—REVIEW BY COURTS.

    Under Stats. 1911, c. 162, sec. 26, courts have no right to
interfere with the public service commission or review its
determination, further than to keep it within the law and protect the constitutional rights of the public service agencies
over which it has been given control.

15. CONSTITUTIONAL LAW—LEGISLATIVE ENCROACHMENT ON COURTS.

    Stats. 1911, c. 162, sec. 26, in so far as it provides that all
rates fixed by the public service commission "shall be deemed
reasonable and just and shall remain in full force and effect
until final determination by the courts having jurisdiction," is
not violative of Const. art. 6, sec. 6, conferring original jurisdiction in all cases in equity upon district courts; such statute
merely establishing a rule of evidence, and not withholding
remedy for imposition of unreasonable rates.

16. CONSTITUTIONAL LAW—LEGISLATURE'S RIGHT TO MAKE RULES OF
    EVIDENCE.

    Legislature has the undoubted right to prescribe such rules
of evidence as may best promote justice in a particular case.

APPEAL from Second Judicial District Court, Washoe
County; *Thomas F. Moran,* Judge.

Action by Paul Garson and others against the Steamboat Canal Company and others. From a judgment
granting a temporary injunction, the named defendant
appeals. **Reversed. Rehearing denied.**

Norcross, Thatcher & Woodburn, for Appellant:

Damages that plaintiffs may sustain by the enforcement of the rate in question are such that they can be easily ascertained by a court and jury. The order granting an injunction pendente lite should be reversed and set aside.

The lower court had no authority to grant an injunction pendente lite against the enforcement of a rate fixed by the public utility commission. Stats. 1911, sec. 26, p. 330. Every reasonable doubt must be yielded in favor of the rate. Missouri Rate Cases, 230 U. S. 474; State v. Railroad, 57 South. 175; Minneapolis R. R. Co. v. Minnesota, 186 U. S. 257; Lady Bryan G. & S. M. Co. v. Lady Bryan M. Co., 4 Nev. 414.

The commission informed all parties that it would use and consider testimony given on former hearings, and the records and data on file in its office. No contention is made that the evidence was irrelevant. The most that can be said against it is that it would be incompetent in a court of law. The rules of competency of evidence, for the purpose of admissibility in hearings before commissions, is entirely different from that of common-law courts. I. C. C. v. Baird, 48 L. Ed. 860; I. C. C. v. Louisville N. R. Co., 57 L. Ed. 434.

If the order of the commission was void, the court should not have granted the injunction, because the new rate fixed by the schedule was in effect, the company having the absolute right to initiate its own rate in the first instance. Stats. 1915, p. 47. The filing and publication of a schedule is for the purpose of affording special facilities to the public for ascertaining the rates in force thereunder and for preventing unjust discrimination and rebates. Oregon R. & N. Co. v. Thisler, 133 Pac. 539; U. S. v. Miller, 56 L. Ed. 568. The absolute right to fix rates is retained by the public utility, subject only to the provisions of the statute. I. C. C. v. Chicago G. W. R. Co., 52 L. Ed. 712; L. & N. R. Co. v. I. C. C., 195 Fed. 541; I. C. C. v. Louisville & N. R. Co., 57 L. Ed.

431; Crescent Coal Co. v. Louisville & N. R. Co., 33 L. R. A. 442.

The lower court usurped the legislative and administrative functions and acted beyond its authority when it fixed a rate for the services performed. The court may not substitute what in its judgment may be the proper rate for the judgment of either the public utility or the commission. Atchison R. Co. v. U. S., 232 U. S. 199; Montana R. Co. v. Morley, 198 Fed. 991; S. P. Co. v. C. F. & I. Co., 101 Fed. 779; S. P. Co. v. Campbell, 230 U. S. 537; Simpson v. Shepard, 57 L. Ed. 1511.

Sardis Summerfield, for Respondents:

The appeal should be dismissed and the lower court permitted to resume the exercise of its original equity jurisdiction.

The appellant, being a mere ditch owner and operator, cannot be included as the owner, operator or controller of a plant or equipment, either in whole or in part. Public Utility Act, sec. 7.

Subdivision a, section 33, public utility act, is violative of the state constitution. The public service commission is a mere supervising and regulating administrative commission, and cannot be empowered by the legislative and executive branches of the state government to usurp the constitutional functions of the courts. Const. Nev. sec. 8, art. 1; sec. 1, art. 3; sec. 6, art. 6. The constitution expressly delegates "original jurisdiction in all cases in equity" to the district courts.

By the Court, DUCKER, J.:

The appellant corporation, the Steamboat Canal Company, is a public utility engaged in the business of delivering water from the Truckee River, through its canal, known as the Steamboat Canal, to a number of users for agricultural and other purposes. In a former year the public service commission of Nevada had established the rate for the delivery and sale of water to such users at $6.50 per miner's inch per annum, and when paid in advance on or before June 1 of each year at $6 per miner's inch. On or before May 18, 1918, the Steamboat Canal Company filed with the public service commission a schedule of rates, and therein established a rate of $10 per miner's inch for the the irrigation season. The public service commission entered an order suspending the proposed rate for a period of sixty days, and cited the Steamboat Canal Company to appear and show cause why the rates in force should be increased. A number of water users served by the company filed a protest against the proposed increase in rates, and upon issue thus made a hearing was held before the commission, at which all parties interested appeared, in person or by attorney. During the pendency of the proceedings before the commission the rate proposed was suspended by its order for an additional sixty days. The hearing commenced on the 5th day of August, 1918. It was thereafter continued to October 8, and closed on October 9, 1918. Thereafter, on December 4, 1918, the commission entered an order denying the application of the Steamboat Canal Company for an increase in rates for water service to $10 per inch, and ordered that the rate be established at $7.50 per miner's inch for irrigation purposes for the season of 1918 and each successive year, unless otherwise ordered by the commission. It was also ordered that, if prepayment should be made on or before June 1 of each year, the charge should be $7.25 per inch.

The protestants, being dissatisfied with the ruling of the commission, commenced this action in the district court against J. F. Shaughnessy and W. H. Simmons, as the public service commission of Nevada, and the Steamboat Canal Company, and obtained an order of the court granting an injunction pendente lite restraining the enforcement or collection of the rate of $7.50 per miner's inch designated by the order of the commission, or collection of any greater rate than $6.50 per miner's inch. From the order granting the temporary injunction this appeal is taken.

1. This action was commenced pursuant to section 26 of an act making the railroad commission of Nevada ex officio a public service commission for the regulation and control of certain public utilities, prescribing the manner in which such public utilities shall be regulated, etc., approved March 23, 1911 (Stats. 1911, c. 162) ; but the respondents contend that the disposition of the appeal must be controlled by the provisions of "An act defining public utilities," etc., approved March 28, 1919 (Stats. 1919, c. 109), for the reason that it expressly repeals the former act. If this contention were correct, we do not see how it could alter our decision, for the reason that all of the provisions in the former act having any application to the facts of this case have been reenacted in the latter act, and no additional provisions enacted therein have any bearing on the issue. But it is not correct to say that the law of 1919 controls this appeal. All of the facts of the case transpired before it became effective, and furthermore express provision is made in section 44 of the law of 1919 that the repeal of the former act shall not "affect any act done, right established, or prosecution or proceeding commenced under and by virtue of" it.

2. Respondents assert that the order of the public service commission is void, because no authority is given it by law to regulate the affairs of the Steamboat Canal Company, in that its canal, through which respondents are served with water, does not come within the meaning of the words "plant" or "equipment," used in the statute in defining certain public utilities over which the commission is given supervision. It is conceded that the statute does not otherwise designate the company's property as a public utility. It will be observed that this contention is a radical departure from the complaint, in which the legal right of the commission to supervise and establish water rates for the Steamboat Canal Company is distinctly recognized. In this respect it is alleged in the complaint that the public service commission has authority to fix reasonable rates for

public utilities operating within the state; that the Steamboat Canal Company is a public utility engaged in the delivery of water for agricultural and other purposes within this state; that the rate heretofore fixed by the public service commission by an order duly made and entered pursuant to law is $6.50 per miner's inch, and that the same is still in force. It is thus seen that respondents have formally asserted in their verified complaint the authority of the public service commission to supervise the water rates of the company, which it now contests. While the statute must control as the source of authority for the commission in this regard, the power to do an act should not be alleged by a party in his pleading and denied by him on appeal.

3. Section 3 of the act of 1911 provides:

"The term 'public utility' within the meaning of this act shall embrace every corporation, company, individual, association of individuals, their lessees, trustees or receivers appointed by any court whatsoever, that now or hereafter may own, operate or control any plant or equipment, or any part of a plant or equipment within the state for the production, delivery or furnishing for or to other persons, firms, associations, or corporations, private or municipal, heat, light, power in any form or by any agency, water for business, manufacturing, agricultural or household use, or sewerage service whether within the limits of municipalities, towns or villages, or elsewhere; and the public service commission is hereby invested with full power of supervision, regulation and control of all such utilities, subject to the provisions of this act and to the exclusion of the jurisdiction, regulation and control of such utilities by any municipality, town or village."

If a precise and technical meaning were accorded to the word "plant," confining it strictly to include only such public utilities of this class which delivered water to consumers through the agency, at least in part, of machinery, as a pumping station or other mechanical apparatus, the intention of the legislature would not, in our opinion, be effectuated. It would contravene the spirit of the act to assume that it was intended to make the right of the consumers served by public utilities of this character to the benefit of the commission's control over rates and service dependent entirely upon whether the water delivered flowed into the ditch or pipe, or was forced into the distributing channel by means of machinery, water wheel, or other apparatus. In Brennan v. Sewerage and Water Board, 108 La. 582, 32 South. 560, it was said that "a system of pipes intended for the distribution of water, but with no provision by which that distribution can be made," may with propriety be called a plant. The term "plant for the delivery of water * * * for agriculture or household use," as used in the statute, is sufficiently comprehensive in its meaning to apply to the canal and business of the Steamboat Canal Company as a public utility, subject under the statute to the supervision and control of the public service commission.

It is also contended by respondents that the order of the commission establishing the rate of $7.50 per miner's inch is void, for the reason that the commission, in determining this rate, took into consideration evidence taken at former hearings and data on file with the commission relative to the Steamboat Canal Company in its dealings with the water users. The following extracts from the record of hearing held on August 5, showing statements made by the commissioners and Mr. Kearney, attorney for the protesting water users, have considerable bearing on the merit of this contention:

"Commissioner Bartine—There is no question of the value of the property. The commission has passed upon that, and determined that the property has a certain value. It is rather hard for me to see how we can depart from that, unless there is a showing made by the company that we are wrong. We will give you any opportunity that you desire to show that it is an overvaluation. You can take any reasonable time for it. These charges are largely a matter of bookkeeping, and, when the decision is finally rendered it will cover the whole thing.

"Commissioner Simmons—I want to say, for this commission, that, in view of no testimony having been introduced in this case bearing upon the valuation of the ditch, the commission will avail itself of the data which it already has, and which are official, with reference to the value of the ditch. If you can show that there is a change in the value of the ditch, other than what we now have before us, then that will be given consideration. But in view of the fact that the question of the valuation of the ditch has not been gone into in this case, either by counsel or stipulation, we would use the data that we already have and which are available, in basing our opinion in the present case.

"Mr. Kearney—In regard to that stipulation I would like to say that, if that testimony is used for the purpose of rehearing and reopening the old case, I would object to it.

"Commissioner Bartine—We do not intend to reopen the old case at all.

"Mr. Kearney—As I understand it, the rate of $6 per inch was fixed upon as a reasonable return for a certain valuation found by the commission, after the testimony had been considered. Now, then, I don't want the commission to reconsider that testimony, and find a different valuation at this time, without having an opportunity to be heard.

"Commissioner Bartine—I do not think it will ever be done; so far as I am concerned it will not be. So far as we have gone into this case, the question of valuation does not cut any figure. The application for an advance in rates is based on figures of cost of material and labor."

It is evident from these statements of the commissioners that the commission had fixed the company's property at a certain valuation at former hearings, and that they intended considering the evidence obtained for this purpose, and would make no change in such valuation without a showing made by the company or the water users. Under the circumstances, no prejudice could have resulted to any of the parties from the action of the commission. Certainly there was nothing in this regard, in view of the full hearing that was held and ruling made upon substantial evidence introduced, that could render the subsequent order of the commission a nullity. Notice of intention to use the former evidence, and the purpose for which it would be considered, was given to all parties at the beginning of the proceedings. They were all present, either in person or by attorney, and were informed that ample time would be given for examination of the proposed evidence and data on file with the commission, or to make any showing against it. More than two months elapsed from the time notice was given until the hearing was closed, and so far as the record discloses no effort was made by the water users to examine the evidence or refute it in any way. Their knowledge of its general character may be fairly assumed from the fact that it was adduced at former hearings held by the commission to establish rates for the Steamboat Canal Company. It was therefore not extraneous evidence, unknown to the parties, but known, available, and specifically called to their attention in ample time for inspection, explanation, or contradiction, and we may assume, from the references made to it in the record, was in the main of a character essential to a proper determination of a reasonable rate for water service.

The facts recited do not bring the case within the ruling advanced in Interstate Commerce Commission v. Louisville Railroad Co., 227 U. S. 88, 33 Sup. Ct. 185, 57 L. Ed. 431, so much relied on by respondents. The government insisted in that case that, as an act of Congress provided that a carrier's rates should be set aside if, after a hearing, the commission shall be of the opinion that the charge was unreasonable, an order based on such opinion was conclusive, and could not be set aside, even if the finding was wholly without substantial evidence to support it. It was further insisted that the commission was required by law to obtain information necessary to enable it to perform the duties and carry out the objects for which it was created, and, having been given legislative power to make rates, it could act, as could Congress, on such information, and therefore its findings must be presumed to have been supported by such information, even though not formally proved at the hearing. These contentions were denied by the court, and it was held that neither of these statutory provisions could in effect empower the commission to decide as to the reasonableness or unreasonableness of rates without a hearing required by the statute at which "all parties must be fully apprised of the evidence submitted, and must be given an opportunity to cross-examine witnesses, to inspect documents, and to offer evidence in explanation or rebuttal." With reference to the latter contention, as to the right of the commission to act upon information gathered for the purposes of investigation, the court said:

"But such a construction would nullify the right to a hearing, for manifestly there is no hearing when the party does not know what evidence is offered or considered, and is not given an opportunity to test, explain, or refute."

The order of the commission was upheld, because there was substantial evidence to support it.

4. In the instant case the order of the commission was not without substantial evidence to support it, nor did the commission base its order upon extraneous evidence, as was asserted to be the power of such administrative boards in Interstate Commerce Commission v. Louisville and Nashville Railroad Co., supra. As previously stated, a full hearing was held, at which all parties were represented, and cognizant of the evidence submitted, and given every reasonable opportunity to introduce witnesses, to cross-examine, to test, explain, or refute any evidence to be considered by the commission. . The consideration of the testimony and data obtained at the former hearings, after due notice that it would be submitted and considered, was an infraction of the strict rules of evidence which prevail in the trial of cases in courts of law, but administrative boards of this character are not hampered by technical procedure. True, they cannot dispense with the essential rules of evidence

which conduce to a fair and impartial hearing, but, from the nature of their organization and the duties imposed upon them by statute they are essentially empowered with liberal discretion in passing upon the competency of evidence.

5. If it were otherwise, the policy of the law, in conferring authority upon the public service commission to supervise and regulate the rates, would be in a large measure frustrated. Interstate Commerce Commission v. Louisville & N. R. R. Co., supra. On the facts of this case we are not prepared to say that the action of the commission in considering the testimony and data complained of by respondents was an abuse of discretion by the commission, or that it deprived respondents of a substantial right.

We now come to a consideration of the injunction pendente lite, which appellants contend the trial court was without authority to grant. The collection of the rate designated in the order of the commission, or of any rate greater than or in excess of $6.50 per miner's inch per annum, was restrained by the injunction. The effect of this order of the district court is to revise and modify the order of the commission establishing a rate of $7.50, and substitute a rate of $6.50 in its stead. Authority for the district court to interfere with the findings of the commission in this case is found in section 26 of the act of 1911, and nowhere therein has the legislature sought to confer upon the courts power to fix the rate of any public utility or change the rate established by the commission. Section 26 reads in part:

"Any party in interest being dissatisfied with an order of the commission fixing any rate or rates, fares, charges, classifications, joint rate or rates, or any order fixing any regulations, practices or services, may within ninety (90) days commence an action in the district court of the proper county against the commission and other interested parties as defendants to vacate and set aside any such order on the ground that the rate or rates, fares, charges, classifications, joint rate or rates, fixed in such order are unlawful or unreasonable, or that any such regulation, practice, or service, fixed in such order is unreasonable. * * *

"(a) No injunction shall issue suspending or staying any order of the commission except upon application to the court or judge thereof, notice to the commission having been first given and hearing having been had thereon; provided, that all rates fixed by the commission shall be deemed reasonable and just and shall remain in full force and effect until final determination by the courts having jurisdiction.

"(b) If, upon the trial of such action, evidence shall be introduced by the plaintiff which is found by the court to be different from that offered upon the hearing before the commission, or additional thereto, the court, before proceeding to render judgment, unless the parties to such action stipulate in writing to the contrary, shall transmit a copy of such evidence to the commission, and shall stay further proceedings in said action fifteen (15) days from the date of such transmission. Upon receipt of such evidence the commission shall consider the same, and may later modify, amend or rescind its order relating to such rate or rates, fares, charges, classifications, joint rate or rates, regulation, practice or service complained of in said action, and shall report its action thereon to said court within ten days from the receipt of such evidence.

"(c) If the commission shall rescind its order complained of, the action shall be dismissed; if it shall alter, modify or amend the same, such altered, modified or amended order shall take the place of the original order complained of, and judgment shall be rendered thereon, as though made by the commission in the first instance. If the original order shall not be rescinded or changed by the commission, judgment shall be rendered upon such original order."

By these provisions the court is empowered only to vacate or set aside any order of the commission on the ground that the rate fixed therein is unlawful or unreasonable, or confirm it if the rate is lawful and reasonable. In fact, it is the policy of the act, as evidenced

from its plain terms, to leave with public utilities **the**
right to initiate rates subject to the revisionary **action**
of the commission.

6. The power to prescribe rates for a common **carrier**
or a public utility company is a legislative function **as**
distinguished from judicial power (Southern Pacific Co.
v. Colorado Fuel & Iron Co., 101 Fed. 783, 42 C. C. A. 12),
which the legislature has really exercised in the first
instance by prescribing that all rates shall be just and
reasonable.

7, 8. The right of public utilities to initiate their own
rates is subject to this statutory requirement and the
public service commission is legally constituted and
given jurisdiction by prescribed procedure to give effect
to the legislative will. The district court to which an
appeal may be taken is therefore, on review, confined to
a determination of the issue of the reasonableness of the
rate challenged. It may ascertain whether the legislative mandate that rates shall be just and reasonable has
become effective through the agency of the commission.
But, being without legislative or administrative functions,
its jurisdiction ends there. It cannot proceed further,
and assume administrative functions in establishing
what, in its judgment, seems to be a reasonable rate.
Spring Valley Waterworks v. City and County of San
Francisco (C. C.) 192 Fed. 144; Madison v. Madison Gas
and Electric Co., 129 Wis. 249, 108 N. W. 65, L. R. A.
(N.S.) 529, 9 Ann. Cas. 819; Reagan v. Farmers' Loan
and Trust Co., 154 U. S. 397, 14 Sup. Ct. 1047, 38 L. Ed.
1014; Pond on Public Utilities, secs. 440–446, and cases
cited; State v. Great Northern Ry. Co., 130 Minn. 57,
153 N. W. 247, Ann. Cas. 1917B, 1201.

As said in the case of Baltimore and Ohio R. R. Co.,
appellant, v. Public Service Commission, 6 Pa. Super. Ct.
403, and commended in Ben Avon Borough v. Ohio
Water Co., 260 Pa. 289, 296, 103 Atl. 744, by the supreme
court of that state:

"Establishing a schedule of the rates or tolls that a
public service company may lawfully demand is one of the
most complicated and important * * * tasks imposed

by the legislature on the public service commission. The proper determination of such questions necessarily involves the consideration of many matters and many things far removed from the atmosphere of an appellate court."

That the court cannot fix the rate itself, however, but is limited in its jurisdiction in determining whether a rate, when fixed, is reasonable and proper, is the generally accepted rule as expressed in the case of Nebraska Tel. Co. v. State, 55 Neb. 627, 76 N. W. 171, 45 L. R. A. 113, decided in 1898, as follows:

"Here the court determines that the respondent shall perform for the relator a specific service for three months for a specific sum of money. This in effect was a determination by the court that $3 per month was a reasonable compensation for the service required to be rendered by the respondent, and a fixing of the compensation for such service at that price for the future. We think the history of the legislation of the entire country shows that the power to determine what compensation public service corporations may demand for their services is a legislative function and not a judicial one."

If it were conceded that the courts of this state could fix or revise the rates a public utility could charge, would not the legislature have performed a vain act in establishing another administrative body for the same purpose? But the courts are precluded by the constitution from performing legislative functions, and the framers of the organic law recognized that power to fix the compensation for common carriers or public utility service was a legislative one. Section 20, article 4, of the state constitution, which precludes the legislature from exercising certain powers, also provides:

"But nothing in this section shall be construed to deny or restrict the power of the legislature to establish and regulate * * * the rates of freight, passage toll, and charges of railroads, toll roads, ditch, flume and tunnel companies incorporated under the laws of this state or doing business therein."

And it is quite clear that the legislature has acted

upon the theory that this power to fix the compensation of common carriers and public service corporations is one vested in it by the constitution. This is evident from its creation of commissions for that purpose, and the powers conferred upon them, as well as from the provisions limiting the courts in review. Nebraska Tel. Co. v. State, supra.

9. It results from what we have said that the district court was without authority to revise the order of the public service commission in this case and fix the rate of service at $6.50 per miner's inch per annum. We also conclude that the court was likewise wrong in vacating the order of the commission establishing the rate of $7.50 per miner's inch and restraining its collection by the Steamboat Canal Company. As already pointed out, section 26 provides:

"That all rates fixed by the commission shall be deemed reasonable and just, and shall remain in full force and effect until final determination by the courts having jurisdiction."

The lower court disregarded this provision of the statute in vacating the order of the commission and in granting an injunction pendente lite. No reason for this action appears from the record, but as the statute is mandatory, and, as counsel for respondents insists in this court, that it is unconstitutional, we assume that the lower court entertained the same view.

10, 11. It is contended that the proviso is violative of section 8 of article 1 of the constitution, guaranteeing that "no person shall be * * * deprived of * * * property, without due process of law," and of section 6 of article 6 of that instrument which confers "original jurisdiction in all cases in equity" upon the district courts. It is urged that the proviso deprives the district court of its equitable powers in this class of cases. We do not share these views and apprehend that may arise partially from a misconstruction of the provision. It is insisted that it is meant by the proviso that the rates shall remain in full force and effect until the final determination in the supreme court. The proviso does not contain the words "court having appellate jurisdiction" or designate the supreme court; yet these would have been natural and appropriate expressions, if the construction claimed by the respondents should prevail. The language is "until final determination by the courts having jurisdiction," and we are persuaded that it was meant to declare that the rates should be maintained pending a final determination by the district courts.

12, 13. A statute should be construed so as to give effect if possible to all its parts; and this construction harmonizes the proviso with the other parts of the section providing for trial and judgment in the district court and gives a reasonable effect to the proviso itself, notwithstanding its language is not exactly accurate in expressing the legislative intent. An absurdity in legislative language is never presumed, nor found by the courts, unless revealed in clear and unmistakable terms. Any reasonable construction which the phraseology of a statute, or a part of a statute, will bear must be drawn to avoid an absurd meaning, upon the theory that legislators are men of ordinarily good sense. If we should construe the proviso to mean that the rates fixed by the commission shall remain in full force and effect until final determination by the supreme court, we should charge the legislature with a gross absurdity in providing for a trial in one part of section 26 and defeating the purpose of the trial in another part of the section.

Section 26 provides that a party, dissatisfied with an order of the commission fixing a rate, may commence an action in the district court "to vacate and set aside any such order" on the ground that the rate is unlawful and unreasonable, and that "judgment shall be rendered upon such original order," or upon any modification, alteration, or amendment of the original order which may be made by the commission pending the trial of the case. Manifestly it was not intended to provide in section 26 for a trial in the district court to test the reasonableness of a rate fixed by the commission giving the court power to vacate the order of the commission fixing it, and then by the proviso to prevent a judgment in case the rate is found to be unreasonable. The purpose of the proviso is, we think, reasonably apparent to maintain the rate during the pendency of the trial and until final judgment in the district court. And this provision does not, in our opinion, trench upon the constitutional guaranty of due process of law. The provision objected to must be taken in connection with the entire act of which it is a part when considered as to its encroachment upon the constitutional guaranty of due process of law. The ultimate purpose of the act is to regulate and control certain classes of business impressed with a public interest.

The public service commission act is the direct outgrowth of an urgent and persistent public demand for prompt, intelligent, and effective public control of public utilities. It is founded on necessity and convenience. Competition did not prove effective in preventing monopoly by public utility companies and its consequent burden on the public in the different classes of public service rendered by them. It is recognized, also, that the rate-making power and the power to regulate and control these enterprises, vested by the constitution in the legislature, could not be conveniently exercised by that body to meet the changing conditions, which make the rates a public utility may lawfully charge for its service vary in value from time to time. These exigencies were met by the legislature in the formation of the governmental agency designated, in the act creating it, as a public service commission. The law presumes that the members of the commission shall be men trained in those lines of business in which public utilities are engaged, and who can fairly and intelligently adjust the complex questions that constantly arise. Necessarily to make the act effective to answer the purposes of its enactment, the commission has been clothed with broad discretionary powers; and to further accomplish these purposes the orders of the commission as to rates

and charges have been made prima facie lawful from
the date of the order until changed or modified by the
commission, or until found to be unreasonable in pursuance of section 26 of the act. Section 25.

"In all actions under this act the burden of proof shall
be upon the party attacking or resisting the order of
the commission to show by clear and satisfactory evidence that the order is unlawful, or unreasonable, as the
case may be." Section 26, subd. e.

14. It was not intended that the courts should interfere with the commission, or review its determinations,
further than to keep it within the law and protect the
constitutional rights of the public service agencies over
which it has been given control. In view of the salutary
public policy of the act, and the ample provision made
for notice and full hearing before the commission, at
which the public utility complained of and the complainant are entitled to appear by counsel, and the ample
provisions made for the production and presentation of
their proofs, it was competent for the legislature to prescribe that the rates fixed by the commission should
abide during the temporary season of a trial to test their
reasonableness. The rates fixed by the commission are
not conclusive. The courts are open for a review of the
proceedings of the commission, and the right is given to
the parties to adduce evidence in addition to that introduced on the hearing before the commission. In order
to facilitate the trial to the end that a speedy determination of the question of the reasonableness of the rates
may be obtained, it is provided in section 26 that:

"All actions brought under this section shall have precedence over any civil cause of a different nature pending in such court, and the court shall always be deemed
open for the trial thereof, and the same shall be tried
and determined as other civil actions."

"Due process of law merely requires such tribunals as
are proper to deal with the subject in hand. Reasonable
notice and a fair opportunity to be heard before some
tribunal before it decides the issues are the essentials of

due process of law." Stettler v. O'Hara, 69 Or. 519, 139
Pac. 746, L. R. A. 1917c, 944, Ann. Cas. 1916a, 217.

We think that none of the essentials necessary to
insure to the parties a full guaranty of due process of
law are absent from the statute, nor impaired by the
provision under consideration.

What we have said as to the nature of the legislation
concerning public utilities applies with equal force to
the objection that the proviso invades the equitable jurisdiction of the district court. The statute makes the
findings of the commission upon questions of fact prima
facie evidence of the reasonableness of rates on review
in the district courts. This in itself might be urged as
some curtailment of equitable jurisdiction, for generally
in equity cases the court may find a fact from the
evidence, and is not bound by a rule that, if there is
evidence to support a fact, it thereby becomes conclusive.

15, 16. But still statutes identical with the provisions
making the findings of the commission prima facie evidence of reasonableness of rates have been uniformly
upheld by the courts against constitutional objections,
upon the theory that no person has a vested right in
any rule of evidence. The legislature has the undoubted
right to prescribe such rules of evidence as may best
promote justice in a particular case. The provision complained of does not prevent parties from exhibiting their
rights on the trial of the case, but merely establishes a
rule of evidence which may not be overcome until issue
is joined and the proofs presented for final determination. The proviso does not withhold a remedy for the
imposition of unreasonable rates. The remedy is merely
deferred for a period of time which, considering the
policy of the law towards the establishment of rates by
the commission, cannot be said to be unreasonable,
especially in view of the fact that the statute acceler-
ates the trial of this class of cases by giving them
precedence over all civil causes of a different nature.

The order of the district court, granting an injunction
pendente lite restraining the collection of the rate of

$7.50 per miner's inch per annum fixed by the order of the public service commission as the rate of service to be charged by the Steamboat Canal Company, and restraining the collection of any greater rate than $6.50 per miner's inch per annum, is hereby reversed.

ON PETITION FOR REHEARING

By the Court, DUCKER, J.:

The petition for rehearing filed by respondents has been given careful attention. It discusses questions that were duly considered and disposed of in the opinion of the court. As we are convinced, after further research and reflection, that these questions were correctly determined, we are impelled to deny the petition.

In the petition our attention has been directed to a certain unguarded statement made in the opinion which we desire to correct. In the course of the discussion of the questions raised, the writer of the opinion referred to an action commenced in the district court to vacate and set aside an order of the commission, as an appeal. That this was an inadvertent expression is apparent from other parts of the opinion, but we desire to expressly correct it, so that no erroneous conclusion might arise from a consideration of the decision. The action commenced in the district court is not an appeal, though it is in some sense a review, for the statute clearly contemplates a consideration by the trial court of the evidence offered upon the hearing before the commission. Section 26 of the act of 1911 (chapter 162) making the railroad commission of Nevada ex officio a public service commission. See, also, section 33 of the act of 1919 (chapter 109) defining public utilities, etc. The opinion is therefore corrected in this respect.

Rehearing in the above-entitled matter is hereby denied.

[No. 2407]

STATE OF NEVADA, Ex Rel. J. G. SCRUGHAM,
AS STATE ENGINEER, RELATOR AND PETITIONER, v.
THE DISTRICT COURT OF THE SIXTH JUDI-
CIAL DISTRICT OF THE STATE OF NEVADA,
IN AND FOR HUMBOLDT COUNTY, THE HON-
ORABLE J. A. CALLAHAN, DISTRICT JUDGE THEREOF,
AND HONORABLE C. J. MCFADDEN, ACTING DISTRICT
JUDGE THEREOF, RESPONDENTS.

[184 Pac. 1023]

1. PROHIBITION—MOOT CASE DISMISSED.
    Where proceedings in prohibition were brought to restrain
    district judge from hearing a motion to dissolve a preliminary
    injunction, the proceeding will be dismissed where, upon hear-
    ing, it appears that the motion had been decided and the
    injunction dissolved by such judge prior to the service upon
    him of the alternative writ.

PROCEEDING in prohibition by the State of Nevada,
on the relation of J. G. Scrugham, as State Engineer,
against the District Court of the Sixth Judicial District
of the State of Nevada, in and for Humboldt County, and
Honorable J. A. Callahan, District Judge thereof, and
Honorable C. J. McFadden, Acting District Judge
thereof. **Proceeding dismissed.**

Leonard B. Fowler, Attorney-General, and *Robert
Richards*, Deputy Attorney-General (*Carey Van Fleet*,
of Counsel), for Petitioner.

Cheney, Downer, Price & Hawkins, for Respondents.

By the Court, DUCKER, J.:

On the petition of the above relator and petitioner,
this court issued an alternative writ of prohibition
restraining the respondents from hearing, trying, or
entering a decree in that certain action entitled "In the
Sixth Judicial District Court of the State of Nevada, in
and for the County of Humboldt, W. C. Pitt et al., Plaintiff, v. J. G. Scrugham, as State Engineer, Defendant,"
and required said respondents to show cause before this

court why they should not be absolutely restrained and prohibited from taking any further proceedings in said action except to dismiss the same. Due return having been made thereto, the matter came on for hearing in this court and was argued and submitted.

It appeared upon said hearing that the motion to dissolve a preliminary injunction theretofore issued in said action and submitted to the respondent Hon. C. J. McFadden for consideration and decision, and which decision was sought to be restrained by said writ, had been decided and the injunction dissolved by him prior to the service upon him of said alternative writ. We are therefore of the opinion that the proceedings in this court are to all intents and purposes resolved into a moot case and should be dismissed.

It will be so ordered.

REPORTS OF CASES

DETERMINED BY

THE SUPREME COURT

OF THE

STATE OF NEVADA

JANUARY TERM, 1920

[No. 2390]

M. REINHART, ADMINISTRATOR WITH THE WILL
ANNEXED OF THE ESTATE OF DOMINGO BENGOA,
DECEASED, APPELLANT, *v.* MARTIN ECHAVE,
RESPONDENT.

[185 Pac. 1070; 187 Pac. 1006]

1. WITNESSES—NO TESTIMONY BY SURVIVING PARTY TO TRANSAC-
TION.

    If one party to an original transaction is precluded from
testifying by death, the other is not entitled to the undue
advantage of giving his own uncontradicted and unexplained
account of the transaction.

2. APPEAL AND ERROR—ERROR IN ADMISSION OF TESTIMONY AS TO
TRANSACTION WITH DECEDENT HARMLESS.

    In a son-in-law's action against his father-in-law on a note
signed by the father and payable to his daughter and the
son-in-law, error in admitting the father's testimony as to
the manner in which his daughter induced him to sign the
note, though the daughter at the time of trial was dead, *held*
harmless and not ground for reversal under Rev. Laws, 5315,
in view of the testimony of the mother of the girl who was
present at the time of the signing.

3. BILLS AND NOTES—DUTY TO OFFER TESTIMONY IN SUPPORT OF
NOTE ATTACKED.

    In a suit on a note made out in printing and three different
handwritings, stripped by evidence of defendant maker of its
commercial character, and based ostensibly on some sort of
a contract between the maker and the plaintiff, his son-in-law,
it was the duty of the plaintiff, having notice of the defenses
against the note, to be prepared on trial to offer some evidence
other than the note itself to entitle him to verdict.

4. BILLS AND NOTES—DUTY TO SHOW WILLING AND INFORMED
SIGNING.

Where plaintiff before his marriage to defendant's daughter
had said he would not marry her except for money, plaintiff,
suing on a note signed by defendant to the order of plaintiff
and defendant's daughter, is under duty to offer some explanation of his conduct consistent with his interest and fair
dealing with defendant to show that the note was signed
willingly and knowingly.

ON PETITION FOR REHEARING

1. GIFTS—GIFT OF DONOR'S OWN NOTE NOT VALID.

One cannot make his own note the subject of a gift to such
an extent that it can be enforced by the donee against the
donor, or against his estate.

APPEAL from Sixth Judicial District Court, Humboldt
County; *Edward A. Ducker,* Judge.

Action by M. Reinhart, administrator with the will
annexed of Domingo Bengoa, deceased, against Martin
Echave, resulting in verdict for defendant. From an
order denying plaintiff a new trial, he appeals. **Affirmed.**
Petition for rehearing denied.

STATEMENT OF FACTS

This action was commenced by Domingo Bengoa
against Martin Echave to recover judgment for the sum
of $4,000 upon a promissory note. The paper was origi-
nally a skeleton note, and is certified with the record
for our inspection. It reads as follows:

"$4,000.00   McDermitt, Nev., Jan. 5, 1911.

"Five years after date without grace, for value
received, I promise *to* pay to *Domingo Bengoa and my
oldest daughter Martina Echave, McDermitt, Nevada,*
the sum of *$4,000.00 four thousand dollars* in gold coin
of the United States, with *no interest* no date until paid;
and in case suit or action is instituted to collect this note
or any portion thereof, I promise to pay all costs and
expenses and such additional sum as the court may
adjudge reasonable as attorney's fees in said suit or
action. *To be paid on the year of 1916,* interest payable.

"Martin Echave."

The portion italicized is written in three different

handwritings. The words "five years after date" and
"Martin Echave" are accounted for. The other is in
the handwriting of one person, but made at different
times. The remainder is in print.

Plaintiff alleges in his complaint that his copayee
sold, assigned, and delivered to him, for value, all her
interest in the note, and that he is the legal owner
thereof; that his copayee died on or about the 27th of
October, 1913.

As against the note the defendant, after denying the
averments of the complaint, set up two affirmative
defenses. One that the payees conspired to cheat and
defraud defendant out of the principal of the note, and
the other, want of consideration.

Plaintiff denied these defenses, and the issues were
submitted to a jury for determination. The verdict was
for defendant. Plaintiff moved for a new trial, which
was denied. Plaintiff died. The cause was revived in
the name of appellant, who prosecutes this appeal from
the order denying plaintiff a new trial.

The evidence for the defendant, aside from his own
testimony, tends very strongly to show that the deceased
payee was for several years under the control and influence of plaintiff. She was about 18 years of age, very
much in love with plaintiff, who was 20 years her senior,
and so much infatuated with him that her parents had
lost control over her. She spent most of her time away
from the home of her parents in company with the
plaintiff. On one occasion defendant telephoned plaintiff that if he was not going to marry his daughter to
send her home. Shortly prior to the date of the note
deceased said to her mother that if she could get money
from her father plaintiff would marry her. She said to
another witness that if she could not get money from
her father to enable her to marry plaintiff she would go
to a bad house. It is undisputed that plaintiff informed
deceased, and on several occasions the defendant, that
he would not marry deceased unless defendant gave him
money; but at no time did plaintiff or deceased state

what amount of money it would require in order to induce plaintiff to marry the deceased. In the conversations when money was suggested defendant informed plaintiff that he had no money and his children would share equally in what he possessed at his death. Plaintiff stated he wanted money then. Defendant at no time promised plaintiff $4,000 to marry his daughter, or any sum, or note, or anything of value.

It appears from the testimony of the mother of deceased that the latter came to her home in the latter part of December, 1910, and in her presence deceased represented to defendant that she had a paper for him to sign for the purpose of establishing a school district or to obtain a school for his vicinity; that the deceased represented that the paper which she then exhibited to defendant was given her by a Mr. Sprague with instructions that it be signed by him and returned the next day; and that if the paper was not in the hands of the proper authorities by the 1st of January, 1911, defendant would get no school. The mother testified that she saw the paper at the time and that it had no writing on it but some printing; that the deceased retained the paper and went with her father into an adjoining room to sign the paper, and the next morning the deceased left her home, taking the paper with her. The mother took no part in the conversation between deceased and defendant. Her testimony was given without objection or cross-examination.

Defendant, over plaintiff's objection, testified that the representation of the deceased as to the character of the paper and its purpose was false and fraudulent; that because of his trust and confidence in his daughter, and relying on her honesty and the truth of her statement, she well knowing his anxiety about obtaining a school for his several children of school age, he was induced to sign the paper without examination or reading it, and he signed the paper supposing it to be for a school purpose. Now it turns out, more than five years after the date of this transaction, that the defendant signed a promissory note, the note sued on. The first intimation the defendant had that the paper was an engagement to pay money was in the spring of 1916, when plaintiff said to him that he had a paper against him, and, when pressed for a statement as to what the paper was, plaintiff replied that it was "the paper you gave to Martina and me."

The deceased delivered the paper to plaintiff shortly after its date. The plaintiff manifestly accepted the note with some suspicion, because he took the paper to a third party, in whom he had confidence, and inquired of him if the paper was all right. Being assured that it was he left it with said party for safe-keeping.

It further appears that for several months after the note was overdue plaintiff and defendant had business dealings whereby plaintiff became indebted to defendant in installments in the sum of several thousand dollars, but the note in question was never adverted to in any of these transactions, and defendant never saw the note until shortly before the suit. When plaintiff left the note with his friend for safe-keeping, the payees, a few days thereafter, between the 10th and 15th of January, 1911, intermarried without the knowledge of deceased's parents.

In rebuttal plaintiff testified that, if he had been informed the note was wrong, he would have obtained another note from the defendant before he married defendant's daughter. The plaintiff introduced the note with the admission of the defendant's signature, proved the death of his copayee, and rested his case without offering any evidence in rebuttal other than that as above stated.

Salter & Robins, for Appellant:

It was error to allow respondent to testify to a transaction when the other party was dead. Rev. Laws, 5419. "The plaintiff was not a competent witness * * *.

The proof necessarily concerned transactions with the deceased about which he could testify, and might testify, differently, and we think he was' rendered incompetent as a witness for any such purpose." Gage v. Phillips, 21 Nev. 156. The act of the legislature prevents living witnesses from establishing communications with parties whose lips have been sealed by death. The decisions upon the statute are unequivocal and numerous. Roney v. Buckland, 5 Nev. 161; Vesey v. Benton, 13 Nev. 284; Schwartz v. Stock, 26 Nev. 128.

"If a note is payable to several jointly, action may be brought by the survivor upon the death of the other. 7 Cyc. 1033; 8 Cyc. 89; Standard Ency., vol. 4, p. 237.

Objection is not waived simply because a witness is cross-examined on matters touched upon in direct examination. Cathay v. Missouri, 33 L. R. A. 103; Laber v. Hotaling, 46 Pac. 1070.

Thomas A. Brandon, for Respondent:

Respondent had a right to testify, and was a competent witness in his own behalf, in so far as he did testify. 40 Cyc. 2301, 2306, 2307, 2318, 2319.

It is the general rule that where two or more persons are parties on the same side of a contract or cause of action, the death of one of them will not exclude testimony against the survivor or survivors. 40 Cyc. 2306; Fulkerson v. Thornton, 68 Mo. 468; Goss v. Austin, 93 Mass. 525; Nugent v. Curran, 77 Mo. 323; Davis v. Dyer, 60 N. H. 400; Sprague v. Swift, 28 Hun, 49; Hines v. C. C. & L. Co., 64 N. E. 886.

One of the main defenses in this action is based upon fraud. Where fraud in the transaction is pleaded, the statute does not apply. Jones on Ev., sec. 774; Caston v. McDowell, 107 N. C. 546.

The fact that one of the parties to a contract is dead furnishes no sound reason for not receiving evidence of the intent of the other party as manifested by his declarations. 40 Cyc. 23. A party to an action against an administrator may testify that he had had numerous conversations with deceased, where the details of these conversations are not given. Williams v. Mower, 14 S. E. 483. Plaintiff may state date and fact of a conversation with decedent's testator. Trimmer v. Thompson, 19 S. E. 291; Barlow v. Buckingham, 26 N. W. 58.

By the Court, SANDERS, J., after stating the facts:

The several assignments of error may be grouped and considered as one, namely, that the trial court, in violation of law, allowed the defendant to testify to a transaction when the other party is dead. Rev. Laws, 5419.

Counsel for respondent urges upon us not to consider the assignment of error because it is not in conformity with the statute. Stats. 1915, p. 164. We are of the opinion that the alleged error is sufficiently designated and must be considered.

1, 2. Appellant's particular grievance, though not in terms so stated, is that the trial court allowed defendant, in support of his defense of fraud in the inception of the note, to testify that his signature thereto was obtained from him by a very gross and fraudulent representation perpetrated upon him by his deceased daughter. It is not denied that, if one party to an original transaction is precluded from testifying by death, the other is not entitled to the undue advantage of giving his own uncontradicted and unexplained account of the transaction. Roney v. Buckland, 5 Nev. 219. But it will be noted that the representation of the deceased concerning the character and purpose of the paper was made in the presence of the defendant's wife, who testified concerning the representation without objection or cross-examination. Her testimony and that of defendant, independent of and unconnected with the transaction, was such that, conceding, but not deciding, that it was error to permit the defendant to give his uncontradicted and unexplained account of the transaction between himself and the deceased payee, it was error of such character that this court would not be justified in disturbing the verdict of the jury on that account. It is not every error occurring at the trial that will warrant the court in reversing the judgment of the trial court. We are admonished by statute to disregard an exception unless it be material and affects the substantial rights of the parties. Rev. Laws, 5315.

3, 4. In opposition to this conclusion, it is in effect argued that when plaintiff introduced the note with the admission of signature he made out a prima facie case, and, with the objectionable testimony removed, was entitled to a verdict. In this contention we are unable to concur. An inspection of the note provokes suspicion of its genuineness to such an extent as to make it incumbent upon plaintiff to offer some explanation of its condition when he first saw it. This the plaintiff deliberately refrained from doing. In a suit on a note circumstanced as this was, stripped by evidence for the defendant of its commercial character, based ostensibly on some sort of a contract, it became and was the duty of the plaintiff, having notice of the defenses against the note, to be prepared at the trial to offer some evidence other than the note itself to entitle him to a verdict. The silence of plaintiff tended to impress the jury that plaintiff was either afraid to speak or preferred to rely upon the law merchant and the death of his copayee to make his case. Though death had sealed the lips of his copayee, the relationship of the payees was such that plaintiff could not plaster his mouth with the note to preclude himself from giving testimony, at least tending to show that he had no notice of the defects or infirmities cast upon the note by competent evidence for the defendant. Plaintiff's conduct prior and subsequent to the delivery of the note to him by the deceased was the subject of investigation. The jury may have regarded his conduct as being suspicious, if not dishonorable. The plaintiff had an opportunity to explain it, and an interest in so doing, yet he failed and refused. It is but reasonable to assume the jury, as it had the right, placed the worst construction on plaintiff's conduct. 10 R. C. L. 888. The plaintiff was an actor in the procurement of the note, as well as the deceased. The odious situation attributable to him and culminating in his possession of the note impelled plaintiff to offer some explanation of his conduct consistent with his honesty and fair dealing with the defendant. The note standing alone does not answer the odious charges against it.

Upon the whole case we are satisfied there was sufficient competent evidence to warrant the verdict. We therefore conclude to affirm the order denying to plaintiff a new trial.

ON PETITION FOR REHEARING

By the Court, SANDERS, J. :

It is urged that the note sued on was in fact and truth a gift from the defendant, Echave, to his daughter and plaintiff Bengoa. If this be true the weight of authority has established that one cannot make his own note the subject of a gift to such an extent that it can be enforced by the donee against the donor in the latter's lifetime, nor against his estate after his death. 1 Dan. Neg. Inst. (6th ed.), sec. 180; 3 R. C. L. 937.

Had the record disclosed positively that the note was a gift, the plaintiff would have been spared criticism by this court simply holding that upon his own showing plaintiff had no cause of action.

DUCKER, J., did not participate.

[No. 2413]

C. E. ROBERTS, LESLIE SMITH, ET AL., PETITIONERS, *v.* THE SECOND JUDICIAL DISTRICT COURT OF THE STATE OF NEVADA, IN AND FOR THE COUNTY OF WASHOE, DEPARTMENT TWO THEREOF; THE HONORABLE THOMAS F. MORAN, ACTING JUDGE THEREIN AND SCHEELINE BANKING AND TRUST COMPANY (A CORPORATION), RESPONDENTS.

[185 Pac. 1067]

1. MANDAMUS—WILL ISSUE ON ERRONEOUS REJECTION OF JURISDICTION.
   Where the lower court's refusal to take jurisdiction of an appeal from a justice court involved no disputed question of fact, but depended upon the court's erroneous view as to time in which an appeal could be perfected, mandamus will issue to require the court to try the action.

2. JUSTICES OF THE PEACE—APPEAL IN UNLAWFUL DETAINER TO BE TAKEN WITHIN TEN DAYS.
   Civil practice act, sec. 659, providing that unlawful detainer appeals from justice court must be taken within ten days after judgment, governs the time for appeal in such actions, and is unaffected by section 846, providing generally that justice court appeals may be taken within thirty days after judgment.

3. LANDLORD AND TENANT—TENANCY FROM MONTH TO MONTH.
   A tenancy for an indefinite term with monthly rentals reserved creates a tenancy from month to month.

4. LANDLORD AND TENANT—NOTICE TO QUIT NECESSARY IN UNLAWFUL DETAINER.
   Under civil practice act, sec. 646, subd. 2, as amended by Stats. 1917, c. 27, authorizing unlawful detainer proceedings against a tenant at will after serving him with notice to quit, the notice is an essential element of the action and must be expressly alleged in the complaint.

5. LANDLORD AND TENANT—NOTICE TO QUIT IN UNLAWFUL DETAINER INSUFFICIENT.
   Under civil practice act, sec. 646, subd. 2, as amended by Stats. 1917, c. 27, requiring a tenant at will to be served with notice to quit before instituting unlawful detainer proceedings, the notice must be clear and unconditional, and a notice that the landlord could not continue to rent the premises "for occupancy as billiard- or poolroom" after a certain date is insufficient.

ORIGINAL PROCEEDING. Application for mandamus by C. E. Roberts and others against the Second Judicial District Court of the State of Nevada in and for the

County of Washoe, Department 2 thereof, Hon. Thomas
F. Moran, Acting Judge therein, and the Scheeline
Banking and Trust Company. Writ issued.

M. J. Scanlan and *James Glynn,* for Petitioner:

Notice to quit must not be conditional, but absolute
and positive. Underhill, Landlord and Tenant, vol. 1,
secs. 118, 119. It must be explicit and positive. Taylor,
Landlord and Tenant, sec. 483. Statutory notice is a
condition precedent. Lacrabere v. Wise, 141 Cal. 555.
Plaintiff must bring himself clearly within the detainer
act. Opera House v. Bert, 52 Cal. 471. Service of notice
to quit is mandatory. Paul v. Armstrong, 1 Nev. 98.
Notice must be absolute. Ayres v. Draper, 11 Mo. 548.

Notice to quit is a request from a landlord to his
tenant to quit the premises leased and give possession to
the landlord at a time therein mentioned. The words of
the notice must be clear and decisive, without ambiguity
or alternative to the tenant. Bouvier's Law Dict.;
Adams on Ejectment, 120–122; Bouvier's Amer. Law,
vol. 1, 2d ed., secs. 1799, 1800.

Tenant has a right to stand upon proof of the exact
service required by statute. Lowman v. West, 36 Pac.
258. Where a party brings an action for the possession of property which he claims as being unlawfully
detained from him, he must allege and prove not only
that he has the right of and is entitled to possession,
but that such property is being unlawfully detained,
after notice to quit has been served as provided by law.
Barnes v. Cox, 41 Pac. 557.

Harlan L. Heward and *James T. Boyd,* for Respondents:

This is not a proper case for the issuance of a writ
of mandamus. Treadway v. Wright, 4 Nev. 119; Breckenridge v. Lamb, 34 Nev. 275. Jurisdiction of the district court is fixed by the constitution. Const. Nev. sec.
6, art. 6. Though the decision of the district court be
erroneous, it may not be corrected by writ of mandamus.
Floyd v. District Court, 36 Nev. 352.

An appeal must be taken within the statutory time. Weinrich v. Porteous, 12 Nev. 102; Reinhart v. Co. D, 23 Nev. 369; Luke v. Coffee, 31 Nev. 165; Candler v. Ditch Co., 28 Nev. 15. This is especially true in regard to actions for forcible entry and detainer. "The law applicable to forcible entry and detainer and appeal therefrom must be rigidly complied with to give the supervising court jurisdiction." Holman v. Hogg, 83 Mo. App. 370; Purcell v. Merrick, 158 S. W. 478.

Respondents did not waive objection that appeal was not taken within the statutory time. Parties cannot even stipulate that appeal was taken in time, where the records show that it was not taken in time. Estate of More, 143 Cal. 493; 2 Hayne, New Trial and Appeal, p. 1084. "The jurisdiction of the district court on appeal in actions of forcible entry and detainer, being derivative only, is not aided by consent of parties." Bably v. Musser, 89 N. W. 742.

By the Court, DUCKER, J.:

This is an application for a peremptory writ of mandamus to compel one of the respondents, District Judge Thomas F. Moran, to proceed with the trial of a certain action appealed from the justice court to the district court in which said judge presides.

The petition shows that the respondent Scheeline Banking and Trust Company commenced an action against the petitioners in the justice's court of Reno township for the restitution of certain premises situated in the city of Reno, Nevada, let by said company to petitioners. Prior to the commencement of this action the Scheeline Banking and Trust Company served petitioners with a notice, of which the following is a copy:

"Scheeline Banking and Trust Company.
                    "Reno, Nevada, Feb. 27, 1919.
  "Mr. C. E. Roberts, No. 116 E. Commercial Row, Reno, Nevada—Dear Sir: Please take notice that on account of noise made by operating room at No. 116 E. Commercial Row as a billiard or pool room interfering with our

other tenants in same building, we cannot continue to rent room for occupancy as billard or pool room after the 31st day of March, 1919. Please be governed accordingly.

"Yours very truly,   H. Lewers, Cashier."

A verdict and judgment were entered in the action in the justice's court in favor of the respondent company on the 16th day of July, 1919, and thereafter, on the 2d day of August, 1919, a notice of appeal was served by petitioners, and filed in said district court on the 5th day of August, 1919. On motion of the respondent Scheeline Banking and Trust Company, the appeal was dismissed by the district court. The ground of the ruling of the court below in dismissing the appeal was that notice thereof was not filed in the district court within ten days from the judgment rendered, in accordance with section 5601 of the Revised Laws of Nevada, concerning actions for unlawful detainer.

1. Petitioners contend that the action was not for unlawful detainer, but for possession and damages, and that, as the appeal was duly perfected within thirty days from the rendition of judgment in the justice's court, as provided by section 5788 of the Revised Laws, the ruling of the district court was error, which can be corrected by mandamus.

Counsel for respondents insist that the action of the district court in dismissing the appeal was a judicial act, within its jurisdiction conferred by the constitution, and, even if erroneous, cannot be remedied by mandamus. This contention is sustained by several decisions of this court, the latest of which is the case of Ex Parte Breckenridge, 34 Nev. 275, 118 Pac. 687, Ann. Cas. 1914B, 871; but these have all been expressly overruled by the decision in the case of Floyd v. District Court, 36 Nev. 349, 135 Pac. 922. It was there held that mandamus would lie to compel the district court to proceed with the trial of a case on appeal from the justice's court, where it had acquired jurisdiction, but had erroneously decided that it was without jurisdiction. No question of fact pertaining to jurisdiction was involved in the case of Floyd v. District Court. The lower court based its action on what this court conceived to be a misconstruction of the statute prescribing statutory requirements in taking an appeal from the justice's court, and tantamount to a refusal to take jurisdiction. We are asked to overrule Floyd v. District Court. If the contention were conceded, then the district court has power, by a misconstruction of some statute governing appeals from the justice court, to determine that it has no jurisdiction when the appellant is entitled to a trial on the merits. If it has power to thus divest itself of jurisdiction, then, as a logical consequence, it ought to have discretion by a misconstruction of the law to acquire jurisdiction when it has not. That it has no power to thus invest itself with jurisdiction is a rule of law too well recognized to be paraded in citations.

The proposition is pointedly stated in the dissenting opinion of Justice Paterson, concurred in by Chief Justice Beatty, in the case of Buckley v. Superior Court of Fresno County, 96 Cal. 119, 31 Pac. 8, decided by the Supreme Court of California:

"If the ruling of the court in the first case was merely erroneous, why was it not merely erroneous in the second case supposed? The court had jurisdiction to hear and decide the motion in the first case, and for that reason it is said its ruling was mere error, although it affirmatively appeared on the record that the court had jurisdiction to hear the appeal. Is it not equally true that in the second case the court had jurisdiction to hear and determine the objection and the motion before it? If its ruling in the one case was merely erroneous, was it not merely erroneous in the other? The error of the court rests in the assumption that, in determining that it has not jurisdiction, although the record affirmatively shows that it has, the superior court may exercise discretion, while it is admitted in determining that it has jurisdiction, when the record shows affirmatively that it has not, there is no discretion in the court, and its order is void. If it be true that a court has no power to say it has jurisdiction when the record shows it has not, the converse of the proposition must be true—that, if the record shows it has jurisdiction, it has no right to say it has not. The question of discretion or error is entirely foreign to the discussion. If the record shows it has jurisdiction, that is the end of it; the court must proceed. It has no power to say that it will not. If the record shows affirmatively that it has not jurisdiction, it has no power to say that it will proceed. In each case the court is bound by the jurisdictional facts appearing of record; it cannot ignore or dispute them. As said in Levy v. Superior Court, 66 Cal. 292, 5 Pac. 353: 'The case is not like those which are dependent upon the existence of facts aliunde.' "

This reasoning seems to us to be entirely sound, and the views expressed were said to be warranted by the authorities in the case of Golden Gate Tile Co. v. Superior Court, 159 Cal. 474, 114 Pac. 978, which overruled the Buckley case.

The rule declared in the case of Golden Gate Tile Co. v. Superior Court, supra, that a superior court may not, on an appeal regularly taken from a justice court, divest itself of jurisdiction by dismissing the appeal under a mistaken view of the law, was recognized and approved in the case of Edwards et al. v. Superior Court of Alameda County, 159 Cal. 710, 115 Pac. 649. In the latter case a dismissal of the appeal under such circumstances was declared to be a refusal to perform a plain statutory duty to decide a cause, the remedy for which is a writ of mandate.

In Griffin Co. v. Howell, 38 Utah, 357, 113 Pac. 326, also cited in Floyd v. District Court, this doctrine is upheld. While it must be admitted that there is a diversity of opinion among the authorities on the question, we are in accord with the rule declared in Floyd v. District Court, and will adhere to it. It is controlling in this case before us as to the propriety of the writ of mandate, if the lower court has jurisdiction and has sought to renounce it, for here, as there, the record shows affirmatively that there is no controverted question of fact upon which jurisdiction is dependent; only a question of law is presented as to whether, under prescribed procedure, the notice of appeal was filed in the district court within the required time. We will examine this question.

2. Chapter 65 of the civil practice act of this state, relating to forcible entry and detainer and unlawful detainer, treats of summary proceedings for obtaining possession of real property. These proceedings are governed by the provisions of this chapter wherever they are inconsistent with the other provisions of the civil practice act. In this regard section 661 of the civil practice act, included in chapter 65, provides that:

"The provisions of this act, relative to civil actions, appeals, and new trials, so far as they are not inconsistent with the provisions of this chapter, apply to the proceedings mentioned in this chapter."

Section 846 of the civil practice act, which provides that an appeal in a civil action in a justice court may be taken to the district court at any time within thirty days after notice of entry of judgment, can therefore have no application, if the action is one for unlawful detainer, for section 659 of the civil practice act, relating to this kind of an action, prescribes that the appeal must be taken within ten days from the rendition of judgment. This section is controlling. Hunsaker v. Harris, 37 Utah, 226, 109 Pac. 1, and cases cited.

Do the allegations of the complaint show that petitioners are guilty of unlawful detainer? Its allegations show that the Scheeline Banking and Trust Company was at the times mentioned, and still is, the owner and entitled to the possession of the premises, and describes them with certainty; that the company rented said premises to C. E. Roberts, one of the petitioners, by the month, for $75 per month, payable in advance on the 1st day of each month; that he entered into possession of the said premises under said rental, and ever since and

up to the 1st day of June, 1919, has continued to occupy
and conduct a business of pool- and billiard-parlor and
saloon business in and on said premises; that on the
27th day of February, 1919, the company notified him in
writing that he could not continue to occupy said premises after the 31st day of March, 1919, as a billiard-
or poolroom, and at the same time notified him that
they would not continue to rent him the said premises,
or permit him to occupy the said premises as a billiard-
or poolroom, after the said 31st day of March, 1919;
that he had continued to occupy said premises after said
31st day of March, 1919, and up to and until the 1st day
of June, 1919, has continued to conduct a billiard- and
pool-parlor therein, and has refused and still refuses to
surrender and deliver up said premises to the company.
Then follow the allegations that since the 1st day of
June, 1919, the other petitioners have been in charge of
the premises, and occupying the same, and conducting a
business of pool- and billiard-parlor and saloon business
therein, and now holding said premises for themselves
and said Roberts, and that they and each of them have
refused and still refuse to surrender and deliver up said
premises to the company; that the sum of $150 is due
for rent and unpaid. The prayer is for the restitution
of the premises, for judgment for the unpaid rent,
damages for the unlawful occupation and detainer of the
premises, and for costs.

3. The complaint discloses a tenancy from month to
month. A tenancy for an indefinite term, with monthly
rent reserved, creates a tenancy from month to month.
24 Cyc. 1034. If it alleges an action for unlawful
detainer, it must be by reason of section 646, subd. 2, as
said section was amended by an act of the legislature
approved February 20, 1917. Stats. 1917, p. 31. Section
646, as amended, in the subdivision reads:

"A tenant of real property, for a term less than life, is
guilty of an unlawful detainer: *   *   *

"2. When, having leased real property for an indefinite time, with monthly or other periodic rent reserved,

he continues in the possession thereof, in person or by subtenant, after the end of any such month or period, in cases where the landlord, fifteen days or more prior to the end of such month or period, shall have served notice requiring him to quit the premises at the expiration of such month or period. * * * "

4. Before a landlord can resort to the summary remedy of an action for unlawful detainer under subdivision 2, he must terminate the tenancy by serving a notice to quit possession as required therein. The notice to quit, being a part of the statutory definition of the offense, necessarily enters into the gist of the action, and must be made to appear by express averment in the complaint. Martin v. Splivalo, 56 Cal. 128. In the case of Lacrabere v. Wise, 141 Cal. 554, 75 Pac. 185, the court said:

"It is an essential prerequisite to the maintenance of an action for unlawful detainer, under section 1161 of the çode of civil procedure, that a three days' notice, demanding payment of the rent due, or possession of the leased premises, should be served upon the defendants, as subdivision 2 of that section requires. It is equally essential to allege the service of such demand in the complaint, and, if controverted, prove it on the trial."

5. In order to effect a termination of the tenancy that will make the detention of the premises thereafter unlawful under subdivision 2 of the statute, the notice to quit the possession must be specific and peremptory. A conditional or uncertain notice will not answer the requirements of the statute. Unless the notice is clear and unconditional, the element of unlawful detention is not established. Mr. Taylor, in his work on Landlord and Tenant, at page 70, says:

"The notice must be explicit and positive, fulfilling strictly the requirements of the statute. It should not give the tenant the mere option of leaving the premises, or require him to enter into a new contract on certain conditions, or the like."

In an action for unlawful detainer, it was held in Baltimore Dental Association v. Fuller, 101 Va. 627, 44 S. E.

771, a notice to terminate a tenancy must be explicit and positive; a conditional notice is not sufficient.

"A notice to quit must be plain and unequivocal in its terms, leaving no doubt as to the intention of the party giving it, so that the other party may safely act thereon." 2 Tiffany, Landlord and Tenant, p. 1443.

Tested by the statute itself and applicable principles, we are of the opinion that the complaint does not set forth an action in unlawful detainer.

One who seeks the summary remedy allowed by the statute must bring himself clearly within the terms of the detainer act. Opera House Association v. Bert, 52 Cal. 471. The complaint nowhere avers that the detention of the premises is unlawful, within the meaning of the detainer act. This is not accomplished by the averment of notice as alleged therein. The averment is, to say the least, ambiguous, and petitioners may have reasonably believed therefrom, and also from the notice served, that the objection to their possession of the premises was only to the manner of the occupancy as a billiard- and pool-parlor. Viewed from respondent's most favorable standpoint, it cannot be said that the allegations of the complaint or the proof in support thereof constitute a positive and unconditional notice to quit the premises, fulfilling the requirements of the statute.

As the complaint does not bring the action clearly within the detainer act, and the appeal having been perfected within the time allowed by section 846 of the civil practice act, it follows from our conclusions that the respondent court was without power to divest itself of jurisdiction, and should proceed to a trial of the action.

Let the writ of mandate issue accordingly.

[No. 2425]

IN THE MATTER OF THE APPLICATION OF JOHN J. WILLIAMS FOR A WRIT OF HABEAS CORPUS.

[186 Pac. 673]

1. INDICTMENT AND INFORMATION—LEAVE GRANTED TO FILE NEW INFORMATION ON MOTION OF DISTRICT ATTORNEY.

Under the information act (Stats. 1913, c. 209, secs. 6, 9, and 10) and Rev. Laws, 7101, though the trial court on sustaining demurrer to original information did not direct that another information be filed, it had jurisdiction to grant district attorney's motion for leave to file new information. motion to dismiss which as filed without due authority was properly denied.

ORIGINAL PROCEEDING. Application of John J. Willaims for a writ of habeas corpus. Writ **discharged, petition dismissed, and petitioner remanded to custody.**

Ryland G. Taylor, for Petitioner:

Petitioner claims the protection of habeas corpus, for the reason that the district court is without jurisdiction, under the facts related and as shown by the record. Ex Parte Dela, 25 Nev. 346; In Re Williams, 116 Cal. 512; Ex Parte Baker, 88 Cal. 84.

The court having sustained a demurrer, with mere leave to file another information, such leave to file is not sufficient direction or order by the court, as contemplated by the statute. Rev. Laws, 7101. Such permissive order is not equivalent to a direction or command. In Re Williams, supra; People v. Jordon, 63 Cal. 219; People v. O'Leary, 77 Cal. 30.

The sustaining of the demurrer was a final judgment, from which an appeal may be taken. Even if the district attorney is directed to file a new information, such information cannot be filed until and unless the case is submitted de novo to the proper magistrate for examination on preliminary hearing. Rev. Laws, 7101; Stats. 1915, c. 209, sec. 6. The court has no right to add to or detract from an indictment. State v. Chamberlain, 6 Nev. 257; In Re Parker, 88 Cal. 84.

H. H. Atkinson, for Respondent:

The matter to be considered by this court is whether or not the statute has been complied with by the proceeding in the district court.

As soon as the demurrer has been sustained, the district attorney announced to the court that he had prepared another information, and asked leave of the court then and there to file it. This leave was immediately granted. The several steps were all one proceeding, and amounted to a direction of the court to the district attorney to file another information. Everything contemplated by the statute was done, and the petitioner was not in any manner prejudiced. "We think that the order granting him leave to file a new information, whether made at his request or not, is tantamount to the resubmission of the matter to him, which is all that the statute contemplates should be done in case of an indictment to which a demurrer has been sustained; and we fail to see wherein any substantial right of the petitioner was prejudiced." In Re Pierce, 67 Pac. 316.

Resubmitting the case to the committing magistrate for another examination upon preliminary hearing is purely optional. "After such order of resubmission the defendant may be examined before a magistrate." Stats. 1919, c. 232, sec. 37.

By the Court, COLEMAN, C. J.:

Petitioner was informed against for embezzlement. To the information a demurrer was filed which, after argument, was sustained by the court. The district attorney, anticipating the result, had prepared a new information, and at the time the demurrer was sustained asked leave of court to fine a new information, which was granted. Thereafter counsel for defendant made a motion to dismiss the information upon the ground that it had been filed without due authority of law. After argument and due consideration, the motion was denied.

Thereupon the defendant filed his original petition for a writ of habeas corpus, upon the ground that he is illegally restrained of his liberty, for the reason that the court at the time of sustaining the demurrer to the original information did not direct that a new information be filed; and to sustain his contention reliance is had upon section 7101 of the Revised Laws of 1912. This section reads:

"If the demurrer is allowed, the judgment is final upon the indictment demurred to, and is a bar to another prosecution for the same offense, unless the court, being of the opinion that the objection on which the demurrer is allowed may be avoided in a new indictment, directs the case to be submitted to the same or another grand jury; provided, that after such order of resubmission, the defendant may be examined before a magistrate, and discharged or committed by him, as in other cases."

It is contended that, while the court might direct the filing of a new information, it had no jurisdiction to grant leave to the district attorney to file it. In support of the contention our attention is directed to the cases of In Re Williams, 116 Cal. 512, 48 Pac. 499, People v. Jordon, 63 Cal. 219, and People v. O'Leary, 77 Cal. 30, 18 Pac. 856.

It will be seen that the section quoted makes no allusion to situations arising because of the sustaining of a demurrer to an information, but our information act (Stats. 1913, p. 293) provides that all provisions of law applying to prosecutions upon indictments shall apply to informations, as near as may be.

The Jordon case is not in point, for the reason that the second information was filed without any order whatever having been made by the court permitting or directing the filing of the same. Nor is the O'Leary case in point, because an entirely different question was involved there than that here presented. Furthermore, it appears from the opinion in that case that "the court directed the district attorney to file a new information. * * *"

From a reading of Ex Parte Williams, we are of the

opinion that it cannot be said that it is directly in point "in fact as well as in law," as stated in one of the briefs. There is this difference: In the case at bar the district attorney, anticipating that the demurrer would be sustained to the first information, prepared a new information which he had in court when the order sustaining the demurrer was entered by the court, and immediately asked leave to file the same, which was granted, and the information was instantly presented and examined by the court, while in the California case in question the demurrer was sustained with leave to the district attorney to file a new one. So far as appears from the opinion in the Williams case, the district attorney did not signify any desire at that time to so proceed. The reasoning of the court in that case does not apply to the situation presented in the instant case. There it was said that the order made was an attempt to transfer the duty of deciding, that if the district attorney failed to act, had he been directed to file a new information, he would have been guilty of misfeasance or nonfeasance, but that if he had refused to act under a permissive order, there would have been no liability—all of which is no doubt true.

But in Ex Parte Hughes, 160 Cal. 388, 117 Pac. 437, in an opinion by Henshaw, J., who wrote the opinion in the Williams case, it was practically held that it was not a jurisdictional requirement that the court direct that a new information be filed; for it was held in that case that it was sufficient where the court said that it was of the "opinion that a new information should be filed, which would do away with the objection and be sufficient in all respects." In the Hughes case the court neither granted leave to file a new information nor directed the filing of one, but merely expressed its opinion as to what should be done.

It will be noted that two of the judges expressed an opinion that the rule declared in the Williams case should have been expressly overruled. As we construe the opinion of the court, it was clearly an abandonment of the position taken in the Williams case, and paves the way for an ultimate reversal thereof.

In a case in which the facts were identical with those in the Williams case, supra, the Supreme Court of Idaho (In Re Pierce, 8 Idaho, 183, 67 Pac. 316) refused to adopt the views of the California court, and the logic of the Idaho case appeals to our reason. In that case the court said:

"In the case under consideration the order which sustained the demurrer to the information granted leave to the prosecuting attorney to file a new information. This was, in effect, directing the district attorney to reconsider the matter, and if, in his judgment, it was proper to file a new information, to do so. If the petitioner had been prosecuted by indictment instead of by information, the order sustaining the demurrer to the indictment should have directed the resubmission of the case to the grand jury, but it would not have been proper for the court to have directed the grand jury to find a new indictment. The county attorney is an officer of the court, and to some extent subject to the control of the court. We think that the order granting him leave to file a new information, whether made at his request or not, is tantamount to the resubmission of the matter to him, which is all that the statute cited supra contemplates should be done in case of an indictment to which a demurrer has been sustained; and we fail to see wherein any substantial right of the petitioner was prejudiced."

We would feel perfectly justified in resting our conclusion upon the Idaho case, but we might say that in our opinion there is another reason why we should not follow the Williams case. As we have said, section 6 of our information statute provides that all provisions of our law applying to prosecutions upon indictment shall apply to prosecutions by information, as near as may be. While section 7101, above quoted, contemplates the filing of a second indictment, the reason which might justify us in holding that the provision as to directing the submission of the matter to the same or another grand jury is mandatory would not apply where the prosecution is by information. It is our duty, as far as possible, to harmonize the information statute and the provision of law alluded to in section 6 thereof, whereby the existing law is made applicable so far as may be. There is every reason why, prior to the adoption of the information system, the law should have provided that the court might direct that a case be submitted to the same or another grand jury, for that direction is to the district attorney to resubmit to a body which is left free and independent to exercise its own judgment and discretion in determining whether or not another indictment should be found; but for the court to direct the district attorney to file a new information would be for the court to usurp the discretion usually vested in that official. That such was not the intention of the information statute, except in extreme cases, is evident, for the reason that in no case can an information be filed except by leave of court first had (section 9), and section 10 provides the cases in which, and the conditions upon which, the court may require the filing of an information. Section 10 of the statute was no doubt meant to meet a situation caused by the wilful neglect and refusal of the district attorney to act in an extreme case. The court having no jurisdiction to require the filing of an information except upon the conditions mentioned in section 10, it would have no such jurisdiction where a demurrer has been sustained to an information, unless it were filed pursuant to the provisions of section 10.

It is ordered that the petition be dismissed, the writ discharged, and that the petitioner be remanded to the custody of the sheriff.

[No. 2409]

WILLIAM J. SMITH, RESPONDENT, *v.* JOHN LUCAS, ALIAS T. E. INGHAM, ALIAS ROY CHURCHILL; JOHN D. HILLHOUSE AND M. B. MOORE, APPELLANTS.

[186 Pac. 674]

1. APPEAL AND ERROR—BILL OF EXCEPTIONS ALLOWED AFTER ASSEMBLING OF JUDGMENT ROLL NOT PART OF IT DISPENSING WITH ASSIGNMENT.

    A bill of exceptions, settled and allowed after entry of judgment and denial of new trial, is not part of the judgment roll, so as to obviate necessity of assignments of error, though appeal is from the judgment only: Civ. Prac. Act, sec. 331, subd. 2, making part of such roll all bills of exceptions "taken and fixed," relating to the time for assembling the roll.

2. APPEAL AND ERROR—ASSIGNMENT OF ERROR OF INSUFFICIENCY OF EVIDENCE NECESSARY.

    Assignment of error is required by Stats. 1915, c. 142, sec. 13, as amended by Stats. 1919, c. 40, sec. 2, though the only objection is insufficiency of the evidence to justify the verdict or decision.

3. APPEAL AND ERROR—SEASONABLE SERVICE AND FILING OF ASSIGNMENT OF ERRORS JURISDICTIONAL, AND NOT WAIVABLE.

    Seasonable service and filing of assignment of errors, as required by Stats. 1915, c. 142, sec. 13, as amended by Stats. 1919, c. 40, sec. 2, is jurisdictional, and absence thereof may not be waived.

APPEAL from Second Judicial District Court, Washoe County; *James A. Callahan*, Judge.

Action by William J. Smith against John Lucas and others. From an adverse judgment, M. B. Moore, intervening defendant, appeals. **Assignment of errors stricken, and judgment affirmed.**

Ayres & Gardner, for Appellant:

.   The present case, not involving "error in law occurring at the trial," does not require any assignment of error. There is no "error" within the statutory limitation of that word. The motion should, therefore, be denied, and the appeal determined upon the merits. Coffin v. Coffin, 40 Nev. 345; Gardner v. Pacific Power Co., 40 Nev. 343; Talbot v. Mack, 41 Nev. 245.

This appeal is from the judgment only. A motion for a new trial was made and denied, but no appeal was taken from the order denying the motion for a new trial. The motion was made upon the insufficiency of the evidence to justify the decision and that it is against law. The evidence was preserved in the bill of exceptions and is presented to the court upon the appeal from the judgment. Therefore the appeal is upon the judgment roll only. Rev. Laws, 5273. The act of 1915 did not inferentially repeal any portions of the practice act. Gill v. Goldfield Con. M. Co., 43 Nev. 1.

There is no reason why the assignment of errors filed in the supreme court should be any more comprehensive than that presented to the trial judge. Rev. Laws, 5322. The requirement that a motion for a new trial based upon the insufficiency of the evidence must be made before an appeal can be taken on such grounds, shows that the trial judge must be given an opportunity to correct any alleged error. Rev. Laws, 5328.

The motion to dismiss has been waived by the respondent. Miller v. Walser, 42 Nev. 497.

Whether the assignment of errors is jurisdictional or not is immaterial under the present discussion, for the court will entertain an appeal on the merits where the acts of the parties justify it, even though there may be a question of jurisdiction. Dixon v. Pruett, 42 Nev. 345.

Norcross, Thatcher & Woodburn and *M. A. Diskin,* for Respondent:

The assignment of errors must be filed in the supreme court ten days after the transcript on appeal has been filed. In this case it was not filed until after the time allowed by law had expired. Stats. 1913, p. 166; Stats. 1919, p. 55. "If the party fails to file such assignment within the time limited, no error shall be considered by the supreme court." An appeal will be dismissed if the assignment of errors has not been filed within the time allowed by law. Not only should the assignment of errors be stricken, but inasmuch as no complaint is made of any error that might be ascertained from an examination of the judgment roll, the appeal should be dismissed, for there is no error for the court to consider, and the judgment of the lower court should be affirmed. Coffin v. Coffin, 40 Nev. 345; Gardner v. Pacific Power Co., 40 Nev. 343.

By the Court, DUCKER, J.:

This is an action in replevin. A motion for a new trial was denied in the lower court, but the appeal is taken from the judgment alone by M. B. Moore, who was an intervening defendant.

The record on appeal was filed with the clerk of this court on the 6th day of August, 1919, and thereafter, on the 24th day of August, 1919, appellant filed his assignment of errors with said clerk. On the 13th day of September, 1919, respondent filed a motion for an order striking the assignment of errors, dismissing the appeal, and affirming the judgment. The ground of the motion, as set forth in the notice thereof, is that no assignment of errors was served on respondent, or filed with the clerk of the supreme court, within ten days after the transcript of the record on appeal was filed in this court, as required by law. In this respect section 2 of an act to amend sections 10 and 13 of an act entitled "An act supplemental to and to amend an act entitled 'An act to regulate proceedings in civil cases in this state and to repeal all other acts in relation thereto,' approved March 17, 1911," approved March 16, 1915, approved March 10, 1919, provides:

"Within ten (10) days after the transcript of the record on appeal has been filed in the supreme court, the party or parties appealing shall serve upon the adverse. parties and file with the clerk of the supreme court an assignment of errors, which assignment shall designate generally each separate error, specifying the lines or folios, and the pages of the record wherein the same may be found. Any error not assigned shall not be considered by the supreme court. If the party fails to file such assignment within the time limited, no error shall be considered by the supreme court. The assignment of errors herein provided for shall be typewritten or printed, paged, and the lines or folios numbered, and the appellant shall furnish three copies thereof for filing in the supreme court." Stats. 1919, p. 55.

1. Counsel for appellant concede that the assignment of errors was not served or filed within the time required by said section 2, but they take the position that no assignment of errors is necessary in this case. This contention is based upon the assumption (1) that the bill of exceptions is a part of the judgment roll, and that under the rulings of this court in Talbot v. Mack, 41 Nev. 245, 169 Pac. 25, and Miller v. Walser, 42 Nev. 497, 181 Pac. 437, no errors need be assigned which appear upon the face of the judgment roll; (2) that, as the only errors assigned are insufficiency of evidence to justify the decision, and that the decision is against law, section 13 of the act of 1915 is not applicable, for the reason that the only errors in law occurring at the trial and excepted to by the party making the application are contemplated by this section.

We cannot acquiesce in either of these contentions and think that they were decided adversely to appellant's view in the case of Coffin v. Coffin, 40 Nev. 345, 163 Pac. 731, in which the appeal was dismissed for failure to serve and file an assignment of errors, within the time allowed by section 13 of the act of 1915. The only substantial change in the section as amended by the act of 1919 is that, in the latter act the time in which an assignment of errors must be served and filed begins to run after the transcript of the record on appeal has been filed in the supreme court, instead of from the time the appeal has been taken from the order or judgment, and ten days is allowed, instead of twenty as in the former act.

In so far as the question on motion to dismiss is concerned, there is no distinction in principle between the case of Coffin v. Coffin and the case at bar. Both were tried on the merits in the district court, and in each a motion for a new trial was made and denied. The only difference is that in the former case the appeal

was taken from the judgment and order of the court
denying the motion for a new trial, while in the case
under consideration the appeal is from the judgment
alone. This difference can have no bearing on the
question before us. In each case the bill of exceptions
was prepared, served, filed, and settled and annexed to
a copy of the judgment roll, after a motion for a new
trial was denied. As previously stated, the assignment
of errors, in the instant case, is based on the grounds
that the evidence is insufficient to justify the decision
and that it is against law. A like assignment of errors
was filed in the Coffin case, with the additional assignment that the complaint did not state facts sufficient to
constitute a cause of action. We see no room for distinction between the two cases; but as the points made in
this case were not raised or discussed in Coffin v. Coffin,
and as they have been ably presented and argued by
counsel for appellant, we deem them worthy of careful
consideration, especially in view of this court's attitude
against deciding a case otherwise than on its merits.

The cases of Talbot v. Mack and Miller v. Walser,
supra, are easily disinguishable from the case at bar.
In each of those cases the appeal was from an order
sustaining a demurrer to the complaint and judgment
thereon, while in the instant case the appeal was taken
after a trial on the merits in the district court. In both
of the former cases it was held that, where the appeal
is upon the judgment roll alone, the errors appearing
upon the face of the judgment roll need not be presented
by an assignment of errors. It was not held or intimated
in either of these cases that a bill of exceptions, as contemplated by the act of 1915, necessarily becomes a part
of the judgment roll, obviating the requirement of an
assignment of errors. Such a ruling would render section 13 of the act requiring an assignment of errors of
no force and effect in any case, manifestly against the
plainly expressed mandate of the statute. True, in
Talbot v. Mack this court recognized that the bill of
exceptions taken to the order sustaining the demurrer,

and allowed by the trial judge, and filed on the date of
the entry of judgment, was a part of the judgment roll.
Such a bill of exceptions is made a part of the judgment
roll by virtue of subdivision 2 of section 331 of the
civil practice act, which prescribes what shall constitute
the judgment roll, in cases where the complaint is
answered by any defendant. This part of the section
reads:

"In all other cases, the pleadings, a copy of the verdict
of the jury, or finding of the court or referee, all bills of
exceptions, taken and filed. * * * "

Counsel insist that the bill of exceptions in this case,
and in all cases when properly taken and allowed,
becomes a part of the judgment roll by force of the
foregoing section, requiring the clerk to include "all
bills of exceptions taken and filed" in the roll. We
cannot concede this interpretation. This section prescribes a definite time when the clerk shall make up
and file the judgment roll, and designates the papers to
be then included therein. It reads:

"Immediately after the entry of judgment, the clerk
must attach together and file the following papers, which
constitute the judgment roll."

Then follows a designation of the papers. A bill of
exceptions, or more than one, may or may not have been
taken and filed at or prior to the time this act of assembling the judgment roll is required to be done. If so
taken and filed, all are required to be included therein.
A bill of exceptions which may thereafter be settled and
allowed in accordance with the act of 1915 becomes no
part of the judgment roll, but must be annexed to a
copy thereof, if the appeal be from a judgment, as provided in section 11 of said act. It appears from the
record in this case that the bill of exceptions was settled
and allowed long after the entry of judgment, and after
a motion for a new trial had been denied. Though
properly a part of the record on appeal, it is no part of
the judgment roll.

2. We come, now, to the other phase of the contention;

that is, that no assignment of errors is necessary, because the provision requiring it is inapplicable to this case, for the reason that only errors at law occurring at the trial, and to which exceptions have been taken, are intended. To ascertain the intention it is necessary to consider the language used, "assignment of errors," in connection with its function and purpose. The office of an assignment of errors is to apprise the appellate court and the adverse party of the errors relied upon for a reversal of the case. It accomplishes a twofold object: It serves the convenience of the appellate court, and affords protection to the adverse party. The duty of searching the record for error does not devolve upon the appellate court, but is placed upon the party complaining to point it out by an assignment of errors, and by a bill of exceptions to furnish the evidence to prove it. The requirement of an assignment of errors and its service upon the opposite party enables him to be prepared to meet the questions raised on appeal, and to be secure from the risk of unpreparedness for new or unexpected points raised at the hearing. As said by the court in Orr v. Pennington, 93 Va. 268, 24 S. E. 928:

"The petition required [petition for an appeal containing assignment of errors] is in the nature of a pleading, and should state the case which the party applying for the appeal wishes to make in the appellate court. It ought to assign clearly and distinctly all the errors relied on for a reversal of the case, so that the opposite party may know what questions are to be raised in the appellate court, and not have new questions sprung upon him at or just before the hearing of the cause, when there may not be sufficient time or opportunity for meeting them."

It is urged that the purpose of the statute is accomplished by rule 11 of the supreme court rules, requiring the filings of points, and with authorities, which shall contain such brief statement of the facts as may be necessary to explain the points made. Even if we were to concede this, the facts remains that the legislature has enacted the proposition into concrete law and has made its provisions mandatory. If we keep the purpose of the statute in mind, there appears no reason why an error in rendering a verdict or decision on insufficient evidence, which on appeal requires a consideration of all the evidence and testimony, should not be assigned, as well as other errors at law, which often involve a consideration only of a small portion of the evidence. The one is just as essential for the information of the court and the opposite party as the other.

If we correctly understand the position of counsel, they assert that in the civil practice act, prior to the amendatory and supplemental act of 1915, errors at law occurring at the trial have been so defined as cause for a new trial, and that all other causes for a new trial have been classified as grounds. From this, and other premises which we will hereafter mention, they deduce the conclusion that, in the enactment providing for an assignment of errors, the term is employed in the same sense and embraces such errors to the exclusion of all causes for a new trial that fall into a different category. Without conceding the assertion that the civil practice act does not allude to errors at law occurring at the trial as a ground for a new trial, we think that, even if it does not, the assumption that the legislature by the act of 1915 therefore intended only those errors to be embraced in an assignment of errors is too shadowy to be indulged as a legitimate inference. It ignores the office and purpose of an assignment of errors, to point out for the benefit of the court and opposite party the errors relied upon for a reversal.

Counsel concede, or must concede, that a verdict or decision based on insufficient evidence is an error, notwithstanding the practice act in relation to new trials designates it a cause, and also as a ground for a new trial. No reason appears why it should not be assigned, as well as any other error upon which a party relies. In the absence of a satisfactory reason for giving to the term "assignment of errors," as employed in the statute, the special and limited meaning contended for, we presume that the legislature used it in its well-understood meaning in law.

A review of the practice acts of this state, and amendments, reveals that insufficiency of the evidence to support the verdict has long been required in an assignment of errors. In the old practice act, adopted in 1869 (Stats. 1869, c. 112, sec. 197), the particulars wherein it was thus deficient were required to be specified. By the amendment to this act in 1893 (Stats. 1893, c. 89) it was provided that it was sufficient assignment of error in that respect to specify that the verdict or decision is not supported by the evidence, or is contrary to the evidence. In sections 389 and 390 of the present civil practice act, relating to a statement on appeal, specification of error on this ground was necessary. These sections of the practice act have been repealed by the act of 1915, which was designed, as said by this court in Gill v. Goldfield Consolidated Mines Co., 43 Nev. 1, 176 Pac. 784, "to be and to operate as a complete revision of the practice then in vogue respecting statements on appeal, and to substitute therefor in toto a system of bills of exception."

Assignments of error as to insufficiency of the evidence having been constantly embodied in the practice acts, the old and the new, from 1869 forward, it is not unreasonable to assume that, if it were intended by section 13 of the act of 1915 to make a radical change by omitting the requirement from the practice, such intention would have been clearly expressed. It is argued that the intention to embrace only errors at law occurring at the trial is also inferable from that part of the language of said section 13, as amended by the act of 1919, which provides that the "assignment shall designate generally each separate error, specifying the lines or folios, and the pages of the record wherein the same may be found"; that this cannot be complied with when the objection is that the evidence is insufficient to justify the verdict or decision, as the absence of evidence cannot be indicted by line or page. We do not regard this language as having an important bearing upon the question. It was evidently designed to require a specification of error to be made with as much definiteness as the nature of the matter would admit. This provision can be complied with literally as to a number of errors that might be sufficient to warrant a reversal of a case, which in our judgment must be assigned, other than errors at law occurring at the trial and insufficiency of evidence. If it cannot be complied with literally in the latter instance, a substantial compliance would be sufficient.

3. The next two points made by counsel for appellant are that an assignment of errors is not jurisdictional, and in this case has been waived by counsel for respondent. They may be considered together, and in this regard we reiterate what was said by this court in Coffin v. Coffin, supra:

"The statute is express and peremptory in its terms; it is not a mere matter of form that can be waived or dispensed with by the agreement of the parties or lenity of the court, but it is one of substance."

The contention that an assignment of errors was waived is based on the fact that counsel for appellant requested and procured from the attorneys for respondent an extension of time to file their reply brief. They cite the case of Miller v. Walser, supra, as an authority for this proposition. There one of the grounds of the motion to dismiss was the failure to file a transcript of the record on appeal within the time required by rule 2 of this court. The attorneys for respondent, after the transcript on appeal was filed, obtained two stipulations from counsel for appellant extending time to serve and file points and authorities, reserving therein no objections as to the time when the transcript on appeal was filed. No timely motion to dismiss the appeal was made on the ground stated. We held that these facts were sufficient to operate as a waiver of the objection that the transcript was not filed in time. The facts are entirely different in that case, and it is therefore not in point.

Counsel for respondent in the case at bar insist that, when an assignment of errors designates as error insufficiency of the evidence to justify the verdict or decision, it must specify wherein the evidence is insufficient. This question is not before us. No assignment of errors was filed within the time specified by statute, and the question is as to whether such an assignment is necessary, when the error complained of is based on the ground of insufficiency of the evidence to justify the decision, or that it is against law, and not as to the sufficiency of the assignment. It follows, from our conclusions, that we have no alternative but to grant the motion.

It is therefore ordered that the assignment of errors filed herein be stricken from the files, and the judgment appealed from be affirmed.

Points decided

[No. 2398]

T. B. CLARKE, APPELLANT, v. JULIUS JOHNSON AND J. G. CRUMLEY, RESPONDENTS.

[187 Pac. 510]

1. REPLEVIN — COUNTER-CLAIM FOR REPAIRS AND REPLACEMENTS INSTALLED PERMISSIBLE.

In an action for claim and delivery, which would be replevin at common law, the property is the subject of the action, so that under the liberal provisions of the practice act as to counter-claims, in an action for possession of automobiles, a defendant, having caused repairs and replacements to be installed, could interpose a counter-claim therefor.

2. WORK AND LABOR—PLAINTIFF RECOVERING AUTOMOBILES IN REPAIRED CONDITION NOT LIABLE ON IMPLIED PROMISE TO DEFENDANT FURNISHING REPAIRS.

In an action by the seller in claim and delivery for recovery of automobiles, plaintiff is not liable as for a voluntary acceptance of services to the purchaser who had caused the machines to be repaired, since plaintiff in taking the machines had no choice but to accept them in their repaired condition, and there was no implied promise to pay for such services.

3. APPEAL AND ERROR—ERRONEOUS JUDGMENT CANNOT BE SUSTAINED ON A THEORY CONTRARY TO EXPRESS FINDING.

Where in replevin action by conditional seller against buyer for recovery of automobiles court erroneously found that seller was liable for repairs incorporated in the automobile on theory of acceptance of services, appellate court cannot sustain decision on theory that seller was liable on theory that transaction constituted a mortgage and mortgagor was entitled to use the automobiles, and that such created implied authority to incur expense of repairs.

4. ACCESSION—TIRES AND REPLACEMENTS UPON AUTOMOBILES SOLD UNDER CONDITIONAL CONTRACT NOT ACCESSIONS AS AGAINST THIRD PARTY FURNISHING THEM.

Since, under a conditional contract for sale of motor trucks, providing that any equipment, repairs, tires, or accessories placed upon the trucks during the continuance of the agreement should become a component part thereof and the title thereto should become vested in seller, tires and replacements were regarded by the parties as separable and severable and not accessions, upon seller's recovering possession of the trucks such equipment did not become the seller's property by accession, but remained the property of defendant, who had furnished, but not sold, them to the buyer.

APPEAL from Fifth Judicial District Court, Nye County; *Mark R. Averill*, Judge.

Action by T. B. Clarke against Julius Johnson and another. Judgment for the plaintiff as against the

defendant Johnson, and against plaintiff in favor of
defendant J. G. Crumley, from which and from an order
denying a new trial upon defendant Crumley's cross-
action the plaintiff appeals. **Judgment modified by
reduction and affirmed.**

STATEMENT OF FACTS

This is an action in claim and delivery to recover the
possession of two motor trucks. At the commencement
of the action the plaintiff took possession of the property under an act entitled "Claim and Delivery," and
thereafter removed the property from the jurisdiction
of the court.

The facts of the case are as follows:

On the 25th of July, 1917, the Leach-Frawley Motor
Company of San Francisco, called the vendor, and Julius
Johnson, styled the vendee, entered into a written contract, admitted to be a conditional sale agreement,
whereby the motor company agreed to sell to Johnson,
and Johnson agreed to purchase from the company, two
G. M. C. motor trucks at the agreed price of $3,550 each,
the terms of sale being $1,100 in cash upon the execu-
tion of the instrument, and the balance payable in
monthly installments of $257.45 on each truck until the
full purchase price had been paid, whereupon the seller
agreed to execute and deliver to the purchaser a bill of
sale of the property. The contract contains the usual
covenants against loss and injury, conditions and remedies of the seller in case of default or breach on the part
of the buyer. It was distinctly understood and agreed
that the buyer would operate and control the trucks in
accordance with the law, statutes, and ordinances relating to automobiles in the State of California, and the
buyer would not take the property out of said state.
It was also expressly provided that—

"The purchaser agrees that any equipment, tires or
accessories of any character placed on said automobiles
during the continuance of this agreement shall be and
become a component part thereof and the title thereto

shall immediately become vested in said seller and be included under the terms of this agreement."

Upon the execution of the contract the trucks were delivered to Johnson on the receipt of his cash payment. Johnson made no further payment, other than one installment of $257.45, paid on or about the 27th of September, 1917. Johnson, after using the trucks in and about his business in California for several months, without notice to seller and without its assent, secretly and clandestinely took the trucks out of the State of California, as we are impressed with the evidence, with the intent to cheat and defraud the owner and its assigns out of the property. Johnson brought the trucks into Nevada, and left or abandoned them, temporarily at least, at Carson City, on or about October 20, 1917, until on or about November 28, 1917, whereupon the trucks were removed to Tonopah, Nevada. Johnson's arrival at that place preceded that of the trucks. Johnson in the interim had found employment in one of the mines in Tonopah. It appears that one J. G. Crumley, president of the Tonopah Sewer Company, and engaged in the real estate business at that place, had in contemplation the purchase of 300 cords of wood located about fifty miles distant from Tonopah, and, if some satisfactory arrangement could be found by which the wood could be transported to market in Tonopah, he would close a contract for its purchase. Crumley was informed of Johnson's having two trucks, and thereupon sought an introduction, as the result of which such negotiations were had between them as that it was agreed and understood that Crumley would bear the expense of bringing the trucks from Carson City to Tonopah, place upon the trucks the necessary repairs, equipment, and accessories to get them in good running condition, and Johnson and Crumley would close the deal for the purchase of the 300 cords of wood, and divide the profits arising from the enterprise, it being understood that Johnson would operate the trucks and Crumley would be reimbursed for all money expended in

getting the trucks in condition for the particular services
out of the profits of the venture, and that the trucks
during the performance of the contract would be under
the control and direction of Crumley. When about
twenty cords of wood had been hauled, plaintiff, on the
13th of December, 1917, after making diligent search
for the whereabouts of Johnson and the trucks, located
Johnson with the trucks at Tonopah. On being advised
of the fact of Johnson's default and wrongdoing in violation of his contract, some propositions passed between
Crumley and the plaintiff looking to a compromise of
Crumley's alleged interest in the property. Thereafter
this action was brought against Johnson and Crumley
for the possession of the trucks. The complaint contains the usual averments incident to an action of this
nature under the statute. Johnson, upon due service of
summons, defaulted, and his default for failure to
answer was entered, and at the time of trial of the
action his whereabouts was unknown to either of the
parties in interest. Crumley answered. After making
certain admissions and denials of the averments of the
complaint, for further answer and counter-claim against
plaintiff's action he set up in detail a full history of his
connection with the property, his dealings with his codefendant Johnson, and demanded judgment and decree
for the specific enforcement of his wood-hauling contract with his codefendant, and, failing from any cause
in obtaining this relief, demanded that he be adjudged
to be the owner and entitled to the possession of two
tires of the value of $441.80, six connecting-rod bearings
worth $23.60, and clutch-facing of the value of $12,
placed by Crumley upon the trucks, and that he be paid
the sum of $339.40, the reasonable value of the moneys
expended by him for mechanic's work and labor upon
each of said trucks, and, in lieu of his failure to recover
possession of the tires and parts as aforesaid, that he
be adjudged the full value thereof, the cost of labor and
repairs, aggregating the total sum of $816.40.

Plaintiff demurred to the answer and counter-claim,

upon the grounds that it did not state facts sufficient to constitute a counter-claim or defense, and that it did not state a cause of action against the plaintiff, and made a motion to strike it out, but the court overruled the demurrer and denied the motion. Thereupon plaintiff for a reply denied the new matter contained in the answer, and pleaded the breach of the conditions of the conditional sales contract in bar of Crumley's counter-claim. Upon the calling of the case for trial, plaintiff moved for judgment on the pleadings, which motion was overruled. Thereupon a trial was had before the court without a jury. The court decided that plaintiff was entitled to judgment against defendant Johnson for the possession of the trucks, except as to the tires and parts placed thereon by defendant Crumley, and the latter was entitled to a judgment for the return to him of the tires and parts so furnished, and the cost of work and labor performed upon each of the trucks. In accordance with its decision, the court rendered judgments, one against Johnson in favor of plaintiff, and against plaintiff in favor of Crumley. From the judgment in favor of Crumley, and from an order denying to plaintiff a new trial in Crumley's cross-action, the plaintiff appeals.

Frank K. Pittman and *H. B. M. Miller,* for Appellant:

The contracts were and are good and valid in law; title to the property was in the seller; rights of the seller were and are good, not only as against the buyer, but even against his creditors. Ann. Cas. 1916A, 332; Shaw v. Webb, 174 S. W. 273; Baughman v. Emanuel, 73 S. E. 511.

Any liens are subordinate to the right of the conditional vendor. Cardinal v. Edwards, 5 Nev. 37.

A buyer under a contract of conditional sale, by which the title remains in the seller until full payment, has no attachable interest in the property until he has fully complied with the condition relating to payment of the purchase price. Morris v. Allen, 121 Pac. 690; Dillon v. Grutt, 144 Pac. 741; Stats. 1917, p. 402.

H. R. Cooke, for Respondents:

The plaintiff's conditional sale agreement affirmatively shows that parties contemplated the trucks were to be put to work. Plaintiff impliedly authorized necessary repairs and accessories, and the party furnishing same is entitled to hold a lien and to recover the reasonable value of the equipment furnished. Watts v. Sweeney, 22 Am. St. Rep. 165; Tucker v. Werner, 21 N. Y. Supp. 264; Rappert v. Zang, 62 Atl. 998; Hammond v. Danielson, 126 Mass. 294. The common-law lien of a mechanic for repairs, under the special circumstances such as exist in the case at bar, where the parties contemplated the use of the property, may be superior to prior existing liens. 3 R. C. L. 56; Drummond C. Co. v. Mills, 69 Am. St. Rep. 719; Kirtley v. Morris, 43 Mo. App. 144.

There is a distinction between the effect of a common-law lien and the statutory lien of a mechanic. "The former, as a general rule, attaches to the property itself without any reference to ownership." Sullivan v. Clifton, 20 L. R. A. 719; Reeves v. Russel, 148 N. W. 654.

Respondent expressly reserved title to the tires and accessories placed on the trucks. Alley v. Adams, 44 Ala. 609.

Respondent had no notice or knowledge of conditional sale or of plaintiff's reserved title rights. Small v. Robinson, 31 Am. Rep. 299; Baughman Auto Co. v. Emanuel, 38 L. R. A. 97.

Detachable accessories do not become a part of personalty. 24 R. C. L. 455. The tires and equipment placed on the trucks by respondent could have been readily detached. Clarke v. Wells, 12 Am. Rep. 187.

By the Court, SANDERS, J., after stating the facts:

1. This is an action which at common law would have been called replevin. In an action of replevin the property is the subject of the action. Therefore, under the quite liberal provisions of the practice act (Rev. Laws, 5046–5052) as to counter-claims, and upon the authority

of Lapham v. Osborne, 20 Nev. 168, 18 Pac. 881, we are of the opinion that the demurrer interposed to the answer and counter-claim, the motion to strike it out, and the motion for judgment upon the pleadings were properly overruled and denied. It follows, therefore, that the court did not err in permitting respondent to testify as to how he happened to cause the repairs to be made and the replacements installed.

2. The case is divided by the trial court into two branches. One represents respondent's right to have judgment for the repairs item, and the other the respondent's right to the recovery of the possession of the tires and replacements or their value.

The court found that respondent was entitled to judgment for the repairs item because plaintiff took away the trucks, took respondent's tires and replacements, and took the benefit of the money he had expended to put them in condition for use, stating that they were bettered at Crumley's expense, and that if a man accept the benefit of another man's work and money he should pay for what he gets. It is fair to assume from this general statement taken from the court's opinion, read in connection with its decision as requested, that the court attempted to apply the rule of voluntary acceptance of services as creating a liability to pay the reasonable and fair value thereof. This rule applies, however, only where the party to whom the services are rendered is free to take their benefit or to reject it. If the services are of such nature as he has no choice but to accept them, he cannot be said to accept them voluntarily. Such acceptance, therefore, creates no liability. 2 Page on Contracts, sec. 776.

The court in its opinion states:

"What should be done about the repairs item presents more difficulty, because that amount represents value or property that cannot be removed from the trucks."

This is true. The repairs, at the time plaintiff took possession of the trucks, had gone into and become a constituent part of the property. In this situation the

owner had no alternative, no choice but to accept the
services. This being the fact, there was no implied
promise on the part of the owner to pay for the services,
nor did the law create one. Riddell v. Ventilating Co.,
27 Mont. 54, 69 Pac. 241.

Upon this branch of the case we conclude the court
erred in rendering judgment in favor of respondent and
against appellant for the amount of the repairs item,
to wit, $339.40.

3. Counsel for the respondent insists that the judgment should be sustained upon the several grounds:
First—That the transaction between the conditional
vendor and vendee was in its essence a mortgage,
Johnson becoming the mortgagor and the Leach-
Frawley Company the mortgagee, and argues from this
premise that as the possession of the trucks was delivered to the mortgagor and he was entitled to use them,
and did use them, as his own, the law created an implied
authority upon Johnson to incur the expense of keeping
the property in a necessary state of repair during the
period of the contract. Second—That, Johnson being
the apparent owner of the property, and Crumley having
dealt with him, as he had the right to do, as an owner,
Crumley is entitled to the protection of a court of equity
upon the maxim that where one of two innocent persons
must suffer by the wrong of another, the one who
enables such other to commit the wrong must bear the
consequences. In view of the court's findings, we are
precluded from substituting the conclusions of counsel
for that of the court, and make a different finding.

4. As to the other branch of the case, we conclude that
the court was correct in adjudging and decreeing
Crumley to be the owner and entitled to the return of
the tires and replacements, not so much, however, on the
ground that both fair dealing and the law required
the return of Mr. Crumley's property to him as upon
the proper construction of the covenant in the sales
contracts, whereby it is expressly provided:

"That any equipment, repairs, tires or accessories of any character placed upon said trucks during the continuance of said agreement shall be and become a component part thereof, and that the title thereto shall immediately become vested in the seller and be included under the terms of said agreements."

From this it is apparent that the seller itself regarded tires and replacements as being separable and severable distinct parts, and not accessions. The vendor recognized that the vendee might acquire a separate property interest in tires and replacements during the period of the contract; otherwise there would have been no necessity for the provision.

"Where the seller of an automobile under a contract of conditional sale retakes the automobile upon default of the buyer to keep the terms of the contract, he is entitled to any tires or other replacements which the purchaser placed on the machine while it was in his possession, provided the title to such parts passed to the purchaser when he acquired them." Berry, Automobiles (2d ed.) 793.

The lower court found Crumley to be the owner of the tires and replacements, and nothing is offered in opposition to this finding, other than the sale contract, to which Crumley was not a party.

We conclude that the judgment must be reduced, and the respondent have judgment for the sum of $816.40, less the sum of $339.40, making a total of $477.

[No. 2410]

IN THE MATTER OF THE APPLICATION OF PLINY H. PHILLIPS FOR A WRIT OF HABEAS CORPUS.

[187 Pac. 311]

1. DIVORCE—ORDER IN CONTEMPT PROCEEDING NOT MODIFICATION OF ORIGINAL DECREE.

　　An order in a contempt proceeding, providing that a divorced husband pay alimony provided for in original decree or go to jail, was not a modification of the original decree, and it was immaterial that the court had not reserved the right to modify or amend the original decree.

2. CONSTITUTIONAL LAW—IMPRISONMENT FOR FAILURE TO PAY ALIMONY NOT IMPRISONMENT FOR "DEBT."

　　Alimony does not constitute a "debt" within the meaning of Const. art. 1, sec. 14, providing that there shall be no imprisonment for debt, a debt in the sense used in the constitution alluding to an obligation growing out of a business transaction, and not to an obligation arising from the existence of the marital status.

3. DIVORCE—ALIMONY MAY BE GRANTED WIFE.

　　The statutes permit the court on granting a divorce to allow alimony to the wife.

ORIGINAL PROCEEDING. Application by Pliny H. Phillips for writ of habeas corpus. **Proceeding dismissed, and petitioner remanded.**

H. V. Morehouse and *H. W. Huskey,* for Petitioner:

The alimony in the judgment is enforceable by execution. It is nothing but a debt. The decree is a judgment at law; it cannot be enforced by contempt. The orders of the lower court are void. The alimony order becomes a debt enforceable by execution. Not being founded on fraud or libel, the debt cannot be enforced by imprisonment. An action at law can be had on the judgment, execution can be issued upon it, and it can be filed as a claim in probate proceedings. It is therefore a debt; no method of reasoning can change it into anything else. Being a debt, the petitioner cannot be imprisoned for its nonpayment. Leeder v. State, 75 N. W. 541; Seager v. Seager, 36 N. W. 536; Marsh v. Marsh, 70 N. E. 154.

It appears from the original judgment that the marriage between the parties has been wholly dissolved; that the judgment is not subject to the further order of the court. When the judgment became final, all jurisdiction over it ended, and the court could not make any order concerning the enforcement of the judgment. Any such order is beyond the jurisdiction of the court. Daniels v. Daniels, 12 Nev. 121; White v. White, 62 Pac. 1062; Howell v. Howell, 37 Pac. 770; Kamp v. Kamp, 59 N. Y. 220; Erkenbrach v. Erkenbrach, 96 N. Y. 456; Bassett v. Bassett, 67 Am. St. Rep. 863; Ætna Ins. Co. v. McCormick, 20 Wis. 265; Salter v. Hilgen, 40 Wis. 363; Bacon v. Bacon, 43 Wis. 197; Day v. Mertlock, 87 Wis. 577.

The jurisdiction over the parties is at an end after the suit, and the award of alimony is final and cannot be changed (Smith v. Smith, 45 Ala. 264; Kerr v. Kerr, 59 How. Pr. 255; Shepherd v. Shepherd, 58 N. Y. 644; Peterson v. Thomas, 28 Ohio St. 596; Hardin v. Hardin, 38 Tex. 516), unless the court reserves the right to make such change in the decree (Severn v. Severn, 7 M. C. Ch. 109; Fries v. Fries, 1 McArthur, 291; Lockbridge v. Lockbridge, 3 Dana, 28; Williams v. Williams, 29 Wis. 517), or unless the statute gives the right to the court to make such change (Mitchell v. Mitchell, 20 Kan. 665; Bacon v. Bacon, 33 Wis. 197).

The court cannot proceed by contempt, because the original decree is only a judgment or order for the payment of money, and the law has provided that the enforcement of such a judgment or order is by execution. Rev. Laws, 5280, 5284, 5366; 21 Pac. 954, 1095; Coughlin v. Ehlert, 39 Mo. 285.

The very claim the court is asked to enforce by contempt is set out as a debt. "There shall be no imprisonment for debt, except in cases of fraud, libel or slander." Const. Nev. sec. 14, art. 1; Rev. Laws, 5088. "Alimony decreed to a wife in a divorce or separation * * * is as much a debt of record, until the decree has been

recalled, as any other judgment for money." Barber v.
Barber, 16 L. Ed. 226. "Whatever, therefore, the
law orders any one to pay, that becomes instantly a
debt." Powell v. Oregon R. R. Co., 36 Fed. 726; Gran-
holm v. Sweigle, 57 N. W. 509; Rhodes v. O'Farrell, 2
Nev. 60; 13 Cyc. 393; Conrad v. Everich, 40 Am. St.
Rep. 679; Trowbridge v. Spinning, 62 Pac. 125; Lynde v.
Lynde, 76 Am. St. Rep. 332; Arrington v. Arrington,
80 Am. St. Rep. 795; Wetmore v. Wetmore, 149 N. Y. 560.

A judgment of alimony has the same force and effect
as a judgment at law. Coulter v. Lumpkin, 21 S. E. 461;
Sapp v. Wightman,.103 Ill. 150; Tyler v. Tyler, 34 S. W.
898; Dufrene v. Johnson, 82 N. W. 107; Kunze v.
Kunze, 59 Am. St. Rep. 857.

L. D. Summerfield, for Respondent:

The decree as entered is enforceable by way of contempt. Phillips v. Philips, 180 Pac. 907; Lake v. Bender,
18 Nev. 361; Tiedeman v. Tiedeman, 158 N. Y. Supp.
851, 36 Nev. 494; Powell v. Campbell, 20 Nev. 238, 2
L. R. A. 615; Ex Parte Spencer, 83 Cal. 460; In Re Cave,
26 Wash. 213.

Enforcement of a decree is not a modification of it.
A court has power to enforce its decrees at any time.
Walker v. Walker, 49 N. E. 664; 14 Cyc. 799; Ruge v.
Ruge, 165 Pac. 1063; Lyon v. Lyon, 21 Conn. 184;
Andrew v. Andrew, 20 Atl. 817.

There is statutory authority for granting the court
continuing power. "Final orders" are within the power
of the court to enter in a divorce action. Rev. Laws,
5842. Such a "final order" being lawfully entered, the
statute functions continuously with respect to it, and
without limitation as to time, whereby "disobedience or
resistance to any lawful writ, order, rule, or process
issued by the court or judge at chambers" is deemed
a contempt and is punishable as such. Rev. Laws, 5394.
The almost unanimous weight of authority is against

the proposition that any order for imprisonment made in this hearing would violate the constitutional inhibition against imprisonment for debt. "Nor does the imprisonment of the husband as a result of contempt proceedings violate a constitutional provision against imprisonment for debt." 14 Cyc. 799; Ex Parte Jontsen, 154 Cal. 540; Ex Parte Hall, 125 Ark. 309; Ex Parte Canavan, 17 N. W. 100; Chadwick v. Chadwick, 170 App. Div. 328; Smith v. Smith, 95 S. E. 199. "The decree is not because of an indebtedness, but is on the ground of personal duty." Andrew v. Andrew, 20 Atl. 817. It is not sought to punish petitioner by imprisonment for debt. The punishment is for a refusal to obey a lawful order of court requiring him to perform a personal duty toward respondent, which the court specifically found he could comply with.

While execution is a proper remedy in these cases, it is not exclusive. Under the statutes of this state, and the adjudicated cases under similar statutes, execution is not the exclusive remedy, but only one of the remedies open to the respondent, contempt being another, at her option. Walker v. Walker, supra; 14 Cyc. 799; Ruge v. Ruge, supra; Lyon v. Lyon, supra; Andrew v. Andrew, supra.

By the Court, COLEMAN, C. J.:

This is an original proceeding in habeas corpus.

On September 17, 1913, Ruth Phillips obtained a decree of divorce from the petitioner, and in said decree the court ordered and directed that the petitioner (the defendant in the divorce action) pay to the plaintiff as alimony a fixed sum on the 15th day of each month. On or about the 19th day of November, 1918, contempt proceedings were instituted in the court in which the divorce had been granted, on account of the failure of the petitioner to comply with the decree awarding alimony. A hearing was had in that proceeding, and on December 3, 1918, the court found that the petitioner had not fully complied with the order directing the payment of alimony, that he was able to make certain payments thereupon and pay in the future a monthly sum on account thereof, and accordingly entered an order that he pay forthwith the sum of $500 and thereafter make certain monthly payments to plaintiff in the action. Failing to comply with the last-mentioned order, plaintiff was, on August 11, 1919, adjudged in contempt of court, and as punishment it was ordered that he be confined in the county jail unless a certain payment were made. Failing to make the payment, a commitment was issued to the sheriff, who took petitioner into custody, from which he seeks to be discharged.

It is the contention of counsel for petitioner that the orders of the court of December 3, 1918, and August 11, 1919, are null and void and of no force or effect. Two reasons are urged in support of the contention: First, because when the final decree of divorce was entered in December, 1918, no right to modify or amend the same having been reserved, the court lost all jurisdiction of the matter; and, second, that by the contempt proceedings it is sought to collect a debt, and that no person can be imprisoned for the nonpayment of a debt, under our constitution.

1. As to the first contention, counsel is in error. The court did not seek, by either the order of December 3 or August 11, to modify its original decree. It merely sought to compel a compliance with that order. There is a wide distinction between modifying a decree and compelling a party to comply with its terms. If we accept the premise of counsel for petitioner—that the orders in question are modifications of the original decree—it would necessarily follow that petitioner would have to be discharged, for we held in Sweeney v. Sweeney, 42 Nev. 431, 179 Pac. 638, that a final decree of divorce cannot be modified, except in certain instances, none of which exists in the instant case.

2. As to the second contention, it may be observed that section 14, article 1, of our constitution provides

that "there shall be no imprisonment for debt," except in certain specified cases. We think it safe in saying that it has been the uniform practice in this state to resort to contempt proceedings where a husband has failed to comply with the decree awarding alimony, when able to do so, and the overwhelming weight of authority is in support of the jurisdiction of the court to so proceed; it being the rule of law that alimony does not constitute a debt within the meaning of that term as used in the constitutional inhibition against imprisonment for debt.

A debt in the sense used in the constitution alludes to an obligation growing out of a business transaction, and not to an obligation arising from the existence of the marital status, such as alimony; nor is alimony given as a judgment. It is a mere allowance for support and maintenance—a duty growing out of the marriage status; a duty which sound public policy sanctions to compel one who is able so to do, possibly as a result of the cooperation (during coverture) of his former wife, to prevent such former wife from becoming a public charge or dependent upon the charity of relatives or friends. "It has frequently been insisted," says Mr. Nelson, "that a decree for alimony is in fact a debt, and therefore payment should be enforced by an attachment for contempt where the constitution prohibits imprisonment for debt. But it is uniformly held, and such is the doctrine, that the decree for alimony is an order of the court to the husband, compelling him to support his wife by paying certain sums, and thus perform a public as well as a marital duty. Such a decree is something more than an ordinary debt or judgment for money. It is a personal order to the husband, similar to an order of the court to one of the officers or to his attorney. The imprisonment is not alone to enforce the payment of money, but to punish the disobedience of the party; and the order is not, therefore, a debt, within the meaning of the constitution." Nelson, Div. & Sep. sec. 939.

The Supreme Court of the United States, in Audubon

v. Shufeldt, 181 U. S. 575, 21 Sup. Ct. 735, 45 L. Ed.
1009, held that neither alimony nor arrears at the time
of an adjudication in bankruptcy, nor alimony accruing
thereafter, was a debt provable in bankruptcy or barred
by the discharge. The same court, in Gompers v. Buck's
Stove and Range Co., 221 U. S. 418, 31 Sup. Ct. 492, 55
L. Ed. 797, 34 L. R. A. (N.S.) 874, in speaking of such
contempt proceedings, said:

"If a defendant should refuse to pay alimony, or to
surrender property ordered to be turned over to a
receiver, or to make a conveyance required by a decree
for specific performance, he could be committed until
he complied with the order. * * * The order for
imprisonment in this class of cases, therefore, is not to
vindicate the authority of the law, but is remedial, and
is intended to coerce the defendant to do the thing
required by the order for the benefit of the complainant.
If imprisoned, as aptly said in Re Nevitt, 54 C. C. A. 622,
117 Fed. 451, 'he carries the keys of his prison in his
own pocket.' He can end the sentence and discharge
himself at any moment by doing what he had previously
refused to do."

Such is the uniform ruling of the courts of the
country, and numerous authorities may be found to sustain the rule in the following books: 14 Cyc. 799; 1
R. C. L. p. 960, and 7 Ency. Law (2d ed.) 41.

The cases of Segear v. Segear, 23 Neb. 306, 36 N. W.
536, and Coughlin v. Ehlert, 39 Mo. 285, are not in conflict with the rule we have declared. Those decisions are
based upon the statute of the particular state. Neither
of them undertakes to repudiate the general rule
which we have invoked, nor alludes to it. So far as
appears from those decisions, but for the statute of
Nebraska and of Missouri, the courts of those states
would be in harmony with the general rule enunciated.

3. It is urged that the trial court had no authority to
allow the plaintiff alimony in the divorce action, and
hence there was no jurisdiction in the court to punish
for contempt. The courts of this state have for years

construed our statute as conferring such right (Phillips
v. Phillips, 42 Nev. 460, 180 Pac. 907) ; and, even if we
were convinced that such construction is not the correct
one, we would not feel justified at this time in laying
down a contrary rule.   This determination is amply
justified, for the reason that, had there been dissatisfaction with the prevailing construction, the legislature
would long ago have amended our statute so as to
remove all doubt as to the legislative intent.

Certain matters that have transpired during the
pendency of this proceeding have been called to our
attention, but, as they are not jurisdictional, they cannot
be considered on this hearing.

For the reasons given, it is ordered that the proceedings be dismissed, and the petitioner remanded.

[No. 2408]

CLOVER VALLEY LAND AND STOCK COMPANY (A CORPORATION), RESPONDENT, *v.* S. G. LAMB AND C. L. TOBIN, J. SHEEHAN, G. W. SUMMERFIELD, T. D. BROWN, B. J. LIONAZ, AND MOSES REINHART, APPELLANTS.

[187 Pac. 723]

1. SHERIFFS AND CONSTABLES—NOT ENTITLED TO COMMISSIONS ON
   FORECLOSURE SALE UNDER DECREE.
   Under Rev. Laws, 2009, as to "commissions for receiving
   and paying over money on execution or process where lands
   * * * have been levied on, advertised and sold," and in
   view of section 2019, a sheriff is not entitled to commissions
   for receiving and paying over money on the sale of real property sold pursuant to a decree and order of sale made upon
   the foreclosure of a mortgage; an execution and levy being
   entirely supererogatory in a foreclosure proceeding where the
   lien on the property has already attached by reason of the
   mortgage contract.

2. OFFICERS—STRICT CONSTRUCTION OF FEE STATUTES.
   Statutes allowing public officers fees for services are strictly
   construed in favor of the person from whom fees are sought
   to be collected.

3. STATUTES—LEGISLATURE PRESUMED TO KNOW LAW.
   The legislature is presumed to have knowledge of the state
   of the law upon the subject upon which it legislates.

4. STATUTES — CONTEMPORANEOUS CONSTRUCTION UNAVAILABLE
   WHERE LANGUAGE UNAMBIGUOUS.
     Contemporaneous construction, as shown by long practice
   by the legal profession and officers, and acquiescence therein
   by the legislature, is to be resorted to only when the statutory
   language is of doubtful import.

APPEAL from Sixth Judicial Court, Humboldt County;
James A. Callahan, Judge.

Action by the Clover Valley Land and Stock Company
against S. G. Lamb and others. From judgment for
plaintiff, defendants appeal. **Affirmed.** SANDERS, J.,
dissenting.

Thomas E. Powell, for Appellants:

A "decree and order of sale" is "process," within the
meaning of the statutes. Rev. Laws, 2009; Bank v.
Wall, 91 N. W. 525; Holmes v. Crooks, 76 N. W. 1073;
National F. I. Co. v. Chambers, 32 Atl. 663; Sauer v.
Steinbauer, 14 Wis. 70; Savage v. Oliver, 36 S. E. 54;
Harmon v. Childress, 11 Tenn. 327; Southern Cal. L.
Co. v. Ocean Beach H. Co., 29 Pac. 627. "The word
'process' as found in the statute is equivalent to the
sheriff's authority." People v. Nash, 1 Idaho, 206;
Blumauer-Frank D. Co. v. Branstetter, 43 Pac. 575.
"We have only to decide whether the sheriff does receive
and pay over money on process when he sells mortgaged
property to the judgment creditor at a foreclosure sale.
We find that the sheriff performed his whole duty in the
premises, and that the judgment creditor has, by the
levy and sale, acquired that which, as between him and
the mortgagor, is money received and paid over on
process." Jurgens v. Houser, 47 Pac. 809.

"If a statute is valid it is to have effect according to
the purpose and intent of the lawmaker. The intent is
the vital part, the essence of the law, and the primary
rule of construction is to ascertain and give effect to
that intent." Lewis's Sutherland, Stat. Constr., 2d ed.,
sec. 363; State v. Ross, 20 Nev. 61.

The court may consider extraneous facts in aid of construction. "If the statute has been in force for a long

period, it may be useful to know what the contemporary
construction was; its practical construction; the sense
of the legal profession in regard to it; and the course
and usages of business which it will affect." Bagley v.
Ward, 37 Cal. 137.

Warren & Hawkins, for Respondent:

A levy in making a judicial sale is a vital element. In
this case the sale was made without levy. Appellants
must therefore justify the sheriff by referring to some
statute authorizing him to collect a commission on a
sale made pursuant to a decree of a court of equity and
without a levy. Statutes relating to fees and compensation of public officers are strictly construed, and an
officer is entitled only to what is clearly given by law.
Fusier v. Mayor, 3 Nev. 58; Berry v. Kiefer, 133 Pac.
1126. "No other fees shall be charged than those specially set forth herein, nor shall fees be charged for any
other services than those mentioned in this act." Rev.
Laws, 2019. "No rule of law is better settled than the
one that an officer can only demand such fees as the law
has fixed and authorized for the performance of his
official duties." Washoe County v. Humboldt County, 14
Nev. 131.

There is a distinction between a sale under execution
and one under an order of sale. Rev. Laws, 5284. No
levy is necessary in the sale of mortgaged premises on
foreclosure. "The only object of the levy is to create a
lien upon the land * * * to subject the lands to the
payment of the plaintiff's debt. If this has already been
done, the levy is supererogatory." Freeman on Executions, 2d ed., vol. 2, sec. 280; Southern Cal. L. Co. v.
Ocean Beach H. Co., 29 Pac. 627; Smith v. Schwartz,
60 Pac. 305; 27 Cyc. 1671; Dennis v. Moore, 52 Pac. 333.

The decision of the lower court fully disposes of the
arguments of the appellants, and is conclusive of the
case on its merits. It is clear and logical, and should be
accepted by this court as the correct construction of the
law involved.

By the Court, DUCKER, J.: .

The plaintiff in the court below, respondent here, brought this action to recover from S. G. Lamb, as sheriff of Humboldt County, and his bondsmen, the sum of $1,040.93, with interest thereon from December 21, 1918, and costs.

Appellant's demurrers to the complaint were overruled and upon failure to answer within the time allowed by the court, judgment was entered for the amount stated against the appellants. From the judgment entered this appeal is taken.

1. The facts out of which this action arose are substantially as follows: Respondent, who was the holder and owner of a note and mortgage given to it to secure part payment on the purchase price of certain lands situate in Humboldt County sold by respondent to one W. H. Johnson, obtained a decree of foreclosure. Pursuant to the judgment, decree, and order of sale said sheriff duly advertised and sold the mortgaged premises to respondent for the sum of $136,291, the amount found to be due and owing to the respondent in the foreclosure proceedings.

The sheriff demanded from respondent for his services the sum of $1,116.63. This amount included the sum of $1,040.93 which he claimed as commissions under the statute hereinafter discussed. Respondent tendered to the sheriff and offered to pay the sum of $74.70, the total amount of costs, expenses, and fees claimed by him exclusive of commissions, and demanded a certificate of sale of the property sold to him. The sheriff declined to accept the amount tendered him and refused to execute and deliver such certificate of sale until the full sum claimed by him was paid; whereupon the respondent paid him under an acknowledged protest the sum of $1,040.93 claimed as his commissions and obtained a certificate of sale.

The clause of the statute under which the sheriff claims these commissions, and the clauses immediately preceding and succeeding it, read:

"For making and posting notices, advertising for sale, on execution or order, any judgment or order of sale, not to include the cost of publication in a newspaper, one dollar and fifty cents; for commissions for receiving and paying over money on execution or process where lands or personal property have been levied on, advertised and sold, on the first five hundred dollars, three per cent; not exceeding one thousand dollars, but over five hundred, one and one-half per cent; and on all sums over fifteen hundred dollars, three-fourths of one per cent; for commissions for receiving and paying over money on execution without levy, or when the lands or goods levied on shall not be sold, one-half of one per cent." Section 2009, Revised Laws of Nevada.

The sheriff did not act under an execution and made no levy upon the property, but, as stated, advertised and sold it pursuant to the decree and order of sale issued and made in the foreclosure proceedings. In fact, a levy for the purpose of dedicating the property to the purpose of the judgment, if made, would have been a superfluity; for the lien on the property had already attached by reason of the mortgage contract between the parties. Freeman on Executions (2d ed.) vol. 2, sec. 280.

As it is conceded that no levy was actually made or attempted, the question of even a constructive levy cannot arise. The sheriff claims commissions under the second clause of the statute cited. The question for determination is therefore thus presented: Is a sheriff legally entitled to commissions for receiving and paying over money on the sale of real property sold pursuant to a decree and order of sale made upon the foreclosure of a mortgage?

The learned trial court decided this question in the negative, and in his written decision which appears in the record, held that by the terms of the statute the class of services wherein the sheriff is allowed to charge the commissions thus authorized is limited to where "lands have been levied on, advertised and sold." We think the court was correct in this conclusion, and as the reasoning by which it is reached is clear, concise, and logical, we have adopted a portion of the decision which deals with the intent of the legislature. The trial court, after pointing out that the sheriff fee act was first enacted in 1861 (Stats. 1861, p. 247), and again in 1865 (Stats. 1864–1865, p. 336), and lastly in 1883 (Stats. 1883, p. 59), and that the first clause of the statute we have quoted has remained practically unchanged by these enactments, and the second and third clauses wholly unchanged except as to the rate of commissions, proceeds:

"We have thus three different legislative bodies, in three successive acts of the legislature, passed at three different times, in a period of twenty-four years, using substantially the same language respecting the point at issue, and under such circumstances the court cannot assume that they overlooked the fact that a levy is unnecessary in executing a mortgage foreclosure order of sale, nor can the court assume they they unintentionally omitted the term 'order of sale' in the second and third clauses hereinbefore set out. Pursuing further the question of the intention of the legislature, we find that in clause 1 a fee of $1.50 is provided for making and posting notices, and advertising for sale on order (under) any order of sale. It seems unlikely that three different legislative bodies having had an 'order of sale' in mind in framing clause 1, and in providing fees to the sheriff for making and posting notices and advertising for sale should have entirely forgotten an 'order of sale' in framing clauses 2 and 3, which are the next two succeeding clauses in the act; thereafter the term 'order of sale' must have been intentionally omitted by the legislature in framing clauses 2 and 3. Force is added to this conclusion when we consider the language of clause 3,· which reads, 'for commissions for receiving and paying over money on execution without levy, or where the lands levied on shall not be sold, one-half of one per cent.' In this clause both the terms 'process' and 'order of sale' are entirely omitted. If in framing clause 2 the legislature intended that in executing an order of sale in a mortgage foreclosure proceeding the sheriff should have commissions equivalent to those allowed in levying and selling under an execution, then why, in framing clause 3, and providing for certain commissions for specified acts done under an execution, should it not have provided for similar commissions for similar acts done under an order of sale?

"Under the language of clause 3, if the sheriff, in executing an order of sale, had posted his notices and advertised the mortgaged property for sale, but did not sell the mortgaged property because before the sale actually occurred the mortgagor paid the amount of the judgment and costs, it is clear that the sheriff would be entitled to no commissions, because the clause clearly provides for commissions to be paid the sheriff only in executions; i. e., 'for receiving and paying over money on executions without levy or where the lands levied on shall not be sold.' If the demurrers in this action were to be sustained, section 2009 would have to be construed thus: If the sheriff receive and pay over money on execution, where lands have been levied on, advertised, and sold, he shall receive the higher rate of commissions. If he sell the lands under an order of sale, then, by assuming that he made a levy, he would receive like commissions. If he receive and pay over money on execution without levy, or where the lands levied on have not been sold, he shall receive the lower rate of commissions, but, if he receive and pay over money on an order of sale where the lands have not been sold, he shall receive no commissions whatever, notwithstanding the fact that the services performed in the latter two instances are just as nearly like each other as are the services performed under the former two instances. Clearly this would be an intentional omission on the part of the legislature, and a court would be making a wide departure in saying that such an omission was the result of an oversight on the part of three legislative bodies, where a different plain construction of the statute is apparent, without indulging in the presumption that such an oversight was made.

"It therefore seems to be the more reasonable conclusion that the legislature did not intend that the sheriff should receive any commission in executing an order of sale in a mortgage foreclosure proceeding."

The learned district attorney, counsel for appellants, attacks this conclusion and the reasons assigned for it because no effect whatever is given to the word "process" in the clause under which the sheriff claims commissions, thereby depriving him of compensation for a most important official act, namely, receiving and paying over money obtained from a sale of lands under a decree and order of sale. He contends that a decree and order of sale comes within the meaning of "process" and that, as a levy cannot be made under a decree and order of sale in foreclosure proceedings, the words of the clause "where lands or personal property have been levied on, advertised and sold" must be held to relate to the word "execution," in order to effect the purpose of the legislature in section 2009 to give to the sheriff compensation for all of his official acts.

We are not unmindful of the statutory rule of construction involved in these contentions that a statute must be given such reasonable construction as will, if possible, make all its parts harmonize with each other and render them consistent with its scope and purpose. The purpose of section 2009 is undoubtedly to give the sheriff compensation in full for all of his official acts, but it is apparent from a consideration of the section and the duties devolving upon him that it was not the intention to compensate him by a particular fee for every official act. Without specifying the official acts he was required to perform without fee when the statute of 1883 was enacted, aside from receiving and paying over money obtained from the execution of an order of sale, which in our judgment is included, it is sufficient to say that in section 17 of the act it was recognized that officers under the fee system were required to perform certain services without charge. It provides:

"No other fees shall be charged than those specially

set forth herein, nor shall fees be charged for any other services than those mentioned in this act." Stats. 1883, sec. 17, p. 65; Rev. Laws, 2019.

2. So it cannot be said that the construction placed upon the clause in question limiting the services to be compensated by commissions to instances where the lands have been levied on, advertised, and sold is contrary to the intent of the statute. If we were to transpose the language of the clause so as to effect the relation of the phrase "levied on," etc., to the word "execution," it would nevertheless be a strained construction to believe that the legislature, having provided for a small fee for making and posting notices of an order of sale in the preceding clause, would have resorted to the general term of "process" to indicate an order of sale in the succeeding clause, where large commissions might be involved. Statutes of this kind are, as a rule, strictly construed in favor of the person from whom fees are sought to be collected. 2 Lewis's Sutherland, Statutory Construction (2d ed.) sec. 714. To be allowed they must be clearly expressed. The tendency of public officers entitled to fees for their services to construe the statutes allowing them liberally may be at the foundation of this rule.

3. The legislature is presumed to have a knowledge of the state of the law upon the subjects upon which it legislates. It must have known that a levy is unnecessary where property is sold under an order of court to satisfy a mortgage; and, indulging this presumption, if it intended that commissions should be charged in such a case, it would not have used language clearly indicating that a levy is necessary.

The purpose of the law in allowing commissions for receiving and paying over money on execution and withholding compensation for the same services performed pursuant to a sale under order of court in foreclosure proceedings is not obscure. As pointed out by the trial court, an officer acting under such an order, if he obeys it strictly, incurs no liability, while, on the other hand, he is liable for the consequences of an illegal levy. It is therefore quite probable that the legislature believed that the sheriff was entitled to commissions on executions on account of the liability to which he was exposed. Counsel for appellants contend that this inference is refuted by other provisions of the section which provide compensations for all official acts incident to levy and sale. An examination of the fees provided for such services, which do not appear to be proportionately larger than for other services in section 2009, convinces us that they were intended as compensation for expense and trouble, and not allowed upon the basis of contingent liability.

The case of Jurgens v. Hauser, 19 Mont. 184, 47 Pac. 809, is cited by counsel for appellant as an authority against our construction of the statute. In the Montana case there had been a foreclosure sale to the judgment creditor, and the action was for collection of commissions under a clause substantially the same as the clause in question in this case. The Montana statute in respect to commissions (omitting the rates) provides:

"For commissions for receiving and paying over money on execution or other process, when lands or personal property have been levied on and sold * * *. For commissions for receiving and paying over money on process without levy or when the lands or goods levied on are not sold." * * * Pol. Code, 1895, sec. 4634.

The question decided in Jurgens v. Hauser was that the sheriff was entitled to commissions on the theory that he does receive and pay over money on process when he sells mortgaged property to the judgment creditor at a foreclosure sale, whether the money actually passes from the latter to him or not. In deciding this question the court must have concluded that commissions were due under the clause of that statute which is similar to the one in question here. But it appears from the opinion in that case that a levy was actually made by the sheriff, notwithstanding the sale was pursuant to foreclosure proceedings. The court said:

"An order of sale and execution was duly issued."

And again in another part of the opinion the court said:

"Adopting this reasoning to our statutes, we find that the sheriff performed his whole duty in the premises, and that the judgment creditor has, by the levy and sale, acquired that which, as between him and the mortgagor, is money received and paid over on process," etc.

The weakness of Jurgens v. Hauser as an authority for appellant on the construction of the clause in question is apparent, because, so far as the opinion discloses, the court did not regard an execution and levy as entirely supererogatory in a foreclosure proceeding, and further because the question before us was incidentally decided there.

4. It is insisted that long practice by the legal profession and officers, and acquiescence by the legislature in the appellants' construction of the clause, should have weight in ascertaining the legislative intent. Contemporaneous construction of this kind is often resorted to where the language of the statute is of doubtful import (Lewis's Sutherland, Statutory Construction, sec. 472), but the meaning of the clause to allow the sheriff commissions only when the lands or personal property have been levied on, advertised, and sold is too plain to invoke this extraneous aid.

The judgment of the court is affirmed.

SANDERS, J., dissenting:

We must assume that the legislature used the words "execution or process" with full knowledge of their legal meaning. They are as old as courts. Under our practice there are but two ways to enforce a final judgment. One is by execution, and the other is by a certified copy of the judgment. Rev. Laws, 5284. The first is the proper mode where the judgment is for the payment of money; and the second is the proper mode where the judgment requires the performance of any other act. A judgment which directs the sale of specific property to satisfy a mortgage or other lien upon it falls within the second class, and is to be enforced by the proper officer under a

certified copy of the judgment. Heyman v. Babcock, 30
Cal. 367. The decree or judgment is not self-executing.
It must be enforced by some person authorized by law.
The sheriff of the county where the incumbered property
is situated is that person. Rev. Laws, 5501. A judgment of foreclosure directing the sale of mortgaged
premises by the sheriff in "process," and, by analogy
to the former equity practice, includes "order of sale."
Tregear v. Etiwanda Water Co., 76 Cal. 537, 18 Pac.
658, 9 Am. St. Rep. 245; Weinstein v. Herman, 81 N. J.
Eq. 236, 86 Atl. 974. In this sense the term "process" is
used in the particular provision of the general law concerning the compensation of sheriffs. It is added to the
term "execution" designedly, and as thus inserted is
intended to comprehend something more than mere
execution. It is not mere tautology and must be allowed
an operation as extensive, if not more extensive, than
"execution"; otherwise there would be no purpose for
its having been inserted in the provision. But my associates, by a too rigid interpretation of the word "levied"
as applied to the term "process," have excluded the latter
from the provision altogether—I think in opposition to
the context, spirit and purpose of the law.

It must be conceded that the sheriff does not bear such
relation to the court that he must take notice of its
orders and judgments and without process carry into
effect those that require the aid of a ministerial officer.
Heyman v. Babcock, supra. The general rule is that
process is the authority of the sheriff to act. Whether
it be styled execution or process is immaterial, and when
a statute allows him a specified compensation for executing either in any case that involves the receipt and
paying over of money, if he is guilty of no dereliction in
the full and complete performance of the mandate of
the court, no legal reason is suggested why he should not
receive the compensation specified.

In support of the conclusion reached by my associates,
it is in effect reasoned that, since the object of a levy is
to create a lien upon the land, to indicate by some act of
the officer the particular property which he intends to

sell, and that, since the judgment itself designates the property to be sold, there is no occasion for levy in case of foreclosure. I concede that it is not necessary for the sheriff in such case to go upon the land to make a formal levy, but my attention has not been directed to any authority that dispenses with the necessity or requirement that the sheriff must by some unequivocal act manifest the intent to appropriate the described property to sale for the satisfaction of the writ or process where the judgment is already a lien upon the property to be sold. The rule is well established that, where the judgment under which real property is sold under execution is a lien upon the land sold, it is a sufficient seizure and levy under the execution to give the statutory notice of sale of the land under execution. Lehnhardt v. Jennings, 119 Cal. 192, 48 Pac. 56, 51 Pac. 195; Crocker on Sheriffs, sec. 500. The same rule applies upon a foreclosure decree. By the advertisement the seizure becomes complete and renders the property subject to the judgment or decree. Union Dime S. I. Co. v. Anderson, 83 N. Y. 174. In the absence of some special provision in the judgment or decree to execute a sale of real property under a judgment of foreclosure, the procedure is the same as that provided for sale under writs of execution issued against real property of the judgment debtor. The order of the court in such case is accompanied with like duties and responsibilities in one case as in that of the other and is followed by like consequences in case of dereliction.

This construction of the provision is in accordance with the intention of the legislature and that applied for more than a half century by gentlemen of the profession and persons affected by its operation. I concede that it may be that in some instances, by reason of this construction, the sheriff is the best paid officer in the state, and I am impressed that, since it is now the policy of the law to place such office upon a salary basis, the provision as it now reads is properly a subject for future legislation, but this is a matter that does not concern courts.

[No. 2388]

THE STATE OF NEVADA, Ex Rel. John Sparks, Et Al., Plaintiffs, *v.* STATE BANK AND TRUST COMPANY (a Corporation), Et Al., Defendants.

FRANK L. WILDES, as Receiver of the State Bank and Trust Company, Appellant, *v.* THE STATE OF NEVADA, Et Al., Respondents.

|187 Pac. 1002]

1. Banks and Banking—Statute Governing Compensation of Receiver Not Retroactive.

Where receiver of bank, ordered into involuntary liquidation under banking act of 1907, sec. 10, was appointed and duly qualified in 1908, and is still actively engaged in the performance of his duties, his compensation is not governed by act of March 29, 1915 (Stats. 1915, c. 286) ; said act not being retroactive.

2. Statutes—Will Not Be Construed as Retrospective.

As a general rule, a statute will not be construed to operate upon past transactions, but in futuro only.

3. Statutes—Every Reasonable Doubt Resolved Against Retroactive Operation.

Every reasonable doubt is resolved against a retroactive operation; and, if all the language of a statute can be satisfied by giving it prospective action only, that construction will be given it.

4. Receivers—Statute as to Compensation Prospective.

The act of March 29, 1915 (Stats. 1915, c. 286), as to compensation of receivers of corporations involuntarily liquidated, seeks to enact a new rule of civil conduct, entirely prospective in its nature, and the rule against retrospective construction must be given full effect.

APPEAL from First Judicial District Court, Ormsby County; *Frank P. Langan,* Judge.

Controversy between the State of Nevada, on the relation of John Sparks and others and the State Bank and Trust Company, a corporation and others, submitted on an agreed statement of facts. From the decision rendered, Frank L. Wildes, as receiver of the State Bank and Trust Company, appeals. **Reversed.**

Mack & Green and *Brown & Belford,* for Appellants:

A law can be given no retrospective or retroactive operation, unless by the language of the statute it is

clearly made to have such effect. In either or any case
it will be denied such operation if the effect is to impair
the obligation of a contract entered into before the
enactment or to deprive any person of property without
due process of law, or to impose new obligations, liabili-
ties or responsibilities not existing at the time of the
enactment. Century Digest, vol. 44, sec. 344; Decennial
Digest, vol. 18, sec. 263; 36 Cyc. 1205; 26 Am. & Eng.
Ency. Law, p. 683; Sedgwick, S. & C. Law, pp. 188–191;
Lewis's Sutherland, Stat. Constr., vol. 1, sec. 12; Merrill
v. Sherburne, 1 N. H. 204; Elliott, Contracts, vol. 3, sec.
2725; Cooley, Const. Lim. 77.

The statute of 1915 (Stats. 1915, p. 507) is unconstitutional. The legislature cannot pass any special law
"regulating the practice of courts of justice," or any
law "where a general law can be made applicable."
Const. Nev. sec. 20, art. 4; State v. Boyd, 19 Nev. 43;
State v. Donovan, 20 Nev. 75. It would be difficult to
find any law more violative of the constitutional provision inhibiting special or local laws than the act in question. People v. C. P. R. R. Co., 83 Cal. 393; Cullen v.
Glendora W. Co., 113 Cal. 503; City v. Havern, 126 Cal.
226; Strong v. Digman, 207 Ill. 385; Board v. Bank, 40
Pac. 894; Bear Lake v. Budge, 75 Pac. 614; Dawson v.
Eustace, 36 N. E. 87; Jones v. Chicago, R. I. & P. Co.,
83 N. E. 215. The legislation must be appropriate to the
classification and embrace all within the particular class.
State v. Boyd, supra; Vulcanite P. C. Co. v. Allison, 69
Atl. 855. As to the subjects enumerated, the constitutional prohibition is absolute. Williams v. Bidleman, 7
Nev. 68; Schweiss v. District Court, 23 Nev. 226; Knopf
v. People, 185 Ill. 20; Wolf v. Humboldt County, 32 Nev.
174; Kraus v. Lehman, 170 Ind. 408; State v. Parsons,
40 N. J. Law, 1; Longview v. Crawfordsville, 68 L. R. A.
622; Bedford Quarries v. Bough, 14 L. R. A. 418;
Edmonds v. Herbransen, 50 N. W. 970; Seaboard Air
Line v. Simon, 56 Fla. 545; 8 Cyc., sec. 1075.

The act of 1915, as applied to the case at bar, is unconstitutional and void, being an attempted legislative usur-
pation of the jurisdiction of the courts. Const. Nev.

sec. 1, art. 3, sec. 6, art. 6. Application of the act would be an attempt to vacate, alter or modify a final judgment of a constitutional court. The fact that the case is still pending does not alter or change the character of the decree as a final decree. Life I. Co. v. Auditor, 100 Ill. 478; Martin v. South Salem L. Co., 26 S. E. 591. Any vacation, alteration or modification of a judgment of any court, or any change of the rights of the parties thereunder, by an act of the legislature, is an unconstitutional infringement upon the judicial power. Ex Parte Darling, 16 Nev. 98; Skinner v. Holt, 69 N. W. 595; Butler v. Supervisors, 26 Mich. 22; Radcliffe v. Anderson, 31 Grat. 105; Gaines v. Executors, 9 B. Mon. 295; Roche v. Waters, 72 Md. 248.

The act is unconstitutional and invalid because it impairs the obligations of a contract under which the receiver was appointed, rendered services and earned compensation. "No state shall pass any law impairing the obligations of contracts." Const. U. S., sec. 10, art. 1. "No * * * law impairing the obligation of contracts shall ever be passed." Const. Nev. sec. 15, art. 1; Security L. I. Co. v. LeClerc, 31 Hun, 36; Montgomery County v. Talley, 169 S. W. 1141. "But after the official services have been rendered, a contract to pay for them at the legal rate exists which cannot be impaired even by the legislature." 29 Cyc. 1427; Hill County v. Sauls, 134 S. W. 267.

The law in force at the time of the performance of the services by the receiver provided for a "reasonable compensation," to be fixed by the court. Rev. Laws, 1199. He cannot be deprived of such "reasonable compensation" by any law enacted after the services have been performed. If no compensation was fixed by law at the time of the performance of the services, he is entitled to a reasonable compensation. Bohart v. Anderson, 103 Pac. 742; Washoe County v. Humboldt County, 14 Nev. 123; Toronto v. Salt Lake County, 10 Utah, 410, 27 Pac. 587.

Leonard B. Fowler, Attorney-General, and *Robert Richards,* Deputy Attorney-General, for Respondent:

The act of 1915 is retroactive, and not merely prospective; and in any event, the compensation of the receiver is in the nature of costs. The law is well settled that costs are governed by the law in effect at the termination of the proceeding. 36 Cyc. 1219.

The very intent and purpose of the act is that it should be given a retrospective effect. The language is plain as to the intent of the legislature. A statute must not be defeated by a "forced and overstrict construction." Ex Parte Prosole, 32 Nev. 378. "It is a rule of statutory construction that all statutes are to be construed as having only a prospective operation, unless the purpose and intention of the legislature to give them a retrospective effect is expressly declared or is necessarily implied from the language used. 36 Cyc. 1205.

The right to compensation of the receiver was not vested, in any sense. Under his appointment there was secured to him only the power to act as receiver. His compensation depended upon the due fulfilment of his trust, the judgment of the court fixing the same, and the rules of procedure that might from time to time be entered by legislative authority. His rights in this regard were merely inchoate, subject to vesting pursuant to legislative will. Endlich, Inter. Stats., secs. 281, 290; 36 Cyc. 1226, 1233.

The statute attacked regulates procedure, a matter "in the nature of costs." These are always within legislative control. 36 Cyc. 1219; Lew v. Bray, 81 Conn. 213; Turley v. Logan County, 17 Ill. 151; Bonney v. Reed, 31 N. J. Law, 133; Hepworth v. Gardner, 4 Utah, 439.

By the Court, DUCKER, J.:

This case is submitted for consideration and decision upon an agreed statement of facts. It appears therefrom that the State Bank and Trust Company was a banking corporation, organized and existing under and by virtue of the laws of this state, and on the 18th day of May, 1908, was ordered into involuntary liquidation under the provisions of section 10, c. 119, of the banking act of 1907, by the district court of the First judicial district of this state. The appellant, Frank L. Wildes, was at the same time duly apointed by the court as receiver of the property and assets of said corporation for the purpose of winding up and liquidating its business and affairs. He duly qualified, and ever since said 18th day of May, 1908, has been, and still is, actively engaged in the performance of his duties.

On the 6th day of August, 1914, appellant filed in said district court his petition, praying for an order fixing his compensation as such receiver. Thereafter, on the 29th day of January, 1919, the said court in a written decision held that the compensation of the receiver for all services rendered during his receivership is governed by the act of 1915, regulating the compensation of receivers of corporations in cases of involuntary dissolution or liquidation, approved March 29, 1915. It reads:

"A receiver of a corporation appointed in any proceeding heretofore or hereafter instituted for the involuntary liquidation or dissolution of such corporation and the winding up of its affairs, in addition to his necessary expenses, shall receive as compensation for his services not to exceed two per cent of all moneys or sums received by him, and an additional two per cent of all moneys paid out by him in dividends; provided, however, in case of extraordinary services rendered by the receiver the court may allow him an additional one per cent upon final accounting of all moneys disbursed by him by way of dividends. Any order, judgment, decree, or proceeding allowing any greater or further compensation than that provided in this act to any receiver of any insolvent corporation appointed in a proceeding for its involuntary liquidation or winding up shall be void." Stats. 1915, p. 507.

1. Appellant contends that his compensation as such receiver is not regulated or limited by the provisions of this act. Hence this appeal.

2. It is urged primarily that the statute of 1915 is prospective in its operation and has no retrospective effect. As a general rule, a statute will not be construed to operate upon past transactions, but in futuro only. It is a maxim, which is said to be as ancient as the law itself, that a law ought to be prospective, not retrospective, in its operation. Retrospective legislation is not favored, and, except when resorted to in the enactment of curative laws, or such remedial acts as do not create new rights or take away vested ones, is apt to result in injustice. The reason is well expressed in Jones v. Stockgrowers' National Bank, 17 Colo. App. 79, 67 Pac. 177:

"Every citizen," says the court, "is supposed to know the law, and to govern his conduct, both as to business affairs and otherwise, in accordance with its provisions. It would be a manifest injustice if, after rights had become vested according to existing laws, they could be taken away, in whole or in part, by subsequent legislation."

3. From a consideration of the pronounced policy of the law against retrospective legislation, there has been evolved a strict rule of construction in this regard.

"There is always a presumption that statutes are intended to operate prospectively only, and words ought not to have a retrospective operation unless they are so clear, strong, and imperative that no other meaning can be annexed to them, or unless the intention of the legislature cannot be otherwise satisfied. Every reasonable doubt is resolved against a retroactive operation of a statute. If all of the language of a statute can be satisfied by giving it prospective action only, that construction will be given it." United States v. Heth, 3 Cranch, 399, 2 L. Ed. 479; United States v. Alexander, 12 Wall. 177, 20 L. Ed. 381; United States v. Burr, 159 U. S. 78, 15 Sup. Ct. 1002, 40 L. Ed. 82; United States Fidelity Co. v. United States, 209 U. S. 306, 28 Sup. Ct. 537, 52 L. Ed. 804; People v. O'Brien, 111 N. Y. 1, 18 N. E. 692, 2 L. R. A. 255, 7 Am. St. Rep. 684; Ducey v. Patterson, 37 Colo. 216, 86 Pac. 109, 9 L. R. A. (N.S.)

1066, 119 Am. St. Rep. 284, 11 Ann. Cas. 393; White
Sewing Machine Co. v. Harris, 252 Ill. 361, 96 N. E. 857,
Ann. Cas. 1912D, 536; Lawrence v. City of Louisville, 96
Ky. 595, 29 S. W. 450, 27 L. R. A. 560, 49 Am. St. Rep.
309; 6 Am. & Eng. Ency. Law, 939; 36 Cyc. 1205–1208;
25 R. C. L. 787, 788, 789.

"This rule," says Paterson, J., in United States v.
Heth, supra, "ought especially to be adhered to, when
such a construction [retrospective operation] will alter
the preexisting situation of parties, or will affect or
interfere with their antecedent rights, *services,* and
remuneration, which is so obviously improper that nothing ought to uphold and vindicate the interpretation
but the unequivocal and inflexible import of the terms,
and the manifest intention of the legislature." (The
italics are ours.)

4. It is apparent that the statute does not deal with
anything which is ordinarily the subject-matter of legitimate retrospective legislation, but seeks to establish a
different rule of compensation for the services of receivers in a particular class of cases from that which was
in force at the time of the enactment. In other words,
it seeks to enact a new role of civil conduct entirely prospective in its nature. So the rule against retrospective
construction must be given full effect. The language of
the statute, "A receiver of a corporation appointed in
any proceeding heretofore or hereafter instituted * * *"
could have been transposed by the legislature so that no
doubt would be left of the intention to give it retroactive
operation. If it read, "A receiver of a corporation heretofore or hereafter appointed in any proceeding instituted, * * *" all doubt would have been removed. It
would be reasonable to assume that such a simple and
natural transposition of a few words of the same language, clarifying and rendering unmistakable the
intention of the legislature, would have been made, if
retrospective operation of the statute were meant. The
words of the statute, "A receiver of a corporation
appointed," are clearly of prospective operation, as are

the words, "proceedings hereafter instituted." The only language in the statute of retrospective operation is the word "heretofore," but this seems to refer to any proceeding instituted, and not to the appointment of a receiver. It is quite possible that a proceeding for the involuntary liquidation or dissolution of a corporation may have been pending in this state when the statute was enacted and a receiver thereafter appointed, so there is nothing incongruous in the view that the legislature intended to provide for such a case, as well as for future proceedings and appointments.

Force is given to this conclusion when we consider the closing sentence of the statute:

"Any order, judgment, decree, or proceeding allowing any greater or further compensation than that provided in this act to any receiver of any insolvent corporation appointed in a proceeding for its involuntary liquidation or winding up shall be void."

There is nothing retroactive in this language. It cannot be said that the legislature meant to declare any order, judgment, or decree of court, fixing the compensation of a receiver made prior to the enactment, void. Such a construction is unwarranted by the language of the sentence, and, furthermore, would render the provision so palpably unconstitutional as to preclude the idea that retrospective operation was intended by the legislature. If it did not mean the statute to have retrospective operation as to orders, judgments, or decrees of court fixing a receiver's compensation, it is fair to assume, in the absence of compulsory language to the contrary, that it did not intend such retroactive effect as to the receivership itself. The intention must be deduced from a view of the whole statute and from the material parts of it. On the whole, it cannot be said that there is anything on the face of the statute putting it beyond doubt that the legislature meant it to operate retrospectively. Cooley, Const. Lim. (6th ed.) 77.

As we conclude that the statute is prospective in its operation, and therefore not applicable to the case under consideration, we will not pass upon the constitutional questions raised by appellant. The lower court erred in holding that the compensation of the receiver is regulated and limited by the act of 1915, for which a reversal is ordered.

[No. 2418]

NEVADA LINCOLN MINING COMPANY, Petitioner, *v.* THE DISTRICT COURT OF THE EIGHTH JUDICIAL DISTRICT OF THE STATE OF NEVADA; Honorable T. C. HART, District Judge of said District and Judge of said Court, and FRANK WILSON, Respondents.

[175 Pac. 1006]

1. Certiorari—Only Question Open to Inquiry Whether Proper Service Was Obtained on Petitioner Seeking to Review Judgment.

   In an original proceeding by certiorari to inquire into the jurisdiction of the district court to render a judgment against petitioner, the only question which the supreme court can examine is whether or not service of summons was obtained upon petitioner in the action sought to be reviewed, so as to give the court jurisdiction to proceed.

2. Certiorari—Issuance of Writ Discretionary and Not Matter of Right.

   Writ of certiorari does not issue as a matter of right, but in the sound discretion of the court.

3. Certiorari—Dismissal of Proceedings where Equity Can Better Afford Relief.

   In an original proceeding by certiorari to inquire into the jurisdiction of the district court to render judgment against claims of a mining company, where the supreme court, in view of all the facts, reaches conclusion that a court of equity is more capable of affording adequate relief and doing justice in the matter, the proceedings will be dismissed.

ORIGINAL PROCEEDING. Petition for certiorari by the Nevada Lincoln Mining Company against the District Court of the Eighth Judicial District of the State of Nevada, Hon. T. C. Hart, District Judge of the district and Judge of such court, and Frank Wilson. **Proceedings dismissed.**

August Tilden, for Petitioner:

The certificate of the clerk purporting to give his version of counsel's testimony must be ignored as gratuitous. Mechler v. Fialk, 82 Atl. 330; Cook v. Court, 59 South. 483. The petition has served its purpose and ceased to be a factor in the proceedings. Donovan v. Board, 163 Pac. 69. The issue is presented by the writ and the return. Idem.

Did the court below "regularly pursue its authority" in rendering the assailed judgment? Rev. Laws, 5690. On such inquiry nothing can be considered except the papers required by law to be in the judgment roll; therefore the court may not examine the certificate of the secretary of state, found in the return. Willey v. Benedict Co., 79 Pac. 270. Such certificate is provided for in the statute governing service on foreign corporations. Rev. Laws, 5025. It is not provided for in the statute governing service on domestic corporations. Rev. Laws, 1188, as amended, Stats. 1913, p. 65.

The recitals in the so-called default and judgment, purporting to find that due service was made, must be read in connection with, and be controlled by, the return of service. Cheely v. Clayton, 28 L. Ed. 298; Venner v. Denver Co., 63 Pac. 1061; Settlemier v. Sullivan, 24 L. Ed. 1110; Hobby v. Bunch, 20 Am. St. Rep. 301; Reinhart v. Lugo, 86 Cal. 395; Lonkey v. Keyes S. M. Co., 21 Nev. 312. The court will not hear parol evidence, nor any evidence dehors the judgment roll. Reinhart v. Lugo, supra. Nor in the face of direct attack entertain presumptions in favor of the validity of the judgment. Radovich v. French, 136 Pac. 341 ; Rich v. Superior Court, 161 Pac. 291. It will be presumed that the return states all of the facts of record. 182 S. W. 996. The burden is on the respondents to show that the court had jurisdiction to render the assailed judgment. Rue v. Quinn, 66 Pac. 216.

To indulge presumptions in favor of jurisdiction * * * "would be against all sound principle." City

v. Fairfax, 24 L. Ed. 583. Conceding that the statute is valid, plaintiff departed materially from its requirements in attempting service. State v. State Bank, 37 Nev. 55; Lonkey v. Keyes S. M. Co., supra; Coffin v. Bell, 22 Nev. 169; Vance v. Maroney, 3 Colo. 47.

The courts uniformly hold that a showing of non-residence made too long before the making of an order of publication is fatal to the validity of the service. Rockman v. Ackerman, 85 N. W. 491; Roosevelt v. Land Co., 84 N. W. 157; Cohn v. Kember, 47 Cal. 144. Therefore a showing made any time after the service must be void.

If this court is embarrassed by the question of appeal, no like embarrassment applies to the writ of mandate. Rev. Laws, 5696; Stoddard v. Court, 41 Pac. 278. If the lower court, acting under rule 45, illegally divested itself of jurisdiction to purge this void judgment from its records, mandamus will lie. Floyd v. District Court, 36 Nev. 349. Where the justice of the case requires it, a petition for a writ of certiorari will be permitted to stand as a petition for a writ of mandamus and the appropriate relief awarded. Tel. Co. v. Superior Court, 114 Pac. 978. Contrary to the respondents' contention, "when the duty is mandatory and no discretion is vested, its performance and the manner of its performance both may be compelled." 26 Cyc. 160, 215.

A. L. Haight and *Cheney, Downer, Price & Hawkins,* for Respondents:

The judgment of the district court is a valid judgment. Even if invalid, the discretionary writ of certiorari, which is intended only to subserve the purposes of justice, ought not to issue.

The failure of the corporation to appoint an agent to receive process indicated its willingness to have notice given to the secretary of state. Olender v. Crystalline M. Co., 86 Pac. 1082. If this court had believed such service was invalid, it would have been very easy to say so. Brooks v. Nevada Nickel Syndicate, 24 Nev. 311; Lonkey v. Keyes, 21 Nev. 312.

The writ of certiorari is not a writ of right. It is a discretionary writ. In granting or withholding it, courts exercise equitable jurisdiction. Woodworth v. Gibbs, 16 N. W. 287. There is no authority for the issuance of the writ if there is an appeal or any plain, speedy and adequate remedy. The lower court denied the motion to set aside the judgment. Appeals lie from rulings made on applications to set aside defaults and judgments. Haley v. Eureka County Bank, 20 Nev. 410; Horton v. New Pass Co., 21 Nev. 184. The writ is exceptional and is allowed only to prevent a failure of justice. White v. Boyce, 50 N. W. 302. The writ will be denied after lapse of time when it would do more harm than good. Hagar v. Yolo County, 47 Cal. 222. The writ will not issue because the summons is defective or the service irregular. St. Louis I. M. & S. Co. v. State, 17 S. W. 806.

The record shows that the execution was returned fully satisfied. It therefore has formed the basis of settled rights and cannot be vacated upon certiorari. State v. Washoe County, 14 Nev. 66. A satisfied judgment cannot be set aside on motion. Maclay v. Meads, 112 Pac. 195. Where property has been sold on a judgment, equity is the only remedy. Foster v. Hauswirth, 6 Pac. 19.

Respondents are not asking that petitioner be denied its right to a full hearing as to the validity of the judgment in question. The petitioner, however, demands that the important rights involved be determined without an opportunity to respondents to present their side of the matter. "But it does not ask to defend; it merely asks that it be allowed to escape the necessity of making a defense." Olender v. Crystalline M. Co., 86 Pac. 1083.

By the Court, COLEMAN, C. J.:

This is an original proceeding in certiorari to inquire into the jurisdiction of the respondent court to render the judgment in question.

It appears that on July 12, 1917, Frank Wilson, one of the respondents, commenced an action in the Eighth judicial district court, in and for Churchill County, against the Nevada Lincoln Mining Company, a corporation organized under the laws of this state, to recover judgment in the sum of $1,050 for services rendered to, and money expended in behalf of, the said corporation. It appears also that the summons which was issued on the day mentioned was placed in the hands of J. H. Stern, sheriff of Ormsby County, Nevada, on the 9th day of August, 1917, and that on that day, after receiving from George Brodigan, secretary of state of the State of Nevada, a certificate stating that the Nevada Lincoln Mining Company, a corporation, had never filed a list of its officers or the name of an agent in this state upon whom process might be served, he served the summons in the action upon the Nevada Lincoln Mining Company, a corporation, by delivering a copy of the same, to which was attached a copy of the complaint in the action, to the said George Brodigan, secretary of state.

There also appears the affidavit of M. L. Wildes, sheriff of Churchill County, certifying to his being over the age of 21 years, the duly elected and acting sheriff, etc., and that on October 1, 1917, he had posted in the office of the county clerk of Churchill County and ex officio clerk of the district court in and for said county, at Fallon, Nevada, a full, true, and correct copy of the original summons in said action, to which was attached a certified copy of the complaint filed therein.

It also appears that on November 2, 1917, the case of Frank Wilson, Plaintiff, v. Nevada Lincoln Mining Company (a corporation), Defendant, was called for hearing before the respondent court, and that at that time the default of the defendant company was entered and judgment rendered in favor of the plaintiff and against the defendant, as prayed in the complaint.

The judgment of the court recites that "it appearing that service of process upon the defendant corporation could not be had by delivering a copy thereof personally to the president, cashier, secretary, or resident agent of such corporation, or by leaving the same at the principal place of business of said corporation in this state," service was made in the manner stated herein.

It also appears that after judgment had been rendered an execution was issued thereupon, and that the mining claims mentioned were levied upon as the property of the judgment debtor, and that after due notice they were sold and disposed of to satisfy said judgment.

Section 87 of the corporation act (Rev. Laws, 1188, as amended, Stats. 1913, p. 65, sec. 1) reads:

"Service of legal process upon any corporation created under this act or subject to its provisions shall be made by delivering a copy thereof personally to the president, cashier, secretary or resident agent of such corporation, or by leaving the same at the principal office or place of business of the corporation in this state. Service by copy left at the said principal office or place of business in this state, to be effective, must be delivered thereat at least thirty days before the return of the process, and in the presence of an adult person; and the officer serving the process shall distinctly state the manner of service in his return thereto, naming such person; provided, that process returnable forthwith must be served personally; and provided further, when for any reason service cannot be had in the manner hereinbefore provided, then service may be made by delivering a copy to the secretary of state at least thirty days before the return of process and by posting a copy of such process in the office of the clerk of the court in which such action is brought or pending, at least thirty days before the return of such process."

1. The only question which we could inquire into in this proceeding would be as to whether or not such service of summons was obtained upon defendant in the action sought to be reviewed as gave the court jurisdiction to proceed. Kapp v. District Court, 31 Nev. 444, 103 Pac. 235.

Upon the hearing in this matter respondents urged various reasons why a writ of certiorari should not issue in this case.· Among them it was contended that since the alleged sale of the property third parties had acquired whatever title passed thereby, had expended large sums of money in developing the property, and had opened up a valuable mine. It was also urged that the petitioner had not acted, in applying for this writ, with reasonable diligence, and that great and irreparable injury would be done should the writ issue herein. It was also contended by counsel for respondent that the petitioner had an adequate remedy in equity.

2. While the law applicable to the situation presented · herein seems clear, the question of determining just what our order should be is one which has caused us a great deal of trouble and anxiety. The writ of certiorari does not issue as a matter of right, but in the sound discretion of the court. Hagar v. Yolo County, 47 Cal. 222; St. Louis ·v. State, 55 Ark. 200, 17 S. W. 806; Spelling, Extr. Rem. (2d ed.) sec. 1897; Bailey, Hab. Corp. & Spec. Rem. p. 648; 5 R. C. L. 254.

3. After numerous conferences, in view of all the facts we have reached the conclusion that a court of equity is more capable of affording adequate relief and of doing justice in the matter than is this court in a proceeding of this character. We are therefore of the opinion that these proceedings should be dismissed.

It is so ordered.

[No. 2380]

IN THE MATTER OF THE DETERMINATION OF THE RELATIVE RIGHTS TO THE WATERS OF BARBER CREEK AND ITS TRIBUTARIES IN DOUGLAS COUNTY, NEVADA.

EUGENE SCOSSA, APPELLANT, v. CLARISSA CHURCH AND BARBER ESTATE, RESPONDENTS.

[182 Pac. 925]

1. WATERS AND WATERCOURSES — DETERMINATION OF RIGHTS — ORDERS APPEALABLE.

   An order of determination of the state engineer in a proceeding to determine the relative rights of persons to water is not appealable, the only appeal allowable, under Stats. 1915, c. 253, sec. 6, in such a case being from the decree of the court affirming or modifying such order.

2. WATERS AND WATERCOURSES—DETERMINATION OF RIGHTS—DISMISSAL OF APPEAL.

   Assuming that the rules prescribed by civil practice act, as amended by Stats. 1915, c. 142, apply to the hearing of an issue raised by a notice of exceptions to an order of determination of the state engineer duly filed with the clerk under Stats. 1915, c. 253, sec. 6, in a proceeding to determine relative rights to water, it does not follow that the failure to preserve errors by a bill of exceptions must result in the dismissal of an appeal from a decree affirming the order of determination of the engineer, although such failure might result in an affirmance of the decree.

3. APPEAL AND ERROR—NOTICE OF UNDERTAKING—DISMISSAL OF APPEAL.

   Since Rev. Laws, 5330, does not require that an undertaking on appeal be served on the adverse party, the supreme court is not authorized to dismiss an appeal for want of service.

4. APPEAL AND ERROR—LACK OF MOTION FOR NEW TRIAL—GROUNDS FOR DISMISSAL OF APPEAL.

   Since the supreme court, on appeal from a decree, can look to the judgment roll to ascertain whether any error appears, an appeal will not be dismissed because it appears from the record that it is based on the ground that the evidence is insufficient to justify the decision of the court, and that no motion for a new trial was made and determined before the appeal was taken, under Rev. Laws, 5328.

IN the Matter of the Determination of the Relative Rights to the Waters of Barber Creek and its Tributaries in Douglas County. From a decision of the First Judicial District Court, Frank P. Langan, Judge, Eugene

Scossa appealed. Clarissa Church and the Barber Estate move to dismiss the appeal. **Motion denied.**

Chartz & Chartz, for Appellant:

The motion to dismiss the appeal should be denied. All proceedings from date of judgment have been taken in the same manner and with the same effect as in civil cases. A notice of appeal has been filed and served, likewise an undertaking on appeal, and the entire record certified to this court. There was no trial before the district court, and therefore no motion for a new trial could be made. All the court could do was to enter a decree affirming or modifying the order of determination made by the state engineer. Stats. 1915, p. 381, sec. 36. The water law provides for summary proceedings and that appeals may be taken from the judgment of the district court in the same manner and with the same effect as in other civil cases. Stats. 1915, p. 384, sec. 75.

Platt & Sanford, for Respondents:

The appeal from the order of determination entered by the state engineer should be dismissed: (1) because it is not a final order and judgment in the case, and (2) because it is an order and judgment not appealable to this court, and this court has no jurisdiction on said appeal. The entire appeal should be dismissed because (1) no bill of exceptions was either agreed upon or settled in the lower court or filed, (2) there was no service of an undertaking, and (3) because this court has no jurisdiction over said appeal. The order of determination made by the state engineer does not purport to be a judicial decree. Stats. 1915, p. 381.

Appeals must be taken in accordance with the method prescribed by statute. This rule is universally followed. Gill v. Goldfield Con. M. Co. 43 Nev. 1; Coffin v. Coffin, 40 Nev. 347; Gardner v. Pacific P. Co., 40 Nev. 344; Ward v. Silver Peak, 39 Nev. 89.

By the Court, SANDERS, J.:

This is a motion to dismiss an appeal. The notice of appeal is as follows:

"To Contestees, Clarissa Church, acting for herself and as guardian for Benjamin Barber, and George C. Russell, executor of the estate of Lyman Barber, deceased, and to George Springmeyer, their attorney:

"Please take notice that contesant, Eugene Scossa, in the above-entitled proceeding hereby appeals to the Supreme Court of the State of Nevada from the order of determination, and from the supplemental order of determination of the State Engineer in the above-entitled proceeding, filed and returned in the above-entitled court, and from the whole thereof, and also appeals from the decree of the above-entitled court, confirming, approving, and affirming said relative determination, and as amended and modified by the supplemental order of determination as made and entered by the State Engineer of the State of Nevada and filed in the above-entitled court, made and entered January 30, 1919, and from the whole thereof, said decree being in favor of defendants, and against said plaintiff, contestant.

"Dated March 12, 1919."

The respondents move to dismiss the appeal on several grounds, and for convenience we shall dispose of them in their order.

1. First—The order of determination of the state engineer is not an appealable order. This is correct. The only appeal allowed by law in such a case as this is an appeal from the decree of the court affirming or modifying the order of the state engineer. Section 6 (section 36), Stats. 1915, p. 381. An appeal direct to this court from the order of the state engineer is irregular and of no effect.

2. Second—"That no bills of exception were either agreed upon or settled in the lower court, and in the time allowed by law, practice, and procedure, and no bill of

exception was filed herein." It is obvious from the notice of appeal that this is also an appeal from a decree entered on the 30th of January, 1919, affirming an order of determination of ·the state engineer. Conceding, but not deciding, that the rules prescribed by the civil practice act, as amended by Statutes of 1915, p. 164, applies to the hearing of an issue raised by the notice of exceptions to the order of determination of the state engineer, duly filed with the clerk of the court (section 6 [sec. 36], Stats. 1915, pp. 378, 381), it does not follow that the failure to preserve errors by a bill of exceptions must result in the dismissal of an appeal. The appeal being from the decree, such failure might result in the affirmance of the decree, but not necessarily in the dismissal of the appeal taken from the decree.

3. Third—"That there was no notice of an undertaking herein." To make an appeal effectual an undertaking must be filed within five days after service of the notice of appeal. Rev. Laws, 5330. In the absence of a requirement that such undertaking be served upon the adverse party we are not authorized to dismiss an appeal upon this ground.

4. Fourth—That this court has no jurisdiction of the appeal, in that it appears from the record that the appeal is based upon the ground that the evidence is insufficient to justify the decision of the court, and, it appearing that no motion for a new trial was made and determined before the appeal was taken, the appeal must be dismissed. Rev. Laws, 5328.

Gill v. Goldfield Consolidated Mines Co., 43 Nev. 1, 176 Pac. 784, is cited as an authority .in support of this position. It is proper to state in this connection that that case is now pending upon an order granting a rehearing therein.

This case being an appeal from a decree, we can look to the judgment roll to ascertain whether any error appears. This being true, the appeal should not be dismissed.

The motion to dismiss the appeal is denied.

———

[No. 2380]

IN THE MATTER OF THE DETERMINATION OF THE RELATIVE RIGHTS TO THE WATERS OF BARBER CREEK AND ITS TRIBUTARIES IN DOUGLAS COUNTY, NEVADA.

EUGENE SCOSSA, APPELLANT, v. CLARISSA CHURCH AND BARBER ESTATE, RESPONDENTS.

[187 Pac. 1004]

1. JUDGMENT—DECREE OF DISTRICT COURT ON EXCEPTIONS TO DETERMINATION OF STATE ENGINEER DETERMINING WATER RIGHTS TOO INDEFINITE.

    In proceedings for the determination of water rights initiated before the state engineer pursuant to the water law, decree of the district court, on exceptions, pursuant to section 35, as amended by Stats. 1915, c. 253, to the determination of the engineer, reading that the court had reviewed all the proof and the facts and the relative determinations by the engineer, and had reached conclusions on the law and facts coincident with the determination of the engineer, and directing decree affirming his order of determination, despite section 36, as amended by Stats. 1915, c. 253, held in no sense a decree which in a water case should be as definite as language can make it and should dispose of each issue raised by the exceptions to the determination of the state engineer.

2. WATERS AND WATERCOURSES—FINDINGS OF STATE ENGINEER IN DETERMINING WATER RIGHTS ENTITLED TO RESPECT, BUT NOT SUPERSEDING POWER OF COURT.

    In proceedings for the determination of water rights pursuant to the water law, the ultimate findings of the state engineer are entitled to great respect, but do not take from the district court on exceptions the power to grant relief to a party whose rights may have been infringed by the engineer.

3. APPEAL AND ERROR—AUTHENTICATION OF RECORD SOLELY BY CLERK OF DISTRICT COURT NOT SUFFICIENT.

    On appeal from decree of the district court affirming an order of the state engineer determining water rights, the certificate of the clerk of the district court attached to the original documents, files, and records in the original proceeding indicates only prima facie correctness, and by analogy to a record certified by an official reporter it must be authenticated by the court or judge to be made a part of the record, in view of Stats. 1915, c. 142.

APPEAL from First Judicial District Court, Douglas County; *Frank P. Langan*, Judge.

In the Matter of the Determination of the Relative Rights to the Waters of Barber Creek and its Tributaries in Douglas County, between Eugene Scossa and Clarissa Church and the Barber Estate. From a decree affirming the determination of the State Engineer, Scossa appeals. **Cause remitted to the district court, which is directed to reopen the case to make findings and enter decree.** COLEMAN, C. J., dissenting.

Chartz & Chartz, for Appellant:

As a matter of law, the contestant is entitled to all the water developed and conserved by him and his predecessors. He has a prescriptive right, besides, to all said waters diverted at point C, to the extent that he can beneficially use the same. The issues decided by the state engineer, and confirmed, approved and affirmed by the district court, were adjudicated in the former suit and are res adjudicata. The state engineer had no jurisdiction over the subject-matter of the action. His findings and determination of the relative rights of the parties to the waters in dispute are contrary to the evidence, and contrary to law.

Platt & Sanford, for Respondents:

Determination of the state engineer and its affirmance by the district court is amply sustained by the judgment roll; and if this court is of the opinion that questions of evidence and proof of alleged errors upon the hearing and trial should be considered, the order of determination and judgment should be affirmed.

This court can consider the judgment roll only, which consists of such documents and papers as are required by statute. Rev. Laws, 5273. "Where the appeal is from the judgment alone, the question of sufficiency of the evidence to sustain the findings will not be considered." State v. Northern Belle M. & M. Co., 15 Nev. 385; Reinhart v. Co. D, 23 Nev. 369; Peers v. Reed, 23 Nev. 404.

"A finding of fact in an equity suit, supported by the evidence, is conclusive on the supreme court." Costello

[No. 2374]

J. B. DIXON, APPELLANT, *v.* CITY OF RENO, GEORGE C. BRYSON, AND JOHN D. HILL-HOUSE, RESPONDENTS.

[187 Pac. 308]

1. FALSE IMPRISONMENT—COMPLAINT INSUFFICIENT.

   In an action for false imprisonment, a count based on lack of jurisdiction of a municipal court *held* insufficient, in that it failed to allege facts showing wherein municipal court was without jurisdiction; plaintiff · having stated that he was arrested and proceeded against on a warrant issued upon a complaint filed with a duly constituted magistrate.

2. PLEADING—CONCLUSION OF PLEADER.

   Allegation in an action for false imprisonment that municipal judge "had no jurisdiction or power" is not a statement of facts, but a conclusion of the pleader.

3. MALICIOUS PROSECUTION—COMPLAINT MUST ALLEGE WANT OF PROBABLE CAUSE.

   A count of complaint *held* to amount to an action on the case for the malicious arrest and imprisonment of the plaintiff in the nature of a conspiracy and to be insufficient where it failed to allege want of probable cause.

4. CONSPIRACY—COMMON-LAW ACTION OBSOLETE.

   The common-law action of conspiracy is obsolete, and in lieu thereof an action on the case in the nature of a conspiracy has been substituted.

5. CONSPIRACY—JUDGMENT—JUDGMENT AGAINST JOINT DEFENDANTS.

   In an action for false imprisonment, judgment may be entered against a single defendant, though the conspiracy charged be not proven; but it cannot be entered against joint defendants without such proof.

6. ACTION—THERE MAY BE JOINDER OF COUNTS IN CASE AND TRESPASS.

   In an action for false imprisonment to include in one action a count in case and count in trespass, the counts must arise from the same state of facts.

COLEMAN, C. J., dissenting in part.

APPEAL from Second Judicial District Court, Washoe County; *George A. Bartlett*, Judge.

Action by J. B. Dixon against the City of Reno and others. Judgment for defendants, and plaintiff appeals. **Affirmed and remanded. Petition for rehearing denied.**

J. M. Frame, for Appellant:

"Normally any and every natural person, including legislators, and irrespective of his public or private character or his personal status or personal relationship, is liable in an action for false imprisonment whenever such person appears to have unlawfully detained another." 19 Cyc. 332, 333, 335, 336. Judicial officers are exempt from liability only when clearly within the pale of their authority. 19 Cyc. 333; 23 Cyc. 568. "The weight of authority is still to the effect that such inferior judges are liable where they attempt to exercise authority where they have none, or assume jurisdiction without any power. 23 Cyc. 569.

Under general demurrers no point can be considered except the single one of whether or not there are sufficient facts set up to constitute a cause of action in favor of the plaintiff and against defendants. Rev. Laws, 5040, 5041, 5065, 5066. The complaint is in accordance with the provisions of the statute. It states all such facts as are necessary to constitute a cause of action against all defendants. 3 Sutherland, Cr. Pl., secs. 3838–3852; 8 Ency. Pl. & Pr., pp. 841–849; 19 Cyc., pp. 319–343; 2 Bates, Pl., secs. 560–565; Strozzi v. Wines, 24 Nev. 389.

The chief changes in the amended complaint, in the first cause of. action, consist in the averments that defendant Bryson, being without jurisdiction or power, acted merely as a private individual; and that defendant Hillhouse was an officer of the municipal court, and had notice and knowledge that appellant, as defendant in the municipal court, had objected to and called in question and denied the jurisdiction of the municipal court and of the defendant Bryson. Telefsen v. Boughton, 5 Wend. 170; Piper v. Pearson, 2 Gray, 120; Clarke v. May, 2 Gray, 410; Allison v. Rheam, 3 S. & R. 137; Wachsmuth v. M. N. Bank, 96 Mich. 426.

The second cause of action does not set out the proceedings in the municipal court, but proceeds more on the lines of a common-law action. This is the better form of complaint. 1 Estee, sec. 1649; 1 Kinkead, Pl., sec. 560; 2 Bates, Pl., secs. 1657–1661; 19 Cyc. 357–359; 8 Ency. Pl. & Pr. 842–849.

W. D. Jones, for Respondents:

The original, as also the amended, complaint fails to state anything but conclusions. "Unless the matters averred show the acts complained of to be unlawful or wrongful, such words are superfluous verbiage." Going v. Dinwiddie, 86 Cal. 638; Pratt v. Gardner, 48 Am. Dec. 652; Harness v. Steele, 159 Ind. 286.

The city of Reno is not liable in the action. Little Rock v. Willis, 27 Ark. 572; Parks v. Greenfield, 44 S. C. 168. The city is not liable for false imprisonment. 4 Dillon, sec. 1656; 28 Cyc. 1300. "The general rule exempting municipal corporations from liability in tort for conduct in the performance of governmental functions resulting in damages to individuals extends to improper arrests made under police power by constables or police officers generally." 19 Cyc. 336; Ex Parte Dixon, 161 Pac. 737; City v. Prunelle, 46 Pac. 949.

The demurrers were properly sustained. "The common law affords to all inferior tribunals and magistrates complete protection in the discharge of their official functions, so long as they act within the scope of their jurisdiction, even though it is alleged that the acts complained of were done maliciously and corruptly." 15 R. C. L., sec. 33, p. 547–549; 23 Cyc. 568; 19 Cyc. 333, 334.

The judgments in favor of the defendants are correct. Lake Bigler R. Co. v. Bedford, 3 Nev. 403.

By the Court, SANDERS, J.:

This is an action to recover damages for false imprisonment. To the original complaint a separate demurrer was filed by each of the defendants, and after argument said demurrers were sustained. The plaintiff filed an amended complaint, wherein it was attempted to state two causes of action, to which general demurrers were filed by each of the defendants and sustained by the court. Thereupon judgment was entered in favor of the defendants and against the plaintiff. Plaintiff appeals.

1. The first cause of action of the amended complaint

alleges that the defendant city of Reno caused plaintiff to be arrested on a warrant issued by the defendant Bryson, judge of the municipal court of said city, upon a complaint sworn to by its assistant city clerk; that thereafter he was brought to trial upon said complaint, over his objection to the jurisdiction of such court to hear and determine the matter complained of; that the defendant Bryson wrongfully and unlawfully pretended to assume jurisdiction, and heard and received certain evidence upon such trial and adjudged plaintiff guilty of a misdemeanor, and that he be fined in the sum of $25, and in default of the payment thereof that he be imprisoned for the term of twenty-five days, and that the said Bryson did thereupon issue and deliver to the defendant Hillhouse a warrant of commitment without having jurisdiction or power so to do; that thereafter the defendant Hillhouse did unlawfully and wrongfully arrest and imprison plaintiff and deprive him of his liberty; that at all such times the said Hillhouse was chief of police of said city of Reno; and that prior to and at the time of such arrest and imprisonment he had notice and knowledge that plaintiff had objected to the jurisdiction of said municipal court and of the defendant Bryson.

It is further alleged that the complaint upon which plaintiff was arrested and tried charged the breach of an ordinance of the city of Reno; that prior to the trial plaintiff filed with said Bryson a motion to set aside the complaint upon which he had been arrested, and afterwards filed a demurrer thereto, in which the validity of said ordinance was raised and the jurisdiction of said court and Bryson to try said plaintiff on said complaint was questioned.

Other matters are alleged for the evident purpose of forming the basis for punitive damages. The allegation of the said first cause of action of the amended complaint, wherein it is sought to charge the lack of jurisdiction of the municipal court of Reno, and the defendant Bryson, as the magistrate thereof, is as follows:

"Plaintiff avers that said court and said defendant Bryson had no jurisdiction or power to try plaintiff on said complaint or charge, and had no jurisdiction or power to adjudge plaintiff guilty or to impose upon him any fine or penalty or imprisonment or to issue any warrant of commitment of plaintiff; but that in the action he took as aforesaid, he was merely a private individual."

2. The so-called first cause of action does not state a cause of action, for the reason that it fails to allege facts showing wherein the municipal court was without jurisdiction. The mere allegation that the said court and Bryson "had no jurisdiction or power" is not a statement of facts, but merely a statement of a conclusion of the pleader. The plaintiff having stated that he was arrested and proceeded against upon a warrant issued upon a complaint filed with a duly constituted magistrate, it was incumbent upon him to plead facts showing the lack of jurisdiction of such magistrate to entertain such proceedings, and, failing to do so, the so-called first cause of action of the amended complaint is not good. This question was determined by the Supreme Court of California in Going v. Dinwiddie, 86 Cal. 633, 25 Pac. 129, the court saying:

"It is clear that the acts complained of were done by the defendant in his official capacity as a judicial officer, and there is no averment, in terms, that said acts were without or in excess of his jurisdiction, nor are any facts averred from which such want of jurisdiction appears. And that a judicial officer is not liable for acts done in his official capacity and within his jurisdiction is as thoroughly established as any other principle of law. One of the best expositions of that principle is found in the opinion of Shaw, C. J., in Pratt v. Gardner, 2 Cush. (Mass.) 68, 48 Am. Dec. 652. This court has also had frequent occasions to state the principle. Downer v.

Lent, 6 Cal. 94, 65 Am. Dec. 489; Turpen v. Booth, 56
Cal. 68, 38 Am. Rep. 48."

In the case of Barker v. Anderson, 81 Mich. 508, 45
N. W. 1108, the court declared the general rule to be
that in an action for damages for false imprisonment it
is necessary to show only that the plaintiff had been
imprisoned or restrained of his liberty, for the reason
that it must be presumed that such restraint was illegal;
but, when the plaintiff shows that such restraint was
exercised pursuant to a complaint made before a magistrate, the issuing of a warrant thereupon, and a trial
and conviction, the burden then rests upon the plaintiff
to show facts entitling him to recover. See, also, Snow
v. Weeks, 75 Me. 105; Petit v. Colmery, 4 Pennewill
(Del.) 266, 55 Atl. 344; Barhydt v. Valk, 12 Wend.
(N. Y.) 145, 27 Am. Dec. 124.

3. The plaintiff, for a second cause of action, alleges:
"(B) That the defendants city of Reno, George C.
Bryson, and John D. Hillhouse conspired together
against the plaintiff to deprive him of his liberty, and
did, on or about the 5th day of July, 1916, unlawfully
and wrongfully deprive the plaintiff of his liberty and
kept him so deprived, against his will and protest, for
a long time thereafter, and did jointly, unlawfully, and
wrongfully, cause him to be arrested and imprisoned
for a long time thereafter; and did thereafter, on or
about the 23d day of August, 1916, further jointly,
unlawfully, and wrongfully, deprive the plaintiff of his
liberty and kept him so deprived of his liberty for a
long time; and did jointly, unlawfully, and wrongfully
and against the plaintiff's will and protest, conspire
together and cause the plaintiff to be assaulted, arrested,
and imprisoned for a long time thereafter."

4-6. To acquaint the court with the full meaning and
purport of the charge, counsel for appellant points out
in his brief that paragraph B proceeds more on the lines
of a common-law action, and resembles more a mere
second count in a common-law declaration. The common-law action of conspiracy is obsolete, and in lieu

By the Court, COLEMAN, C. J.:

This is an appeal from an order denying a motion for a change of the place of trial of the above-entitled action from the county of Washoe to the county of Pershing. The motion was based upon the ground that it appears from the face of the amended complaint that the subject of the action, or some part thereof, is situated in Pershing County, and that no part thereof is situated in Washoe County.

1. Preliminary to disposing of the appeal upon the merits, it becomes necessary to determine whether or not the court has the authority to consider such appeal upon its merits at this time. The transcript on appeal was filed in the office of the clerk of this court on February 4, 1920. On February 7 counsel for respondents served upon counsel for appellants a notice to the effect that on February 13, 1920, they would move the court to proceed to hear the appeal taken from the order denying the motion for a change of place of trial. On the date last mentioned counsel for appellants did not appear, but a letter was presented, wherein they objected to the court's considering the matter, upon the grounds that the time for the filing of the assignment of errors and of an opening brief had not expired. Counsel for respondents appeared and argued the matter. The Statutes of 1919, p. 55, provide that the appealing party shall, within ten days after the transcript on appeal shall have been filed, file his assignment of errors; and rule 11 of this court provides that the appellant shall, within fifteen days after the filing of the transcript on appeal, serve and file his brief. The statute fixing the time for the filing of the assignment of errors does not apply in this case. While in Coffin v. Coffin, 40 Nev. 345, 163 Pac. 731, we took the position that an assignment of errors was indispensable, in the case of Talbot v. Mack, 41 Nev. 245, 169 Pac. 25, we held that, the appeal being from the judgment roll, an assignment of errors was not necessary, and refused to dismiss the appeal; which ruling was adhered to in Miller v.

Walser, 42 Nev. 497, 181 Pac. 437, and Smith v. Lucas et al., 43 Nev. 348, 186 Pac. 674.

Though the appeal in this case is not on what is technically known as the judgment roll, it is substantially the same. The record consists of the amended complaint, demand for change of venue, affidavit in support of the motion, written stipulation, and the order appealed from. The reasoning in the Talbot-Mack case applies with equal force to the matter now before us.

2. The objection based upon rule 11, relative to the time allowed for the filing of the opening brief by appellant, is not well taken. Rule 23 of this court provides that appeals from orders denying or granting a change of venue will be heard upon three days' notice when the parties live within twenty miles from Carson City, and when the party served resides more than twenty miles from Carson City one additional day's notice will be required. Ample notice was given of this hearing. Rule 23, when invoked, supersedes rule 11. The latter rule was made to govern in ordinary appeals, but rule 23 is a special rule, applying to the situation here presented, and controls, and was made to expedite hearings in this court upon appeals from an order granting or denying a motion for a change of venue, and other interlocutory orders.

3. We come now to the merits of this appeal. Section 69 of our civil practice act (Rev. Laws, 5011), which is made the basis of the motion for a change of venue, provides that actions for the recovery of real property shall be tried in the county in which it is situated. The affidavit which is the basis of the motion for a change of venue reads:

" * * * That all of the mining claims and property situated thereon, referred to in the amended complaint, * * * is situated in the county of Pershing. * * * "

A perusal of the amended complaint discloses the fact that the action is not to recover real estate, nor any interest in real estate, but pertains solely to shares of stock in certain corporations owning mining claims situated in Pershing County, Nevada. It is now almost universally held that shares of stock in a corporation are personal property (10 Cyc. 366; 4 Thomp. Corp. [2d ed.] sec. 3465), and by statute in this state are expressly made so. Stats. 1913, p. 42. There was no foundation whatever for the motion for a change of venue in this case, and the order appealed from was properly entered.

4. It is also contended by respondents that at the time the application for a change of venue was made the time for the filing thereof had expired, and to sustain this contention reliance is had upon the case of Connolly v. Salisberry, 43 Nev. 182, 183 Pac. 391. While it is very probable that the contention is well founded, we are unable to decide the question, for the reason that we are not advised as to when the summons was served in the case, or whether any was served at all. The time within which a party must make a demand for a change of venue begins to run from the date of the service of summons, as pointed out in the Connolly-Salisberry case. We do not means to hold that where a defendant waives the service of summons, and stipulates as to the time in which he shall appear and plead, the time so agreed upon might not control; but such is not the situation here.

5. It is contended that the appeal was taken for the purpose of delay, and that appellants should be penalized. Paroni v. Simonsen, 34 Nev. 26, 115 Pac. 415. We are unable to say that the appeal was so taken, unless we are justified in saying that the original motion for a change of venue was for delay. While we are of the opinion that the affidavit for a change of venue is utterly without merit, we do not feel justified in indulging the presumption that counsel and defendants did not have confidence in their application therefor.

For the reasons given, the order appealed from is affirmed, respondents to recover their costs.

[No. 2402]

WILLIAM AUSTIN KEYWORTH, APPELLANT, *v.* NEVADA PACKARD MINES COMPANY (A CORPORATION), RESPONDENT.

[186 Pac. 1110]

1. INFANTS—PURPOSE OF STATUTE AS TO CONVEYANCES OF MINING CLAIMS BY MINORS.

   The real purpose of Rev. Laws, 1103, 1104, relative to conveyances of mining locations and claims by minors, was to subject minors under the age of 21 and over 18 who convey interests in mining claims to the same consequences as attach to persons over 21 who convey such property.

2. ESTOPPEL—PRINCIPAL MUST SUFFER FROM WRONGFUL CONDUCT OF AGENT HELD OUT AS OPTIONEE.

   Where the owner of a mining claim put another in position to hold himself out as holder of an option to sell, and purchasers dealt with such other on the assumption, the owner cannot urge the agency of such other and his misconduct as ground for setting aside his deed to the purchasers, since one who makes it possible for a person to perpetrate a wrong on another must suffer the consequences.

3. PARTNERSHIP—AGREEMENT OF PURCHASERS OF MINING CLAIM OPTION TO PAY OPTIONEE PART OF CONSIDERATION IN PROMOTION STOCK NOT CREATING PARTNERSHIP.

   · Where the optionee of mining claims sold his interest in the option in consideration that purchasers should make the initial payment on the option and organize a company to take title to the claims and divide with him the promotion stock, no partnership was thereby created between the parties, any more than if the whole consideration had been paid in cash; so that such purchasers could not be charged as partners, with optionee's knowledge of facts.

4. CORPORATIONS—KNOWLEDGE OF DIRECTOR'S FRAUD WHILE ACTING FOR HIMSELF NOT CHARGEABLE TO COMPANY.

   Where the holder of an option on mining claims became director and officer of a company formed to operate such claims after exercise of the option, the company was not charged with knowledge of the officer's fraud on the owner of the claims; he having acted wholly for himself.

APPEAL from Sixth Judicial District Court, Humboldt County; *James A. Callahan*, Judge.

Action by William Austin Keyworth against the Nevada Packard Mines Company. From judgment for defendant, plaintiff appeals. **Affirmed. Petition for rehearing denied.**

Hoyt, Norcross, Thatcher, Woodburn & Henley, for Appellant:

The judgment of the lower court should have been for appellant. Upon the evidence and admitted facts, no other judgment is warranted than that prayed for by the plaintiff, and such a judgment should be ordered by this appellate court. Every material issuable fact was found in favor of plaintiff. A correct application of the law to the facts will require the direction of a judgment to be entered in favor of the plaintiff, according to the prayer of the complaint.

It was fraud upon the plaintiff, requiring the setting aside of the deed, for Ray to negotiate the sale without first informing plaintiff of the discovery made by or known to Ray. Norris v. Taylor, 49 Ill. 17; Holmes v. Cathcart, 60 L. R. A. 734; Lichtenstein v. Case, 99 App. Div. (N. Y.) 570; Daniel v. Brown, 33 Fed. 849; Gruber v. Baker, 20 Nev. 453, 23 Pac. 858, 9 L. R. A. 302; Hanelt v. Sweeney, 109 Fed. 712; Hall v. Gambrill, 88 Fed. 709, 92 Fed. 32, 37; Hobart v. Sherburne, 66 Minn. 171; Jansen v. Williams, 36 Neb. 869; Crompton v. Beedle, 75 Atl. 333; Gross on R. E. Brokers, sec. 144; Rev. Laws, 1103, 1104; 4 R. C. L. 269.

The purchase of property for a sum very greatly less than its actual value is a badge of fraud, and in this case is alone sufficient to set aside the deed. It is especially true where one of the parties is an infant. Maloy v. Berkin, 27 Pac. 442; Chamberlain v. Stern, 11 Nev. 272.

Ray was in position of a real estate broker selling on commission. As such he was charged with the utmost good faith, and was bound to notify his principals of anything which might affect the value of the property or acquaint them of the fact if he himself should become the purchaser. 4 R. C. L., p. 269, secs. 19–26, 41, 62, 64; Gross on R. E. Brokers, secs. 144, 256, 260; Holmes v. Cathcart, supra; Hall v. Gambrill, supra; Ruckman v. Bergholz, 37 N. J. Law, 440; Neighbor v. Pac. R. Assn., 124 Pac. 523.

All who formed the partnership for the acquiring of the mining claims are chargeable with knowledge and the acts or fraud of any one in respect thereto. Krumm v. Beach, 96 N. Y. 398; 30 Cyc. 526, 527; 16 Cyc. 588; 10 R. C. L. 627.

The defendant corporation took title to the property in controversy with full notice of the fraud perpetrated upon the plaintiff. McCaskill Co. v. United States, 216 U. S. 504; Linn T. Co. v. United States, 236 U. S. 574; Hoffman C. Co. v. Cumberland Co., 16 Md. 456; 10 Cyc. 1059; Southern R. I. Co. v. Walker, 211 U. S. 603; Wilson Coal Co. v. United States, 188 Fed. 545.

Appellant, under the facts of the case, is entitled to all the rules of law respecting transactions with infants. Rev. Laws, 1017, 1103, 1104; 22 Cyc. 512, 530, 539, 540; Lee v. Bank, 171 Pac. 677.

Cheney, Downer, Price & Hawkins, for Respondent:

This case being one in equity, tried fully and fairly, and in which the court has resolved every question material to plaintiff's right to recover against the plaintiff, the judgment should be affirmed.

The granting of the relief sought by plaintiff would be inequitable. Gamble v. Silver Peak, 34 Nev. 429.

"There is no principle of law that obligates one who has made an honest contract with another to communicate to that other anything subsequently happening that might be of inducement to that other to repudiate his contract." Fulton v. Walters, 216 Pa. St. 56; Gross on R. E. Brokers, sec. 145.

At the time of the execution of the deed plaintiff was over the age of 18 years. Therefore he was of lawful age under the statute and executed the deed conveying the mining claims or his interest therein. Rev. Laws, 1103, 1104.

"Canceling an executed conveyance is the exertion of a most extraordinary power in courts of equity, and when asked for on any ground it will not be granted unless the ground for its exercise most clearly appears."

Bispham's Equity, sec. 475; Culton v. Asher, 149 S. W. 946; Virginia I. C. & C. Co. v. Crigger, 201 S. W. 298.

"If he assented to the formation of the corporation and the transfer of the mine to it, he clearly waived his right to reclaim an interest in the mine itself." Johnston v. Standard M. Co., 148 U. S. 360; Cline v. James, 101 Fed. 737, 109 Fed. 961.

The contention of a partnership is without foundation in fact or law. Under the agreement the parties were to do whatever was therein provided as individuals. Hawley v. Tesch, 59 N. W. 670; Stringer v. Stevenson, 240 Fed. 892; Bienenstok v. Ammidown, 49 N. E. 321; National Bank v. Thomas, 47 N. Y. 15; Benedick v. Arnow, 49 N. E. 326; 1 Lindley, Partnership, 158, 30 Cyc. 523, 524; Neill v. Shamburg, 27 Atl. 992.

Plaintiff's claim of agency is based upon presumptions and not facts. Moore on Facts, vol. 1, sec. 545, p. 516.

There was no obligation to disclose to plaintiff the alleged discovery; and if such discovery was made and not disclosed, it does not give plaintiff any grounds to recover. Black on Rescission and Cancelation, secs. 66, 467. The arrangement did not create an agency requiring disclosure. Steel v. Lawyer, 91 Pac. 958; Fulton v. Walters, 64 Atl. 861; Texas B. Co. v. Barclay & Co., 109 S. W. 101; Black on Rescission, 1129–1130; Neill v. Shamburg, 27 Atl. 992.

Concealment of evidence of speculative value, even by a coowner occupying confidential relations, is held to be no fraud. Richardson v. Henney, 157 Pac. 980.

Under the law, upon his own theory, plaintiff ratified the sale and conveyance by failing to promptly disaffirm it upon becoming of age. 22 Cyc. 544; Henry v. Root, 33 N. Y. 526; Boyden v. Boyden, 9 Met. 519; Lynd v. Budd, 2 Page Ch. 191; Buchanan v. Hubbard, 21 N. E. 538; Shappiro v. Goldberg, 192 U. S. 232.

Plaintiff's action is barred by the statute of limitations. Rev. Laws, 4951, 4956, 4967, 4970; Gibson's Chancery, secs. 113, 114, 115. It is barred also under

the doctrine of laches. Gamble v. Silver Peak, 34 Nev.
427; Johnston v. Standard M. Co., 148 U. S. 360; Riker
v. Alsop, 155 U. S. 448; Patterson v. Hewitt, 195 U. S.
309; Curtis v. Lakin, 94 Fed. 251; Graft v. Portland
T. & M. Co., 54 Pac. 854. When essential facts might be
learned by due diligence, ignorance thereof will afford
no excuse. Notes 19 Am. & Eng. Cases, 110, 113; Lang
Syne M. Co. v. Ross, 20 Nev. 126; 25 Cyc. 1186.

By the Court, COLEMAN, C. J.:

This action was brought to recover an undivided one-
fourth interest in the Packard No. 1, Packard No. 2, and
Packard Fraction mining claims, situated in Rochester
mining district, Humboldt County, Nevada. The plaintiff, on March 29, 1913 (being then past 18 years of
age), together with H. R. Lund, Dick Keyworth, and
Donald C. Wheeler, gave R. L. Ray an option on the said
mining claims for the sum of $5,000, with the under-
standing that, in case said option were taken up, a
corporation should be formed to take title to said property, and that 2 per cent of the capital stock of such
company should be issued and delivered to the plaintiff
and his coowners. Five hundred dollars of said cash
consideration was to be paid on or before April 10, 1913,
and the balance within one year thereafter. It was
further agreed that upon the making of the payment of
$500 Ray or his assigns should have possession of the
property, with the privilege of working the same, and
should pay to said owners a royalty of 10 per cent on
the net proceeds; the royalty payments to be credited
upon the deferred payment of $4,500.

Simultaneously with the execution of said option,
another and separate agreement was made, whereby it
was understood that in case Ray should make a sale he
should receive a commission of 20 per cent. At the same
time said owners executed a deed to Ray for said property, which was to be put in escrow upon the making of
the initial payment of $500; said deed to be delivered

to him when the terms of the option agreement were complied with by Ray or his assigns. The execution of said deed and option was procured by Ray with the view of interesting one Gottstein in the property; but, the latter failing to take over the property, Ray sought a written extension of time in which to dispose of it. This the owners refused to grant, but Ray was informed that, if he found a purchaser for the property before the owners did, the terms of such option would be complied with.

Ray succeeded in interesting one Frank Margrave in the property, who on April 19, 1913, paid the owners the sum of $500, in accordance with the agreement of March 29' 1913, and the said deed was at that time placed in escrow with the Mercantile Banking Company of Lovelock, Nevada, to be delivered when the terms of the escrow agreement were complied with.

Ray received from plaintiff and his coowners $100 of the $500 so paid them. Immediately after the said payment had been made and said deed placed in escrow, Ray, Margrave, and Mark Walser, who was associated with Margrave in the transaction, entered into possession of the property and proceeded to prospect the same and to extract and ship ore therefrom. In July, 1913, Ray, Margrave, and Walser organized the defendant corporation and became directors and officers thereof.

By deed of July 11, 1913, Ray transferred the said mining claims to Walser and Margrave, who by deed of the same date conveyed the property to the defendant company, both of which deeds were recorded on said date of execution. On April 19, 1914, the deed of March 29, 1913, held in escrow as above mentioned, was delivered, in accordance with the escrow agreement, upon the payment of the balance due, less $810 which the defendant claimed the right to withhold, being the balance claimed by Ray as commission, the defendant contending that as between it and Ray it was entitled to the same, and plaintiff and his coowners waiving all claim thereto.

It is alleged by plaintiff that Ray, between April 10 and 19, 1913, made a discovery of ore upon said mining claims which "would have the effect of greatly increasing their sale value," and intentionally declined to communicate to said owners the knowledge thereof, for the purpose of inducing them to carry out the terms of the agreement of March 29, 1913, and that on April 18 Ray took said Margrave upon the said mining claims and disclosed to him his (Ray's) knowledge of such discovery, and, for the purpose of preventing said owners from learning of such discovery, exacted of Margrave a promise to keep it secret in case he did not become interested in the property. Walser is also charged with knowledge of such facts at the time of the making of said first payment, as is defendant company as of the time of its organization.

Knowledge on the part of Ray, Margrave, and Walser of plaintiff's minority is alleged as of April 19, 1913, when said $500 payment was made, and that the defendant was aware thereof at the time of its organization.

It is also alleged that at the time of the making of said first payment said claims were of great value, and that plaintiff did not acquire knowledge of said discoveries of said Ray until on or about April 18, 1917.

A judgment having been entered in favor of the defendant, and a motion for a new trial having been denied, the plaintiff has appealed.

Sections 1 and 2 of "An act concerning conveyances of mining locations and claims by minors," approved February 29, 1869 (Rev. Laws, 1103, 1104), reads:

"SECTION 1. In all cases in this state, since the first day of July, A. D. eighteen hundred and sixty-seven, where minors over the age of eighteen years have sold interests acquired by them in mining claims or locations by virtue of their having located such claims, or having been located therein by others, and have executed deeds purporting to convey such interests, such deeds, if otherwise sufficient in law, shall be held valid and sufficient to convey such interest fully and completely, notwithstanding the minority of the grantor, and without any power or right of subsequent revocation; provided, that this section shall not apply to cases where any fraud was practiced upon such minor, or any undue or improper advantage taken by his purchaser or any other person to induce such minor to execute such deed; and, provided further, that this section shall not apply to or affect any suits which may now be pending in any courts of this state, in which the legality or validity of such deeds may be involved.

"SEC. 2. All minors in this state, over the age of eighteen years, are hereby authorized and empowered to sell and convey by deed such interests as they may have acquired, or may hereafter acquire, in mining claims or mining locations within this state, by virtue of locating the same, or being located therein, and such deed shall, if otherwise sufficient in law, be held valid and sufficient to convey such interest fully and completely, and without the right of subsequent revocation, notwithstanding the minority of the grantor, subject however, to the same provisions and limitations contained in the first section of this act."

1. In view of the fact that plaintiff was of the age of 18 years at the time of the making of the sale on April 19, 1913, it becomes necessary that we inquire as to the real purpose of the foregoing act.

In approaching a consideration of this question, we must first determine the purpose of the statute which we have quoted. We may speculate as much as we please as to circumstances which led to the adopting of the statute mentioned. It may be that experience had taught that youths, during their minority, frequently became the locators of mining property, and that it was difficult in many instances for a prospective purchaser to accurately determine the age of one from 18 to 21, and that it might have happened that in some instances young men under the age of 21 had represented themselves as over that age to facilitate the transfer of their interest in mining claims, and thereafter repudiated the transaction as the act of an infant, and either caused a great deal of trouble or an outlay of considerable amount.

Be this as it may, the legislature sought to safeguard purchasers of mining property who took deeds from all persons over the age of 18, and enacted the law giving the same force to the deed of a person under 21, but over 18 years of age, conveying an interest in a mining claim, as that given to the deed of a person over 21, provided that no fraud was practiced upon the minor or undue advantage taken of him. In view of the fact that prior to the enactment of the statute it was the law of the state that any conveyance, even of an adult, might be set aside where fraud or undue influence had been practiced to procure it, the proviso contained in the act quoted was not for the purpose of declaring a new rule, but was put in as a precautionary measure to make sure that the rule then in existence would be made applicable to any transactions had under the statute in question. The real purpose of the act, then, was to subject minors under the age of 21· years, and over 18, who conveyed an interest in a mining claim, to the same consequences as attached to persons over 21 who conveyed mining property.

It is insisted that the failure of Ray to disclose to the plaintiff the discovery made by Ray between April 10 and 19, 1913, of rich float upon the ground in question constituted a fraud upon plaintiff for which he should be adjudged the owner of the interest in question. In support of the contention, we are directed to numerous authorities which declare it to be the law that an agent or broker engaged in negotiating the sale of property must act with the utmost good faith, and that he is under a legal obligation to disclose to his principal facts within or which may come to his knowledge which might influence the principal in the transaction. As to this general rule of law there can be no dispute; but, conceding for the purpose of this case (without so deciding) that the facts disclosed bring it within the general rule stated, we are of the opinion that the judgment should be affirmed.

Plaintiff and his coowners had executed an option and

deed, both of which were to be placed in escrow upon the payment by Ray or his assigns of the sum of $500. Margrave and Walser, learning the facts, and having inspected the property, got the owners and Ray together and went to the bank, where the $500 was paid and the instruments placed in escrow as agreed. This was all done while Margrave and Walser, so far as appears, were laboring under the impression that Ray was simply an optionee, and not an agent of the plaintiff and his coowners to sell the property. There is no evidence in the record to the contrary; but plaintiff testified that in August succeeding the date of the transaction Walser informed him that knowledge had just been acquired to the effect that Ray was getting a commission from the selling, and requested that the owners waive the payment to the bank on account of the escrow agreement of the sum of $810, an amount equal to the balance claimed by Ray as commission, which was afterwards done. This being the fact, it appears conclusively that Margrave and Walser had been acting all of the time upon the assumption that Ray was not agent of the plaintiff and his coowners, but was merely an optionee of the property, and that they took the property just as though such was the fact.

2. In view of this undisputed state of facts, whatever the law may be upon the question of agency, the plaintiff cannot recover, for the reason that, having put Ray in the position to hold himself out as the holder of an option, and parties having dealt with him upon that assumption, he cannot urge now the agency of Ray and his misconduct as a ground for setting aside the deed, for the reason that, where one of two persons must suffer for the wrong of another, he who makes it possible for such person to perpetrate a wrong must be the sufferer. Paraphrasing the language of the court in Scott v. Gallagher, 14 Serg. & R. (Pa.) 333, 16 Am. Dec. 508, the interpolated words being italicized:

"Courts of justice view secret agreements with a jealous and scrutinizing eye. * * * There would be no hardship in the case on *Keyworth,* because it was his own folly to place himself and others in the power of *Ray.* If any person suffers it should be *Keyworth,* and not *defendant,* for this plain and obvious reason, that he has been the cause *which made the perpetration of the fraud possible.* Equity says, if one of two innocent persons must suffer, he who has been the cause shall bear the loss."

See, also, Magee v. Manhattan L. I. Co., 92 U. S. 98, 23 L. Ed. 699; Reed v. Munn, 148 Fed. 761, 80 C. C. A. 215; American Bonding Co. v. Pueblo Inv. Co., 150 Fed. 23, 80 C. C. A. 97, 9 L. R. A. (N.S.) 557, 10 Ann. Cas. 357; Hendry v. Cartwright, 14 N. M. 72, 89 Pac. 309, 8 L. R. A.(N.S.) 1056; Gass v. Hampton, 16 Nev. 185.

In this connection it might not be out of place to say that, while plaintiff was under 21 years of age, the entire negotiations in the transaction were left to him by his partners, one of whom, at least, is a man of large affairs.

3. It is contended that, in view of the fact that prior to the time the initial payment of $500 was made by Margrave and Walser an agreement was entered into by and between them and Ray, to the effect that they should make said initial payment and at their own expense should organize a company to take title to said property and divide between themselves and Ray the promotion stock thereof, a partnership was created among them, and that such partnership was charged with knowledge of all of the facts known to Ray. We do not consider this transaction a partnership. The agreement did not create a partnership, any more than it would have done had it called for the payment of a cash consideration for the option. Money might have been the consideration to have been paid for his option, and if such had been the fact, it could not be contended that a partnership was created; and it is equally clear to our minds that the agreement to issue to Ray a certain amount of stock for his interest, in lieu of cash, and the making of him a director of the company, did not create a partnership.

4. But, conceding the correctness of the plaintiff's contention that such a partnership did exist (without expressing any opinion as to the legal effect thereof), he is in no position to complain, because, as we have said, by giving Ray the option he was enabled, as a matter of fact, to mislead Margrave and Walser as to his true status in the transaction, and through them the defendant company which took over the property, which acquired its title before knowledge of the alleged fraud had been gained.   The mere fact that Ray became a director and officer of the company was not enough to charge it with knowledge of the fraud of Ray; for during all of the negotiations he was acting for himself, and not for Margrave, Walser, or defendant corporation.   The rule applying to such a situation is declared in Edwards v. Carson Water Co., 21 Nev. 469, 483, 34 Pac. 381, 385, as follows:

"Instead of acting for the corporation, they [the officers of the company] executed a note purporting to be a valid obligation to the company, when in fact it was to secure the individual indebtedness of its president for money which the corporation had intrusted to him to pay its debts, and which he testifies he was permitted to retain to his own use, with the knowledge and consent of the debtor, Wright.   Under such circumstances, at the time of the giving of the note of 1886, Helm was acting for himself, and he was not, with respect to the transaction, an agent at all; and the corporation is not, as to that matter, bound by his acts, nor it is chargeable with his knowledge."

The Court of Appeals of Kansas, in First National Bank v. Skinner, 10 Kan. App. 517, 62 Pac. 705, quotes approvingly from Thompson on Corporations, as follows:

"The knowledge acquired by the officers or agents of the corporation, while not acting for the corporation, but while acting for themselves, is not imputable to the corporation."

See, also, 7 R. C. L. p. 657, and extended note to Bank of Pittsburg v. Whitehead, 36 Am. Dec. 191.

In Franklin Mining Co. v. O'Brien, 22 Colo. 129, 43
Pac. 1016, 55 Am. St. Rep. 118, the court says:

"The general rule undoubtedly is that a corporation
is not affected with notice or knowledge of facts merely
because some of its promoters who organized the corporation had knowledge of such facts, or merely because
some of its stockholders had notice; and a corporation
is not charged with notice of facts known or acquired
by its officer or agent in a transaction in which he acts
for himself, and not for the corporation. To this effect
we are referred to the case of Davis Wagon Wheel Co. v.
Davis Iron Wagon Co. (C. C.) 20 Fed. 699."

See, also, Zang v. Adams, 23 Colo. 410, 48 Pac. 509, 58
Am. St. Rep. 249.

While laches, estoppel, and the statute of limitations
were pleaded by the defendant, they will not be considered, because, entertaining the views which we do,
the judgment must necessarily be affirmed.

It is so ordered.

DUCKER, J., did not participate, having presided at the
trial in the lower court.

ON PETITION FOR REHEARING

Per Curiam:

Rehearing denied.

Points decided

[No. 2371]

PAT MOONEY AND DESERT PRODUCE COMPANY (A CORPORATION), RESPONDENTS, *v.* S. H. NEWTON, APPELLANT.

[187 Pac. 721]

1. APPEAL AND ERROR—EXCEPTIONS MUST BE TAKEN AT TIME RULING IS MADE TO ENTITLE PARTY TO REVIEW.

   When an exception is necessary to a ruling of the court, it must be taken when the ruling is made, unless by permission of the court it is allowed to be taken at a later time.

2. APPEAL AND ERROR—ORDER SETTLING BILL OF EXCEPTIONS NOT ORDER ALLOWING EXCEPTIONS TO BE TAKEN.

   An order of the court settling a bill of exceptions is in no sense an order allowing exceptions to be taken at that time.

3. APPEAL AND ERROR—BILL OF EXCEPTIONS NOT SETTING OUT MATTER RULED ON INSUFFICIENT.

   A bill of exceptions not setting out the matter on which the ruling was made is insufficient; a mere reference to other parts of the transcript being insufficient.

4. COURTS—DISTRICT COURT HAS JURISDICTION OF SUIT IN INTERPLEADER INVOLVING LESS THAN $300.

   Under Civ. Prac. Act, sec. 63 (Rev. Laws, 5005), the district court has jurisdiction of an action in interpleader, although the amount involved is less than $300, such suit being equitable, and district courts having original jurisdiction in all chancery cases.

5. INTERPLEADER—PLAINTIFF ENTITLED TO COSTS OUT OF FUND DEPOSITED.

   In an action in interpleader under Civ. Prac. Act, sec 63 (Rev. Laws, 5005), the plaintiff, if the interpleader is granted, is entitled to his costs out of the fund deposited in court, to be ultimately paid by the unsuccessful party, and the defendant not in fault is entitled to a decree against the other defendant for the costs so taken out of the fund, as well as his own costs.

6. INTERPLEADER—PLAINTIFF NOT ENTITLED TO ATTORNEY FEE AS COSTS.

   The plaintiff in an action in interpleader, if the interpleader is granted, is not entitled to an attorney fee to be paid by the losing party; the allowance of an attorney fee being a subject of statutory regulation.

7. APPEAL AND ERROR—DEFENDANT CANNOT COMPLAIN OF ERRORS AFFECTING CODEFENDANT ONLY.

   A defendant appellant cannot on appeal complain of an error affecting a codefendant only.

APPEAL from Fifth Judicial District Court, Nye County; *Mark R. Averill,* Judge.

Interpleader suit by Pat Mooney against the Desert

Produce Company and S. H. Newton. From an adverse judgment, the last-named defendant appeals. **Affirmed. Petition for rehearing denied.**

O. H. Mack and *C. L. Richards*, for Appellant.

H. R. Cooke and *Frank T. Dunn*, for Respondents.

By the Court, DUCKER, J.:

The respondent Pat Mooney brought an interpleader suit in the district court of Nye County against Desert Produce Company, a corporation, C. Craig and S. H. Newton and Henry Martin. The substance of the complaint appears in the following statement: On December 8, 1916, plaintiff made and delivered to defendant Craig two promissory notes of $100 each, with interest at 12 per cent per annum, and on the 11th day of September, 1917, said notes were overdue and still in the possession of Craig. The defendant Desert Produce Company on the last date mentioned served upon plaintiff at Tonopah, Nevada, a writ of garnishment against the money owing by plaintiff to said Craig upon the notes, which writ issued out of the district court of the Fifth judicial district of the State of Nevada in and for Nye County, in an action brought by the said company against the said Craig. Shortly thereafter one of the defendants, Henry Martin of Tonopah, Nevada, made a demand upon plaintiff for the payment of said notes to him, which demand was refused for the reason that the sums due upon the promissory notes had already been attached. On the 21st day of June, 1918, an action was commenced in the justice's court of Reno township, Washoe County, Nevada, entitled S. H. Newton v. Pat Mooney, wherein said Newton alleges that he is the owner and holder of said notes. On said last-mentioned date Newton caused a writ of attachment to issue out of said justice's court and to be delivered to the constable of Tonopah township, Nye County, Nevada, who did then and there on the 25th day of June, 1918, levy upon and attach the property and effects of respondent. Respondent further alleges in his complaint that he has no beneficial interest in or claim upon the sums of money due upon said notes, and was ready and willing on the 11th day of September, 1917, and at all times thereafter, to take up and pay said notes, but does not know to which of said claimants he ought of right to pay the money due thereon and cannot safely pay the same to any one of them without hazard to himself; that he is ready and willing and does herewith tender to and deposit with the clerk of the said district court said full sum of $200 as principal due upon the notes, and the sum of $18 as interest from the date thereof to September 11, 1917, the date upon which the said sums of money were first attached by the Desert Produce Company, to be subject to such further orders or disposition as the court may deem meet and proper to make in that behalf; that this suit is not brought by collusion with either or any of the defendants.

The prayer asks judgment and decree; that defendants be restrained by injunction from further prosecuting or instituting proceedings or process against respondent in relation to said sums of money; that they be required to interplead concerning such claims and set forth their several titles, and settle and adjust their demands between themselves; that the clerk of said district court, or some other suitable person, be authorized to receive and hold said money pending such litigation, and also to demand and receive said notes and deliver the same to respondent; that he be discharged from all liability in the premises; that he be paid his costs out of said sum of money; and for general relief.

The Desert Produce Company answered. After admitting most of the allegations of the complaint, for a further answer and affirmative defense and by way of cross-complaint against the respondent and its codefendant, it alleges, in substance, the commencement of an action against its codefendant, Craig, in said court on the 8th day of September, 1917, and the recovery of a judgment against him in the sum of $8,854.96 on the 18th day of April, 1918; that during the pendency of the action a writ of attachment was duly issued and levied on all of the right, title, and interest of Craig in and to the said promissory notes; and that a writ of garnishment was duly served upon respondent Mooney, and return made thereto by him to the substance and effect that he was personally indebted to Craig in the sum of $200 upon said promissory notes which were then due and ready to be paid; that after the rendition and entry of judgment an execution was duly issued to the sheriff of the county, which was levied by him and demand made on respondent for the payment of said $200 and accrued interest, who refused to pay the same on the ground that the said promissory notes were not delivered up for cancelation; that said judgment still remains in full force and effect and unsatisfied to the amount of $7,822.96; and that the company was entitled to have payment of said $200 and accrued interest thereon made to the sheriff of the county to be applied in satisfaction upon said judgment. Judgment is demanded that the codefendants be adjudged to have no right, title, interest, or claim in or to said $200 or accrued interest or the notes evidencing said indebtedness; that said notes be ordered delivered to the clerk of the court for cancelation and surrender to respondent Mooney upon the payment by him to said sheriff of the money due on such notes; and for other relief.

A demurrer was interposed by appellant to the complaint herein on the grounds that it does not state facts sufficient to constitute a cause of action; that the court has no jurisdiction of the persons of the parties, or the subject-matter of the action; and that it is ambiguous, unintelligible, and uncertain. A demurrer was also interposed by appellant to the company's affirmative defense and cross-complaint on the first two grounds mentioned. These demurrers were overruled by the court, and appellant's default for failure to answer within the time required was duly entered. Martin and Craig made no appearance. The case was tried before the court upon the issue made by the complaint and answer, and judgment entered that the interpleader suit was properly and necessarily commenced by the respondent Mooney by reason of the unfounded claim to said $218 made by said Newton. An attorney fee fixed at $50 and costs amounting to $10.30, aggregating the sum of $60.30, were allowed respondent Mooney to be deducted by the clerk and paid from the sum of $218 deposited. Judgment was also rendered in favor of the defendant company and against Newton for the residue of said sum deposited, to wit, $157.70, and for the said sum of $60.30 deducted as Mooney's costs and attorney fee. From the judgment entered, this appeal is taken by said Newton.

The foregoing statement is sufficient to present the questions necessary for determination on this appeal.

It appears from the transcript of the record on appeal that no exceptions were taken by the appellant within the time required by law, so as to entitle a bill embodying them to be settled and allowed by the lower court.

No exceptions were taken to adverse rulings of the court by appellant before trial, and, being in default, he did not participate in the trial. Final judgment was entered on the 17th day of December, 1918.

1-3. Two rulings adverse to appellant on his motions were made after judgment, respectively, on December 28, 1918, and January 14, 1919, but no exceptions were taken or embodied in a bill of exceptions until January 18, 1919. It was served and filed two days later, and on April 5, 1919, was presented to the court and settled and allowed. When an exception is necessary to a ruling of the court, it must be taken when the ruling is made, unless by permission of the court it is allowed to be taken at a later time. An order of the court settling a bill of exceptions is in no sense an order allowing exceptions to be taken at that time. If it be contended that some of the exceptions were taken to rulings deemed to be excepted to by law, the bill of exceptions settled by the court is entirely deficient in not setting out the matter on which the ruling was made. A mere reference to it and the ruling of the court as appearing in other parts of the transcript is insufficient. On December 30 an objection was taken by counsel to the ruling made on December 28 denying the motion to strike the decision and judgment. If this can be considered an exception, the bill is nevertheless deficient in this respect in not setting out any matter with reference to the motion on which the ruling was made; in other words, the court could not learn from the evidence presented by the bill of exceptions whether the ruling on the motion was error or not. The bill of exceptions in this case bears a very close resemblance to an assignment of errors. Seasonable objections were taken to the proposed bill of exceptions in the district court, and also in this court, on the grounds mentioned. For the reasons stated, we are precluded from considering the errors alleged in it, and will confine ourselves to the judgment roll.

4. It was assigned as error, and the principal question argued on the hearing, that the district court had no jurisdiction of the subject-matter of the action, because the amount involved is less than $300. The action is an interpleader suit under the statute and clearly equitable. In this respect the statute provides:

"And whenever conflicting claims are or may be made upon a person for or relating to personal property or the performance of an obligation or any portion thereof, such person may bring an action against the conflicting claimants to compel them to interplead and litigate their several claims among themselves." Section 63, Civil Practice Act (Rev. Laws, 5005).

The equity of an action in interpleader is that the conflicting claimants should litigate the matter amongst themselves, without involving the plaintiff in their dispute, with which he has no interest. 4 Pomeroy's Eq., sec. 1320 (4th ed.) ; 2 Story's Eq., sec. 1117 (14th ed.) ; Shaw v. Coster, 35 Am. Dec. note, 697.

In all chancery cases the district courts have original jurisdiction, whatever may be the amount in controversy. Wilde v. Wilde, 2 Nev. 306. It is therefore obvious that the contention that the district court is without jurisdiction is untenable.

5. A cause of action is sufficiently stated in the complaint to entitle the respondent Mooney to the relief demanded. Appellant's demurrer to the complaint was properly overruled. His demurrer to the answer of his codefendant, the Desert Produce Company, is without merit. There is no error in the judgment as to costs. The plaintiff in this kind of an action, if the interpleader is granted, is entitled to his costs out of the fund deposited in court to be ultimately paid by the unsuccessful party, and the defendant not in fault is entitled to a decree against the other defendant for the costs so taken out of the fund as well as for his own costs. 15 R. C. L. 223.

This disposes of all the alleged errors presented by the judgment roll, except the question as to the allowance of an attorney fee to respondent Mooney out of the fund deposited in court.

6. This was error. The allowance of an attorney fee to be paid by the losing party is a subject of statutory regulation. While the legislature has provided for the recovery of an attorney fee by the plaintiff or prevailing party in certain actions in this state, the case at bar does not fall within any of these special statutes.

7. The error, however, is not prejudicial to appellant. Having failed to recover in the action in the lower court,

he cannot be heard to complain of an error which affects his codefendant only.

The judgment of the district court is affirmed.

ON PETITION FOR REHEARING

Per Curiam:

Rehearing denied.

———

[No. 2420]

VERD KINGSBURY, APPELLANT, *v.* JOHN V. COPREN, AND JOHN V. COPREN, AS ADMINISTRATOR OF THE ESTATE OF THOMAS J. HIGGINS, DECEASED, RESPONDENT.

[187 Pac. 728]

1. PLEADING—COMPLAINT AGAINST ADMINISTRATOR. BOTH IN REPRESENTATIVE AND PERSONAL CAPACITY, NOT DEMURRABLE FOR UNCERTAINTY.

Where defendant in claim and delivery, or replevin, was sued both as an individual and as administrator, the fact was not a ground of demurrer for uncertainty or ambiguity.

2. EXECUTORS AND ADMINISTRATORS—COMPLAINT IN CLAIM AND DELIVERY AGAINST ADMINISTRATOR HELD NOT TO STATE CAUSE OF ACTION IN INDIVIDUAL CAPACITY.

Complaint in action in claim and delivery, or replevin, against an administrator, both personally and in his representative capacity, which charged that defendant, having obtained the property from plaintiff by false representations, thereafter caused it to be inventoried and appraised as the property of the estate, etc., did not state a cause of action against defendant as an individual.

3. EXECUTORS AND ADMINISTRATORS—COMPLAINT AGAINST ADMINISTRATOR IN PERSONAL AND REPRESENTATIVE CAPACITY MUST STATE CAUSE OF ACTION AGAINST HIM IN BOTH.

Though in some circumstances a defendant may be sued both as an individual and as administrator, in such a suit the complaint must state a cause of action against the party in both capacities, or be demurrable.

4. EXECUTORS AND ADMINISTRATORS — ADMINISTRATOR NOT LIABLE IN BOTH PERSONAL AND REPRESENTATIVE CAPACITY FOR WITHHOLDING PROPERTY.

An administrator could not hold possession of plaintiff's personal property both as an individual and as administrator, nor could plaintiff in claim and delivery charge the administrator with holding the property in both capacities.

5. PLEADING—PLAINTIFF SEEKING RECOVERY OF PERSONALTY FROM ADMINISTRATOR MUST ALLEGE IN WHAT CAPACITY IT IS HELD, THOUGH KNOWN TO DEFENDANT.

The mere fact that defendant in claim and delivery, sued in his personal and representative capacity, knows in which capacity he claims the property sought by plaintiff, does not relieve plaintiff from the necessity of alleging in which capacity defendant holds it; the rule that facts peculiarly within the knowledge of defendant need not be alleged with the usual degree of exactness not applying when the allegation is essential to prima facie right of recovery.

6. PLEADING—COMPLAINT AGAINST ADMINISTRATOR NOT UNCERTAIN AS TO CAPACITY IN WHICH DEFENDANT HELD PROPERTY.

Complaint in claim and delivery against an administrator in his personal and representative capacity, alleging, first, that defendant listed and described the property in question as that of his decedent's estate, and, second, that he claimed it as the property of such estate, while there was a total absence of any allegation that he held or claimed as an individual, was not uncertain or ambiguous as to the capacity in which it charged defendant with holding the property.

ON PETITION FOR REHEARING

1. PLEADING—PRAYER FOR RELIEF NO PART OF CAUSE OF ACTION.

The prayer for relief in a complaint is no part of the statement of a cause of action.

2. PLEADING—PLAINTIFF BOUND BY MATERIAL ALLEGATIONS.

A plaintiff is bound by the material allegations in his complaint, charging defendant in a particular capacity.

APPEAL from Second Judicial District Court, Washoe County; *Thomas F. Moran,* Judge.

Action by Verd Kingsbury against John V. Copren, individually and as administrator of the estate of Thomas J. Higgins, deceased. From a judgment for the defendant on demurrer to the complaint, plaintiff appeals. **Reversed, with instructions. Petition for rehearing denied.**

Mack & Green, for Appellant:

There is a single cause of action; a single person defendant, though sued in two capacities—in his individual capacity and in his representative capacity. It is alleged that he obtained possession of the chattels by representing in his individual capacity that he had made application for letters of administration, and falsely represented that it was necessary for him to have possession of the property; that he promised to return it promptly, but thereafter listed it as belonging to the estate. He obtained the property by false and fraudulent representations made in his individual capacity, and claimed it in a representative capacity, and was therefore properly joined in both capacities. He is the defendant and not the plaintiff. His claim, if any, is a matter of defense, as well as the capacity in which he claims. 30 Cyc. 98, 99, 127. "A person may be a party in two different capacities under the same circumstances that two different persons might be joined." 20 Standard Proc. 880; Smith v. Stevenson B. Co., 100 N. Y. Supp. 672; Bamberger v. Fillebrown, 33 N. Y. Supp. 614.

The capacity in which the defendant claimed the property was a matter within his knowledge, and of which the plaintiff had no knowledge, and was therefore purely a matter of defense. 31 Cyc. 48; 21 R. C. L. 485. "It is a general rule that facts peculiarly within the knowledge of the adverse party need not be pleaded." Owen v. Geiger, 2 Mo. 39; Dow v. City, 134 Pac. 197; Doe v. Sanger, 78 Cal. 150; Brashear v. Madison, 142 Ind. 685.

"An action may be maintained against a person in his individual capacity, and as executor." Roark v. Turner, 29 Ga. 456. "Here the defendant ought not to complain that the plaintiff has commenced but one suit against him, when he ought to have commenced two." Armstrong v. Hall, 17 How. Pr. 78.

Platt & Sanford, for Respondent:

The trial court sustained defendant's demurrer upon the grounds of uncertainty, unintelligibility, and ambiguity. The court did not err. It cannot be ascertained whether the defendant as an individual or the estate is directly assailed by the complaint. The complaint is so contradictory and so involved and uncertain that the demurrer was necessary to clear it of all vagueness, ambiguity, and uncertainty. "Demurrers were very properly sustained * * * to a complaint * * * from which it could not be ascertained whether the acts complained of were committed by defendants in their individual capacity or in one of the capacities in which they were alleged to have. acted." Lapique v. Ruef, 158 Pac. 339.

There is no dispute over the legal contention that the defendant may be sued in an individual and representative capacity, but the allegations must be drawn with such definiteness and certainty as to properly inform the defendant with respect to the exact nature of the complaint against him.

By the Court, COLEMAN, C. J.:

This is an action in claim and delivery, or replevin, as known at common law.

As appears from the title of the action, it was instituted against the defendant both in his individual and representative capacities. The complaint alleges the death of Higgins and the appointment and qualification of Copren as administrator of the estate of the deceased. It is then alleged that at the time of bringing the suit plaintiff was, and for a long time prior thereto had been, the owner of a certain diamond ring and stick-pin, of the aggregate value of $1,100. It is then alleged:

"IV. That on the 6th day of January, 1919, at the city of Reno, county of Washoe, State of Nevada, the said defendant wrongfully obtained and came into possession of said personal property by falsely representing to plaintiff that he would promptly return the same; that he had made application for letters of administration of the estate of Thomas J. Higgins, deceased; that it was necessary for him to have the possession of said property in order to satisfy all persons interested in said estate that all property heretofore owned by said deceased was being properly administered; that plaintiff was ignorant of the requirements of such administration and delivered said property to said defendant, in faith upon his promise to promptly return the same,

and said defendant did promise to promptly return the
same, but ever since and still retains the possession
thereof, and has neglected and refused and still neglects
and refuses to deliver the same to plaintiff, and thereafter listed and described the same in the inventory and
appraisement of the estate of Thomas J. Higgins as the
property of said estate, and claims the same as property
thereof."

The complaint then alleges that plaintiff demanded of
defendant the possession of said personal property, but
that he refused, and still refuses, to deliver the same to
her. It is also alleged that the personal property in question was not taken for a tax, assessment, or fine pursuant to statute, or seized under any execution or judgment
against the property of the plaintiff.

The complaint concludes with the usual prayer for
possession of the personal property in question, or, in
case possession cannot be had, for damages.

To the complaint a demurrer was filed, setting forth
four grounds, one being that the complaint is ambiguous
and uncertain in that—

"It cannot be understood from said complaint whether
the defendant in this action is being sued personally or
whether he is being sued in his official capacity. Nor
does it state whether or not judgment is desired from
the personal estate of the defendant or from the estate
he is officially managing."

The court sustained the demurrer upon the ground of
uncertainty. Plaintiff declining to amend her complaint,
judgment was entered in favor of defendant for his
costs. From this judgment an appeal has been taken.

1. To the contention of respondent, as stated in the
first sentence of the matter which we have quoted from
the demurrer, we think we need devote but little consideration. It is clear that the defendant was actually
sued both as an individual and as administrator. This
is not a ground of demurrer for uncertainty or ambiguity. If defendant is improperly joined in two capacities, or if the complaint fails to state a cause of action

against him in either of the capacities in which he is
sued, it may be that the demurrer should have been
sustained upon one or more of the other grounds stated
therein.

2. The complaint does not state nor undertake to state
a cause of action against the defendant as an individual,
but it does undertake to state a cause of action against
him as administrator. We held in the recent case of
Nielsen v. Rebard, 43 Nev. 274, 183 Pac. 984, that to
state a cause of action in replevin it must be shown that
the specific property is in possession of the defendant at
the time of bringing the suit. Nowhere in the complaint
is there a statement of a fact from which it might be
inferred that plaintiff sought to charge that defendant
had possession of the property in question in his individual capacity. On the other hand, the allegation of
the complaint negatives that idea, wherein it is charged
that the defendant "thereafter listed and described the
same [the property in question] in the inventory and
appraisement of the estate of Thomas J. Higgins as the
property of said estate, and claims the same as property
thereof."

3, 4. While it is true that in some circumstances a
defendant may be sued both as an individual and as
administrator, it is also true that when so sued the complaint must state a cause of action against the party in
both capacities, or suffer the consequences. In the very
nature of things, the defendant could not hold possession of the personal property in question both as an
individual and as administrator, nor could plaintiff
charge the defendant with holding the property in both
capacities, because such an allegation would be inconsistent as to a matter of fact. Nelson v. Smith, 42 Nev.
302, 176 Pac. 261, 178 Pac. 625.

5. And the mere fact that defendant knows in which
capacity he claims the property would not relieve the
plaintiff from the necessity of alleging in which capacity
he holds it; for, while it is a general rule that facts
peculiarly within the knowledge of the defendant do

not have to be alleged by the plaintiff with the same degree of exactness as if such were not the fact, when the matter is such that its allegation "is essential to the apparent or prima facie right of recovery," this rule has no application. 21 R. C. L. 486.

6. In view of the allegation of the complaint, from which it appears (1) that the defendant listed and described the property in question as the property of the estate, and (2) that he claims it as property thereof, and of the further fact that there is a total absence of any allegation that the defendant holds or claims the property as an individual, we think it cannot be said that the complaint is uncertain or ambiguous as to the capacity in which the complaint charges the defendant with holding the property.

It follows that the judgment must be reversed.

It is ordered that the judgment be reversed, with instructions to the lower court to permit the plaintiff to reform her complaint in such manner as she may be advised.

ON PETITION FOR REHEARING

By the Court, COLEMAN, C. J.:

The respondent asks for a rehearing, and assigns as grounds thereof: (1) That we overlooked the fact that the complaint asks relief of the defendant without designating in which capacity it is sought; and (2) because the order of reversal directed the lower court to permit appellant to amend her complaint as she may be advised.

1, 2. We might well deny the petition without comment; but, in view of the position taken by both parties to the action, as manifested in the petition and the answer thereto, we deem it proper to say that in preparing our former opinion we had in mind the well-recognized rule that the prayer for relief in a complaint is no part of the statement of a cause of action (21 R. C. L. 489; 31 Cyc. 110) ; and having held that no cause of action was alleged against the defendant in his individual capacity, and that in view of the fact that it is an impossibility for the defendant to hold the property in question in both capacities, we concluded that it appeared from the complaint itself, as a matter of law, that there was no uncertainty as to the capacity in which plaintiff seeks to hold the defendant responsible, as she is bound by the material allegations of her complaint (Christensen v. Duborg, 38 Nev. 410, 150 Pac. 306).

As to the second point made, it may be that we might as well have made no order as to an amendment; but we think it goes without saying that any amendment which may be made must be in accordance with the law. Such was the view we entertained at that time.

At least one question is presented by the record in this case which we were not called upon to determine because not assigned as error; but we think from what we did say it can be inferred what our ruling would have been had the point been presented. The law is clear, and a disregard of it will simply entail useless expense.

Petition for rehearing is denied.

GENERAL INDEX

GENERAL INDEX

ABSURD MEANING TO BE AVOIDED. See STATUTES, 3.

ACCESSION.
1. TIRES AND REPLACEMENTS UPON AUTOMOBILES SOLD UNDER CONDITIONAL CONTRACT NOT ACCESSIONS AS AGAINST THIRD PARTY FURNISHING THEM.

Since, under a conditional contract for sale of motor trucks, providing that any equipment, repairs, tires, or accessories placed upon the trucks during the continuance of the agreement should become a component part thereof and the title thereto should become vested in seller, tires and replacements were regarded by the parties as separable and severable and not accessions, upon seller's recovering possession of the trucks such equipment did not become the seller's property by accession, but remained the property of defendant, who had furnished, but not sold, them to the buyer. *Clarke* v. *Johnson*, 359.

ACQUIESCENCE OF LEGISLATURE IN CONTEMPORANEOUS CONSTRUCTION. See STATUTES, 6.

ACTION.
1. THERE MAY BE JOINDER OF COUNTS IN CASE AND TRESPASS.

In an action for false imprisonment to include in one action a count in case and count in trespass, the counts must arise from the same state of facts. *Dixon* v. *City of Reno*, 413.

See PLEADING, 5.

ACTION AGAINST ADMINISTRATOR. See EXECUTORS AND ADMINISTRATORS, 2, 3.

ACTION BY SUBCONTRACTOR AGAINST SURETY OF CONTRACTOR. See CONTRACTS, 1; PLEADING, 9.

ACTION FOR COMMISSION. See BROKERS, 1.

ACTION FOR FALSE IMPRISONMENT. See PLEADING, 3.

ACTION FOR MALICIOUS PROSECUTION. See MALICIOUS PROSECUTION, 1.

ACTION FOR PURCHASE PRICE. See SALES, 1, 3.

ACTION FOR SPECIFIC PERFORMANCE. See SPECIFIC PERFORMANCE, 1, 2.

ACTION FOR SUPPORT AND MAINTENANCE. See HUSBAND AND WIFE, 4, 5, 6; PLEADING, 4.

ACTION IN CLAIM AND DELIVERY. See REPLEVIN, 1; WORK AND LABOR, 1.

ACTION IN CLAIM AND DELIVERY AGAINST ADMINISTRA-
TOR. See PLEADING, 1, 2, 7.

ACTION IN REPLEVIN. See APPEAL AND ERROR, 9.

ACTION IN TROVER AND CONVERSION. See TROVER AND CON-
VERSION, 1.

ACTION IN UNLAWFUL DETAINER. See JUSTICES OF THE
PEACE, 1; LANDLORD AND TENANT, 1, 2.

ACTION OF DISTRICT COURT IN CERTIORARI. See CERTI-
ORARI, 1.

ACTION TO QUIET TITLE TO MINING CLAIMS. See MINES
AND MINERALS, 2, 3.

ACTS CONSTITUTING ELECTION OF REMEDIES. See ELEC-
TION OF REMEDIES, 1.

ADMINISTRATOR NOT LIABLE IN BOTH PERSONAL AND
REPRESENTATIVE CAPACITY. See EXECUTORS AND ADMIN-
ISTRATORS, 1, 2, 3.

ADMISSIBILITY OF EVIDENCE. See SALES, 1, 3.

ADMISSIBILITY OF PAROL EVIDENCE. See EVIDENCE, 1.

ADOPTION OF WRITTEN CONTRACT. See CONTRACTS, 1.

ADVERSE PARTY NOTIFIED OF APPLICATION FOR WRIT.
See CERTIORARI, 12.

AGREEMENT FOR SALE OF HAY. See SALES, 1, 3, 4.

AGREEMENT SETTLING RIGHTS IN COMMUNITY PROP-
ERTY. See HUSBAND AND WIFE, 1.

ALIMONY. See CONSTITUTIONAL LAW, 4.

ALIMONY MAY BE GRANTED WIFE. See DIVORCE, 1, 2.

ANSWER ALLEGING WANT OF CONSIDERATION SUFFI-
CIENT. See BILLS AND NOTES, 1.

APPEAL. See STATUTES, 17.

APPEAL FOR PURPOSES OF DELAY. See COSTS, 1.

APPEAL FROM ORDER OF DETERMINATION OF STATE
ENGINEER. See WATERS AND WATERCOURSES, 2, 3.

APPEAL IN UNLAWFUL DETAINER TO BE WITHIN TEN
DAYS. See JUSTICES OF THE PEACE, 1.

APPEAL AND ERROR.
  1. ASSIGNMENT OF ERROR OF INSUFFICIENCY OF EVIDENCE NECESSARY.
       Assignment of error is required by Stats. 1915, c. 142, sec.
       13, as amended by Stats. 1919, c. 40, sec. 2, though the only
       objection is insufficiency of the evidence to justify the verdict
       or decision. *Smith* v. *Lucas.* 348.

2. Assignments of Error Not Necessary where Appeal Is on Judgment Roll.

Notwithstanding Stats. 1919, p. 55. requiring the appellant to file the assignments of error within ten days after transcript on appeal shall have been filed, an appeal from an order denying motion to change place of trial will not be dismissed because of appellant's failure to file assignments of error where, though the appeal was not on what is technically known as the judgment roll, it was substantially the same, the record consisting of the amended complaint, motion for change of venue, affidavit in support thereof, etc. *Page v. Walser*, 422.

3. Authentication of Record Solely by Clerk of District Court Not Sufficient.

On appeal from decree of the district court affirming an order of the state engineer determining water rights, the certificate of the clerk of the district court attached to the original documents, files, and records in the original proceeding indicates only prima facie correctness, and by analogy to a record certified by an official reporter it must be authenticated by the court or judge to be made a part of the record, in view of Stats. 1915, c. 142. *In Re Waters of Barber Creek*, 407.

4. Bill of Exceptions Allowed after Assembling of Judgment Roll Not Part of It Dispensing with Assignment.

A bill of exceptions, settled and allowed after entry of judgment and denial of new trial, is not part of the judgment roll, so as to obviate necessity of assignments of error, though appeal is from the judgment only: Civ. Prac. Act, sec. 331. subd. 2, making part of such roll all bills of exceptions "taken and fixed," relating to the time for assembling the roll. *Smith v. Lucas*, 348.

5. Bill of Exceptions Not Setting Out Matter Ruled on Insufficient.

A bill of exceptions not setting out the matter on which the ruling was made is insufficient; a mere reference to other parts of the transcript being insufficient. *Mooney v. Newton*, 441.

6. Change of Theory on Appeal.

An act should not be alleged by a party in his pleading and denied by him on appeal. *Garson v. Steamboat Canal Co.*, 298.

7. Defendant Cannot Complain of Errors Affecting Codefendant Only.

A defendant appellant cannot on appeal complain of an error affecting a codefendant only. *Mooney v. Newton*, 441.

8. Determination of Right to Appeal before Hearing on Merits.

Ordinarily questions not pertaining to the regularity and efficacy of an appeal, but affecting its merit, should not be determined on motion to dismiss; but a party's right to be heard on the merits is statutory, depending entirely on whether he or she is within the general class designated by the statute. and the question should be determined in advance of hearing on the merits. *In Re McKay's Estate*, 114.

APPEAL AND ERROR—*Continued.*

9. ERRONEOUS JUDGMENT CANNOT BE SUSTAINED ON A THEORY CONTRARY TO EXPRESS FINDING.

Where in replevin action by conditional seller against buyer for recovery of automobiles court erroneously found that seller was liable for repairs incorporated in the automobile on theory of acceptance of services, appellate court cannot sustain decision on theory that seller was liable on theory that transaction constituted a mortgage and mortgagor was entitled to use the automobiles, and that such created implied authority to incur expense of repairs. *Clarke v. Johnson,* 359.

10. ERROR IN ADMISSION OF TESTIMONY AS TO TRANSACTION WITH DECEDENT HARMLESS.

In a son-in-law's action against his father-in-law on a note signed by the father and payable to his daughter and the son-in-law, error in admitting the father's testimony as to the manner in which his daughter induced him to sign the note, though the daughter at the time of trial was dead, *held* harmless and not ground for reversal under Rev. Laws, 5315, in view of the testimony of the mother of the girl who was present at the time of the signing. *Reinhart v. Echave,* 323.

11. EXCEPTIONS—CERTIFICATE.

A trial court's certificate that statement and bill of exceptions contains all material evidence, except documentary evidence, is insufficient to authorize review of evidence, which will be presumed to support findings and judgment. *Love v. Mt. Oddie U. M. Co.,* 61.

12. EXCEPTIONS MUST BE TAKEN AT TIME RULING IS MADE TO ENTITLE PARTY TO REVIEW.

When an exception is necessary to a ruling of the court, it must be taken when the ruling is made, unless by permission of the court it is allowed to be taken at a later time. *Mooney v. Newton,* 441.

13. FINDINGS—CONCLUSIVENESS.

A finding of fact based on a substantial conflict in material evidence is conclusive upon appeal. *Cassinelli v. Humphrey Co.,* 208.

14. FINDINGS—CONCLUSIVENESS.

A finding based upon undisputed facts or the construction of a written instrument is not binding upon appeal. *Idem.*

15. JURISDICTION ACQUIRED BY APPEAL ON JUDGMENT ROLL.

Though an appeal was taken on the judgment roll alone, and the appellate court did not acquire jurisdiction to review errors other than those appearing on the face of the judgment roll, the appellate court acquired jurisdiction of the appeal. *Gill v. Goldfield Con. M. Co.,* 1.

16. LACK OF MOTION FOR NEW TRIAL—GROUNDS FOR DISMISSAL OF APPEAL.

Since the supreme court, on appeal from a decree, can look to the judgment roll to ascertain whether any error appears, an appeal will not be dismissed because it appears from the record that it is based on the ground that the evidence is insufficient to justify the decision of the court, and that no

motion for a new trial was made and determined before the
appeal was taken, under Rev. Laws, 5328. *In Re Waters of
Barber Creek*, 403.

17. METHOD OF APPEAL—STATUTES.

Where the method of appeal is prescribed by statute, it must
be followed, and the assumption that a ceremony is useless will
not justify a departure therefrom. *Gill v. Goldfield Con. M.
Co.*, 1.

18. NO CONSIDERATION ON REHEARING OF QUESTION NOT URGED ON
ORIGINAL HEARING.

A question not urged in the supreme court on original hearing of the appeal cannot be considered on rehearing. *In Re
Forney's Estate*, 228.

19. NOTICE OF UNDERTAKING—DISMISSAL OF APPEAL.

Since Rev. Laws, 5330, does not require that an undertaking
on appeal be served on the adverse party, the supreme court
is not authorized to dismiss an appeal for want of service.
In Re Waters of Barber Creek, 403.

20. OBJECTION MADE FIRST TIME ON APPEAL.

An objection that complaint utterly failed to state a cause
of action may be raised for the first time on appeal. *Nielsen
v. Rebard*, 274.

21. ON APPEAL ON DENIAL OF CHANGE OF VENUE BRIEF MUST BE
FILED AS REQUIRED BY COURT RULE 23.

Where on appeal from an order denying change of venue,
respondent invoked court rule 23, and filed the notice provided, rule 11, providing that the appellant shall within fifteen
days after filing the transcript serve and file his brief, was
superseded, and the appellant must file his brief within the
time fixed by rule 23. *Page v. Walser*, 422.

22. ORDER SETTLING BILL OF EXCEPTIONS NOT ORDER ALLOWING
EXCEPTIONS TO BE TAKEN.

An order of the court settling a bill of exceptions is in no
sense an order allowing exceptions to be taken at that time.
Mooney v. Newton, 441.

23. RAISING DEFENSES NOT MADE IN TRIAL COURT.

Where, in an action for breach by lessor of his oral contract to furnish horses for making a crop, the matter of estoppel to set up the invalidity of the oral agreement under the
statute of frauds because of the changed position of plaintiff
was not a matter of evidence or contest at the trial, it cannot
be relied on, on appeal. *Nehls v. Stock Farming Co.*, 253.

24. REHEARINGS.

Rehearings in the supreme court are not granted as a matter
of right, and are not allowed for the purpose of reargument,
unless there is reasonable probability that the court may have
arrived at an erroneous conclusion. *Pershing Co. v. Humboldt
Co.*, 78.

25. REJECTION OF TESTIMONY HARMLESS ERROR.

In suit to cancel a mother's deed to daughter, refusal to
permit another daughter, who had been joined with grantee
daughter as defendant, to testify to transaction between her
and mother with respect to mother's disposition of her prop-

APPEAL AND ERROR—*Continued.*

    erty, if error, was harmless, where court permitted her statement that deed had been prepared in accordance with mother's directions to stand, and where it was such fact that was sought to be elicited by the rejected testimony. *Adams* v.*Wagoner*, 266.

26. REVERSAL IN EQUITY FOR ERRONEOUS INSTRUCTION.

    In equity cases, a judgment will not be reversed because of an erroneous instruction. *Love* v. *Mt. Oddie U. M. Co.*, 61.

27. REVIEW—ASSIGNMENTS—NECESSITY OF MOTION FOR NEW TRIAL.

    Where an appeal is based upon alleged errors relating to evidence as pointed out under Rev. Laws, 5323 (Civ. Prac. Act, sec. 381), a motion for a new trial must be made and determined before the appeal is taken, as required by section 5328 (section 386). *Gill* v. *Goldfield Con. M. Co.*, 1.

28. SEASONABLE SERVICE AND FILING OF ASSIGNMENT OF ERRORS JURISDICTIONAL, AND NOT WAIVABLE.

    Seasonable service and filing of assignment of errors, as required by Stats. 1915, c. 142, sec. 13, as amended by Stats. 1919, c. 40, sec. 2, is jurisdictional, and absence thereof may not be waived. *Smith* v. *Lucas*, 348.

APPELLATE NATURE OF PROCEEDINGS. See CERTIORARI, 7.

APPLICATION FOR CHANGE OF VENUE. See VENUE, 2, 3.

APPLICATION FOR WRIT. See CERTIORARI, 12.

APPLICATION TO RESET CASE FOR TRIAL. See TRIAL, 1.

ARTIFICIAL AND TECHNICAL ESTATES. See DEEDS, 3.

ASSEMBLING OF JUDGMENT ROLL. See APPEAL AND ERROR, 4.

ASSIGNMENT OF ERRORS. See APPEAL AND ERROR, 27, 28.

ATTORNEY AT LAW. See LICENSES, 1, 3.

ATTORNEY'S FEE IN INTERPLEADER. See INTERPLEADER, 2.

AUTHENTICATION OF RECORD ON APPEAL. See APPEAL AND ERROR, 3.

AUTOMOBILE ACCESSORIES. See ACCESSION, 1.

AUTOMOBILE REPAIRS. See APPEAL AND ERROR, 9; WORK AND LABOR, 1.

AUTOMOBILES. See REPLEVIN, 1.

AVOIDANCE OF INHERITANCE TAX. See TAXATION, 8.

BANKS AND BANKING.

1. STATUTE GOVERNING COMPENSATION OF RECEIVER NOT RETROACTIVE.

    Where receiver of bank, ordered into involuntary liquidation under banking act of 1907, sec. 10, was appointed and duly qualified in 1908, and is still actively engaged in the performance of his duties, his compensation is not governed by act of March 29, 1915 (Stats. 1915, c. 286); said act not being retroactive. *Wilden* v. *State*, 388.

BASTARDS.

1. FOR LEGITIMATION FATHER MUST HAVE FAMILY INTO WHICH CHILD IS RECEIVED.

Under Civ. Code Cal. sec. 230, for legitimation of a bastard, the father must have a family into which the child can be received. *In Re Forney's Estate*, 227.

2. LEGITIMATION CONTROLLED BY LAW OF STATE OF DOMICILE OF FATHER.

Where a bastard child was born in California to a father there resident, and subsequently the father died leaving personalty in Nevada, the child cannot claim such personalty on any theory of legitimation under Nevada law, not having been legitimated in California, whose laws controlled. *Idem.*

3. LEGITIMATION MUST BE VALID IN STATE WHERE BASTARD AND FATHER LIVED.

Legitimation of a bastard must be according to the law of the state in which she and her father had lived during their joint lives, to entitle her to take as his heir personal property which he left in another state. *Idem.*

4. LEGITIMATION, ONCE MADE, CANNOT BE REPUDIATED.

Once a child born illegitimate has been legitimated, from such moment it acquires every legal right which a child born in wedlock can enjoy, its right of inheritance becomes fixed, and the father cannot repudiate his act in legitimating it. *Idem.*

5. WHAT LAW GOVERNS LEGITIMATION.

There can be only one proper state for the legitimation of a child born illegitimate; and, if it is not legitimated according to the laws of such state, it is not legitimated anywhere. *Idem.*

BILL OF EXCEPTIONS. See APPEAL AND ERROR. 4; STATUTES, 17.

BILL OF EXCEPTIONS MUST SET OUT MATTER RULED ON. See APPEAL AND ERROR, 5.

BILLS AND NOTES.

1. ANSWER ALLEGING WANT OF CONSIDERATION SUFFICIENT.

In an action on a note, the answer of the maker *held* sufficient to present as against the payee the defense of want of consideration. *Dixon* v. *Miller*, 280.

2. DUTY TO OFFER TESTIMONY IN SUPPORT OF NOTE ATTACKED.

In a suit on a note made out in printing and three different handwritings, stripped by evidence of defendant maker of its commercial character, and based ostensibly on some sort of a contract between the maker and the plaintiff, his son-in-law, it was the duty of the plaintiff, having notice of the defenses against the note, to be prepared on trial to offer some evidence other than the note itself to entitle him to verdict. *Reinhart* v. *Echave*, 323.

3. DUTY TO SHOW WILLING AND INFORMED SIGNING.

Where plaintiff before his marriage to defendant's daughter had said he would not marry her except for money, plaintiff, suing on a note signed by defendant to the order of plaintiff and defendant's daughter, is under duty to offer some expla-

BILLS AND NOTES—*Continued.*

nation of his conduct consistent with his interest and fair dealing with defendant to show that the note was signed willingly and knowingly. *Idem.*

4. EVIDENCE—WANT OF CONSIDERATION JURY QUESTION.

Ordinarily a mere equality in the number of witnesses does not constitute a balance of evidence, and hence in an action on a note, where defendant urged want of consideration and testified to facts in support of his claim, which testimony was contradicted by plaintiff, the payee, the question is for the jury. *Dixon v. Miller*, 280.

5. WANT OF CONSIDERATION A DEFENSE AGAINST ORIGINAL PAYEE.

As against the original payee who was not a holder of a note in due course, the maker may, under negotiable-instruments law, sec. 28, urge the absence or failure of consideration. *Idem.*

See APPEAL AND ERROR, 10; EVIDENCE, 1; GIFTS, 1.

BONDS FOR LOAN TO LAND OWNERS ILLEGAL. See COUNTIES, 2.

BONDS MUST BE FOR PUBLIC PURPOSE. See COUNTIES. 1.

"BOUGHT." See SALES, 4.

BOUNDARIES OF COUNTIES. See CONSTITUTIONAL LAW, 1, 3; COUNTIES, 3, 4.

BREACH OF CONTRACT. See ELECTION OF REMEDIES, 1; HUS- AND WIFE, 1.

BREACH OF ORAL AGREEMENT. See APPEAL AND ERROR, 23; STATUTE OF FRAUDS, 1, 2, 3.

BRIEFS ON APPEAL. See APPEAL AND ERROR, 21.

BROKERS.
1. ACTION FOR COMMISSION.

In a broker's action for commissions for the sale of land. a finding that the contract was one of general employment to find a purchaser at any price, defendant to pay 5 per cent commission, was not supported by proof of a contract that plaintiff was to find a buyer for the property at a stated price upon which a 5 per cent commission was to be paid. *Campbell v. Vanetti*, 98.

BULK–SALES LAW. See FRAUDULENT CONVEYANCES, 1, 2.

CANAL COMPANY A PUBLIC UTILITY. See WATERS AND WATERCOURSES, 4.

CANCELATION OF DEED. See APPEAL AND ERROR, 25; DEEDS, 4.

CAPACITY IN WHICH ADMINISTRATOR HOLDS PROPERTY. See EXECUTORS AND ADMINISTRATORS, 1, 2, 3; PLEADING, 7.

CAPACITY IN WHICH ADMINISTRATOR IS SUED. See PLEAD- ING, 1, 2, 7.

CARRIERS.

1. LIABILITY FOR LOSS OR DAMAGE—LIMITATION—VALUATION.

A railroad's contract fixing a valuation on intrastate shipment negligently destroyed *held* void, where property's actual value was greater. *Southern Pacific Co.* v. *Haug*, 102.

2. LIMITATION OF LIABILITY FOR NEGLIGENCE—LOSS.

A common carrier cannot, by contract, avoid liability for loss or damage to freight caused by its own negligence or that of its servants. *Idem.*

3. LOSS OF GOODS—DAMAGES—MEASURE.

Irrespective of statute, it is a general rule that measure of damages where goods intrusted to a carrier are destroyed is their value with interest from the date delivery should have been made. *Idem.*

CERTIFICATE AS TO STATEMENT AND BILL OF EXCEPTIONS. See APPEAL AND ERROR, 11.

CERTIORARI.

1. ACTION OF COURT—DUTY TO AID APPELLATE COURT.

On certiorari to review the action of the district court, the latter should not place itself in the position of adverse party, as if it had some personal interest in sustaining its judgment, or throw obstacles in the way to prevent a review of its proceedings, as by failing to give notice to adverse party of proceedings. *Hilton* v. *District Court*, 128.

2. DILIGENCE IN PROCURING RECORD.

Though Rev. Laws, 5686, requires clerk of court to return transcript with writ of certiorari where writ is directed to the court, prosecutor of writ is required to use due diligence in having complete record made out, and on his failure so to do proceedings will be dismissed. *Dixon* v. *District Court*, 159.

3. DILIGENCE OF PETITIONER—DISMISSAL OF PROCEEDINGS.

In certiorari proceedings in supreme court against lower court, where clerk refused to annex transcript to writ because of petitioner's failure to pay fees, court will not dismiss proceedings on ground that petitioner failed to exercise due diligence in having record made out, where petitioner acted in good faith, believing that his duty ended upon issuance of writ, and that it was then the supreme court's duty to require lower court and clerk to return writ with transcript under Rev. Laws, 5686, 5687. *Idem.*

4. DISMISSAL OF PROCEEDINGS WHERE EQUITY CAN BETTER AFFORD RELIEF.

In an original proceeding by certiorari to inquire into the jurisdiction of the district court to render judgment against claims of a mining company, where the supreme court, in view of all the facts, reaches conclusion that a court of equity is more capable of affording adequate relief and doing justice in the matter, the proceedings will be dismissed. *Nevada Lincoln Co.* v. *District Court*, 306.

5. GROUNDS—ERRORS.

A claim that a court erred in determining that a wife's cause of action for support and maintenance was brought

CERTIORARI—*Continued.*

within Stats. 1913, c. 97, was not a claim that the court exceeded its jurisdiction, so as to be reviewable on certiorari. *Hilton* v. *District Court*, 128.

6. ISSUANCE OF WRIT DISCRETIONARY AND NOT MATTER OF RIGHT.

Writ of certiorari does not issue as a matter of right, but in the sound discretion of the court. *Nevada Lincoln Co.* v. *District Court*, 396.

7. NATURE OF PROCEEDINGS.

Proceedings on certiorari are of appellate nature, though not pursued in ordinary and technical form of appeal. *Dixon* v. *District Court*, 159.

8. ONLY QUESTION OPEN TO INQUIRY WHETHER PROPER SERVICE WAS OBTAINED ON PETITIONER SEEKING TO REVIEW JUDGMENT.

In an original proceeding by certiorari to inquire into the jurisdiction of the district court to render a judgment against petitioner, the only question which the supreme court can examine is whether or not service of summons was obtained upon petitioner in the action sought to be reviewed, so as to give the court jurisdiction to proceed. *Nevada Lincoln Co.* v. *District Court*, 396.

9. REVIEW—HARMLESS ERROR—JURY.

Where trial court directed a verdict, that defendant was erroneously compelled to go to trial before a special venire was harmless. *State* v. *McFadden*, 140.

10. TRANSCRIPT—COSTS.

Clerk of court is not required under Rev. Laws. 5686. to annex transcript in returning writ of certiorari directed to the court, unless petitioner in serving writ upon clerk pays the fees prescribed by law for the making of the transcript. *Dixon* v. *District Court*, 159.

11. TRIAL—PROVINCE OF COURT—DIRECTION OF VERDICT.

The trial judge, in the exercise of sound discretion. may in a proper case direct a verdict, and, though the direction of verdict be improper, it is not within the jurisdiction of the court so as to be reviewable on certiorari; and this is so. though there was no mode of review in particular case. *State* v. *McFadden*, 140.

12. WHEN ISSUES—NECESSARY PARTIES.

In the exercise of its discretion the supreme court may issue. under Rev. Laws, 5685, a writ of certiorari to review an action of a district court without notice to the adverse party, but the supreme court should not be asked, in such a proceeding. to annul a judgment granting support and maintenance to a wife, where the adverse party is not made a party to the application for the writ. *Hilton* v. *District Court*, 128.

See JUSTICES OF THE PEACE, 2.

CHANGE OF THEORY ON APPEAL. See APPEAL AND ERROR. 6.

CHANGE OF VENUE. See APPEAL AND ERROR, 21; COSTS. 1: VENUE, 1, 2, 3.

CHANGED POSITION OF PLAINTIFF. See STATUTE OF FRAUDS. 1, 2.

CITY OCCUPATION TAX. See LICENSES. 1, 2, 3.

CLAIM AND DELIVERY. See EXECUTORS AND ADMINISTRATORS, 3; REPLEVIN, 1; WORK AND LABOR, 1.

CLAIM AND DELIVERY AGAINST ADMINISTRATOR. See PLEADING, 1, 2, 7.

CODEFENDANT. See APPEAL AND ERROR, 7.

CODIFICATION AND REVISION. See STATUTES, 16.

COMITY BETWEEN STATES: See TAXATION, 11.

COMMISSION OF BROKER. See BROKERS, 1.

COMMISSIONS ON FORECLOSURE SALE. See SHERIFFS AND CONSTABLES, 1.

COMMON CARRIERS. See CONSTITUTIONAL LAW, 10.

COMMON-LAW NUISANCE. See GAMING, 2.

COMMUNITY PROPERTY. See ELECTION OF REMEDIES, 1; HUSBAND AND WIFE, 1.

COMPENSATION OF RECEIVERS. See BANKS AND BANKING, 1; RECEIVERS, 1.

COMPLAINT AGAINST ADMINISTRATOR. See EXECUTORS AND ADMINISTRATORS, 2, 3; PLEADING, 1, 2, 7.

COMPLAINT FOR FALSE IMPRISONMENT. See FALSE IMPRISONMENT, 1.

COMPLAINT IN ACTION FOR MALICIOUS PROSECUTION. See MALICIOUS PROSECUTION, 1.

COMPLAINT IN UNLAWFUL DETAINER. See LANDLORD AND TENANT, 2.

COMPLAINT NOT STATING CAUSE OF ACTION. See APPEAL AND ERROR, 20.

CONCLUSION OF PLEADER IN ACTION FOR FALSE IMPRISONMENT. See PLEADING, 3.

CONCLUSIVENESS OF FINDINGS. See APPEAL AND ERROR, 13, 14.

CONDITIONAL CONTRACT. See ACCESSION, 1.

CONFLICT IN OBJECTS. See STATUTES, 8.

CONSIDERATION. See BILLS AND NOTES, 1, 5.

CONSOLIDATION OR CREATION OF COUNTIES. See COUNTIES, 3, 4.

CONSPIRACY.
1. COMMON-LAW ACTION OBSOLETE.
The common-law action of conspiracy is obsolete, and in lieu thereof an action on the case in the nature of a conspiracy has been substituted. *Dixon* v. *City of Reno*, 413.

CONSPIRACY—*Continued.*

   2. JUDGMENT—JUDGMENT AGAINST JOINT DEFENDANTS.

     In an action for false imprisonment, judgment may be entered against a single defendant, though the conspiracy charged be not proven; but it cannot be entered against joint defendants without such proof. *Idem.*

   See MALICIOUS PROSECUTION, 1.

CONSTABLES. See SHERIFFS AND CONSTABLES, 1.

CONSTITUTIONAL LAW.

   1. COUNTIES—VESTED RIGHTS—BOUNDARIES OF COUNTIES—RIGHTS OF INHABITANTS.

     The inhabitants of a county have no vested rights as far as the boundaries of the county or the extent of its territory are concerned, and the same may be changed without their consent. *Pershing Co.* v. *Humboldt Co.,* 78.

   2. DETERMINATION OF CONSTITUTIONAL QUESTIONS.

     The constitutionality of statutory provisions should not be passed upon until some right dependent on the particular provision is brought before the court for adjudication. *Idem.*

   3. DIVISION OR CREATION OF NEW COUNTY.

     The whole matter of the division of counties and the creation of new ones is in its nature political, and not judicial, and belongs wholly to the legislative department of the government. *Idem.*

   4. IMPRISONMENT FOR FAILURE TO PAY ALIMONY NOT IMPRISONMENT FOR "DEBT."

     Alimony does not constitute a "debt" within the meaning of Const. art. 1, sec. 14, providing that there shall be no imprisonment for debt, a debt in the sense used in the constitution alluding to an obligation growing out of a business transaction, and not to an obligation arising from the existence of the marital status. *Ex Parte Phillips,* 368.

   5. JUDICIAL AUTHORITY—CONSTRUCTION OF STATUTES.

     Whether a statute was repealed by a later one is a judicial, and not a legislative, question. *Gill* v. *Goldfield Con. M. Co.,* 1.

   6. LEGISLATIVE ENCROACHMENT ON COURTS.

     Stats. 1911, c. 162, sec. 26, in so far as it provides that all rates fixed by the public service commission "shall be deemed reasonable and just and shall remain in full force and effect until final determination by the courts having jurisdiction," is not violative of Const. art. 6, sec. 6, conferring original jurisdiction in all cases in equity upon district courts; such statute merely establishing a rule of evidence, and not withholding remedy for imposition of unreasonable rates. *Garson* v. *Steamboat Canal Co.,* 298.

   7. LEGISLATURE'S RIGHT TO MAKE RULES OF EVIDENCE.

     Legislature has the undoubted right to prescribe such rules of evidence as may best promote justice in a particular case. *Idem.*

   8. POLICY OF LAW MATTER FOR LEGISLATURE.

     The policy or expediency of a law is within the exclusive domain of legislative action, and is a forbidden sphere for the judiciary. *In Re McKay's Estate,* 114.

9. REGULATION OF CHARGES NOT A DENIAL OF DUE PROCESS OF LAW.
Stats. 1911, c. 162, sec. 26, in so far as it provides that all rates fixed by the public service commission "shall be deemed reasonable and just and shall remain in full force and effect until final determination by the courts having jurisdiction," is not violative of Const. art. 1, sec. 8, guaranteeing that no person shall be deprived of property without due process of law. *Garson* v. *Steamboat Canal Co.*, 298.

10. REGULATION OF RATES OF PUBLIC UTILITY A LEGISLATIVE FUNCTION.
The power to prescribe rates for a common carrier or a public utility company is a legislative function, as distinguished from judicial power, which the legislature has really exercised in the first instance, by prescribing that all rates shall be just and reasonable. *Idem*.

11. RIGHT TO QUESTION STATUTE.
One not prejudiced by the enforcement of a statute cannot question its constitutionality or obtain decision as to its validity on the ground it impairs the rights of others, so that a county from whose territory another is formed by the legislature cannot question the validity of the formative statute in its provisions designating officers of the new county, etc. *Pershing Co.* v. *Humboldt Co.*, 78.

12. WHETHER ALLOWING NICKEL-IN-THE-SLOT MACHINES INJUDICIOUS QUESTION FOR LEGISLATURE.
Whether a law allowing nickel-in-the-slot machines to a limited extent is unwholesome is a question for the legislature or the people, and not the courts. *Ex Parte Pierotti*, 243.

See COUNTIES, 5; CRIMINAL LAW, 4, 5; LOTTERIES, 1; PUBLIC SERVICE COMMISSIONS, 5.

CONSTITUTIONALITY OF COUNTY ORGANIZATION. See STATUTES, 19.

CONSTITUTIONALITY OF ENTIRE STATUTE. See STATUTES, 12.

CONSTITUTIONALITY OF OCCUPATION TAX. See LICENSES, 2, 3.

CONSTRUCTION IN LIGHT OF FACTS. See STATUTES, 5.

CONSTRUCTION MUST GIVE EFFECT TO ENTIRE ACT. See STATUTES, 4.

CONSTRUCTION OF BULK–SALES LAW. See FRAUDULENT CONVEYANCES, 1, 2.

CONSTRUCTION OF CONTRACT FOR SALE OF HAY. See SALES, 4, 7.

CONSTRUCTION OF DEED OF TRUST. See TAXATION, 6, 7.

CONSTRUCTION OF DEEDS. See DEEDS, 1.

CONSTRUCTION OF FEE STATUTES. See OFFICERS, 1.

CONSTRUCTION OF REFERENDUM. See STATUTES, 13.

CONSTRUCTION OF STATUTES. See CONSTITUTIONAL LAW, 5; STATUTES, 1, 2.

CONSTRUCTION OF UNIFORM SALES ACT. See SALES, 8.

CONSTRUCTION TO AVOID ABSURD MEANING. See STATUTES, 3.

CONSTRUCTIVE DELIVERY. See SALES, 6, 7.

CONTEMPLATION OF DEATH. See TAXATION, 5, 7.

CONTEMPORANEOUS CONSTRUCTION UNAVAILABLE. See STATUTES, 6.

CONTEMPT FOR FAILURE TO PAY ALIMONY. See DIVORCE, 2.

CONTINGENCY. See STATUTES, 9.

CONTRACT BETWEEN MAKER AND PLAINTIFF. See BILLS AND NOTES, 2.

CONTRACT FOR SALE OF HAY. See SALES, 1, 3, 4.

CONTRACT FOR SALE OF LAND. See BROKERS, 1.

CONTRACT LIMITING LIABILITY. See CARRIERS, 1, 2.

CONTRACT PARTLY PERFORMED. See STATUTE OF FRAUDS, 4, 5.

CONTRACT SETTLING RIGHTS IN COMMUNITY PROPERTY. See HUSBAND AND WIFE, 1.

CONTRACT TO FURNISH HORSES. See STATUTE OF FRAUDS, 1, 2.

CONTRACTS.
1. ADOPTION—EXECUTION.
Parties may adopt a written contract, and thus make it as binding as though formally executed by both, without signing it; and hence in an action by subcontractor against the surety on the contractor's bond, brought after complete performance by subcontractor, the fact that the written subcontract was not executed is no defense. *Reno E. Wks. v. U. S. F. & G. Co.*, 191.
See ACCESSION, 1; APPEAL AND ERROR, 23; ELECTION OF REMEDIES, 1.

CONVEYANCE OF MINING CLAIMS BY A MINOR. See INFANTS, 1.

CONVEYANCE OF PROPERTY TO CHILDREN. See TRUSTS, 1.

CONVEYANCES. See FRAUDULENT CONVEYANCES, 1, 2.

CONVEYANCES IN FEE. See DEEDS, 1, 5.

CORPORATE STOCK PERSONAL PROPERTY. See VENUE, 4.

CORPORATIONS.
1. KNOWLEDGE OF DIRECTOR'S FRAUD WHILE ACTING FOR HIMSELF NOT CHARGEABLE TO COMPANY.
Where the holder of an option on mining claims became director and officer of a company formed to operate such

claims after exercise of the option, the company was not charged with knowledge of the officer's fraud on the owner of the claims; he having acted wholly for himself. *Keyworth v. Nevada Packard Co.*, 428.

2. RATES OF PUBLIC UTILITIES.

The right of public utilities to initiate their own rates is subject to the requirement that all rates shall be just and reasonable. *Garson v. Steamboat Canal Co.*, 298.

COSTS.

1. NO PRESUMPTION THAT MOTION FOR CHANGE OF VENUE WAS MADE WITH INTENT TO DELAY, THOUGH IT WAS NOT WELL TAKEN.

The appellate court cannot indulge presumption that defendants did not have confidence in their application for change of venue, and so impose a penalty on defendants whose appeal from the denial of motion was affirmed on ground that appeal was for delay. *Page v. Walser*, 422.

COSTS IN ACTION OF INTERPLEADER. See INTERPLEADER, 1, 2.

COSTS OF CLERK OF DISTRICT COURT. See CERTIORARI. 10.

COUNTER-CLAIM FOR REPAIRS. See REPLEVIN. 1.

COUNTIES.

1. BONDS TO BE PAID BY TAXATION ILLEGAL UNLESS FOR PUBLIC PURPOSE.

Where county and municipal bonds are issued whose payment is provided for solely by taxation, their validity depends upon the question whether the purposes to which the proceeds of the bonds are to be applied are public purposes. *State v. Churchill County*, 290.

2. BONDS TO RAISE MONEY TO LOAN TO LAND OWNERS ILLEGAL.

Stats. 1919, c. 204, authorizing the county of Churchill to issue bonds to establish a fund to loan to private land owners for the purpose of reclaiming arid lands, is invalid, in that the method provided is ineffective and would result in taxation for private purposes. *Idem.*

3. CHANGE OF BOUNDARIES—CONSOLIDATION OR CREATION.

Unless a limitation exists in the constitution, the power of the legislature is absolute. by general or special statutes, to provide change of boundaries, division, addition, consolidation of existing counties, or the creation and organization of new counties. *Pershing Co. v. Humboldt Co.*, 78.

4. CREATION, EXISTENCE, AND CHANGE—LEGISLATIVE CONTROL.

Since a county is called into existence by the legislature, and therefore is its creature, its territory may be cut up in parcels by the legislature, and its common property and common burden apportioned in such manner as the legislature may deem reasonable and equitable, or its existence as a county may be blotted out, all even against the will of its inhabitants. *Idem.*

COUNTIES—*Continued.*

5. FORMATION OF NEW OUT OF OLD—REFERENDUM—CONSTITUTION— "IN AND FOR."

Stats. 1919, p. 75, creating and organizing the county of Pershing out of a portion of Humboldt County, is not a local law "in and for" Humboldt County, making necessary referendum to the voters of such latter county under Const. art. 19, sec. 3, providing the referendum powers are reserved to the electors of each county as to all local legislation in and for the respective counties. *Idem.*

See CONSTITUTIONAL LAW, 1, 3, 11.

COUNTIES NOT ENTITLED TO REFERENDUM. See STATUTES, 13.

COUNTY ORGANIZATION. See STATUTES, 19.

COURTS.

1. DISTRICT COURT HAS JURISDICTION OF SUIT IN INTERPLEADER INVOLVING LESS THAN $300.

Under Civ. Prac. Act, sec. 63 (Rev. Laws, 5005), the district court has jurisdiction of an action in interpleader. although the amount involved is less than $300, such suit being equitable. and district courts having original jurisdiction in all chancery cases. *Mooney* v. *Newton*, 441.

COURTS OF LIMITED JURISDICTION. See JUSTICES OF THE PEACE, 2.

CREATION OF ESTATES. See DEEDS, 3.

CREATION OF NEW COUNTIES. See CONSTITUTIONAL LAW, 11.

CRIMINAL LAW.

1. HABEAS CORPUS—HEARING ON PETITION.

On an original petition for habeas corpus by an attorney at law, convicted on failure to pay occupation tax, petitioner cannot be permitted to show that the facts proven on the trial at which he was convicted were not sufficient to constitute the crime charged. *Ex Parte Dixon*, 196.

2. HABEAS CORPUS—ORIGINAL PETITION—HEARING.

In an original application for habeas corpus by one convicted of violation of an occupation-tax law, the court cannot consider the abuse of the lower court's discretion in refusing to grant a continuance of the trial in which the petitioner was convicted, or an objection to evidence as incompetent or the exclusion of evidence offered in petitioner's behalf. *Idem.*

3. INDICTMENT AND INFORMATION—LEAVE GRANTED TO FILE NEW INFORMATION ON MOTION OF DISTRICT ATTORNEY.

Under the information act (Stats. 1913, c. 209, secs. 6, 9, and 10) and Rev. Laws, 7101. though the trial court on sustaining demurrer to original information did not direct that another information be filed, it had jurisdiction to grant the district attorney's motion for leave to file new information. motion to dismiss which as filed without due authority was properly denied. *Ex Parte Williams*, 342.

4. LIMITATION ON POWER—SUSPENSION OF SENTENCE.

Where the constitution enumerates certain cases in which the collection of a fine may be suspended, or certain methods whereby it may be done, or confers such power upon certain official or officials, the power so conferred is exclusive. *State v. Moran*, 150.

5. SUSPENSION OF SENTENCE—CONSTITUTIONALITY OF STATUTE.

Rev. Laws, 7259, authorizing the court to suspend sentence except in specified cases, is unconstitutional; there being no constitutional authority therefor, and method of suspending sentence provided for by Const. art. 5, secs. 13, 14, being exclusive. *Idem*.

CROSS–COMPLAINT IN ACTION FOR SUPPORT AND MAINTENANCE. See PLEADING, 4.

DAMAGE TO FREIGHT IN TRANSIT. See CARRIERS, 1, 2, 3.

DAMAGES FOR BREACH OF PAROL AGREEMENT. See STATUTE OF FRAUDS, 3.

DECREE OF DISTRICT COURT AS TO WATER RIGHTS. See JUDGMENT, 1.

DEED OF TRUST. See TAXATION, 6, 7; TRUSTS, 2, 3.

DEED OF TRUST AND WILL EXECUTED SIMULTANEOUSLY. See TAXATION, 7, 8.

DEED OF TRUST TO TRANSFER STOCK. See TAXATION, 1.

DEED OR WILL. See WILLS, 1.

DEED TO MINING CLAIM. See ESTOPPEL, 1.

DEEDS.

1. CONSTRUCTION—FEE.

It is the policy of the law to encourage making conveyances in fee. *In Re Miller's Estate*, 12.

2. DEED OF INCOMPETENT GRANTOR HELD VOID.

Mother's deed to daughter, executed while mother was in her last illness, and at a time when she was not capable of comprehending fully and fairly the nature and effect of the transaction, *held* void. *Adams* v. *Wagoner*, 266.

3. ESTATES WHICH MAY BE CREATED.

There is no natural right to create artificial and technical estates with limitations over, nor has the remainderman any more right to succeed to the possession of property under such deeds than legatees or devisees under a will. *In Re Miller's Estate*, 12.

4. EVIDENCE SHOWING INCAPACITY OF GRANTOR.

In action to cancel mother's deed to daughter, executed by mother while in her last illness and a few hours before her death, evidence *held* to show that mother, at the time of execution of deed, was not possessed of sufficient intelligence to understand fully the nature and effect of the transaction. *Adams* v. *Wagoner*, 266.

DEEDS—*Continued.*
5. LEGALITY.

It is as lawful to create an estate for life with remainder after death of the grantor as it is to convey in fee. *In Re Miller's Estate,* 12.

6. SUFFICIENCY OF EVIDENCE TO SHOW UNDUE INFLUENCE.

Evidence *held* to show that mother's deed to daughter, with whom mother was living at time of her death, executed while mother was in her last illness and a few hours before her death, was procured by undue influence of daughter. *Adams v. Wagoner,* 266.

7. VALIDITY—EFFECT UPON EXECUTION.

A deed to be valid should take effect in interest upon its execution, though the right of possession or enjoyment may not take place until the happening of a certain event. *In Re Miller's Estate,* 12.

See APPEAL AND ERROR, 25.

DEFAULT. See JUDGMENT, 2.

DEFECTIVE SERVICE OF SUMMONS. See CERTIORARI, 8.

DEFENSES NOT MADE IN TRIAL COURT. See APPEAL AND ERROR, 23.

DENIAL OF CHANGE OF VENUE. See APPEAL AND ERROR, 21.

DESCENT AND DISTRIBUTION.
1. GRANDNIECE EXCLUDED FROM INHERITANCE BY NEPHEWS AND NIECES.

Stats. 1897, c. 106, regulating descent, as amended by Stats. 1915, c. 130, sec. 259, providing as to nephews and nieces in the third degree of kinship, excludes a grandniece from any inheritance. so that such grandniece was not an "heir" of testatrix, and section 272, defining the right of representation, does not bear on the former section, except as a statutory rule of interpretation. *In Re McKay's Estate,* 114.

DESERTION OF WIFE AND CHILD. See HUSBAND AND WIFE, 2.

DESTRUCTION OF HAY PENDING DELIVERY. See SALES. 2, 4.

DETERMINATION OF CONSTITUTIONAL QUESTIONS. See CONSTITUTIONAL LAW, 2.

DETERMINATION OF RIGHT TO APPEAL BEFORE HEARING ON MERITS. See APPEAL AND ERROR, 8.

DETERMINATION OF WATER RIGHTS. See WATERS AND WATERCOURSES, 1, 2, 3.

DEVELOPMENT WORK ON GROUP OF CLAIMS. See MINES AND MINERALS, 1, 2, 3.

DILIGENCE OF PETITIONER. See CERTIORARI, 2.

DIRECTED VERDICT. See CERTIORARI, 9, 10.

DIRECTOR'S FRAUD NOT CHARGEABLE TO COMPANY. See CORPORATIONS, 1.

DISCRETION IN ISSUANCE OF WRIT. See CERTIORARI. 6, 12.

DISCRETION OF TRIAL JUDGE. See CERTIORARI. 10.

DISMISSAL OF APPEAL. See APPEAL AND ERROR, 16, 19.

DISMISSAL OF APPEAL FROM DECREE. See WATERS AND WATERCOURSES, 1.

DISMISSAL OF MOOT CASE. See PROHIBITION. 1.

DISMISSAL OF PROCEEDINGS. See CERTIORARI, 2, 4.

DISTRICT COURT JURISDICTION. See PUBLIC SERVICE COMMISSIONS, 5.

DISTRICT COURT TO AID APPELLATE COURT. See CERTIORARI, 1.

DIVISION OR CONSOLIDATION OF COUNTIES. See CONSTITUTIONAL LAW, 3, 11; COUNTIES, 3, 4.

DIVORCE.
1. ALIMONY MAY BE GRANTED WIFE.
    The statutes permit the court on granting a divorce to allow alimony to the wife. *Ex Parte Phillips*, 368.
2. ORDER IN CONTEMPT PROCEEDING NOT MODIFICATION OF ORIGINAL DECREE.
    An order in a contempt proceeding, providing that a divorced husband pay alimony provided for in original decree or go to jail, was not a modification of the original decree, and it was immaterial that the court had not reserved the right to modify or amend the original decree. *Idem.*
    See HUSBAND AND WIFE, 1; ELECTION OF REMEDIES, 1; PLEADING, 4.

DOCTRINE OF PART PERFORMANCE. See STATUTE OF FRAUDS, 4, 5.

DOMICILE OF FATHER CONTROLS IN LEGITIMATION OF CHILDREN. See BASTARDS, 2, 5.

DOUBT RESOLVED AGAINST RETROACTIVE OPERATION. See STATUTES, 7.

DUE PROCESS OF LAW. See CONSTITUTIONAL LAW, 9.

EFFECT MUST BE GIVEN TO ENTIRE ACT. See STATUTES, 4.

EFFECT OF PARTIAL INVALIDITY OF STATUTE. See STATUTES, 12.

EFFECTIVE UPON EXECUTION. See DEEDS, 7.

EFFICACY OF TAX FOR PUBLIC IMPROVEMENT. See TAXATION, 3.

ELECTION OF REMEDIES.
1. ACTS CONSTITUTING AN ELECTION.
    Where plaintiff wife, defendant in divorce suit, instead of bringing action for husband's breach of contract whereby he

ELECTION OF REMEDIES—*Continued.*

agreed to pay her a specified sum in consideration of her agreement not to demand a division of community property, or ask for suit money, instituted proceedings to set aside divorce decree in his favor, *held*, she cannot maintain suit on the con- .tract; the remedies being inconsistent, and she having made an election. *Robertson* v. *Robertson*, 50.

EQUAL AND UNIFORM RATE OF TAXATION. See LICENSES, 3.

EQUIPMENT AND REPAIRS TO MOTOR TRUCKS. See ACCESSION, 1.

EQUITABLE RELIEF. See CERTIORARI, 4.

EQUITY. See APPEAL AND ERROR, 26.

EQUITY JURISDICTION OF DISTRICT COURT. See CONSTITUTIONAL LAW, 6; COURTS, 1.

ERRONEOUS INSTRUCTION IN EQUITY NOT REVERSIBLE ERROR. See APPEAL AND ERROR, 26.

ERRONEOUS JUDGMENT CONTRARY TO EXPRESS FINDING. See APPEAL AND ERROR, 9.

ERRONEOUS VIEW AS TO JURISDICTION. See MANDAMUS, 1.

ERROR OF DISTRICT COURT NOT EXCESS OF JURISDICTION. See CERTIORARI, 5.

ERRORS AFFECTING CODEFENDANT ONLY. See APPEAL AND ERROR, 7.

ESTATE FOR LIFE WITH REMAINDER. See DEEDS, 5.

ESTATES OF DECEASED PERSONS. See BASTARDS, 1, 2, 3; DESCENT AND DISTRIBUTION, 1; EXECUTORS AND ADMINISTRATORS, 1, 2, 3; GIFTS, 1; PLEADING, 1, 2, 7; TAXATION, 1, 7, 8.

ESTATES WHICH MAY BE CREATED. See DEEDS, 3.

ESTOPPEL.
1. PRINCIPAL MUST SUFFER FROM WRONGFUL CONDUCT OF AGENT HELD OUT AS OPTIONEE.
   Where the owner of a mining claim put another in position to hold himself out as holder of an option to sell, and purchasers dealt with such other on the assumption, the owner cannot urge the agency of such other and his misconduct as ground for setting aside his deed to the purchasers, since one who makes it possible for a person to perpetrate a wrong on another must suffer the consequences. *Keyworth* v. *Nevada Packard Co.*, 428.
   See APPEAL AND ERROR, 23; STATUTE OF FRAUDS, 1, 2, 3.

EVIDENCE.
1. PAROL EVIDENCE ADMISSIBLE TO SHOW WANT OF CONSIDERATION.
   The rule that parol evidence is not admissible to contradict or vary an absolute engagement to pay money on the face of a bill or note does not exclude evidence as between the immedi-

ate parties of a total failure or want of consideration, and the negotiable-instruments law, sec. 28, recognizes the right to urge want of consideration. *Dixon* v. *Miller*, 280.

See APPEAL AND ERROR, 1, 10, 13, 14; BROKERS, 1; SALES, 1, 3; TAXATION, 2; TRIAL, 2.

EVIDENCE IN ACTION TO CANCEL DEED. See APPEAL AND ERROR, 25.

EVIDENCE OF LESSORS' CHANGED POSITION. See STATUTE OF FRAUDS, 1.

EVIDENCE OF UNDUE INFLUENCE. See DEEDS, 6.

EVIDENCE OF WANT OF CONSIDERATION. See BILLS AND NOTES, 4.

EVIDENCE ON HEARING BEFORE PUBLIC SERVICE COMMISSION. See WATERS AND WATERCOURSES, 5.

EVIDENCE SHOWING DEVELOPMENT WORK. See MINES AND MINERALS, 2, 3.

EVIDENCE SHOWING INCAPACITY OF GRANTOR. See DEEDS, 4.

EVIDENCE TO ESTABLISH TRUST. See TRUSTS, 1.

EVIL SOUGHT TO BE REMEDIED. See STATUTES, 2.

EXCEPTIONS. See APPEAL AND ERROR, 11, 22.

EXCEPTIONS AT TIME OF RULING. See APPEAL AND ERROR, 12.

EXCEPTIONS TO DETERMINATION OF STATE ENGINEER. See JUDGMENT, 1.

EXCLUSION FROM INHERITANCE. See DESCENT AND DISTRIBUTION, 1.

EXECUTION OF WRITTEN CONTRACT. See CONTRACTS. 1.

EXECUTORS AND ADMINISTRATORS.
1. ADMINISTRATOR NOT LIABLE IN BOTH PERSONAL AND REPRESENTATIVE CAPACITY FOR WITHHOLDING PROPERTY.
   An administrator could not hold possession of plaintiff's personal property both as an individual and as administrator, nor could plaintiff in claim and delivery charge the administrator with holding the property in both capacities. *Kingsbury* v. *Copren*, 448.
2. COMPLAINT AGAINST ADMINISTRATOR IN PERSONAL AND REPRESENTATIVE CAPACITY MUST STATE CAUSE OF ACTION AGAINST HIM IN BOTH.
   Though in some circumstances a defendant may be sued both as an individual and as administrator, in such a suit the complaint must state a cause of action against the party in both capacities, or be demurrable. *Idem.*

EXECUTORS AND ADMINISTRATORS—*Continued.*

3. COMPAINT IN CLAIM AND DELIVERY AGAINST ADMINISTRATOR HELD
   NOT TO STATE CAUSE OF ACTION IN INDIVIDUAL CAPACITY.

   Complaint in action in claim and delivery, or replevin,
   against an administrator, both personally and in his representative capacity, which charged that defendant, having
   obtained the property from plaintiff by false representations,
   thereafter caused it to be inventoried and appraised as the
   property of the estate, etc., did not state a cause of action
   against defendant as an individual. *Idem.*

FAILURE TO PAY ALIMONY. See CONSTITUTIONAL LAW, 4.

FAILURE TO STATE CAUSE OF ACTION. See PLEADING, 5.

FALSE IMPRISONMENT.
1. COMPLAINT INSUFFICIENT.

   In an action for false imprisonment, a count based on lack
   of jurisdiction of a municipal court *held* insufficient, in that it
   failed to allege facts showing wherein municipal court was
   without jurisdiction; plaintiff having stated that he was
   arrested and proceeded against on a warrant issued upon a
   complaint filed with a duly constituted magistrate. *Dixon v.
   City of Reno,* 413.

   See ACTION, 1; CONSPIRACY, 2; MALICIOUS PROSECUTION, 1;
   MINES AND MINERALS, 3; PLEADING, 3.

FEE SIMPLE. See DEEDS, 1, 5.

FEES FOR TRANSCRIPT. See CERTIORARI, 3, 10.

FEES OF ATTORNEY IN INTERPLEADER. See INTERPLEADER, 2.

FEES ON FORECLOSURE SALE. See SHERIFFS AND CONSTABLES, 1.

FILING AND SERVICE OF ASSIGNMENT OF ERRORS NOT
   WAIVABLE. See APPEAL AND ERROR, 28.

FINAL DETERMINATION. See PUBLIC SERVICE COMMISSIONS, 3.

FINDINGS. See APPEAL AND ERROR, 9, 13, 14.

FINDINGS AND JUDGMENT ON DEFAULT. See JUDGMENT, 2.

FINDINGS BASED ON SUBSTANTIAL CONFLICT OF EVI-
   DENCE. See APPEAL AND ERROR, 13.

FINDINGS BASED ON UNDISPUTED FACTS. See APPEAL AND
   ERROR, 14.

FINDINGS OF STATE ENGINEER. See WATERS AND WATER-
   COURSES, 3.

FIXING OF RATES BY PUBLIC SERVICE COMMISSION. See
   CONSTITUTIONAL LAW, 9.

FORECLOSURE PROCEEDINGS. See SHERIFFS AND CONSTA-
   BLES, 1.

FORMATION OF NEW COUNTIES. See COUNTIES, 5.

FRAUD OF DIRECTOR NOT CHARGEABLE TO COMPANY. See CORPORATIONS, 1.

FRAUDS. See STATUTE OF FRAUDS, 1.

FRAUDS, STATUTE OF. See APPEAL AND ERROR, 23.

FRAUDULENT CONVEYANCES.
 1. BULK-SALES LAW—CONSTRUCTION—"VOID."
　　　　Bulk-sales law, declaring certain sales "void," does not pre-
 ● clude the seller from recovering the purchase price of a sale
　　　made in violation of its terms; "void," as used in the statute,
　　　meaning "voidable." *Escalle* v. *Mark*, 172.
 2. BULK-SALES LAW—PURPOSE.
　　　　The main purpose of the bulk-sales law is to protect whole-
　　　salers. *Idem.*

FUNGIBLE GOODS. See SALES, 1–7.

FUTURE INTERESTS. See WILLS, 1.

GAMBLING DEVICES. See LOTTERIES, 1.

GAMING.
 1. NICKEL-IN-THE-SLOT MACHINE GAMBLING DEVICE.
　　　　Nickel-in-the-slot machines, by which a player has a chance
　　　of losing the amount he plays or receiving a larger amount,
　　　are well-known gambling devices. *Ex Parte Pierotti*, 243.
 2. NUISANCE—GAMING-HOUSES NUISANCES AT COMMON LAW.
　　　　While at common law gaming or gambling was not itself
　　　unlawful, and is not now a crime unless so made by statute,
　　　yet at common law public gaming-houses were nuisances, not
　　　only because they were deemed great temptations to idleness,
　　　but because they were apt to draw together numbers of disor-
　　　derly persons. *Idem.*

GIFTS.
 1. GIFT OF DONOR'S OWN NOTE NOT VALID.
　　　　One cannot make his own note the subject of a gift to such
　　　an extent that it can be enforced by the donee against the
　　　donor, or against his estate. *Reinhart* v. *Echave*, 324.

GRANDNIECE. See DESCENT AND DISTRIBUTION, 1.

GRANTOR MUST BE COMPETENT. See DEEDS, 2, 4.

GROUNDS FOR DISMISSAL OF APPEAL. See APPEAL AND ERROR, 16.

GROUNDS FOR ISSUANCE OF WRIT. See CERTIORARI, 5.

GROUNDS OF MOTION FOR NEW TRIAL. See APPEAL AND ERROR, 16.

GROUP OF CLAIMS. See MINES AND MINERALS, 1, 2, 3.

HABEAS CORPUS. See CRIMINAL LAW, 1, 2.

HARMLESS ERROR. See APPEAL AND ERROR, 10, 25; CERTIORARI, 9.

HEARING BY PUBLIC SERVICE COMMISSION. See WATERS AND WATERCOURSES, 5.

HUSBAND AND WIFE.

1. AGREEMENT SETTLING RIGHTS IN COMMUNITY—BREACH.

Plaintiff wife, defendant in divorce suit, by filing motion in divorce proceeding to set aside divorce decree in favor of her husband, together with answer to the merits specifically asking for attorney's fees and other money, violated contract whereby she agreed not to demand a division of community property, or ask for suit money in consideration of husband's promise to pay her a specified sum in settlement of community property rights. *Robertson v. Robertson*, 50.

2. DESERTION—NONSUPPORT—PROSECUTION—VENUE.

Prosecution of husband for desertion and nonsupport of wife and child under Act Pa. March 13, 1903 (P. L. 26). need not be instituted at place of his residence, or county in which offense is alleged to have been committed, but may be instituted wherever relief may be needed; such statute, in view of section 2, and in view of act April 13, 1867 (P. L. 78), to which it is supplementary, being remedial as well as penal, with purpose of affording relief to dependent wives and children. *Ex Parte Brennen*, 165.

3. MAINTENANCE.

To entitle a wife to recover in an action under Stats. 1913. p. 120, for support and maintenance, without applying for divorce, it is incumbent upon her to make a showing of the marriage relation, her needs, and the ability of her husband, as in a suit for divorce. *Hilton v. District Court*, 128.

4. SUPPORT AND MAINTENANCE.

A wife may maintain an action against her husband for support and maintenance without applying for divorce, under Stats. 1913, c. 97. *Idem.*

5. SUPPORT AND MAINTENANCE—RESIDENCE.

The requirement as to residence in section 7 of Stats. 1913. c. 97, giving wife right of action against husband for support and maintenance without applying for a divorce, relates to the venue of the action and not to jurisdiction of the parties, and such residence need be such only that an ordinary action could be maintained by her according to the statute regulating the venue of civil action. so enlarged as to permit her to sue in the county where the husband may be found. *Idem.*

6. SUPPORT AND MAINTENANCE—STATUTE.

The object of Stats. 1913, c. 97, giving wife right of action against husband for support and maintenance without applying for a divorce, is to give the wife a sure and speedy remedy through an independent action when she has any cause of action for divorce against her husband, or when he has deserted her for a period of ninety days, and, being remedial, must be liberally construed with a view to promote its object, the jurisdiction of the court being neither limited nor restricted. *Idem.*

See CERTIORARI, 5, 12; CONSTITUTIONAL LAW, 4; DIVORCE, 1, 2; ELECTION OF REMEDIES, 1; PLEADING, 4.

ILLEGITIMATE CHILDREN. See BASTARDS, 1, 2, 3, 4, 5.

IMPLIED REPEAL. See STATUTES, 8, 14, 15, 17.

IMPRISONMENT FOR DEBT. See CONSTITUTIONAL LAW, 4.

IMPRISONMENT FOR FAILURE TO PAY ALIMONY. See CONSTITUTIONAL LAW, 4.

"IN AND FOR." See COUNTIES, 5.

INCOMPETENT GRANTOR. See DEEDS, 2, 4.

INDEFINITE DECREE AS TO WATER RIGHTS. See JUDGMENT, 1.

INDICTMENT AND INFORMATION. See CRIMINAL LAW, 3.

INFANTS.
  1. PURPOSE OF STATUTE AS TO CONVEYANCES OF MINING CLAIMS BY MINORS.
      The real purpose of Rev. Laws, 1103, 1104, relative to conveyances of mining locations and claims by minors, was to subject minors under the age of 21 and over 18 who convey interests in mining claims to the same consequences as attach to persons over 21 who convey such property. *Keyworth* v. *Nevada Packard Co.*, 428.

INHERENT POWER OF COURT. See MOTIONS, 1.

INHERITANCE. See DESCENT AND DISTRIBUTION, 1.

INHERITANCE TAX. See TAXATION, 1, 6, 7, 8, 11.

INJUNCTION. See PROHIBITION, 1.

INJUNCTION PENDENTE LITE. See PUBLIC SERVICE COMMISSIONS, 3.

INQUIRY ON HABEAS CORPUS. See CRIMINAL LAW, 1, 2.

INSTRUCTIONS IN EQUITY CASES. See APPEAL AND ERROR, 26.

INSUFFICIENCY OF BILL OF EXCEPTIONS. See APPEAL AND ERROR, 5.

INSUFFICIENCY OF COMPLAINT FOR FALSE IMPRISONMENT. See FALSE IMPRISONMENT, 1.

INSUFFICIENCY OF EVIDENCE. See APPEAL AND ERROR, 1, 16.

INSUFFICIENCY OF EVIDENCE SHOWING DEVELOPMENT WORK. See MINES AND MINERALS, 2, 3.

INSUFFICIENCY OF EVIDENCE TO ESTABLISH TRUST. See TRUSTS, 1.

INSUFFICIENCY OF NOTICE TO QUIT. See LANDLORD AND TENANT, 1, 2.

INSUFFICIENCY OF PLEADING. See STATUTE OF FRAUDS, 1, 2.

INTENT OF LEGISLATURE. See STATUTES, 2.

INTENT OF LEGISLATURE AS TO REPEAL. See STATUTES, 14, 15.

INTENTION OF PARTIES. See SALES, 5.

INTERESTS CREATED BY DEATH OF DONOR. See WILLS. 1.

INTERPLEADER.
1. PLAINTIFF ENTITLED TO COSTS OUT OF FUND DEPOSITED.

In an action in interpleader under Civ. Prac. Act. sec 63 (Rev. Laws, 5005), the plaintiff, if the interpleader is granted. is entitled to his costs out of the fund deposited in court, to be ultimately paid by the unsuccessful party, and the defendant not in fault is entitled to a decree against the other defendant for the costs so taken out of the fund, as well as his own costs. *Mooney* v. *Newton*, 441.

2. PLAINTIFF NOT ENTITLED TO ATTORNEY FEE AS COSTS.

The plaintiff in an action in interpleader, if the interpleader is granted, is not entitled to an attorney fee to be paid by the losing party; the allowance of an attorney fee being a subject of statutory regulation. *Idem*.

INTERPLEADER SUIT INVOLVING LESS THAN $300. See COURTS, 1.

INVALIDITY OF AGREEMENT. See STATUTE OF FRAUDS. 1. 2. 3.

INVALIDITY OF PART OF STATUTE. See STATUTES. 12.

IRREVOCABILITY OF TRUST. See TRUSTS. 2. 3.

ISSUANCE OF WRIT DISCRETIONARY. See CERTIORARI. 6.

JOINDER OF COUNTS IN CASE AND TRESPASS. See ACTION. 1.

JUDGMENT.
1. DECREE OF DISTRICT COURT ON EXCEPTIONS TO DETERMINATION OF STATE ENGINEER DETERMINING WATER RIGHTS TOO INDEFINITE.

In proceedings for the determination of water rights initiated before the state engineer pursuant to the water law. decree of the district court, on exceptions, pursuant to section 35. as amended by Stats. 1915, c. 253· to the determination of the engineer, reading that the court had reviewed all the proof and the facts and the relative determinations by the engineer. and had reached conclusions on the law and facts coincident with the determination of the engineer. and directing decree affirming his order of determination, despite section 36. as amended by Stats. 1915, c. 253, *held* in no sense a decree which in a water case should be as definite as language can make it and should dispose of each issue raised by the exceptions to the determination of the state engineer. *In Re Waters of Barber Creek*, 407.

2. DEFAULT—NOTICE OF SUBSEQUENT PROCEEDING.

Where defendant was in default, the fact that the court made findings and entered judgment without notice is no ground of objection, for after default it would be a useless thing to require service of notice on defendant. *Reno E. Wks.* v. *U. S. F. & G. Co.*, 191.

See APPEAL AND ERROR, 9; CERTIORARI, 7.

JUDGMENT AGAINST JOINT DEFENDANTS. See Conspiracy, 2.

JUDGMENT ROLL. See Appeal and Error, 2, 4, 15.

JUDICIAL AND LEGISLATIVE POWERS. See Statutes, 10.

JUDICIAL AUTHORITY TO CONSTRUE STATUTES. See Constitutional Law, 5.

JUDICIAL DETERMINATION AS TO RATES. See Public Service Commissions, 2, 3, 5.

JURISDICTION IN ACTION FOR SUPPORT AND MAINTENANCE. See Husband and Wife, 5, 6.

JURISDICTION OF APPEAL ON JUDGMENT ROLL. See Appeal and Error, 15.

JURISDICTION OF COURTS. See Public Service Commissions, 4.

JURISDICTION OF DISTRICT COURT. See Certiorari, 5, 8, 11.

JURISDICTION OF DISTRICT COURT IN INTERPLEADER. See Courts, 1.

JURISDICTION OF DISTRICT COURT TO RENDER JUDGMENT. See Certiorari, 4.

JURISDICTION OF MUNICIPAL COURT. See False Imprisonment, 1.

JURISDICTION OF TRIAL COURT TO DIRECT NEW INDICTMENT. See Criminal Law, 3.

JURISDICTION ON APPEAL. See Appeal and Error, 28.

JUSTICES OF THE PEACE.
1. Appeal in Unlawful Detainer To Be Taken within Ten Days.

Civil practice act, sec. 659, providing that unlawful-detainer appeals from justice court must be taken within ten days after judgment, governs the time for appeal in such actions, and is unaffected by section 846, providing generally that justice court appeals may be taken within thirty days after judgment. *Roberts* v. *District Court*, 332.

2. Certiorari—Review—Jurisdiction—Record—Presumptions.

Judgment of a justice of the peace against defendants will be held void on certiorari, record or files of the case not affirmatively showing summons was served or that defendants appeared, nothing being presumed in favor of jurisdiction of courts of limited jurisdiction, and it not being permissible to consider affidavits that summons was in fact served. *State* v. *Bonner*, 95.

See Mandamus, 1.

JURY.
1. Jury Trial—Special Venire.

Under Rev. Laws, 4940, declaring that it shall be in the discretion of the court, with the consent of all parties litigant, either to draw the names of the jurors from the box, as provided in the act, or to issue an open venire directed to the

JURY—*Continued.*

sheriff, etc., the court is without authority to order a special venire, which is unknown to the statute law, to try a case over the exceptions of one of the parties. *State* v. *McFadden.* 140.

See CERTIORARI, 9.

LAND CONTRACTS. See STATUTE OF FRAUDS, 5.

LANDLORD AND TENANT.
1. NOTICE TO QUIT IN UNLAWFUL DETAINER INSUFFICIENT.

Under civil practice act, sec. 646, subd. 2, as amended by Stats. 1917, c. 27, requiring a tenant at will to be served with notice to quit before instituting unlawful-detainer proceedings, the notice must be clear and unconditional, and a notice that the landlord could not continue to rent the premises "for occupancy as billiard- or poolroom" after a certain date is insufficient. *Roberts* v. *District Court,* 332.

2. NOTICE TO QUIT NECESSARY IN UNLAWFUL DETAINER.

Under civil practice act, sec. 646, subd. 2, as amended by Stats. 1917, c. 27, authorizing unlawful-detainer proceedings against a tenant at will after serving him with notice to quit, the notice is an essential element of the action and must be expressly alleged in the complaint. *Idem.*

3. TENANCY FROM MONTH TO MONTH.

A tenancy for an indefinite term with monthly rentals reserved creates a tenancy from month to month. *Idem.*

LAW TO TAKE EFFECT IN CONTINGENCY. See STATUTES, 9.

LEAVE TO FILE NEW INFORMATION. See CRIMINAL LAW, 3.

LEGALITY OF DEED. See DEEDS, 5.

LEGALITY OF OCCUPATION TAX. See LICENSES, 1, 2, 3.

LEGISLATION FOR COUNTIES. See STATUTES, 13.

LEGISLATIVE AND JUDICIAL POWERS. See STATUTES, 10.

LEGISLATIVE ENCROACHMENT ON COURTS. See CONSTITUTIONAL LAW, 6.

LEGISLATIVE INTENT AS TO REPEAL. See STATUTES, 14, 15.

LEGISLATURE MAY FIX RATES OF PUBLIC UTILITY. See CONSTITUTIONAL LAW, 10.

LEGISLATURE PRESUMED TO KNOW THE LAW. See STATUTES, 11.

LEGISLATURE SOLE JUDGE IN DIVISION OF COUNTIES. See CONSTITUTIONAL LAW, 3.

LEGISLATURE TO DETERMINE POLICY OF LAW. See CONSTITUTIONAL LAW, 8.

LEGISLATURE'S POWER TO CHANGE BOUNDARIES OF COUNTIES ABSOLUTE. See COUNTIES, 3, 4.

LEGISLATURE'S RIGHT TO MAKE RULES OF EVIDENCE. See CONSTITUTIONAL LAW, 7.

LEGITIMATED CHILDREN CANNOT BE REPUDIATED. See BASTARDS, 5.

LEGITIMATION OF BASTARDS. See BASTARDS, 1, 2, 3, 5.

LEGITIMATION OF BASTARDS CONTROLLED BY LAW OF DOMICILE OF FATHER. See BASTARDS, 2, 3, 5.

LESSOR OF HORSES AND TEAMS. See STATUTE OF FRAUDS, 3.

LIABILITY FOR LOSS OR DAMAGE BY CARRIERS. See CARRIERS, 1, 2.

LIABILITY OF ADMINISTRATOR. See EXECUTORS AND ADMINISTRATORS, 1, 2.

LIABILITY OF CARRIER. See CARRIERS, 1.

LIABILITY OF SELLER. See SALES, 2, 3, 4.

LICENSES.
1. CITY OCCUPATION TAX.
   An admission to the bar of a state is a vested and valuable right, but subject to taxation, including a city occupation tax. *Ex Parte Dixon*, 196.
2. LICENSE TAX ON OCCUPATION—CONSTITUTIONALITY.
   The imposition of a license tax upon an occupation is not illegal, because not expressly authorized by the state constitution, but is permissible, unless prohibited thereby. *Idem.*
3. OCCUPATION TAX—UNIFORMITY—ATTORNEYS.
   A city ordinance, imposing a tax upon the occupation of attorney at law, *held* not in violation of Const. art. 10, sec. 1, providing for an equal and uniform rate of taxation. *Idem.*

LIMITATION OF JUDICIAL POWERS. See STATUTES, 10.

LIMITATION OF LIABILITY. See CARRIERS, 1, 2.

LIMITATION OF POWER TO SUSPEND SENTENCE. See CRIMINAL LAW, 4, 5.

LOANS TO PRIVATE LAND OWNERS ILLEGAL. See COUNTIES, 2.

LOCAL LAW "IN AND FOR." See COUNTIES, 5.

LOCATION WORK ON MINING CLAIMS. See MINES AND MINERALS, 3.

LOSS BY FIRE PENDING DELIVERY. See SALES, 2, 3, 4.

LOSS OF GOODS. See CARRIERS, 1, 2, 3.

LOTTERIES.
1. NICKEL-IN-THE-SLOT MACHINES, THOUGH GAMBLING DEVICES, NOT LOTTERIES.
   A nickel-in-the-slot machine, although a gambling device and expressly brought within the purview of the earlier gam-

LOTTERIES—*Continued.*

bling statutes, is not a lottery, within Const. art. 4, sec. 24, declaring that no lotteries shall be authorized in the state; and hence the state legislature may, as it did in Stats. 1915, except slot machines for the sale of cigars and drinks and no backplay allowed. *Ex Parte Pierotti*, 243.

MAINTENANCE. See HUSBAND AND WIFE, 3, 4, 5, 6.

MALICIOUS PROSECUTION.
1. COMPLAINT MUST ALLEGE WANT OF PROBABLE CAUSE.
   A count of complaint *held* to amount to an action on the case for the malicious arrest and imprisonment of the plaintiff in the nature of a conspiracy and to be insufficient where it failed to allege want of probable cause. *Dixon* v. *City of Reno*, 413.

MANDAMUS.
1. WILL ISSUE ON ERRONEOUS REJECTION OF JURISDICTION.
   Where the lower court's refusal to take jurisdiction of an appeal from a justice court involved no disputed question of fact, but depended upon the court's erroneous view as to time in which an appeal could be perfected, mandamus will issue to require the court to try the action. *Roberts* v. *District Court*, 332.

MANDATORY NATURE OF VENUE STATUTE. See VENUE, 1, 2.

"MANIFEST." See MINES AND MINERALS, 3.

MATERIAL ALLEGATIONS BIND PLAINTIFF. See PLEADING, 6.

MEASURE OF DAMAGES FOR GOODS DESTROYED IN TRANSIT. See CARRIERS, 3.

MEASUREMENT OF HAY. See SALES, 3, 4.

MERITS OF PUBLIC QUESTION. See PROHIBITION, 2.

METHOD OF APPEAL. See APPEAL AND ERROR, 17.

MINES AND MINERALS.
1. DEVELOPMENT WORK ON GROUP OF CLAIMS.
   In the exercise of judgment as to where development work should be done on a group of mining claims and locations, a wide latitude should be allowed the owners of the property. *Love* v. *Mt. Oddie U. M. Co.*, 61.
2. EVIDENCE NOT SHOWING DEVELOPMENT WORK INSUFFICIENT.
   In an action to quiet title to a group of eight mining claims, wherein verdict was rendered in favor of plaintiff relocators for four of the claims, evidence that the development work done in one place by defendant company on such claims was insufficient to prevent forfeiture *held* not such as to sustain the judgment. *Idem.*
3. IMPROVEMENT WORK ON SINGLE LOCATION DEVELOPING ENTIRE GROUP.
   Improvement work within the meaning of the federal statute as to the location of mining claims, is deemed to have been

performed, whether the claim consists of one location or several, when in fact the labor is performed or the improvements are made for the development of the whole claim, that is, to facilitate the extraction of metals, though the labor and improvements may be on ground originally part of only one of the locations, and it is not necessary that the work "manifestly" tend to the development of all the claims in the group; "manifest" meaning evident or obvious to the mind. *Idem.*

4. QUESTION OF FACT WHETHER WORK DONE IMPROVED CLAIMS.

It is purely a question of fact whether or not development work done in a particular shaft by the locator of claims so tended to improve the entire group of claims as to prevent forfeiture thereof. *Idem.*

See CERTIORARI, 4; CORPORATIONS, 1; ESTOPPEL, 1: PARTNERSHIP, 1.

MINING CLAIMS HELD BY MINORS. See INFANTS. 1.

MINING STOCK PERSONAL PROPERTY. See VENUE, 4.

MODIFICATION OF ORIGINAL DECREE. See DIVORCE, 2.

MOOT CASE DISMISSED. See PROHIBITION, 1.

MOTION FOR CHANGE OF VENUE. See COSTS, 1.

MOTION FOR NEW TRIAL. See APPEAL AND ERROR, 16.

MOTION FOR NEW TRIAL BEFORE APPEAL. See STATUTES, 1, 8.

MOTION FOR NEW TRIAL NECESSARY. See APPEAL AND ERROR, 27.

MOTION TO DISSOLVE PRELIMINARY INJUNCTION. See PROHIBITION, 1.

MOTIONS.

1. TRIAL—RESETTING OF CASE—NOTICE.

If considered as a motion, within the meaning of civil practice act, sec. 5362, and rule 10 (Rev. Laws, 4942) of the district courts. an application to reset a case for trial on an earlier date than that fixed should be denied, where the five days' notice required in case of motions was not given, and the action of the court in granting the motion, of which no notice at all was given, although defendant was present in court at.1; the time the application was made, cannot be sustained with the ground that the courts have inherent power to regackard their own docket and control their own business. *McFadden*, 140.

MOTOR TRUCKS. See ACCESSION, 1.   COSTS, 1.

"MOVE." See VENUE, 5.   , VENUE, 4.

MUNICIPAL BONDS. See COUNTIES, 1. 2.   ¿GATIONS. See

NATURE OF TRANSFER TAX. See TAXAT

NECESSARY PARTIES TO WRIT OF CERTIORARI. See CERTI-
ORARI, 12.

NECESSITY OF EXCEPTION AT TIME OF RULING. See
APPEAL AND ERROR, 12.

NECESSITY OF MOTION FOR NEW TRIAL. See APPEAL AND
ERROR, 27.

NECESSITY OF NOTICE TO QUIT. See LANDLORD AND TENANT, 2.

NEGLIGENCE. See CARRIERS, 1, 2.

NEGOTIABLE INSTRUMENTS. See BILLS AND NOTES, 5; EVI-
DENCE, 1.

NEPHEWS AND NIECES. See DESCENT AND DISTRIBUTION, 1.

NEW TRIAL. See STATUTES, 8.

NEW TRIAL PRIOR TO APPEAL. See STATUTES, 1.

NICKEL–IN–THE–SLOT MACHINES. See CONSTITUTIONAL LAW,
12; GAMING, 1; LOTTERIES, 1.

NONSUPPORT. See HUSBAND AND WIFE, 2, 6.

NOTICE OF APPEAL FROM ORDER DENYING CHANGE OF
VENUE. See APPEAL AND ERROR, 21.

NOTICE OF MOTION TO RESET CASE. See MOTIONS, 1.

NOTICE OF PROCEEDINGS SUBSEQUENT TO DEFAULT. See
JUDGMENT, 2.

NOTICE OF UNDERTAKING. See APPEAL AND ERROR, 19.

NOTICE TO QUIT IN UNLAWFUL DETAINER. See LANDLORD
AND TENANT, 1, 2.

NUISANCE. See GAMING, 2.

OBECT OF ACTION IN TROVER AND CONVERSION. See TRO-
VER AND CONVERSION, 1.

OBJECTION MADE FIRST TIME ON APPEAL. See APPEAL AND
ERROR, 20.

OBJECTION THAT COMPLAINT FAILS TO STATE CAUSE
OF ACTION. See PLEADING, 5.

OBJECTION TO SETTING CASE FOR TRIAL. See TRIAL, 1.

OCCUPATION TAX. See CRIMINAL LAW, 1,.2; LICENSES, 1, 2, 3.

OFFICERS.
1. STRICT CONSTRUCTION OF FEE STATUTES.
   Statutes allowing public officers fees for services are strictly
   construed in favor of the person from whom fees are sought
   to be collected. *Clover Valley Co. v. Lamb*, 375.

OMITTED PARTS IN CODIFICATION AND REVISION. See
STATUTES, 16.

OPERATION OF INHERITANCE TAX. See TAXATION, 1.

OPTION ON MINING CLAIMS. See PARTNERSHIP, 1.

OPTION TO SELL MINING CLAIMS. See ESTOPPEL, 1.

ORAL AGREEMENT TO FURNISH HORSES. See STATUTE OF FRAUDS, 1, 2.

ORDER IN CONTEMPT NOT MODIFICATION OF DECREE. See DIVORCE, 2.

ORDER OF DETERMINATION OF STATE ENGINEER. See WATERS AND WATERCOURSES, 1, 2, 3.

ORDER SETTLING BILL OF EXCEPTIONS. See APPEAL AND ERROR, 22.

ORGANIZATION OF COUNTY. See STATUTES, 19.

ORIGINAL JURISDICTION OF DISTRICT COURT. See CONSTITUTIONAL LAW, 6.

ORIGINAL PETITION FOR HABEAS CORPUS. See CRIMINAL LAW, 1, 2.

PARDONING POWER. See CRIMINAL LAW, 4, 5.

PAROL CONTRACT. See STATUTE OF FRAUDS, 1, 2, 3.

PAROL EVIDENCE ADMISSIBLE TO SHOW WANT OF CONSIDERATION. See EVIDENCE, 1.

PART PERFORMANCE. See STATUTE OF FRAUDS, 4.

PARTIAL INVALIDITY. See STATUTES, 12.

PARTICULAR STATUTORY PROVISION MUST BE PRESENTED. See CONSTITUTIONAL LAW, 2.

PARTNERSHIP.
   1. AGREEMENT OF PURCHASERS OF MINING CLAIM OPTION TO PAY OPTIONEE PART OF CONSIDERATION IN PROMOTION STOCK NOT CREATING PARTNERSHIP.
   Where the optionee of mining claims sold his interest in the option in consideration that purchasers should make the initial payment on the option and organize a company to take title to the claims and divide with him the promotion stock, no partnership was thereby created between the parties, any more than if the whole consideration had been paid in cash; so that such purchasers could not be charged as partners, with optionee's knowledge of facts. *Keyworth v. Nevada Packard Co.*, 428.

PASSING OF TITLE. See SALES, 1-7.

PENALTY FOR INTENTIONAL DELAY. See COSTS, 1.

"PERSONAL PROPERTY." See PLEADING, 7; VENUE, 4.

PLAINTIFF BOUND BY MATERIAL ALLEGATIONS. See PLEADING, 6.

PLAINTIFF ENTITLED TO COSTS. See INTERPLEADER, 1.

PLAINTIFF RECOVERING AUTOMOBILE NOT LIABLE FOR REPAIRS. See WORK AND LABOR, 6.

"PLANT." See WATERS AND WATERCOURSES, 4.

PLEADING.

1. COMPLAINT AGAINST ADMINISTRATOR, BOTH IN REPRESENTATIVE AND PERSONAL CAPACITY, NOT DEMURRABLE FOR UNCERTAINTY.

Where defendant in claim and delivery, or replevin, was sued both as an individual and as administrator, the fact was not a ground of demurrer for uncertainty or ambiguity. *Kingsbury* v. *Copren*, 448.

2. COMPLAINT AGAINST ADMINISTRATOR NOT UNCERTAIN AS. TO CAPACITY IN WHICH DEFENDANT HELD PROPERTY.

Complaint in claim and delivery against an administrator in his personal and representative capacity, alleging, first, that defendant listed and described the property in question as that of his decedent's estate, and, second, that he claimed it as the property of such estate, while there was a total absence of any allegation that he held or claimed as an individual, was not uncertain or ambiguous as to the capacity in which it charged defendant with holding the property. *Idem.* 449.

3. CONCLUSION OF PLEADER.

Allegation in an action for false imprisonment that municipal judge "had no jurisdiction or power" is not a statement of facts, but a conclusion of the pleader. *Dixon* v. *City of Reno*, 413.

4. CROSS-COMPLAINT—MATTERS ALLEGED IN COMPLAINT.

If the averments of marriage and residence are necessary and indispensable facts to be stated in a complaint for support and maintenance, they are equally so in a cross-complaint in a divorce action, regardless of the fact that the plaintiff has alleged that there was a marriage and that the parties resided in the state. *Hilton* v. *District Court*, 128.

5. FAILURE TO STATE CAUSE OF ACTION.

An objection that the complaint utterly fails to state a cause of action may be raised at any time. *Nielsen* v. *Rebard*, 274.

6. PLAINTIFF BOUND BY MATERIAL ALLEGATIONS.

A plaintiff is bound by the material allegations in his complaint, charging defendant in a particular capacity. *Kingsbury* v. *Copren*, 449.

7. PLAINTIFF SEEKING RECOVERY OF PERSONALTY FROM ADMINISTRATOR MUST ALLEGE IN WHAT CAPACITY IT IS HELD, THOUGH KNOWN TO DEFENDANT.

The mere fact that defendant in claim and delivery, sued in his personal and representative capacity, knows in which capacity he claims the property sought by plaintiff, does not relieve plaintiff from the necessity of alleging in which capacity defendant holds it; the rule that facts peculiarly within the knowledge of defendant need not be alleged with the usual degree of exactness not applying when the allegation is essential to prima facie right of recovery. *Idem.* 449.

8. PRAYER FOR RELIEF NO PART OF CAUSE OF ACTION.

The prayer for relief in a complaint is no part of the statement of a cause of action. *Idem.*

9. VARIANCE BETWEEN PLEADING AND INSTRUMENT REFERRED TO.

In an action by subcontractor against the surety on contractor's bond, the fact that the bond denominated the subcontractor as the electric works, while the complaint named it as the electrical works, is immaterial under Rev. Laws, 5080, 5081, the variance probably being due to a mere clerical error. *Reno E. Wks. v. U. S. F. & G. Co.*, 191.

See APPEAL AND ERROR, 6; STATUTE OF FRAUDS, 1, 2.

PLEADING IN ACTION FOR FALSE IMPRISONMENT. See ACTION, 1.

POLICY OF LAW MATTER FOR LEGISLATURE. See CONSTITUTIONAL LAW, 8, 12.

POSSESSION AND ENJOYMENT. See DEEDS, 7.

POSSESSION BY DEFENDANT NECESSARY. See REPLEVIN, 2.

POWER OF LEGISLATURE. See STATUTES, 9.

POWER OF STATE TO TAX. See TAXATION, 2.

POWERS OF COURTS AND LEGISLATURE REGARDING VALIDITY. See STATUTES, 18.

PRAYER FOR RELIEF NO PART OF CAUSE OF ACTION. See PLEADING, 8.

PREMISES VIEWED BY COURT. See TRIAL, 2.

PRESUMPTION OF LEGISLATIVE KNOWLEDGE. See STATUTES, 1, 11.

PRESUMPTIONS AS TO INTENT OF PARTIES. See SALES, 8.

PRESUMPTIONS AS TO JURISDICTION. See JUSTICES OF THE PEACE, 2.

PREVENTION OF FRAUD. See STATUTE OF FRAUDS, 2.

PRINCIPAL AND AGENT. See ESTOPPEL, 1.

PROBABLE CAUSE. See MALICIOUS PROSECUTION, 1.

PROCEEDINGS IN CERTIORARI OF APPELLATE NATURE. See CERTIORARI, 7.

PROCEEDINGS IN CONTEMPT. See DIVORCE, 2.

PROHIBITION.

1. MOOT CASE DISMISSED.

Where proceedings in prohibition were brought to restrain district judge from hearing a motion to dissolve a preliminary injunction, the proceeding will be dismissed where, upon hearing, it appears that the motion had been decided and the injunction dissolved by such judge prior to the service upon him of the alternative writ. *State v. District Court*, 320.

PROHIBITION—*Continued.*
2. QUESTIONS OF PUBLIC IMPORT REVIEWABLE ON MERITS.

   On application for prohibition, the supreme court may consider the questions involved on their merits, where the public is vitally concerned and long and expensive litigation will thereby be avoided. *State v. Churchill County*, 290.

PROMISSORY NOTES. See APPEAL AND ERROR, 10; BILLS AND NOTES, 1, 2, 3, 4; GIFTS, 1.

PROOF IN ACTION FOR FALSE IMPRISONMENT. See CONSPIRACY, 2.

PROSECUTION FOR DESERTION OF WIFE AND CHILD. See HUSBAND AND WIFE, 2, 6.

PROSPECTIVE EFFECT. See STATUTES, 20.

PROSPECTIVE OPERATION. See STATUTES, 7.

PROVISIONS EMBRACED BY TITLE. See STATUTES, 19.

PUBLIC IMPROVEMENT. See TAXATION, 3.

PUBLIC OFFICERS. See OFFICERS, 1.

PUBLIC PURPOSE. See TAXATION, 4.

PUBLIC QUESTIONS REVIEWABLE. See PROHIBITION, 2.

PUBLIC SERVICE COMMISSIONS.
1. APPLICABILITY OF ACT OF 1919 TO APPEAL FROM JUDGMENT IN CASE BROUGHT UNDER ACT OF 1911.

   Where the facts involved in action to enjoin enforcement of rates fixed by public service commission under Stats. 1911, c. 162, transpired before the "act defining public utilities," etc. (Stats. 1919, c. 109), took effect, the appeal from the judgment was governed by former act, in view of section 44 of latter act. *Garson v. Steamboat Canal Co.*, 298.
2. RATES TO REMAIN IN FORCE PENDING JUDICIAL DETERMINATION.

   Stats. 1911, c. 162, sec. 26, providing that all rates fixed by the public service commission "shall be deemed reasonable and just and shall remain in full force and effect until final determination by the courts having jurisdiction," does not require that rates remain in full force and effect until final determination in the supreme court, but only pending final determination by district courts. *Idem.*
3. RESTRAINING ENFORCEMENT OF RATES PENDENTE LITE.

   Under Stats. 1911, c. 162, sec. 26, providing that all rates fixed by the public service commission shall be deemed in full force and effect until final determination, district court had no right to grant an injunction pendente lite restraining enforcement of the rate fixed by the commission. *Idem.*
4. REVIEW BY COURTS.

   Under Stats. 1911, c. 162, sec. 26, courts have no right to interfere with the public service commission or review its determination, further than to keep it within the law and protect the constitutional rights of the public service agencies over which it has been given control. *Idem.*

5. REVIEW OF ORDER ESTABLISHING RATES.

Under Stats. 1911, c. 162, sec. 26, and in view of Const. art. 4, sec. 20, district court's jurisdiction, on appeal from order of public service commission, is confined to the reasonableness of the rate change; the court having no right to assume administrative functions in establishing what in its judgment seems to be a reasonable rate. *Idem.*

6. RULES OF EVIDENCE.

Though the public service commission cannot dispense with the essential rules of evidence which conduce to a fair and impartial hearing on the question of rates, they are essentially empowered with liberal discretion in passing upon the competency of evidence. *Idem.*

See CONSTITUTIONAL LAW, 6, 9.

PUBLIC UTILITIES. See WATERS AND WATERCOURSES, 4, 5.

PUBLIC UTILITIES MAY INITIATE RATES. See CORPORATIONS, 2.

"PUBLIC UTILITY." See WATERS AND WATERCOURSES, 4.

PURCHASE OF MINING CLAIM OPTION. See PARTNERSHIP, 1.

PURCHASE PRICE. See SALES, 1, 3.

PURPOSE OF BULK–SALES LAW. See FRAUDULENT CONVEYANCES, 2.

PURPOSE OF STATUTE. See STATUTES, 2.

QUESTION OF FACT AS TO DEVELOPMENT WORK. See MINES AND MINERALS, 4.

QUESTIONS OF PUBLIC IMPORT REVIEWABLE ON MERITS. See PROHIBITION, 2.

QUIETING TITLE. See MINES AND MINERALS, 2, 3.

RAILROAD'S LIABILITY FOR LOSS OF SHIPMENT. See CARRIERS, 1, 3.

RAISING DEFENSES NOT MADE IN TRIAL COURT. See APPEAL AND ERROR, 23.

RATES FIXED BY PUBLIC SERVICE COMMISSION. See PUBLIC SERVICE COMMISSIONS, 1, 2, 3, 5.

RATES OF PUBLIC UTILITIES. See CORPORATIONS, 2.

RATES PENDING JUDICIAL DETERMINATION. See PUBLIC SERVICE COMMISSIONS, 2, 3.

REAL AND PERSONAL PROPERTY. See VENUE, 4.

REAL PROPERTY. See DEEDS, 3, 5.

REAL PROPERTY SOLD UNDER EXECUTION. See SHERIFFS AND CONSTABLES, 1.

REARGUMENT NOT PERMISSIBLE, ON REHEARING. See APPEAL AND ERROR, 24.

REASONABLE CONSTRUCTION. See STATUTES, 3.

REASONABLENESS OF RATES. See PUBLIC SERVICE COMMISSIONS, 5.

RECEIVERS.
1. STATUTE AS TO COMPENSATION PROSPECTIVE.
    The act of March 29, 1915 (Stats. 1915. c. 286), as to compensation of receivers of corporations involuntarily liquidated. seeks to enact a new rule of civil conduct, entirely prospective in its nature, and the rule against retrospective construction must be given full effect. *Wildes v. State*, 388.

See BANKS AND BANKING, 1.

RECLAMATION PROJECT NOT SUFFICIENT BASIS FOR TAX. See TAXATION, 3.

RECORD IN CERTIORARI. See JUSTICES OF THE PEACE. 2.

RECORD ON APPEAL. See APPEAL AND ERROR, 3.

RECOVERY OF SHARES OF CORPORATE STOCK. See SPECIFIC PERFORMANCE, 1.

REFERENDUM. See COUNTIES. 5; STATUTES, 13.

REFUSAL TO TAKE JURISDICTION OF APPEAL. See MANDAMUS, 1.

REGULATION OF CHARGES NOT DENIAL OF DUE PROCESS OF LAW. See CONSTITUTIONAL LAW, 9.

REGULATION OF PUBLIC UTILITIES. See WATERS AND WATERCOURSES, 4, 5.

REGULATION OF RATES OF PUBLIC UTILITY LEGISLATIVE FUNCTION. See CONSTITUTIONAL LAW, 10.

REHEARING FOR QUESTIONS URGED ON ORIGINAL HEARING. See APPEAL AND ERROR, 18.

REHEARING NOT A MATTER OF RIGHT. See APPEAL AND ERROR, 24.

REJECTION OF JURISDICTION. See MANDAMUS, 1.

REJECTION OF TESTIMONY AS TO DEED HARMLESS. See APPEAL AND ERROR, 25.

REMEDIES. See ELECTION OF REMEDIES, 1.

REPAIRS AND REPLACEMENTS. See REPLEVIN, 1.

REPAIRS TO AUTOMOBILE. See APPEAL AND ERROR, 9.

REPEAL BY CODIFICATION. See STATUTES, 16.

REPEAL BY IMPLICATION. See STATUTES, 8, 17.

REPEAL OF STATUTE JUDICIAL QUESTION. See CONSTITUTIONAL LAW, 5.

REPEAL OF STATUTES. See STATUTES. 14, 15.

REPLEVIN.

1. COUNTER-CLAIM FOR REPAIRS AND REPLACEMENTS INSTALLED PERMISSIBLE.

In an action for claim and delivery, which would be replevin at common law, the property is the subject of the action, so that under the liberal provisions of the practice act as to counter-claims, in an action for possession of automobiles, a defendant, having caused repairs and replacements to be installed, could interpose a counter-claim therefor. *Clarke* v. *Johnson*, 359.

2. POSSESSION BY DEFENDANT NECESSARY.

To enable a plaintiff to recover in replevin, the specific property must be in the possession of the defendant at the commencement of the action. *Nielsen* v. *Rebard*, 274.

REPLEVIN AGAINST ADMINISTRATOR. See EXECUTORS AND ADMINISTRATORS, 3.

REPUGNANT ACT. See STATUTES, 15.

RESETTING OF CASE. See MOTIONS, 1; TRIAL, 1.

RESIDENCE. See HUSBAND AND WIFE, 5.

RESTRAINING ENFORCEMENT OF RATES. See PUBLIC SERVICE COMMISSIONS, 3.

RESTRICTIONS ON POWER OF STATE TO TAX. See TAXATION, 2.

RETROACTIVE LAWS. See BANKS AND BANKING, 1.

RETROACTIVE LEGISLATION. See STATUTES, 7.

RETROSPECTIVE EFFECT OF STATUTE. See RECEIVERS, 1; STATUTES, 20.

REVERSAL IN EQUITY FOR ERRONEOUS INSTRUCTION. See APPEAL AND ERROR, 26.

REVIEW BY COURTS. See PUBLIC SERVICE COMMISSIONS, 4.

REVIEW OF ACTION OF DISTRICT COURT. See CERTIORARI, 1.

REVIEW OF DETERMINATION OF STATE ENGINEER. See JUDGMENT, 1.

REVIEW OF DIRECTED VERDICT. See CERTIORARI, 9.

REVIEW OF EVIDENCE. See APPEAL AND ERROR, 27.

REVIEW OF JUDGMENT. See CERTIORARI, 7, 8.

REVIEW OF JUDGMENT OF JUSTICE OF THE PEACE. See JUSTICES OF THE PEACE, 2.

REVIEW OF ORDER ESTABLISHING RATES. See PUBLIC SERVICE COMMISSIONS, 5.

REVISION AND CODIFICATION. See STATUTES, 16.

REVOCABILITY. See TRUSTS, 2, 3.

RIGHT OF INHERITANCE. See BASTARDS, 1, 2, 3, 4.

RIGHT TO APPEAL. See APPEAL AND ERROR, 8.

RIGHT TO QUESTION STATUTE. See CONSTITUTIONAL LAW, 11.

RIGHTS AND OBLIGATIONS AS TO INHERITANCE TAX. See TAXATION, 10.

RIGHTS INFRINGED BY STATE ENGINEER. See WATERS AND WATERCOURSES, 3.

RIGHTS OF ATTORNEYS AT LAW. See LICENSES, 1, 3.

RIGHTS OF INHABITANTS OF COUNTIES AS TO BOUNDARIES. See CONSTITUTIONAL LAW, 1, 3.

RULES OF EVIDENCE PRESCRIBED BY LEGISLATURE. See CONSTITUTIONAL LAW, 7.

SALES.
1. ACTION FOR PURCHASE PRICE—ADMISSIBILITY OF EVIDENCE.

In action for purchase price of hay destroyed by fire, evidence that a stick was placed in the hay to indicate amount covered by the sales agreement *held* immaterial on question whether hay subject to agreement was ascertained so as to pass title, where a subsequent written agreement fixed exact amount of hay sold. *Casinelli v. Humphrey Co.*, 208.

2. DESTRUCTION OF GOODS—SELLER'S LIABILITY.

Under the direct provisions of uniform sales act, secs. 8, 22, the seller must bear the loss of hay covered by a sales agreement, but to which title had not passed, when it burned without the fault of either party. *Idem.*

3. EVIDENCE—ADMISSIBILITY.

In seller's action to recover purchase price of hay which defendant claimed had not been measured so as to pass title before it was accidentally burned, evidence that plaintiff's sons measured the hay after sales contract was executed, but before date agreed upon for measurement, *held* inadmissible to show compliance with contract. *Idem.*

4. PASSING OF TITLE—CONSTRUCTION OF CONTRACT.

A contract under which all hay in certain stacks was sold, excepting thirty tons to be retained by the seller, etc., *held* to make measurement of the hay a condition precedent to the passing of title despite the use of the words "bought" and "sold" in the contract. *Idem.*

5. PASSING OF TITLE—"SPECIFIC OR ASCERTAINED GOODS."

Where all the hay in certain stacks was sold except thirty tons retained by the seller, the hay sold was "specific or ascertained goods" within uniform sales act, sec. 18, providing that the property in such goods is transferred at time the parties intend. *Idem.*

6. PASSING OF TITLE—UNIFORM SALES ACT.

Uniform sales act, sec. 19, rule 5, creating a presumption that title does not pass until the goods have been delivered.

held inapplicable to an agreement under which certain hay was to be constructively delivered immediately after it had been measured. *Idem.*

7. PASSING OF TITLE—UNIFORM SALES ACT.

Uniform sales act, sec. 19, rule 1, creating a presumption that title is intended to pass where there is an unconditional contract to sell certain specific goods in a deliverable state, etc., *held* inapplicable to an agreement to sell all the hay in certain stacks except thirty tons to be retained by the seller. *Idem.*

8. UNIFORM SALES ACT—CONSTRUCTION.

Uniform sales act, sec. 19, prescribing several rules for ascertaining the intent of the parties as to when title passes, merely creates presumptions which give way if a contrary intent appears. *Idem.*

See APPEAL AND ERROR, 9; FRAUDULENT CONVEYANCES, 2.

SALES OF MINING CLAIMS. See PARTNERSHIP, 1.

SCOPE OF JUDICIAL AND LEGISLATIVE POWER. See STATUTES, 18.

SERVICE AND FILING OF ASSIGNMENT OF ERRORS JURISDICTIONAL. See APPEAL AND ERROR, 28.

SERVICE OF NOTICE OF UNDERTAKING ON APPEAL. See APPEAL AND ERROR, 19.

SERVICE OF SUMMONS. See CERTIORARI, 8; JUSTICES OF THE PEACE, 2; VENUE, 6.

SETTING OF CASE FOR TRIAL. See TRIAL, 1.

SHARES OF CORPORATE STOCK. See SPECIFIC PERFORMANCE, 1.

SHARES OF CORPORATE STOCK NOT REAL PROPERTY. See VENUE, 4.

SHERIFFS AND CONSTABLES.

1. NOT ENTITLED TO COMMISSIONS ON FORECLOSURE SALE UNDER DECREE.

Under Rev. Laws, 2009, as to "commissions for receiving and paying over money on execution or process where lands * * * have been levied on, advertised and sold," and in view of section 2019, a sheriff is not entitled to commissions for receiving and paying over money on the sale of real property sold pursuant to a decree and order of sale made upon the foreclosure of a mortgage; an execution and levy being entirely supererogatory in a foreclosure proceeding where the lien on the property has already attached by reason of the mortgage contract. *Clover Valley Co.* v. *Lamb*, 375.

SIGNING OF WRITTEN CONTRACT. See CONTRACTS, 1.

SLOT MACHINE. See GAMING, 1; LOTTERIES, 1.

"SOLD." See SALES, 4.

SPECIAL VENIRE. See CERTIORARI, 9; JURY, 1.

"SPECIFIC OR ASCERTAINED GOODS." See SALES. 5, 7.

SPECIFIC PERFORMANCE.
1. NOT APPLICABLE TO CORPORATE STOCK.
    Shares of corporate stock cannot be recovered in an action
for specific performance, unless they possess peculiar and
unusual value. *Nielsen* v. *Rebard*, 274.

SPECIFIC PROPERTY MUST BE IN POSSESSION OF DEFEN-
    DANT. See REPLEVIN, 2.

STATE ENGINEER. See WATERS AND WATERCOURSES, 1, 2, 3.

STATE ENGINEER'S DETERMINATION AS TO WATER
    RIGHTS. See JUDGMENT, 1.

STATEMENTS ON APPEAL. See STATUTES, 17.

STATUTE AS TO COMPENSATION. See RECEIVERS, 1.

STATUTE MUST BE FOLLOWED ON APPEAL. See APPEAL AND
    ERROR, 17.

STATUTE OF FRAUDS.
1. CHANGED POSITION OF PLAINTIFF INSUFFICIENT TO ESTOP DEFEN-
    DANT FROM PLEADING STATUTE.
    In lessees' action against lessor for breach of an oral con-
tract to furnish horses to plant and harvest a crop, evidence
of lessees' changed position in accepting lease and oral agreement is insufficient to show the working of a fraud, and
thereby estop lessor from setting up the invalidity of the oral
contract under the statute of frauds, where there was no evidence that the plaintiffs could not obtain the identical employment they left to accept the lease and oral contract. *Nehls* v.
Stock Farming Co., 253.
2. ESTOPPEL TO SET UP STATUTE TO PREVENT PERPETRATION OF A
    FRAUD.
    In an action for a breach of an oral contract by which
lessor was to furnish lessee with horses for seeding and harvesting a crop, whatever sum the plaintiffs spent in securing
horses and operating the farm did not induce a change of
position of plaintiffs, but was the result of a change of position, so that the doctrine of estoppel would not apply to prevent the defendant lessor from setting up the invalidity of
the agreement under the statute of frauds, on the ground that
the plea of the statute would work a fraud. *Idem.*
43. LESSOR OF HORSES AND TEAMS NOT ESTOPPED TO SHOW INVALIDITY
    OF CONTRACT.
    Where lessees hired horses to plow and seed land, after
lessor had refused to furnish horses, and without being misled by any act or acts on part of lessor, lessor is not estopped
from setting up invalidity of its parol contract to furnish
horses under statute of frauds in lessees' action for damages
for breach thereof. *Idem.*
4. PART PERFORMANCE HAS NO APPLICATION TO CONTRACT NOT TO
    BE PERFORMED WITHIN A YEAR.
    A contract not to be performed within one year is void
(Rev. Laws, 1075), notwithstanding part performance: the doc-

trine of part performance having no application to such contract, and the statute being aimed exclusively at the time of performance, and not the subject-matter. *Idem.*

5. PART PERFORMANCE TAKES LAND CONTRACTS OUT OF THE STATUTE.
Part performance takes land contract out of statute of frauds when not to enforce the contract would result in a fraud being perpetrated upon a party who has partially performed. *Idem.*

See APPEAL AND ERROR, 23.

STATUTES.
1. CONSTRUCTION—LEGISLATIVE KNOWLEDGE—PRESUMPTION.
It may be presumed that the legislature adopted Civ. Prac. Act, sec. 386 (Rev. Laws, 5328), requiring that a motion for new trial must be made and determined before an appeal based on insufficiency of evidence can be taken, with full knowledge that the existing practice was otherwise. *Gill v. Goldfield Con. M. Co.,* 1.

2. CONSTRUCTION—PURPOSE—INTENT.
In construing a statute the legislative intent controls, and in seeking the intent the evil sought to be remedied should be ascertained. *Escalle v. Mark,* 172.

3. CONSTRUCTION TO AVOID ABSURD MEANING.
Any reasonable construction which the phraseology of a statute, or a part of a statute, will bear, must be drawn to avoid an absurd meaning. *Garson v. Steamboat Canal Co.,* 298.

4. CONSTRUCTION TO GIVE EFFECT TO ENTIRE ACT.
A statute should be construed so as to give effect, if possible, to all its parts. *Idem.*

5. CONSTRUED IN LIGHT OF FACTS.
A legislative enactment must be construed in the light of known facts suggested by the act itself. *State v. Churchill County,* 290.

6. CONTEMPORANEOUS CONSTRUCTION UNAVAILABLE WHERE LANGUAGE UNAMBIGUOUS.
Contemporaneous construction, as shown by long practice by the legal profession and officers, and acquiescence therein by the legislature, is to be resorted to only when the statutory language is of doubtful import. *Clover Valley Co. v. Lamb,* 375.

7. EVERY REASONABLE DOUBT RESOLVED AGAINST RETROACTIVE OPERATION.
Every reasonable doubt is resolved against a retroactive operation; and, if all the language of a statute can be satisfied by giving it prospective action only, that construction will be given it. *Wildes v. State,* 388.

8. IMPLIED REPEAL—CONFLICT IN OBJECTS.
Although Civ. Prac. Act, sec. 386 (Rev. Laws, 5328), and Stats. 1915, c. 142, relate to the same subject, both being designed to correct errors on appeal, the purpose of the former was to require a motion for new trial before taking appeal, while the object of the latter was to provide the method of appeal by bills of exception, so that the latter does not repeal the former by conflict in objects. *Gill v. Goldfield Con. M. Co.,* 1.

STATUTES—*Continued.*

9. LAW TO TAKE EFFECT ON CONTINGENCY—POWER OF LEGISLATURE.

The legislature has power to pass a law to take effect on a contingency expressed in the body of the law; and may designate such contingency as a vote of the people of the territory affected by the law. *Pershing Co.* v. *Humboldt Co.*, 78.

10. LEGISLATIVE AND JUDICIAL POWERS.

So long as the legislature acts within the powers given it, the courts cannot interfere. *State* v. *Churchill County*, 290.

11. LEGISLATURE PRESUMED TO KNOW LAW.

The legislature is presumed to have knowledge of the state of the law upon the subject upon which it legislates. *Clover Valley Co.* v. *Lamb*, 375.

12. PARTIAL INVALIDITY—EFFECT.

Unless the validity of a whole statute depends on the constitutionality of one or more provisions not germane to the title, or are so blended with the scope and purpose of the act as a whole as to affect its validity or any other of its provisions, the invalidity of one or more of such provisions does not defeat the general scope and purpose of the act. *Pershing Co.* v. *Humboldt Co.*, 78.

13. REFERENDUM—CONSTRUCTION.

In construing the referendum as applied to legislation for counties, the usual rules of construction are applicable; the thing to be sought being the thought expressed. *Idem.*

14. REPEAL—LEGISLATIVE INTENTION.

Whether one statute was repealed by another is a question of legislative intention, which is to be determined by acknowledged rules. *Gill* v. *Goldfield Con. M. Co.*, 1.

15. REPEAL—REPUGNANT ACT.

One statute is not repugnant to another unless they relate to the same subject and are enacted for the same purpose. *Idem.*

16. REPEAL BY CODIFICATION—REVISION—OMITTED PARTS.

Where a statute is revised or one act framed from another, some parts being omitted, the omitted parts are considered annulled. *Idem.*

17. REPEAL BY IMPLICATION.

Stats. 1915, c. 142, revises the subject-matter of Rev. Laws, 5343 (Civ. Prac. Act, sec. 401), respecting statements on appeal, and substitutes therefor in toto a system of bills of exception, and hence repeals by implication the earlier statute. *Idem.*

18. SCOPE OF POWERS.

The courts cannot hold a statute valid because it is sanctioned by the legislature and public opinion, where the statute is not within scope of legitimate legislation. *State* v. *Churchill County*, 290.

19. TITLE—ORGANIZATION OF COUNTY—CONSTITUTIONALITY.

Stats. 1919, p. 75, organizing the county of Pershing out of a portion of Humboldt County, and certain of its provisions, *held* not unconstitutional on the ground that such provisions are not embraced by the title, the disputed provisions being incident to the complete organization of the county, and germane to the main object of the act. *Pershing Co.* v. *Humboldt Co.*, 78.

20. WILL NOT BE CONSTRUED AS RETROSPECTIVE.

As a general rule, a statute will not be construed to operate upon past transactions, but in futuro only. *Wildes* v. *State*, 388.

See BANKS AND BANKING, 1; CONSTITUTIONAL LAW, 2, 5, 6, 9, 11; COUNTIES, 3, 5; COURTS, 1; CRIMINAL LAW, 3; DESCENT AND DISTRIBUTION, 1; DIVORCE, 1, 2; HUSBAND AND WIFE. 3, 4, 6; JUDGMENT, 1; JURY, 1; JUSTICES OF THE PEACE, 1; LANDLORD AND TENANT, 1, 2; LOTTERIES, 1; OFFICERS, 1; PLEADING, 9; PUBLIC SERVICE COMMISSIONS, 1, 2, 3, 4, 5; RECEIVERS, 1; SALES, 2, 5, 8; SHERIFFS AND CONSTABLES, 1; STATUTE OF FRAUDS, 4; TAXATION, 1; VENUE, 1, 2, 3, 4; WATERS AND WATERCOURSES, 1, 2, 4.

STATUTORY RIGHT TO HEARING ON MERITS. See APPEAL AND ERROR, 8.

STIPULATION AS TO CHANGE OF VENUE NOT EFFECTIVE. See VENUE, 3, 5.

STOCK TRANSFER. See TRUSTS, 3.

STOCK TRANSFER BY DEED OF TRUST. See TAXATION, 1.

STOCK TRANSFER IN CONTEMPLATION OF DEATH. See TAXATION, 7.

STRICT CONSTRUCTION OF FEE STATUTES. See OFFICERS, 1.

SUBCONTRACTOR MAY SUE SURETY OF CONTRACTOR. See CONTRACTS, 1; PLEADING, 9.

SUBSTANTIAL CONFLICT IN MATERIAL EVIDENCE. See APPEAL AND ERROR, 13, 14.

SUFFICIENCY OF AUTHENTICATION OF RECORD ON APPEAL. See APPEAL AND ERROR, 3.

SUFFICIENCY OF CERTIFICATE AS TO BILL OF EXCEPTIONS. See APPEAL AND ERROR, 11.

SUFFICIENCY OF EVIDENCE TO SHOW UNDUE INFLUENCE. See DEEDS, 6.

SUIT IN INTERPLEADER INVOLVING LESS THAN $300. See COURTS, 1.

SUPPORT AND MAINTENANCE. See CERTIORARI, 5, 12; HUSBAND AND WIFE, 3, 4, 5, 6; PLEADING, 4.

SURVIVING PARTY MAY NOT TESTIFY. See WITNESSES, 1.

SUSPENSION OF SENTENCE. See CRIMINAL LAW, 4, 5.

TAX ON OCCUPATION. See LICENSE, 1, 2, 3.

TAXATION.
  1. INHERITANCE TAX—STATUTE—OPERATION.
    Transfer of stock by deed of trust intended to take effect in possession or enjoyment at or after grantor's death was

TAXATION—*Continued.*

taxable under the inheritance-tax law, although such law had not taken effect at time of execution of deed; the property having vested at time of death and not at the date of the execution of the deed. *In Re Miller's Estate*, 12.

2. RESTRICTIONS ON POWER OF STATE TO TAX.

The only restriction on the power of the state to tax property within its jurisdiction and to direct the purposes for which taxes shall be raised is that the assessment shall be uniform and equal and the purpose a public one. *State* v. *Churchill County*, 290.

3. TAX FOR PUBLIC IMPROVEMENT MUST BE EFFECTIVE.

A tax for a public improvement to be legal must be effective, and a tax designed to accomplish a vast reclamation project must rest upon some safer hypothesis than the volition and individual energy of those upon whom is the duty to make the law authorizing the tax effective. *Idem.*

4. TAX MUST BE FOR PUBLIC PURPOSE.

There can be no lawful tax which is not laid for a public purpose. *Idem.*

5. TAX ON TRANSFER IN CONTEMPLATION OF DEATH.

Whether a transfer by way of trust is one intended to take effect at or after the grantor's death does not depend on whether the trust is revocable, but the test is whether the property passes with all attributes of ownership, independently of the death of the transferor. *In Re Miller's Estate*, 12.

6. TRANSFER TAX—CONSTRUCTION OF DEED OF TRUST.

In determining whether a deed of trust immediately vested legal title so as to exempt transfer from a transfer tax under inheritance-tax law, the deed will be construed, together with a will executed simultaneously therewith as a single instrument. *Idem.*

7. TRANSFER TAX—DEED OF TRUST—CONSTRUCTION.

Deed of trust by 86-year-old invalid after enactment of inheritance-tax law, but shortly before law took effect, transferring stock to trustees with directions to pay income to grantor during his life, with directions as to disposition of property after his death, corresponding to provisions of will executed simultaneously with deed, was intended as disposition of property to take effect at or after grantor's death, within inheritance-tax law. *Idem.*

8. TRANSFER TAX—DEED OF TRUST—WEIGHT OF EVIDENCE.

Where, immediately after execution of the will, testator executed deed of trust directing trustees to pay testator income during his natural life and directed disposal of property following his death by provisions corresponding to those in will, evidence that execution of deed was an afterthought to avoid, if possible, an expected increase in the tax rate in California and a probable inheritance tax of federal government, is entitled to weight in action to impose a transfer tax under inheritance-tax law. *Idem.*

9. "TRANSFER TAX"—NATURE.

The "transfer tax," imposed by inheritance-tax law, is in the nature of an excise tax, to wit, on the transfer of property. *Idem.*

10. TRANSFER TAX—RIGHTS AND OBLIGATIONS.

The rights and obligations of all parties in regard to payment of inheritance tax under inheritance-tax law are determinable as of the time of the death of the decedent. *Idem.*

11. TRANSFER TAX NOT INTERFERENCE WITH COMITY BETWEEN STATES.

Where the devolution of title to property involves a succession or inheritance tax, it is governed and controlled by the laws of the forum imposing the tax, if the transfer sought to be taxed is within the jurisdiction of the tax authorities, and imposition of such tax cannot be denied, on the ground that it would interfere with comity between states, for it is a well-settled rule that no foreign law will be enforced in a sovereign state, if to enforce it will contravene the express statute law or expressed public policy of the forum or is injurious to its interests. *Idem.*

See LICENSES, 1, 2, 3.

TAXATION ILLEGAL UNLESS FOR PUBLIC PURPOSE. See COUNTIES, 1.

TAXATION MUST BE FOR PUBLIC PURPOSE. See COUNTIES, 2.

TENANCY FROM MONTH TO MONTH. See LANDLORD AND TENANT, 2.

TESTIMONY AS TO TRANSACTION WITH DECEDENT. See APPEAL AND ERROR, 10.

TESTIMONY BY SURVIVING PARTY NOT ADMISSIBLE. See WITNESSES, 1.

TESTIMONY NECESSARY IN SUPPORT OF NOTE ATTACKED. See BILLS AND NOTES, 2, 3, 4.

THEORY CONTRARY TO EXPRESS FINDING NOT SUSTAIN-ABLE. See APPEAL AND ERROR, 9.

THEORY OF CASE. See APPEAL AND ERROR, 6.

TIME FOR APPEAL IN UNLAWFUL DETAINER. See JUSTICES OF THE PEACE, 1.

TIME FOR CHANGE OF VENUE. See VENUE, 2, 3, 6.

TIME FOR TAKING EXCEPTIONS. See APPEAL AND ERROR, 22.

TIME FOR PERFORMANCE. See STATUTE OF FRAUDS, 4.

TIME OF TAKING EFFECT OF INHERITANCE TAX. See TAXATION, 10.

TITLE. See STATUTES, 19.

TITLE TO GOODS PENDING DELIVERY. See SALES, 1–7.

TRANSACTION WITH DECEASED PERSON. See APPEAL AND ERROR, 10.

TRANSCRIPT OF PROCEEDINGS IN LOWER COURT. See CERTIORARI, 3, 10.

TRANSFER IN CONTEMPLATION OF DEATH. See TAXATION. 5, 7.

TRANSFER OF STOCK BY DEED OF TRUST. See TAXATION, 1.

"TRANSFER TAX." See TAXATION, 9.

TRANSFER TAX NOT AN INTERFERENCE WITH COMITY BETWEEN STATES. See TAXATION, 11.

TRIAL.
1. SETTING OF CASE FOR TRIAL—RESETTING—WAIVER OF ERRORS.

   Where defendant was present in court at the time plaintiff's counsel applied to reset the case for trial on an earlier date than that originally fixed, and defendant resisted the application solely on the ground that the court was without authority to order the case, which was on the jury calendar, to be tried before a special venire, and that he was entitled to trial before the regular panel, there was a waiver of the failure of the applicant to give the five days' notice required in case of motions. *State* v. *McFadden*, 140.

2. VIEW OF PREMISES BY COURT.

   A view of the premises involved in mining litigation cannot be considered as evidence, but only to enable the court better to understand and comprehend the evidence introduced and intelligently to apply it. *Love* v. *Mt. Oddie U. M. Co.*, 61.

   See MOTIONS, 1.

TRIAL BY JURY. See JURY, 1.

TRIAL JUDGE MAY DIRECT VERDICT. See CERTIORARI, 11.

TROVER AND CONVERSION.
1. OBJECT OF ACTION.

   Trover is an action, not to recover the specific thing, but to recover the value of the property wrongfully converted. *Nielsen* v. *Rebard*, 274.

TRUSTS.
1. EVIDENCE OF CONSULTATION BETWEEN CHILDREN INSUFFICIENT TO ESTABLISH TRUST.

   Evidence of consultation between children, without the knowledge or consent of the mother, whereby children agreed that mother, who was lying on deathbed, should convey property to one of the children, who agreed with the other children to pay the debts of the estate and distribute the residue by proper conveyance equally between other heirs, was not admissible as proof that child to whom property was so conveyed held land in trust for other children. *Adams* v. *Wagoner*, 266.

2. REVOCABILITY.

   It is only in cases where other parties besides the person creating the trust have an interest therein that the trust becomes irrevocable. *In Re Miller's Estate*, 12.

3. REVOCABILITY—DEED OF TRUST.

   Deed of trust transferring stock to trustees, with direction to pay income to grantor during his life and directing disposition after death in manner corresponding to will executed simultaneously, beneficiaries receiving no present interest, grantor could revoke deed of trust. *Idem.*

UNCERTAINTY OF COMPLAINT AGAINST ADMINISTRATOR. See PLEADING, 1, 2, 7.

UNDERTAKING ON APPEAL. See APPEAL AND ERROR, 19.

UNDISPUTED FACTS. See APPEAL AND ERROR, 14.

UNIFORM AND EQUAL PURPOSE ONLY RESTRICTION. See TAXATION, 2.

UNIFORM SALES ACT. See SALES, 2, 6, 7, 8.

UNIFORMITY OF TAXATION. See LICENSES, 3.

UNLAWFUL DETAINER. See JUSTICES OF THE PEACE, 1; LANDLORD AND TENANT, 1, 2.

VALIDITY OF DEED. See DEEDS, 7.

VALIDITY OF ENTIRE STATUTE. See STATUTES, 12.

VALIDITY OF NOTE. See GIFTS, 1.

VALIDITY OF STATUTE DIVIDING COUNTIES. See CONSTITUTIONAL LAW, 11.

VALIDITY OF STATUTES. See STATUTES, 18.

VALUATION OF PROPERTY DAMAGED IN TRANSIT. See CARRIERS, 1.

VARIANCE BETWEEN PLEADING AND INSTRUMENT. See PLEADING, 9.

VENUE.
1. CHANGE—STATUTE.
   Rev. Laws, 5015, relating to change of venue, is mandatory, and a proper application for a change must be granted. *Connolly v. Salsberry,* 182.
2. CHANGE—STATUTE.
   Rev. Laws, 5015, subd. 1, authorizing court on motion to change place of trial in certain cases, does not authorize court to change the venue at any time before trial, in a case where defendant has filed no seasonable written application. *Idem.*
3. CHANGE—TIME.
   Under Rev. Laws, 5015, providing for change of venue upon application made before the time for answering has expired, a stipulation made by attorneys, pursuant to district court rule No. 27, extending defendants' time to answer, did not extend the time to apply for a change of venue. *Idem.*
4. REAL PROPERTY NOT INVOLVED IN SUIT PERTAINING TO MINING STOCK—"PERSONAL PROPERTY."
   Venue of action pertaining to shares of stock of a mining corporation cannot under Civ. Prac. Act, sec. 69, be changed to the county in which the mines owned by the corporation were situated, on the ground that real property was involved,

VENUE—*Continued.*

since shares of corporate stock are personal property. *Page v. Walser,* 422.

5. STIPULATION—CONSTRUCTION—"MOVE."

A stipulation extending defendants' time to appear, demur, answer, or "move" did not extend the time to move for a change of venue as a matter of right. *Connolly v. Salsberry,* 182.

6. TIME FOR DEMANDING CHANGE BEGINS FROM DATE OF SERVICE OF SUMMONS.

The time for demanding change of venue begins to run from the date of service of summons. *Page v. Walser,* 422.

See APPEAL AND ERROR, 21; COSTS, 1.

VENUE IN ACTION FOR SUPPORT AND MAINTENANCE. See HUSBAND AND WIFE, 5.

VENUE IN PROSECUTION FOR DESERTION. See HUSBAND AND WIFE, 2.

VESTED RIGHTS. See LICENSES, 1, 3.

VIEW OF PREMISES BY COURT. See TRIAL, 2.

"VOID." See FRAUDULENT CONVEYANCES, 1.

VOLUNTARY SIGNING. See BILLS AND NOTES, 3.

WAIVER OF OBJECTION IN SETTING CASE FOR TRIAL. See TRIAL, 1.

WANT OF CONSIDERATION. See BILLS AND NOTES, 1.

WANT OF CONSIDERATION DEFENSE AGAINST ORIGINAL PAYEE. See BILLS AND NOTES, 5.

WANT OF CONSIDERATION QUESTION FOR JURY. See BILLS AND NOTES, 4.

WANT OF PROBABLE CAUSE. See MALICIOUS PROSECUTION, 1.

WATERS AND WATERCOURSES.

1. DETERMINATION OF RIGHTS—DISMISSAL OF APPEAL.

Assuming that the rules prescribed by civil practice act, as amended by Stats. 1915, c. 142, apply to the hearing of an issue raised by a notice of exceptions to an order of determination of the state engineer duly filed with the clerk under Stats. 1915, c. 253, sec. 6, in a proceeding to determine relative rights to water, it does not follow that the failure to preserve errors by a bill of exceptions must result in the dismissal of an appeal from a decree affirming the order of determination of the engineer, although such failure might result in an affirmance of the decree. *In Re Waters of Barber Creek,* 403.

2. DETERMINATION OF RIGHTS—ORDERS APPEALABLE.

An order of determination of the state engineer in a proceeding to determine the relative rights of persons to water is not appealable, the only appeal allowable, under Stats. 1915, c. 253, sec. 6, in such a case being from the decree of the court affirming or modifying such order. *Idem.*

3. FINDINGS OF STATE ENGINEER IN DETERMINING WATER RIGHTS ENTITLED TO RESPECT, BUT NOT SUPERSEDING POWER OF COURT.

In proceedings for the determination of water rights pursuant to the water law, the ultimate findings of the state engineer are entitled to great respect, but do not take from the district court on exceptions the power to grant relief to a party whose right may have been infringed by the engineer. *Idem.*

4. REGULATION—"PUBLIC UTILITY"—"PLANT."

A canal company, engaged in the business of delivering water to a number of users for agricultural and other purposes, *held* a "public utility," within Stats. 1911, c. 162, sec. 3, making a corporation, which owns, operates, or controls "any plant or equipment," or part thereof, for delivery of water to other persons a "public utility," and subject to control of public service commission; the word "plant" not having been used in its precise and technical meaning, requiring pumping station or other mechanical apparatus, and being sufficiently comprehensive to apply to the canal and business of such canal company. *Garson v. Steamboat Canal Co., 298.*

5. REGULATION OF RATES—HEARING OF PUBLIC SERVICE COMMISSION.

Public service commission's use, in hearing as to water rates, of testimony and data obtained at former hearings, after due notice that such testimony and data would be considered, and ample time for examination thereof given all the parties to the proceeding, *held* not an abuse of discretion, where a full hearing was held, with full opportunity to all parties to introduce and cross-examine witnesses, and to test, explain, or refute such evidence; the use of such testimony and data not having deprived the parties of any substantial right. *Idem.*

See JUDGMENT, 1.

WEIGHT OF EVIDENCE IN EXECUTION OF DEED OF TRUST.
See TAXATION, 8.

WHOLESALERS. See FRAUDULENT CONVEYANCES, 2.

WIFE MAY BE GRANTED ALIMONY. See DIVORCE, 1, 2.

WILL AND DEED OF TRUST EXECUTED SIMULTANEOUSLY.
See TRUSTS, 2, 3.

WILLS.
1. DEED OR WILL—FUTURE INTERESTS.

Where interests created do not arise until death of donor or some other future time, the instrument cannot be a deed, although so denominated and accompanied by words of immediate grant, a sufficient consideration, and formal delivery. *In Re Miller's Estate, 12.*

See DEEDS, 3; TAXATION, 7, 8.

WITNESSES.
1. NO TESTIMONY BY SURVIVING PARTY TO TRANSACTION.

If one party to an original transaction is precluded from testifying by death, the other is not entitled to the undue advantage of giving his own uncontradicted and unexplained account of the transaction. *Reinhart* v. *Echave*, 323.

WORK AND LABOR.
1. PLAINTIFF RECOVERING AUTOMOBILES IN REPAIRED CONDITION NOT LIABLE ON AN IMPLIED PROMISE TO DEFENDANT FURNISHING REPAIRS.

In an action by the seller in claim and delivery for recovery of automobiles, plaintiff is not liable as for a voluntary acceptance of services to the purchaser who had caused the machines to be repaired, since plaintiff in taking the machines had no choice but to accept them in their repaired condition, and there was no implied promise to pay for such services. *Clark* v. *Johnson*, 359.

WRIT OF CERTIORARI. See CERTIORARI, 1–12.

WRIT OF CERTIORARI NOT ISSUED AS MATTER OF RIGHT. See CERTIORARI, 6.

WRIT OF MANDAMUS. See MANDAMUS, 1.

WRIT OF PROHIBITION. See PROHIBITION, 1.

WRONGFUL CONDUCT OF AGENT. See ESTOPPEL, 1.